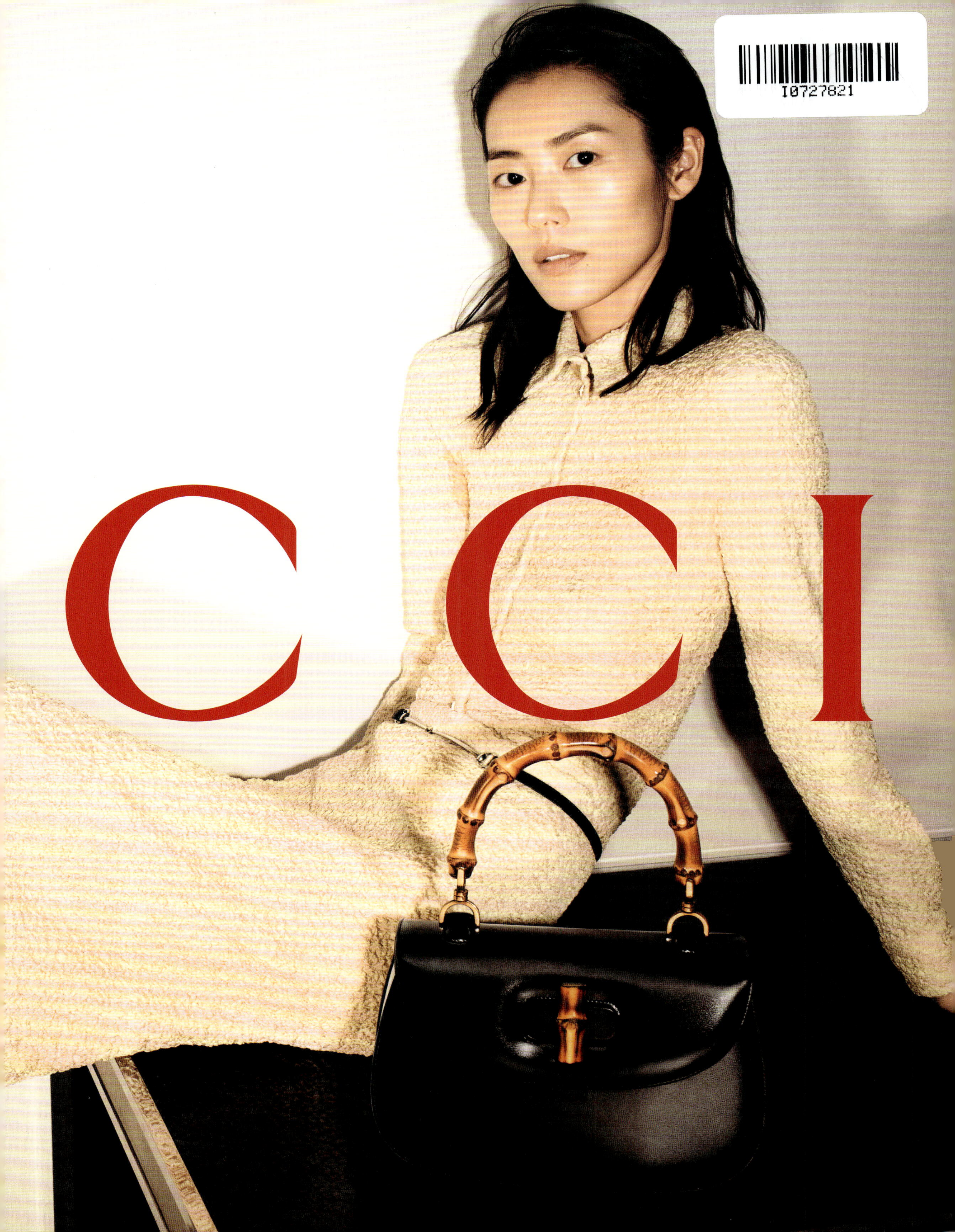

C C I

# Fall 2023
# Accra

## Front



## Back



# Words & Pictures



Front cover:
Carlos Idun-Tawiah, *Flower Boy*, Accra, 2023, for *Aperture*
Courtesy the artist
(See page 72)

Subscribe to *Aperture* and visit archive.aperture.org for every issue since 1952.

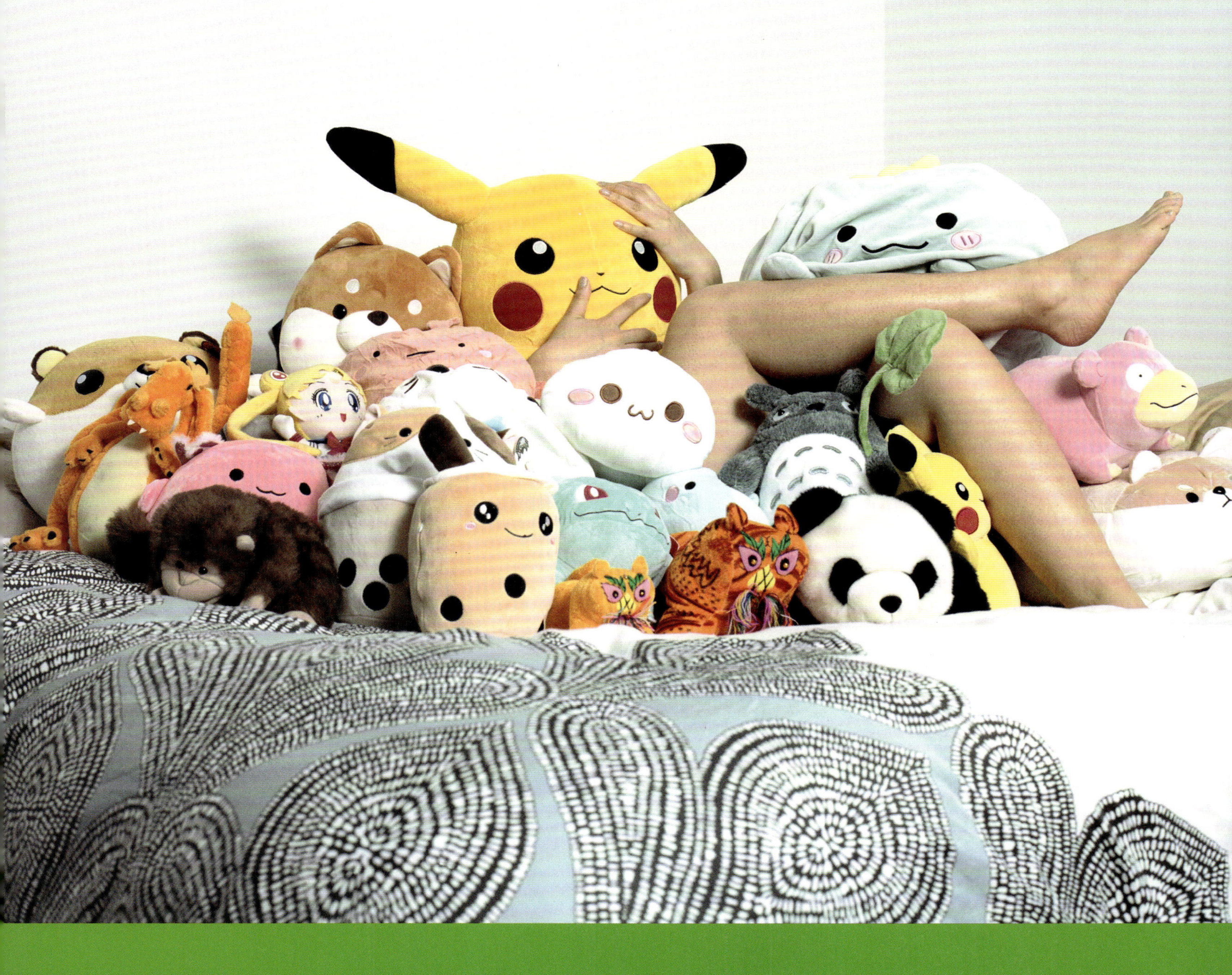

# Kinship
## Photography & Connection

Six photographers capture the intimacy of relationships
in a way that transcends cultural and geographic borders.

On view through November 5, 2023
Buy tickets at **sfmoma.org**

SF MO MA

Aperture, a not-for-profit foundation, connects the photo community and its audiences with the most inspiring work, the sharpest ideas, and with each other—in print, in person, and online.

*Aperture* (ISSN 0003-6420) is published quarterly, in spring, summer, fall, and winter, at 548 West 28th Street, 4th Floor, New York, N.Y. 10001. In the United States, a one-year subscription (four issues) is $75; a two-year subscription (eight issues) is $124. In Canada, a one-year subscription is $95. All other international subscriptions are $110 per year. Visit aperture.org to subscribe. Single copies may be purchased at $24.95 for most issues. Subscribe to the *Aperture Digital Archive* at aperture.org/archive. Periodicals postage paid at New York and additional offices. Postmaster: Send address changes to *Aperture*, P.O. Box 3000, Denville, N.J. 07834. Address queries regarding subscriptions, renewals, or gifts to: *Aperture* Subscription Service, 866-457-4603 (U.S. and Canada), or email custsvc_aperture@fulcoinc.com.

Newsstand distribution in the US is handled by CMG. For international distribution, contact Central Books, centralbooks.com. Other inquiries, email orders@aperture.org or call 212-505-5555.

Become a Member of Aperture to take your interest in and knowledge of photography further. With an annual tax-deductible gift of $250, membership includes a complimentary subscription to *Aperture* magazine, discounts on Aperture's award-winning publications, a special limited-edition gift, and more. To join, visit aperture.org/join, or contact membership@aperture.org.

Credits for "Timeline," pp. 14–15: Gardner photographs: © Library of Congress; *Nightwatch*: Courtesy Miramax/Photofest

Credits for "Curriculum," pp. 20–21: Plumb: © the artist and Robert Koch Gallery; Sultan: © Estate of Larry Sultan and courtesy Yancey Richardson Gallery, New York; Dijkstra: © the artist and courtesy Marian Goodman Gallery, New York



Library of Congress Catalog Card No: 58-30845.

ISBN 978-1-59711-549-0

Printed in Turkey by Ofset Yapimevi

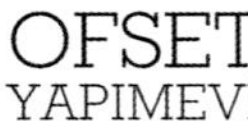


Support has been provided by members of Aperture's Magazine Council: Jon Stryker and Slobodan Randjelović, Susan and Thomas Dunn, Kate Cordsen and Denis O'Leary, and Michael W. Sonnenfeldt, MUUS Collection.

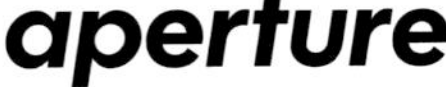


**The Magazine of Photography and Ideas**

**Editor**
Michael Famighetti
**Guest Editors**
Lyle Ashton Harris, Nii Obodai
**Senior Managing Editor**
Brendan Embser
**Assistant Editor**
Varun Nayar
**Contributing Editor,
The PhotoBook Review**
Lesley A. Martin
**Copy Editors**
Donna Ghelerter, Chris Peterson, Claire Voon
**Production Director**
Minjee Cho
**Production Manager**
Andrea Chlad
**Press Supervisor**
Ali Taptık

**Art Direction, Design & Typefaces**
A2/SW/HK, London

**Publisher**
Dana Triwush
magazine@aperture.org

**Director of Brand Partnerships**
Isabelle Friedrich McTwigan
212-946-7118
imctwigan@aperture.org

**Advertising**
Elizabeth Morina
917-691-2608
emorina@aperture.org

**Executive Director,
Aperture Foundation**
Sarah Meister

Minor White, Editor (1952–1974)

Michael E. Hoffman, Publisher and Executive Director (1964–2001)



aperture.org

# FINE ART PRINT ON ALUMINUM DIBOND

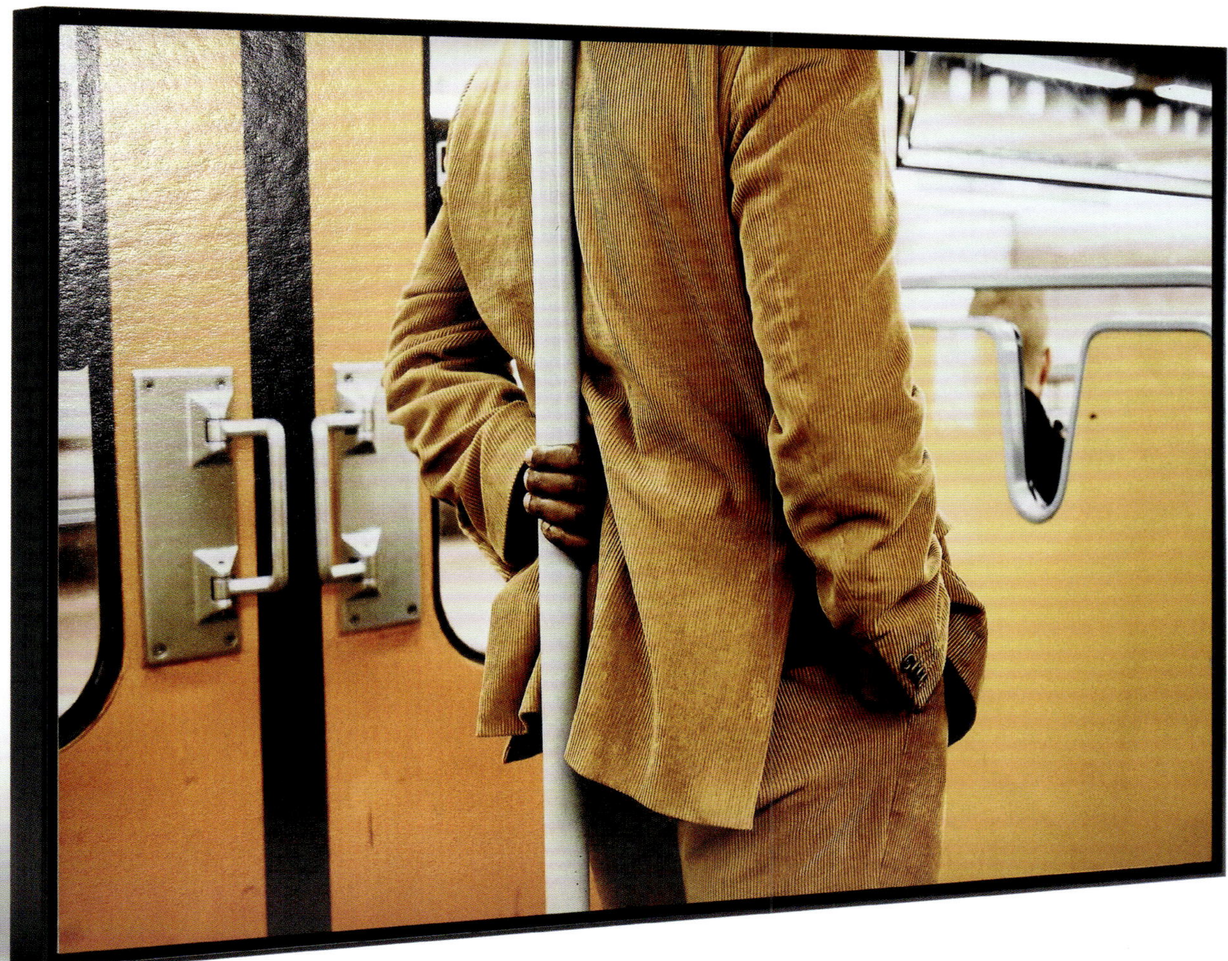

Fine Art Print on Aluminum Dibond | Hahnemühle Fine Art Baryta | 18 x 12 ”
Aluminum ArtBox, 1 ”, black

Present your Fine Art Prints in puristic elegance! Four papers with characteristic surfaces give your photography an individual effect. Our lamination on Alu-Dibond ensures a perfect presentation of your Fine Art Prints on the wall — absolutely flat and, if desired, in a custom-made frame from our manufacture. There are two matt and two glossy variants to choose from, so you can determine the paper according to your preferences and matching the motif.

**The new Fine Art Prints on Aluminum Dibond are available in WhiteWall stores and at WhiteWall.com.**

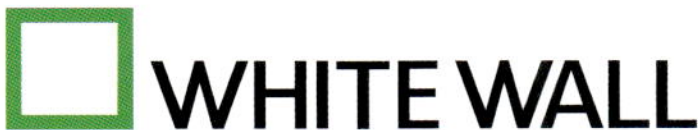

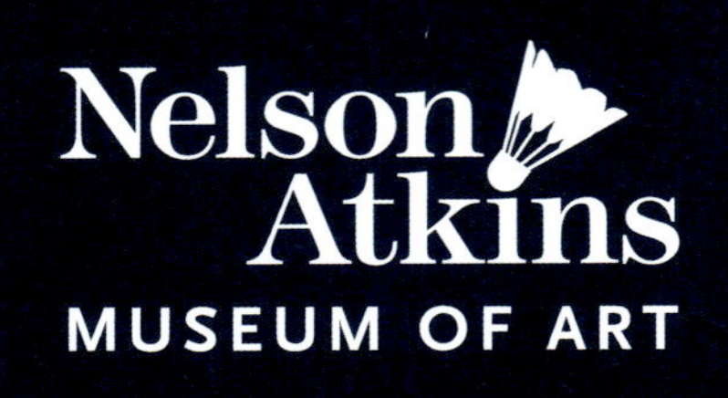


816.751.1278 | nelson-atkins.org
45th & Oak, Kansas City, Missouri

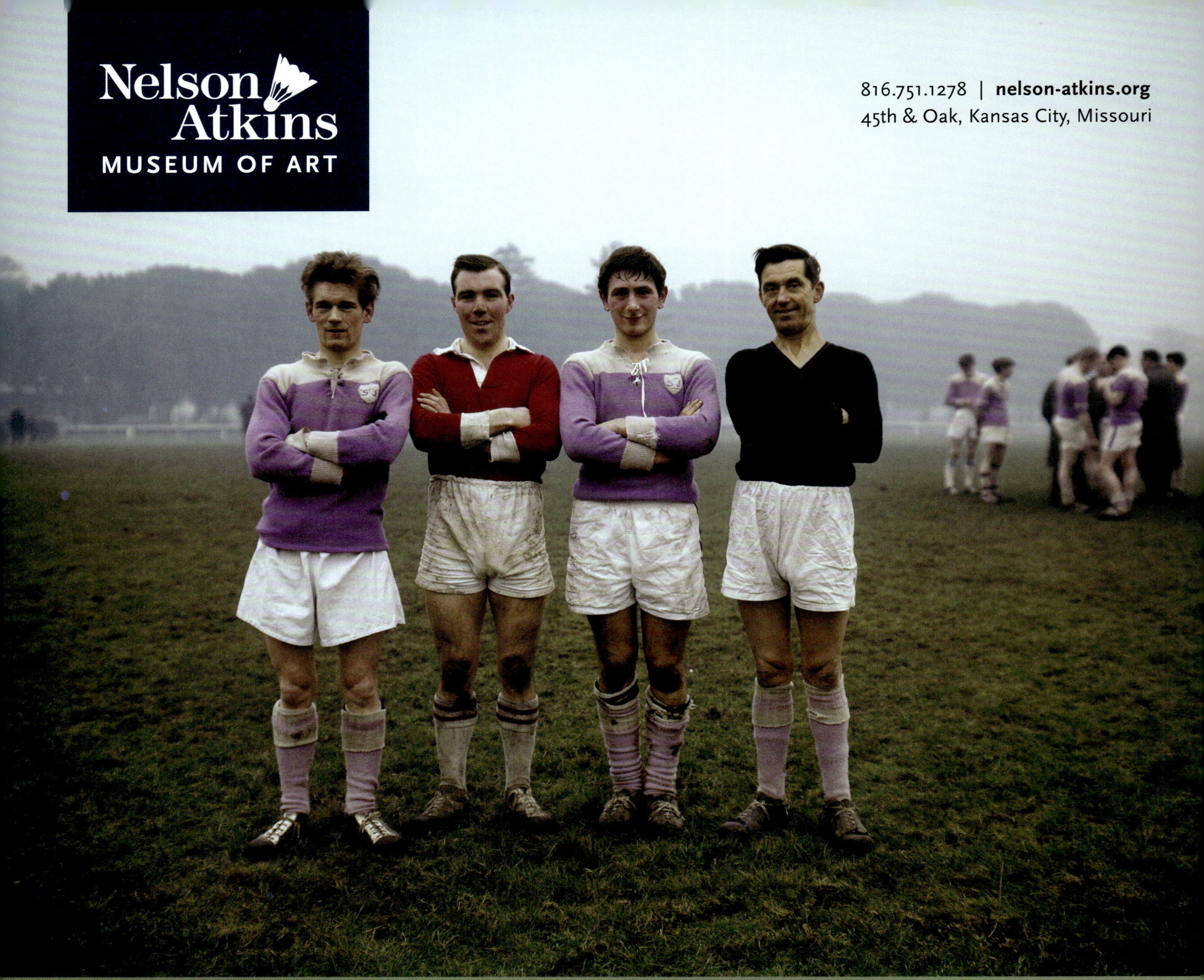

# EVELYN HOFER

## EYES ON THE CITY

Sept. 16, 2023–Mar. 24, 2024

Evelyn Hofer's insightful and sensitive portraits of European and U.S. cities convey the vibrancy and complexity of urban life in the late 1950s and 1960s.

Co-organized by The Nelson-Atkins Museum of Art and the High Museum of Art. In Kansas City, generous support provided by the Hall Family Foundation.

Evelyn Hofer, American, born Germany(1922–2009). *Phoenix Park on a Sunday, Dublin,* 1966.Dye transfer print,13 5/16 × 16 7/16 inches. The Nelson-Atkins Museum of Art, Gift of the Hall Family Foundation,2019.39.14.©Estate of Evelyn Hofer

### Alfredo Boulton

Alfredo Boulton had multiple lives. The Venezuelan photographer, art critic, historian, collector, and publisher was born into a wealthy Caracas family in 1908. As a teenager, he studied and traveled in Europe, where he met avant-garde artists who would shape his vision—and the trajectory of modern art in Venezuela. Boulton is "shockingly underrecognized outside of his home country," notes the curator Idurre Alonso. But that's likely to change with Alonso's exhibition *Alfredo Boulton: Looking at Venezuela (1928–1978)*, drawn from the Getty's acquisition of Boulton's extensive archive in 2020. Boulton's photographs show the influence of modernists such as Man Ray and his fascination with Venezuela's history, expressed in his heroizing images of fishermen and cowboys. In 1952, he photographed the celebrated matador Luis Sánchez Olivares as he was dressing for a bullfight in an elaborate cape embroidered with the Virgin of Caracas. It's an image, Alonso says, that "conveys the idea of the mixture of cultures that happened in Latin America"—and is emblematic of Boulton's desire to portray a uniquely Venezuelan form of beauty.

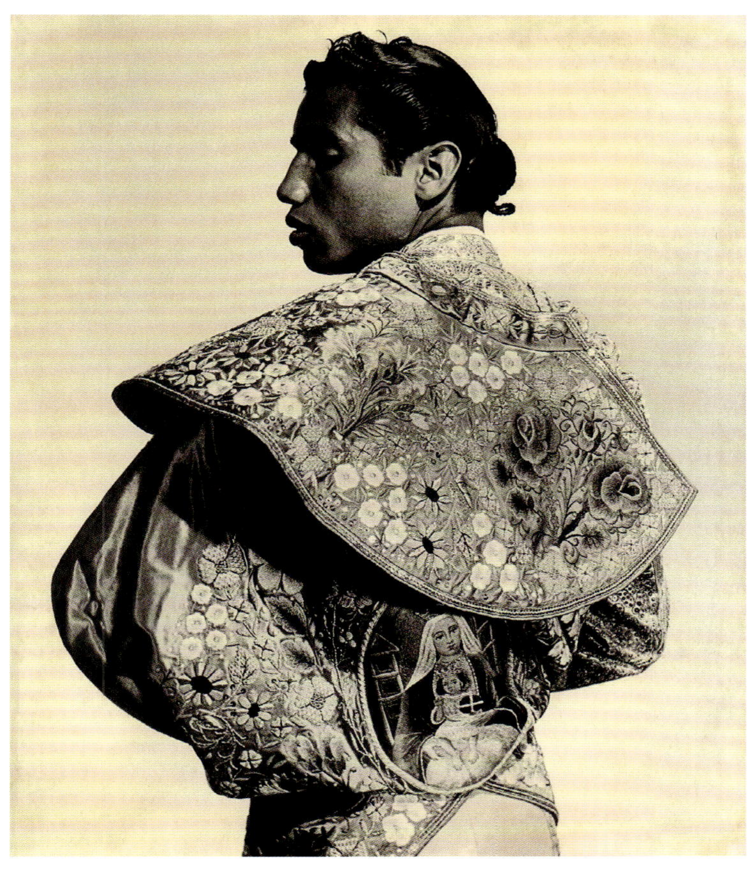

*Alfredo Boulton: Looking at Venezuela (1928–1978)* at the Getty Center, Los Angeles, August 29, 2023–January 7, 2024

Alfredo Boulton, *Luis Sánchez Olivares, "El Diamante Negro," No. 2*, 1952
© J. Paul Getty Trust

Weng Fen, *On the Wall Series: Guangzhou 1*, 2002–3
Courtesy the artist

### A Window Suddenly Opens

In 1996, the artists Rong Rong and Liu Zheng began publishing a magazine called *New Photo*, which tracked how photographers in China were responding to the galvanic changes in their lives and culture that coincided with the rise of globalization and the spectacular growth of cities. "When *concept* enters Chinese photography, it is as if a window suddenly opens in a room that has been sealed for years," they wrote in the magazine's third issue. "We can now breathe comfortably, and we now reach a new meaning of 'new photography.'" What "new" meant in the 1990s is the starting point for the Hirshhorn Museum's survey *A Window Suddenly Opens*, which covers three decades of image making from China as artists shifted from straightforward documentary to kaleidoscopic conceptualism, deploying irreverent humor, digital intervention, and environmental critique. "After decades of prioritizing the collective, a new focus on the individual arose," notes the curator Betsy Johnson, "and with it came a conceptual liberation that freed artists from political and institutional constraints regarding how art is made and what it could be."

*A Window Suddenly Opens: Contemporary Photography in China* at the Hirshhorn Museum and Sculpture Garden, Washington, DC, November 4, 2022–January 7, 2024

## María Magdalena Campos-Pons

Since the 1980s, the Cuban artist María Magdalena Campos-Pons has used a range of sensory strategies to untangle complex histories related to colonialism, memory, migration, gender, and religion. Having grown up in postrevolutionary Cuba, and as the descendant of Nigerians who came to the island through the transatlantic slave trade, Campos-Pons mixes photography, film, painting, performance, and installation with frequent references to the Afro-Cuban Santeria tradition. Working during the emergence of intersectional-feminist discourses in the 1980s, she places special emphasis on the body as a site of trauma and possibility, as well as on its inextricable links to the histories of representing race and sexuality. *María Magdalena Campos-Pons: Behold* is the artist's first survey since 2007 and brings together highlights from nearly four decades of work, emerging from what she calls an "undisciplined" approach to the boundary between media and performance. Through often large-scale and multipaneled works, tactile interventions, and the manipulation of organic material, Campos-Pons, according to the curator Carmen Hermo, "shows us the ache of sublimated violence, the resilience of memory, the bittersweet beauty inherent in the fortitude of survival, continuation, and growth."

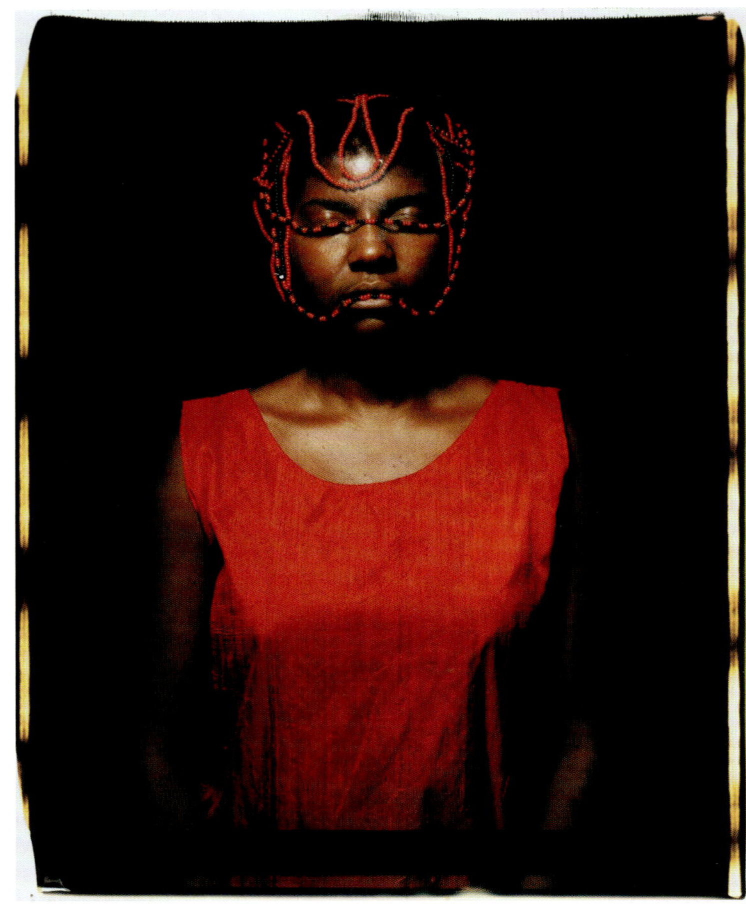

*María Magdalena Campos-Pons: Behold* **at the Brooklyn Museum, September 15, 2023–January 14, 2024**

María Magdalena Campos-Pons, *Red Composition* (detail), from the series *Los Caminos (The Path)*, 1997
© the artist and courtesy Gallery Wendi Norris

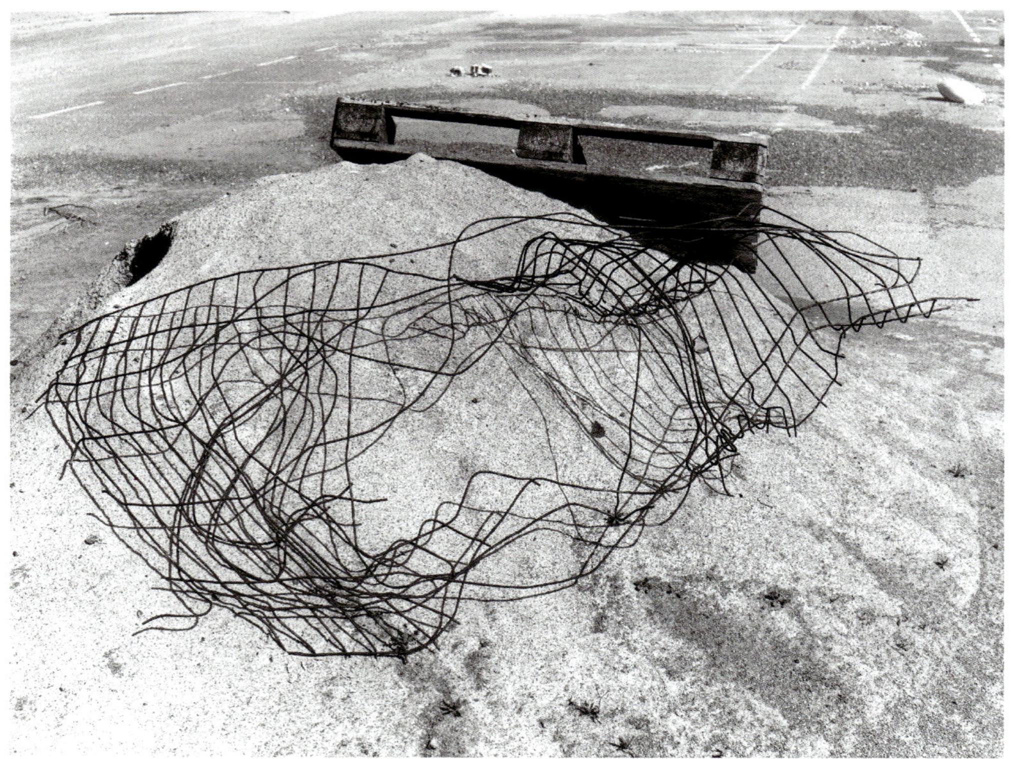

Raymond Meeks, *Untitled*, 2022, from the series *The Inhabitants*
Courtesy the artist

## Immersion

Immersion—a partnership between Fondation Henri Cartier-Bresson in Paris and the International Center of Photography (ICP) in New York—consists of alternating residencies in France and the United States, culminating in an original commission shared through bilingual publications and exhibitions. This year's laureate, Raymond Meeks, spent most of 2022 exploring and photographing the formal and informal infrastructures that underpin immigration in Western Europe. His resulting series, *The Inhabitants*, scans the landscape for traces, pathways, and physical impressions of transit and migration, linking them to the interiority of his own home and studio in northern France. "Each footprint, broken branch, and makeshift eating and sleeping place is a sign, but not just of anxious and fearful passage," says David Campany, the managing director of programs at ICP and a mentor for this edition of Immersion. "It is a sign of the system." In both content and form, the exhibition—presented alongside exhibitions by past laureates Vasantha Yogananthan and Gregory Halpern—addresses the constructed nature of national identity and the many ways landscapes and people shape each other.

*Immersion: Gregory Halpern, Raymond Meeks, and Vasantha Yogananthan* **at the International Center of Photography, New York, September 29, 2023–January 8, 2024**

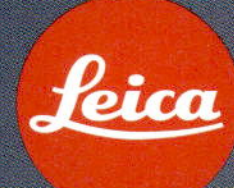


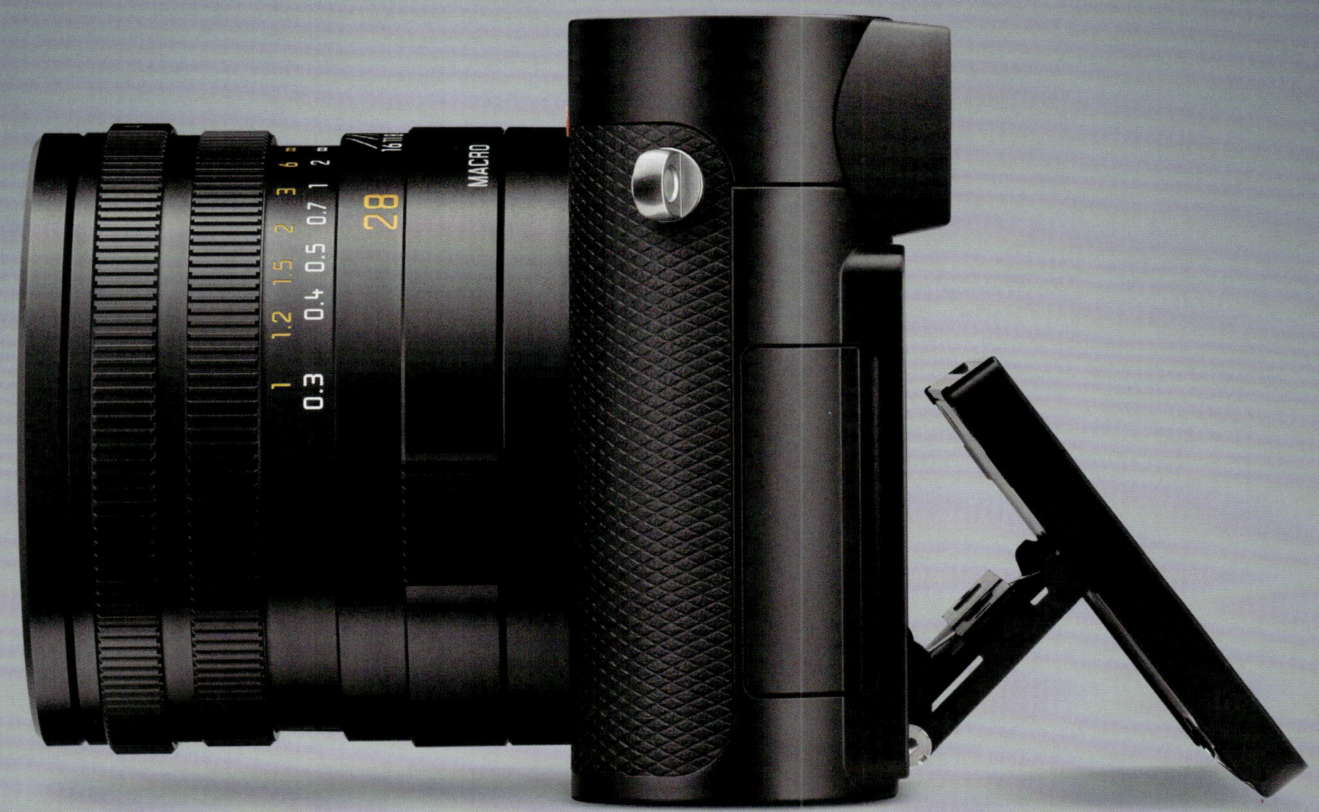


## LEICA Q3

### Unique. Just like you.

Discover a camera as unique as you are.
**leicacamerausa.com**

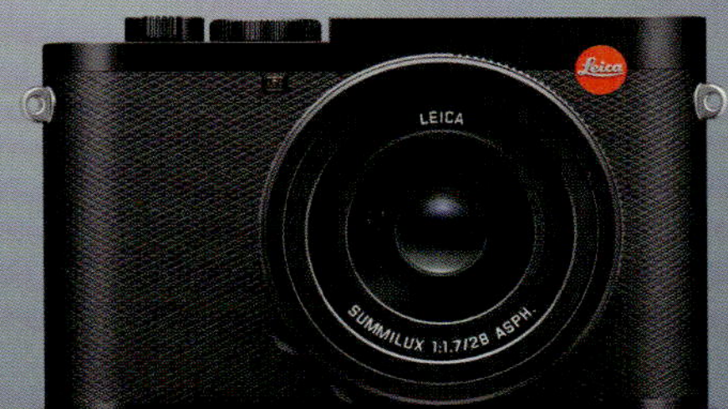


Bellevue | Boston | Los Angeles | Miami | Washington, D.C. | San Francisco | NYC – SoHo
NYC - Meatpacking District (Coming November 2023)

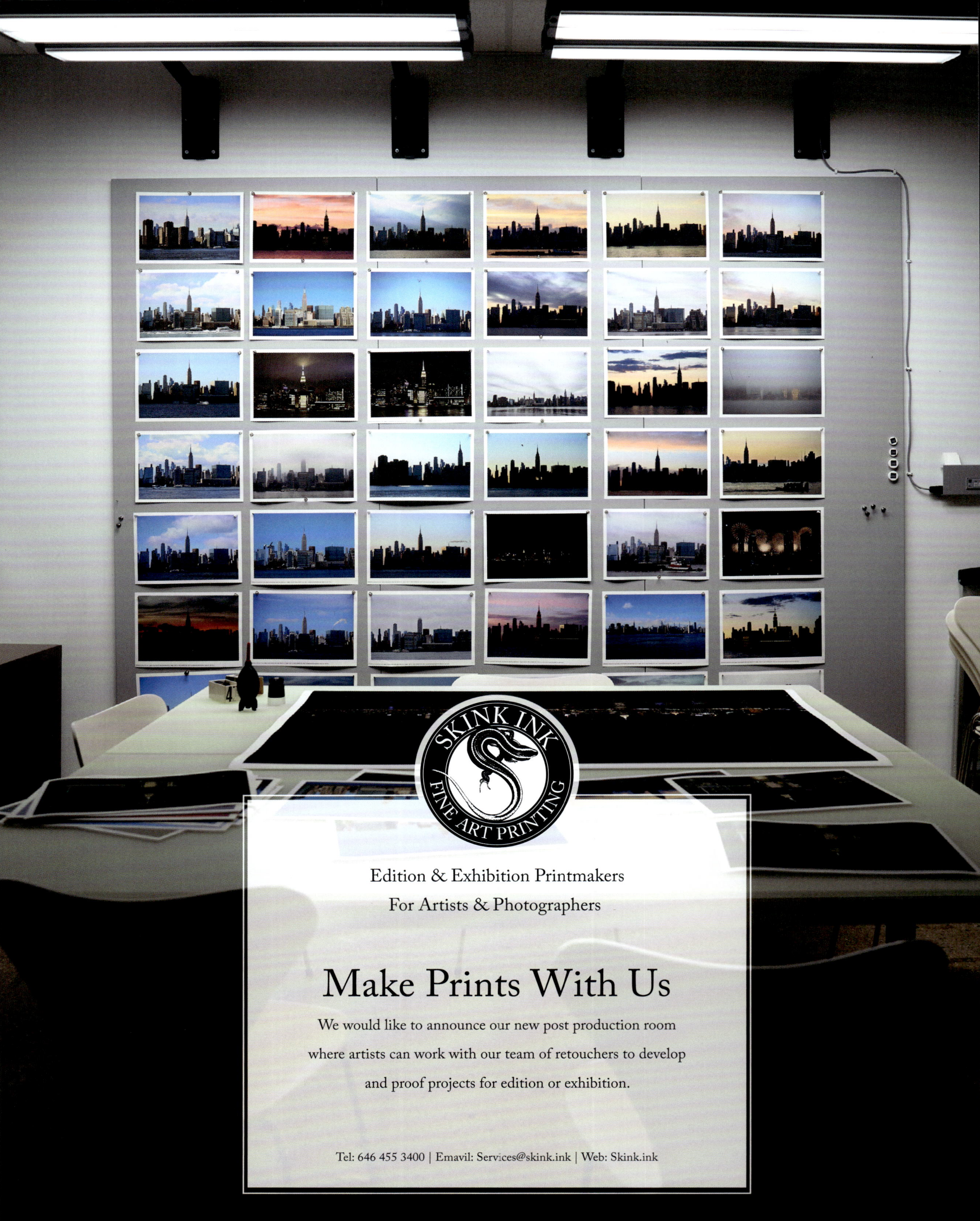

SKINK INK
FINE ART PRINTING

Edition & Exhibition Printmakers
For Artists & Photographers

Make Prints With Us

We would like to announce our new post production room
where artists can work with our team of retouchers to develop
and proof projects for edition or exhibition.

Tel: 646 455 3400 | Emavil: Services@skink.ink | Web: Skink.ink

Artwork by Philip Riley

# Viewfinder

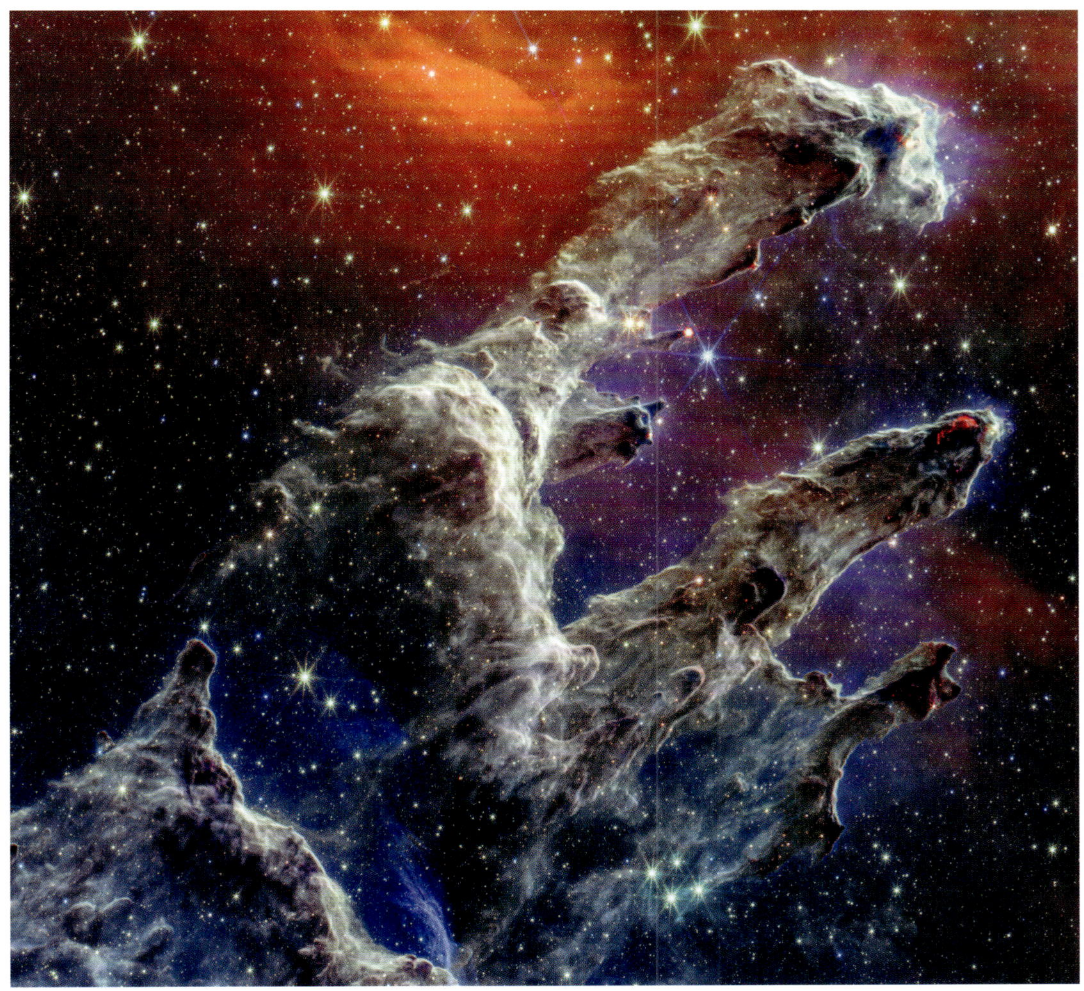

**How do the James Webb Space Telescope's cosmic views represent what we cannot see?**

Elizabeth A. Kessler

In the mid-nineteenth century, William Henry Fox Talbot, one of the inventors of photography, proposed a cutting-edge experiment. Scientists were beginning to study light beyond human vision, light we now describe as infrared and ultraviolet, and Talbot conceived of a way to photograph with these invisible rays. Although photography was less than a decade old, and he never tried the method himself, Talbot was confident that "the eye of the camera would see plainly where the human eye would find nothing but darkness." Jump forward to the twenty-first century, and images from the James Webb Space Telescope deliver on that promise. The telescope, which was launched into orbit in 2021 and relies on methods that echo those proposed by Talbot, observes infrared light with seemingly impressive ease, and its vividly colored, highly detailed images show us what had previously been hidden from view. But to depict what the infrared camera sees plainly requires another jump, a leap from detecting the presence of light to translating it for our eyes.

With its view of the Pillars of Creation, the Webb revisits a star-forming region in the Eagle Nebula made familiar by Hubble Space Telescope images. But now we see more—more of everything. The three immense columns of gas and dust glow with silvery light, highlighted by areas in brilliant red. With close study, one finds stunningly complex and detailed forms within the columns. These are not monoliths but vast and varied topographies that invite exploration. The sky in the background is decorated with an array of colors: deep blue in the lower left, violets

"

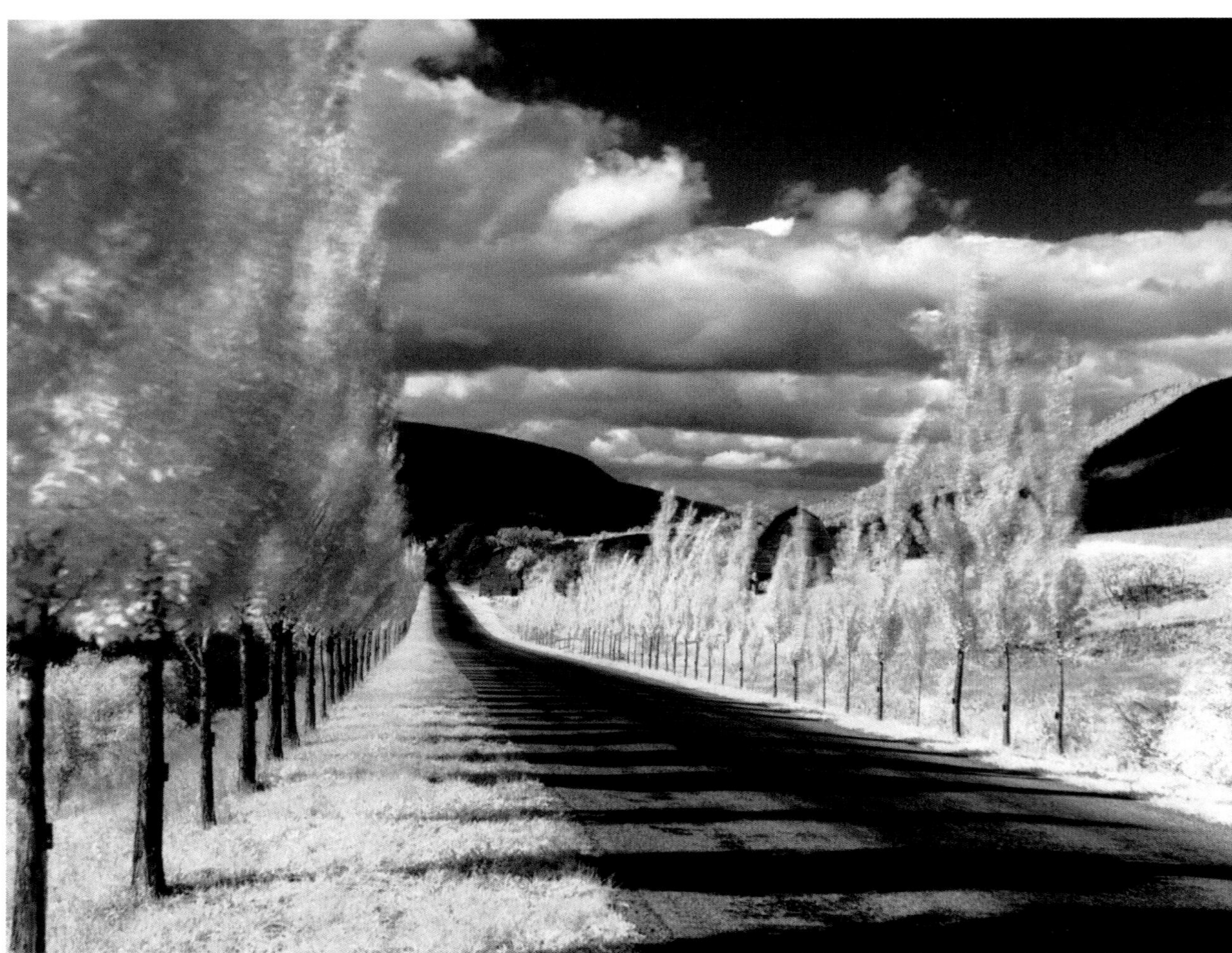



and purples in the middle, and fiery orange along the top. And stars, thousands of points of light in various sizes and hues, speckle the entire field of view.

The appearance of these images depends on careful choices by astronomers and image processors, who adjust contrast, clean up flaws, and choose how to orient the celestial scenes. These decisions help to make evident the scientifically interesting aspects of the observations. They also align these views of distant nebulae, stars, and galaxies with our aesthetic standards and expectations, the visual language we have learned through looking at pictures of our world. The ideal translation then reads in two tongues, as scientifically valid and aesthetically compelling.

The delicate balance of science and aesthetics is most evident in the colors. The Webb's cameras record monochromatic observations, each taken through a filter that registers light at a particular wavelength. To create a color image, astronomers and image processors digitally combine at least three different observations together, assigning a unique hue to each one. The relative wavelengths guide the color choices: typically, blue is assigned to the observation that corresponds to the shortest wavelength of light, red to the one at the longest wavelength, and

green to the one in the middle. When image processors follow the convention exactly, colors can make visible the physical properties of the nebula for those who know the key.

However, the translation is often more complex than such a straightforward example suggests. Webb's resplendent *Pillars of Creation* incorporates nine observations, and image processors introduced other hues—purple, yellow, cyan, and orange—to distinguish between them. The practice of mapping color and relative wavelength guides the choices, but as the colors multiply and combine, it becomes much more difficult to interpret just by looking. Instead, the Webb images' rainbow palette delivers something more esoteric: a glimpse, at least in translation, of the unimaginable hues that lie beyond red.

The photographer Minor White, writing in a journal entry from the 1950s, asked: "How far can camerawork go toward making manifest the invisible? That is its work, but how far can it go?" White experimented with infrared film around the same time, photographing the rural landscapes of upstate New York. In *Road and Poplar Trees* (1955), a banal, even clichéd scene of a poplar-lined lane becomes subtly and compellingly strange. The leaves of the trees vibrate with an

animated brilliance. Dark shadows create unsettling gashes along the pathway. Much like the astronomical images, the representation of light in White's photograph can be interpreted in multiple ways. It makes the physical presence or absence of infrared light visible and also invites us to see the mysterious in the familiar.

For the Webb images, the translation operates in the opposite direction, bringing the alien and otherworldly down to earth and to our human eyes. Since their first release in July 2022, the telescope's images have been met with enthusiasm and excitement, especially for how plainly the camera sees. But it's easy to forget or overlook how far the telescope extends human sight and the strangeness of that experience. Over its lifetime, the Webb will help astronomers address a range of scientific questions. Its images have already responded to another question, one that has engaged photographers as deeply as it has scientists: How to represent what we cannot see?

**Elizabeth A. Kessler is a lecturer in American studies at Stanford University and the author of *Picturing the Cosmos: Hubble Space Telescope Images and the Astronomical Sublime* (2012).**

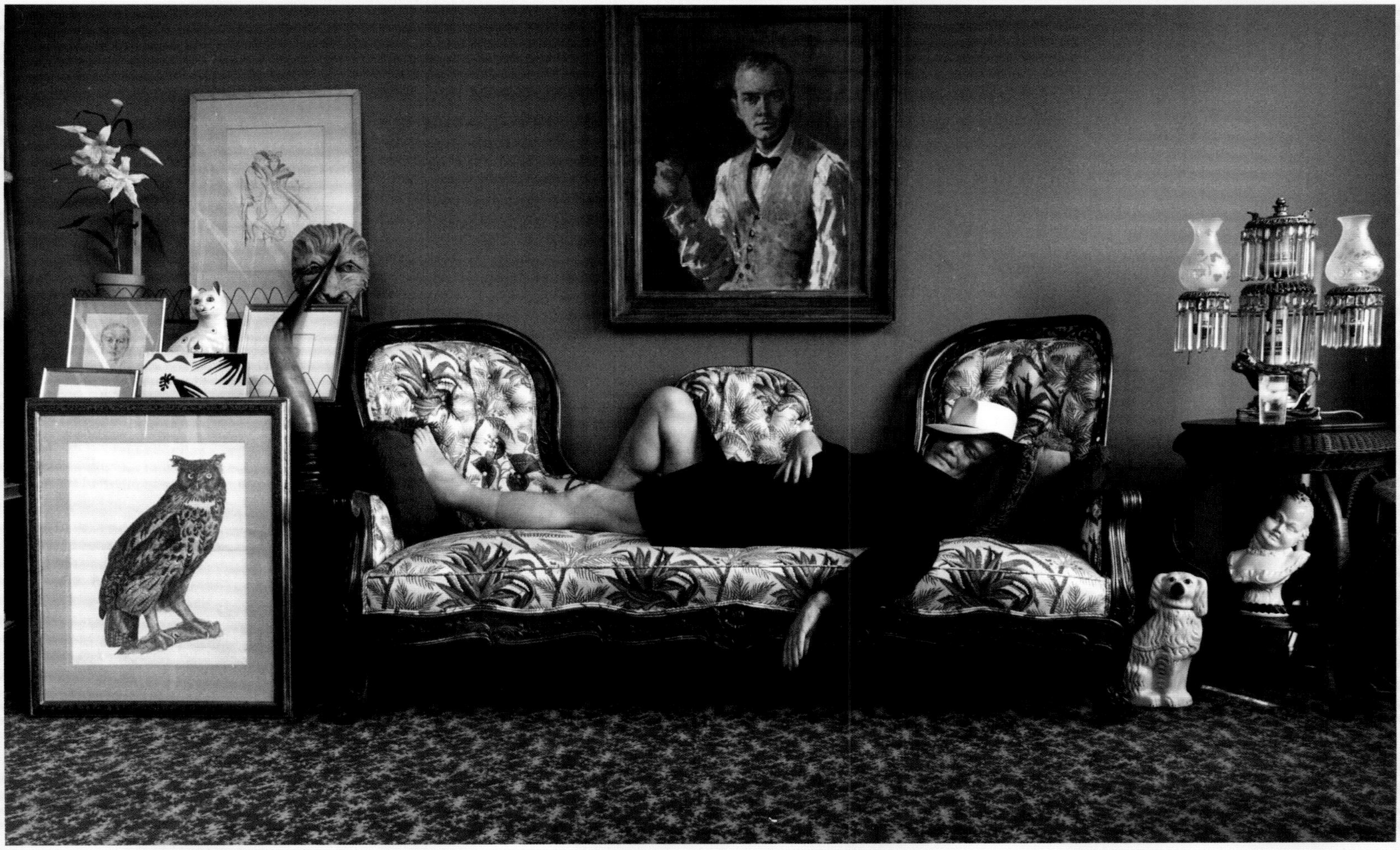

Arnold Newman, *Truman Capote*, 1977. Gelatin silver print. Overall: 40.6 x 50.8 cm. Art Gallery of Ontario. Anonymous Gift, 2012. © Arnold Newman Properties/Getty Images (2023). 2015/3955. Commissioned by *Travel & Leisure*.

# BUILDING ICONS:
# ARNOLD NEWMAN'S
## MAGAZINE WORLD, 1938–2000

October 18, 2023 – January 21, 2024

Organized by the Art Gallery of Ontario

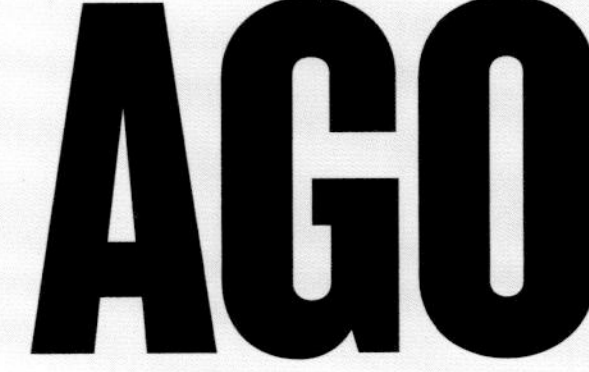

Contemporary programming at the AGO is supported by     Canada Council   Conseil des arts
for the Arts   du Canada

# Timeline

Alexander Gardner's portraits of a former Confederate soldier outnumber even the sitter's long list of aliases. The twenty-one-year-old who plotted with John Wilkes Booth to kill President Lincoln, and brutally attacked Secretary of State William H. Seward, on April 14, 1865, was born Lewis Thornton Powell, though he was also known as Paine, Payne, Hall, and Wood. Powell was executed several months later, but his image has had a long afterlife, extending far beyond Civil War history.
—**Kim Beil**

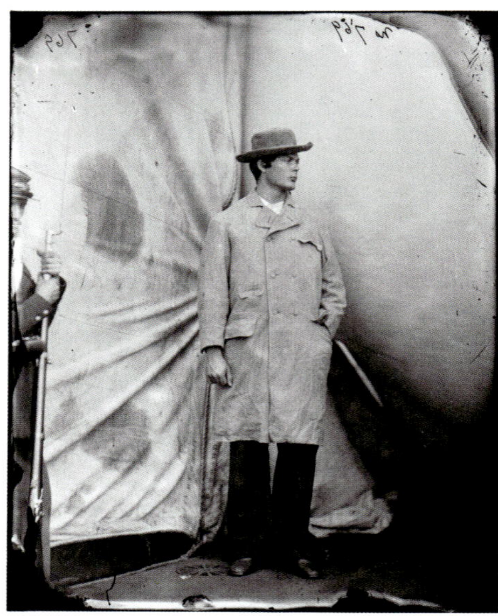

Gardner took this portrait of Powell on the day of his arrest, April 18, 1865, according to documentary research by the historians Barry Cauchon and John Elliott. Powell is posed in front of a canvas awning on the USS *Saugus*, an ironclad warship docked in the Washington Navy Yard. The photo-historian Damian Sutton points out that Powell is dressed in his own clothes; investigators even retrieved Powell's hat from the scene of the crime.

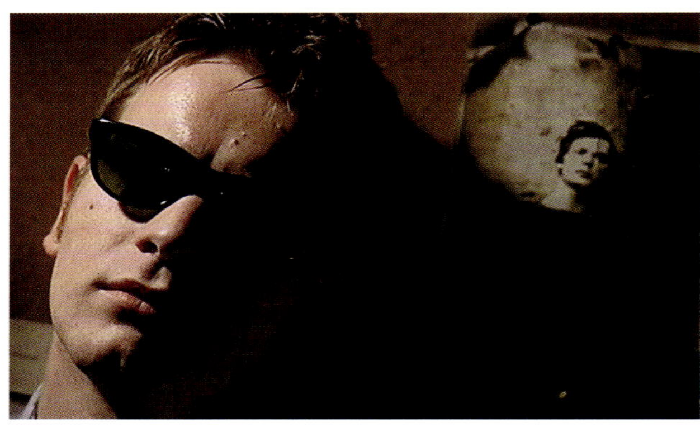

Powell's image lives on. In 1997, it appeared in the film *Nightwatch*. In 2011, Powell became the icon for Michelle Legro's *My Daguerreotype Boyfriend* blog, "where early photography meets extreme hotness." Legro attributes Powell's popularity to the defiant but sultry way he engages Gardner's camera. Back in May 1865, the Washington *Evening Star* reported that Powell "directed a cool impudent stare by turns upon every person in the room." More than 150 years later, Powell's gaze still seems to unsettle time itself.

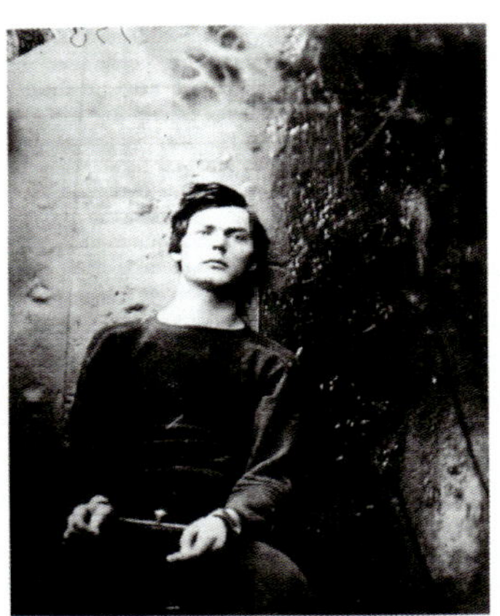



Powell's portraits found more admirers in the twentieth century. This version was cited by Roland Barthes in *Camera Lucida* (1980). Like earlier writers, Barthes admired Powell's fine form: "The photograph is handsome, as is the boy." For Barthes, the photograph's uniquely poignant affect comes from the fact that it shows a man whose death is imminent, illustrating the medium's founding paradox—in photographs, one sees the past and the future at the same time.

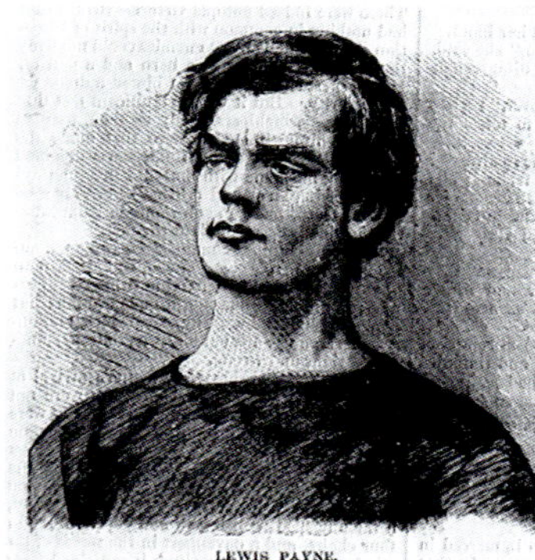



This engraving from *Harper's Weekly*, July 22, 1865, accompanied illustrations of the prisoners on the scaffold and an account of the executions. Other reports of the day described Powell as if the gallows were a catwalk: "His costume showed his fine form to the best advantage, and this . . . brought admiration for his *physique* from those who despised and loathed him for his crimes." The *New York Times* characterized him, instead, as "a wild and savage-looking man, showing no marks of culture or refinement."

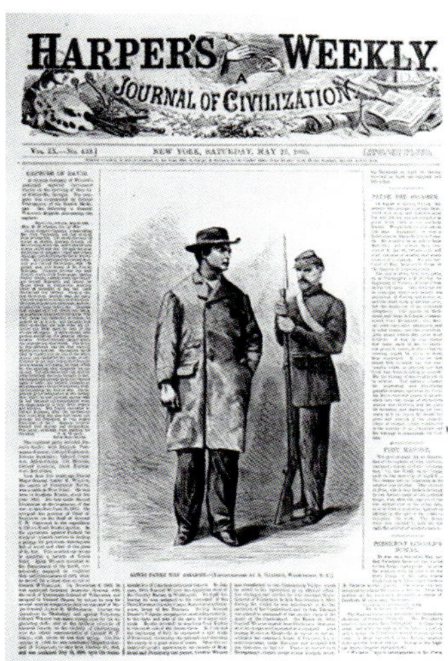

This engraving of Powell made the May 27, 1865, cover of *Harper's Weekly*. Despite the fact that his likeness had been locked down by Gardner's camera, the magazine conceded that Powell's true identity remained mysterious. The article speculated that he was both "an outlaw from Kentucky" and "a hired assassin dispatched from Canada." At the time of printing, he was referred to as Payne, though the magazine ominously questioned "if indeed that be his real name."

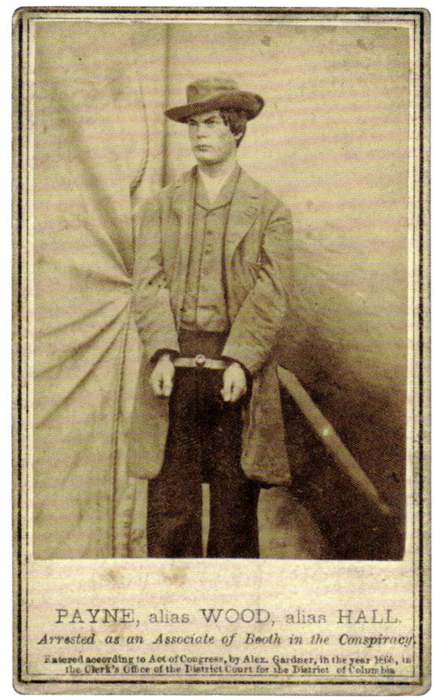

It wasn't only Powell's obscure history that fascinated the public. Even before his identification and arrest, the extreme brutality of his attack on Secretary of State William H. Seward made headlines. Bedridden after a recent carriage accident, the politician was an easy target. Powell fought with and wounded four other men during the encounter. A piece of Seward's bloodied bedsheet, shredded by Powell's bowie knife, is in the collection of the Seward House Museum today.

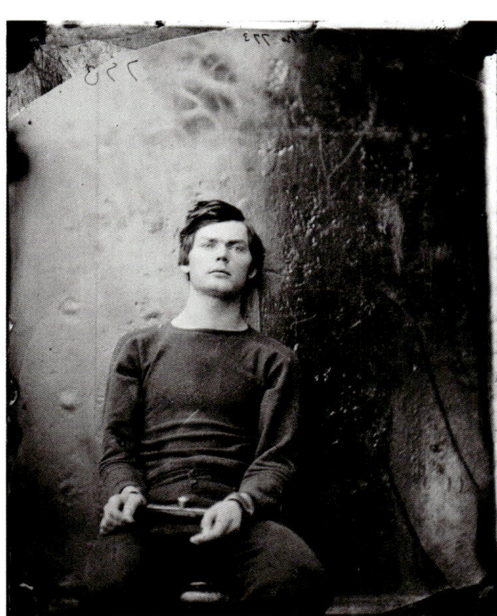

In most of Gardner's portraits, Powell is dressed in the blue woolen top of a Union sailor's uniform, minus the large flap collar. Presaging celebrity trials of the following centuries, the press described Powell's clothing in intimate detail. The Washington *Evening Star* commented, "He seems to affect as rowdyish a dress as possible, and to-day appeared in nothing but a close-fitting collarless blue woolen undershirt, pants of the same color and material, stocking and shoes."

**Kim Beil teaches art history at Stanford University. She is the author of *Good Pictures: A History of Popular Photography* (2020).**

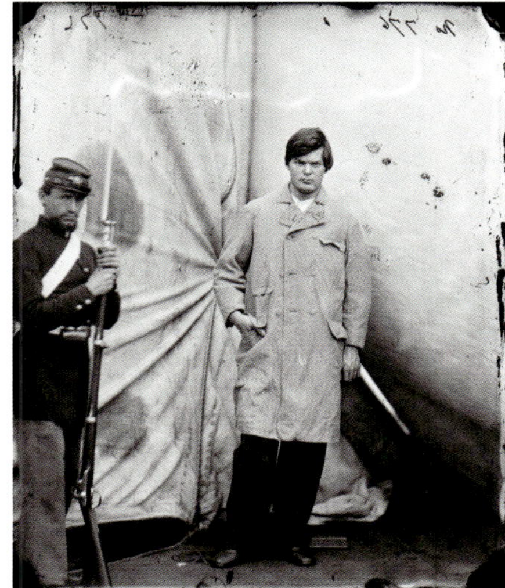

Authorities and the public were desperate for more information about the man witnesses repeatedly described as "large" and "powerful." Gardner's photographs conformed to these expectations, emphasizing Powell's height and muscular build in comparison to the guard. Gardner was perhaps taken with Powell too. In addition to at least six variations of the standing portrait, five of which Gardner copyrighted and sold as cartes-de-visite, he also took four seated portraits of Powell in front of the gun turret on the USS *Saugus*.

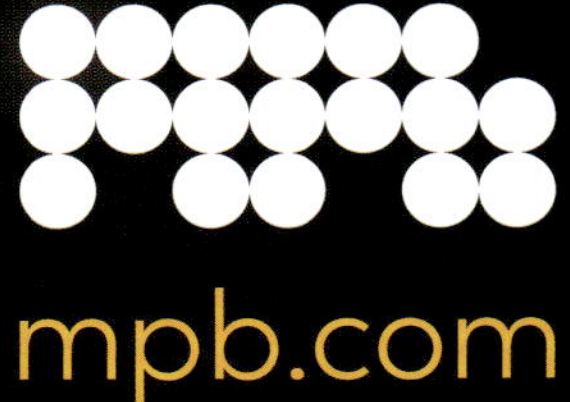

# MPB **values** your camera gear

**Free shipping, fast payment, fully insured.**

Our dynamic pricing engine provides the right price for any camera or lens.

Selling to MPB is completely risk free. Your gear is always fully insured. You can change your mind at any point before you get paid and we'll return your gear for free.

Drop off your gear and get paid within days.

See how much money you can get for your gear.

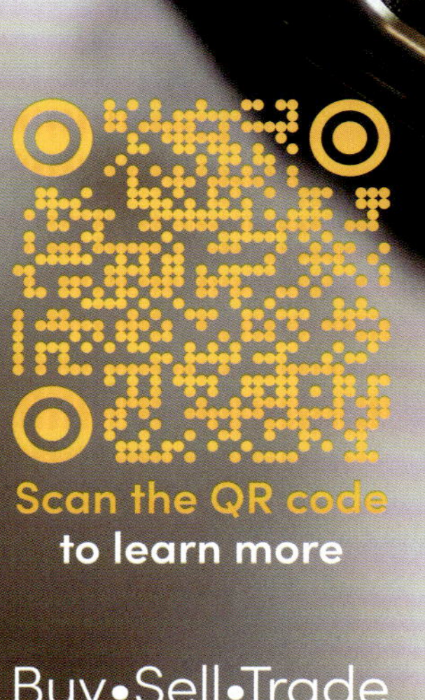


Buy•Sell•Trade
Create

# Dispatches

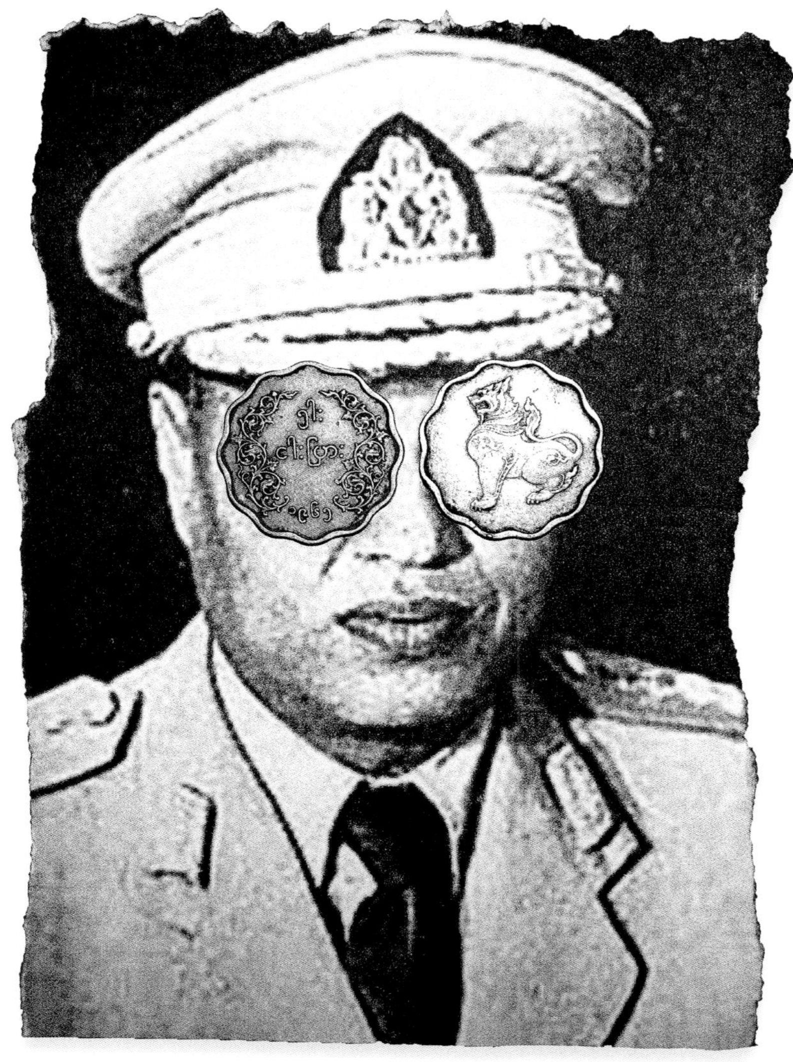

**Following a brutal and ongoing coup in 2021, photographers from Myanmar attempt to make sense of a troubling new reality.**
Tin Htet Paing

In the early hours of February 1, 2021, Myanmar's military began knocking on the doors of dissidents. The Tatmadaw, as they are officially known, had launched a brutal coup that swiftly overthrew the democratically elected government. Within weeks, the military transformed the country into a full-fledged dictatorship, suppressing peaceful protests with lethal force and arresting anticoup activists. The move was reminiscent of the junta that had ruled Myanmar in various

forms from 1962 to 2011, evoking a familiar horror for those who had lived through previous takeovers. For the younger generation, which had come of age in a relatively democratic and free Myanmar, the coup represented an existential crisis. Due to the junta's ongoing efforts to repress citizens' freedom—including enforced disappearances, long prison sentences, and executions—the majority of Myanmar's population remains opposed to the military regime.

Sai [redacted], a multidisciplinary artist who works under a partially redacted pseudonym (*sai* means "mister" in a Shan dialect) for his family's safety and to highlight Myanmar's censorship of its citizens, was in the former capital, Yangon, when the military arrived at his family home in the country's Shan State. His father—a chief minister and senior member of the National League for Democracy party—was promptly arrested, forcing Sai into hiding. In May

2021, the artist secretly returned to his home, where his mother had been placed under house arrest. After a brief reunion, he fled again to avoid possible arrest, as military intelligence was keeping the family members of detained leaders under close watch.

His series *Trails of Absence* (2021–ongoing) uses a physical gap to portray family trauma, fear, and the void left by his father's imprisonment. The artist stages portraits where he and his mother appear with a string running between them. Their faces are obscured by pieces of fabric woven in the style of a traditional Shan carpet. These fabrics, originally worn by those being held—and effectively disappeared—in Myanmar's notorious prisons after the February 2021 coup, were given to Sai through personal connections. "I asked to get some sort of evidence that can represent their existence," he told me recently. "They gave me their clothes."

For those in Myanmar who oppose the coup, there has been a lot of frustration over the Western media's coverage. Despite the fact that ordinary citizens are subjected to daily armed violence and arbitrary detentions, the focus has seemed to remain on high-profile political figures. In 2022, Sai's father was sentenced to twenty years of imprisonment and hard labor. "The series is a call to action for the world to take notice of political prisoners in Myanmar," the artist says. "Can the world still sweep us under the carpet if we become the carpet?"

For the photographer Ri—who also works under a pseudonym—Myanmar's political present is both deeply personal and historically bound. While her previous images focused on community, queer relationships, and Myanmar's landscape, after that February's events, she felt the need for a change. While photographing anticoup demonstrations in Yangon in 2021, Ri wanted to move beyond a documentary approach and instead explore the historical power structures perpetuating oppression. "I felt like I had a responsibility to do something when the coup happened," she says. "It was partly because of survivor's guilt."

In her multimedia piece *What We Remember, When We Remember* (2021–ongoing), Ri uses archival imagery, original photographs, and collage to explore the impact of nearly half a century of military rule on the country's collective psyche. She spoke with a range of subjects—those who have embraced the Tatmadaw along with those who fear and despise them—asking, "When did you learn to hate or be afraid of the military?" One issue that came up often was money. The previous military, led by the dictator General Ne Win, instituted a swathe of policies, including the devaluing of select banknotes from Myanmar's currency, ultimately weakening the cash-based national economy. Ri's mother, who worked in a state-owned factory then, was affected by these changes, losing all of her life savings. In one piece from the series, two defunct coins cover the former dictator's eyes, a commentary on the economic stresses placed on ordinary people.

Despite broad national resistance to the coup, Myanmar's population is

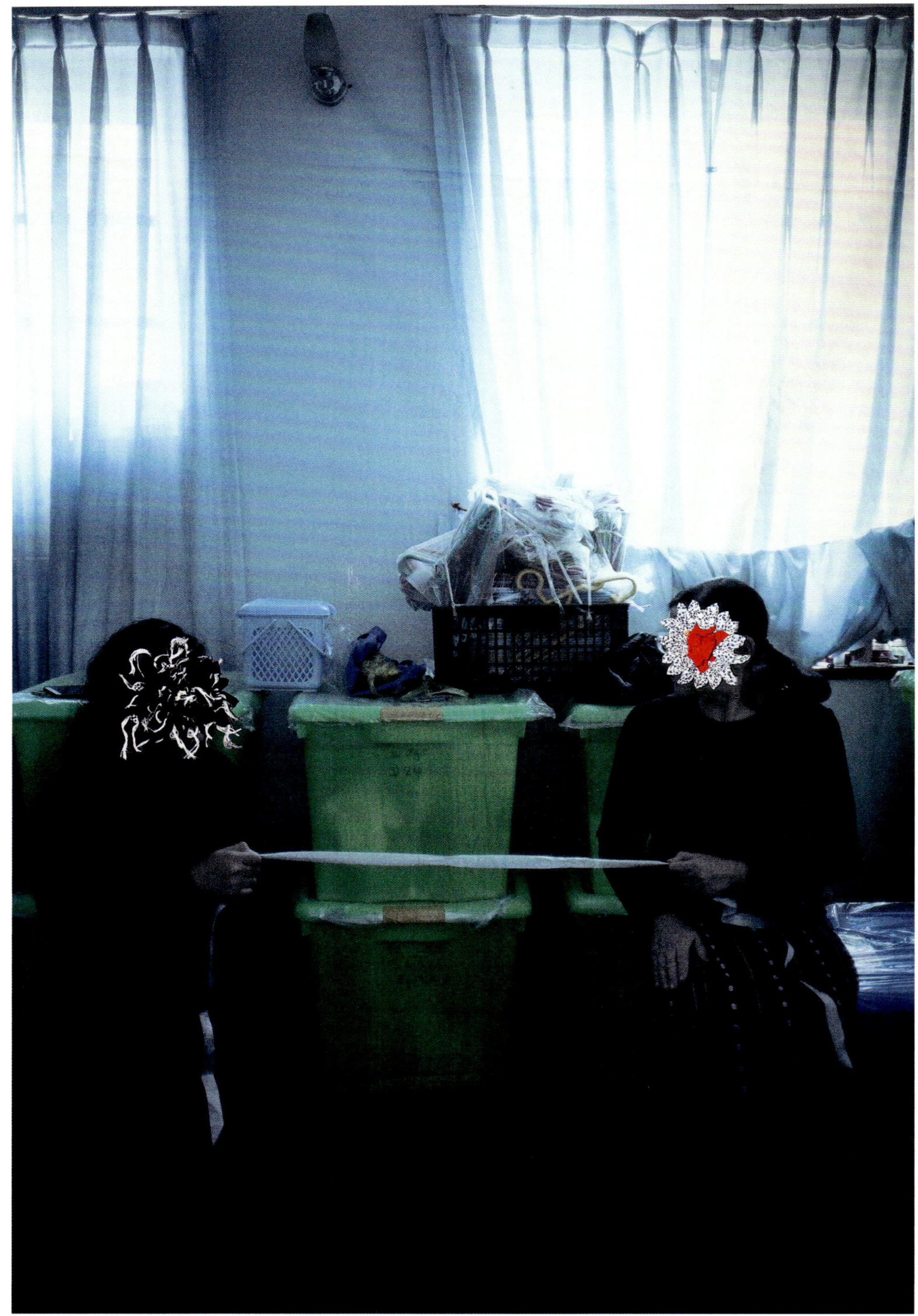

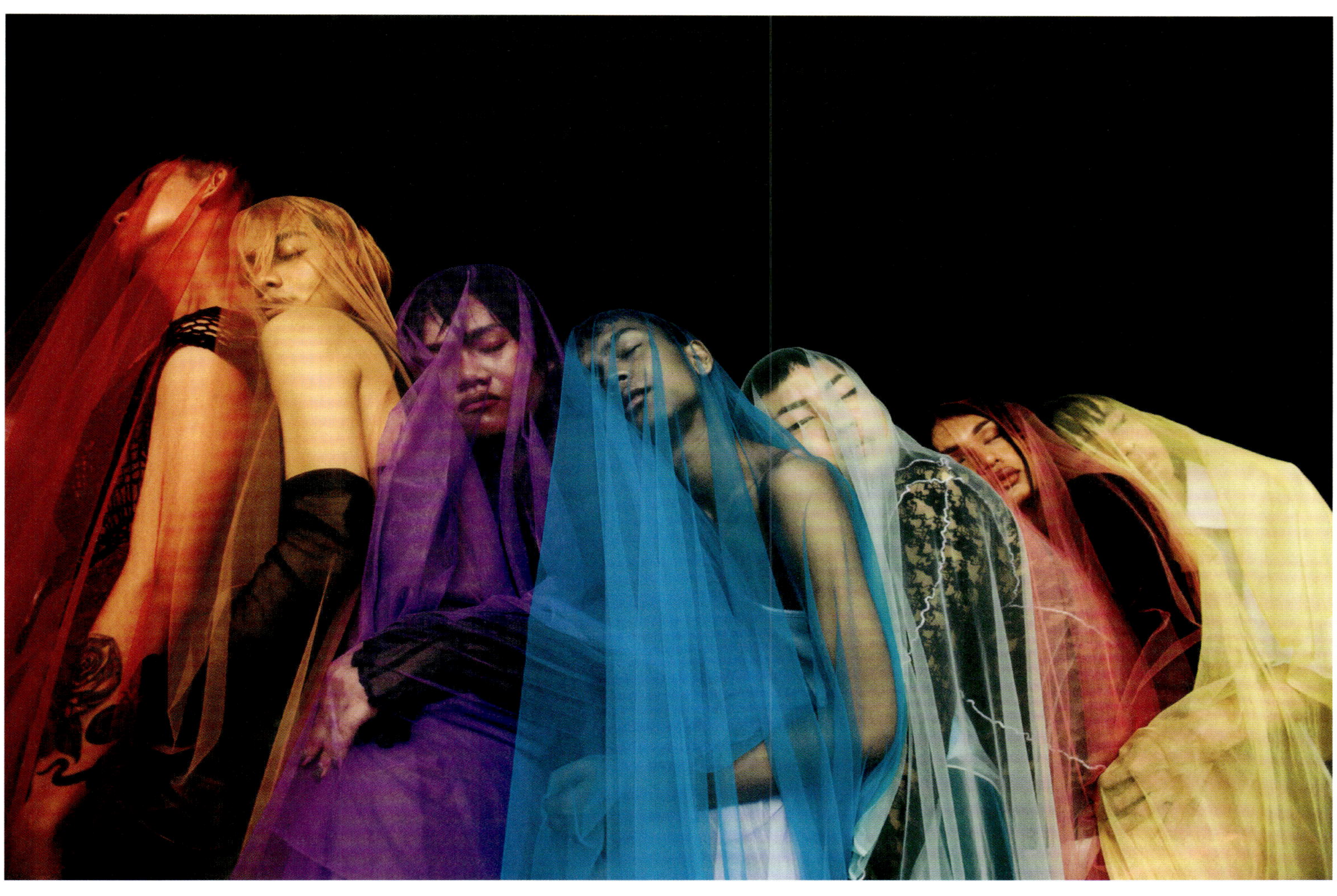



# These artists belong to a generation that has experienced both partial democracy and dictatorship.

far from a monolith, with more than 135 ethnic groups across several states. Currently living between Bangkok and Yangon, the photographer Zicky Le is half Burmese and half Karen, an ethnic minority with a long history of conflict with Myanmar's governments that dates back to the country's independence from British rule in 1948. Zicky has been a fashion and editorial photographer for nearly a decade, with work published in *Vogue Italia* and the Madrid-based *Sicky* magazine. The series *We Are Who We Are* (2022) expresses his frustration with how queer people are portrayed—often, with mockery—in Myanmar's popular culture and mainstream media. In response, Zicky photographs his queer friends with vibrant color and lighting to celebrate their beauty, diversity, and truth. "I want to contribute to a cultural revolution that overthrows sexism, transphobia, and homophobia," Zicky says. "Representation is not the end of liberation but a means."

Young artists such as Sai, Ri, and Zicky have grown up in the shadow of two Myanmars, belonging to a generation that has experienced both partial democracy and dictatorship. Like them, many artists in the country have begun to self-censor their endeavors under a junta-ruled Myanmar. Some, also using pseudonyms, have worked exclusively with foreign institutions or exiled outlets. Several photographers have fled to neighboring countries, including Thailand, while others have joined the armed revolt. In their own context, each has contributed to the creation of informal communities of support that challenge the political systems and ideologies inherited from decades of military rule. For these artists, photography is a crucial tool for solidarity, resistance, and visibility—and it is one of many.


**Tin Htet Paing is an exiled Myanmar journalist and photographer currently based in Melbourne, Australia.**

# Curriculum
## Mimi Plumb

The illicit thrills and dusty landscapes of suburban California are the raw material of Mimi Plumb's arresting black-and-white photographs. Girls sneak a cigarette, boys play amid tires, freeways spiral into the sky, and the threat of wildfire looms endlessly. Buildings are bombed out and punks dance all night. Plumb grew up in the Bay Area and taught at the San Francisco Art Institute. Lately, her work from the 1970s and '80s, which eerily predicted environmental chaos and the transformations of the American West, has received retrospective treatment through the photobooks *Landfall* (2018), *The White Sky* (2020), and *The Golden City* (2021). In Plumb's eye, the future has already arrived, and the end is already beginning.

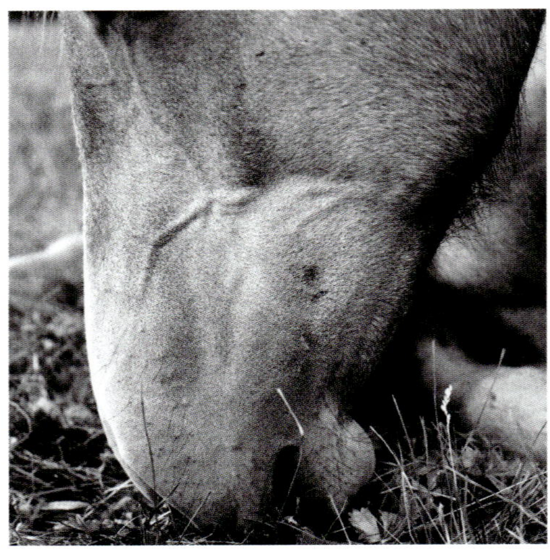

### Cricket, the lead mare

For several years, Cricket always avoided me. She was the lead mare of a herd of horses roaming a meadow in California's John Muir Wilderness, high in the Sierra Nevada, during the summer months I spent there. Photographing the horses one afternoon, I felt a light touch on my neck from behind. It was Cricket. She dropped her head onto my shoulder and breathed deeply. We stood stock-still together for twenty minutes. I marvel at the memory of it.

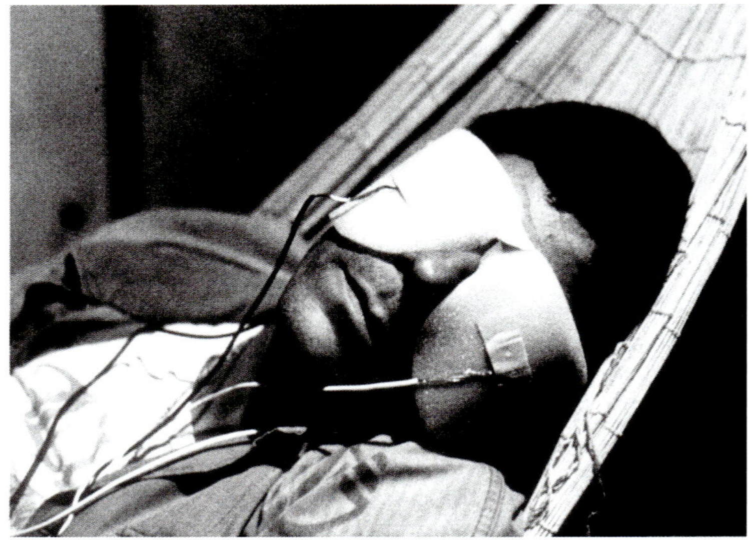

### *La Jetée*

I don't remember when I first saw *La Jetée* (1963), the French science-fiction film by Chris Marker made almost entirely of still black-and-white images. I think it's one of the great stories told with photographs. Visually, the film is stunning, ominous, and seductive—a tale of love and desire set in an apocalyptic future. *La Jetée*, around twenty-seven minutes long, can be found online and is well worth several viewings.

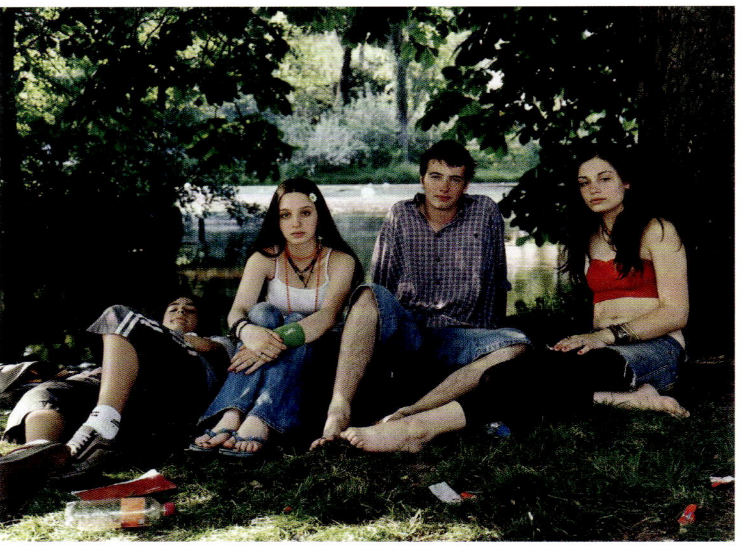

### Sandra S. Phillips

Sandra "Sandy" Phillips joined the San Francisco Museum of Modern Art as a curator of photography in 1987 and stepped down from her senior curator position at the museum in 2016. I idolize Sandy to the extent that, at times, I am still tongue-tied in her presence. The Rineke Dijkstra retrospective, in 2012, was my favorite of her shows. It was a feast for the eyes—room upon room of larger-than-life portraits, precisely described from large-format film. The sitters' youthful faces conveyed both their vulnerability and their sweetness—and at times, particularly in the videos, their wild, raw energy. In the exhibitions she curated, Sandy seemed to know in her bones the best way to present an artist's work.

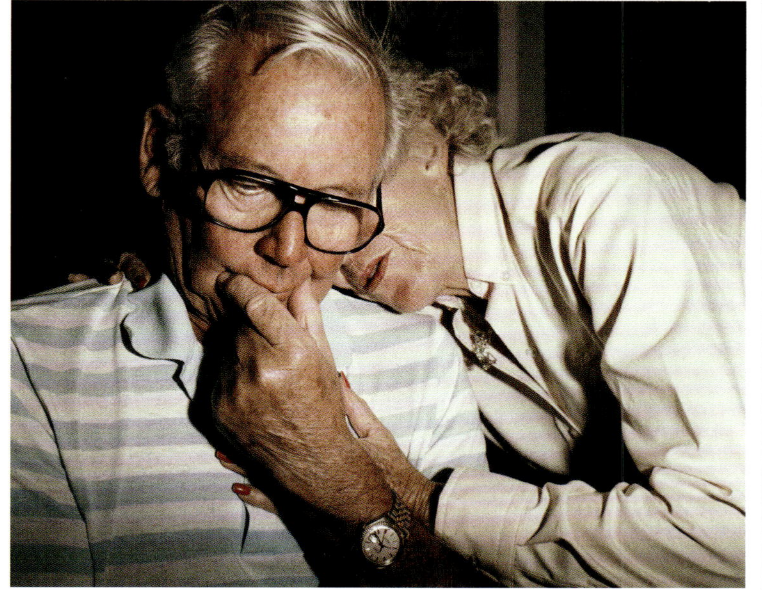

## Larry Sultan

Larry Sultan, my mentor and teacher in graduate school, and I often discussed, What is to be done? How does one navigate and photograph an upside-down world? He never pretended to know the answer, but he loved the question. One of Larry's great gifts was his sharing of this vulnerability in class. He would sometimes call me late at night, wondering how he had come across to the students. His sensitive demeanor seemed to be particularly important to young men; it directly challenged the idea of stoic masculinity.



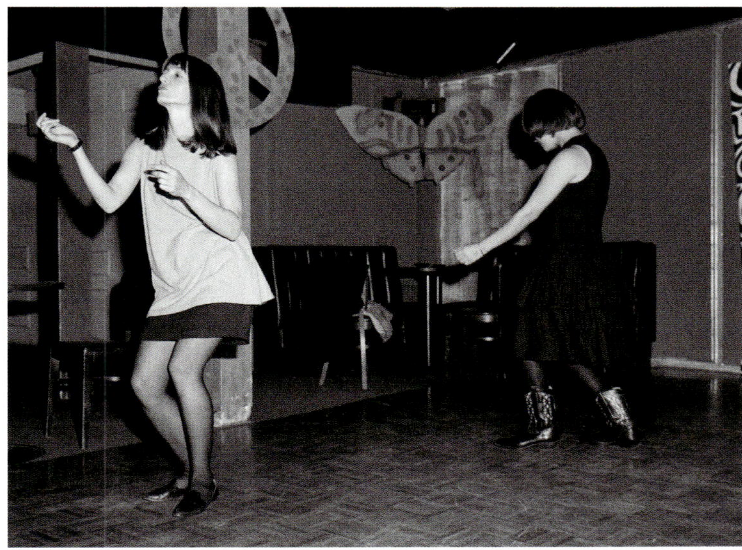

## The Mission District

The Mission District in San Francisco in the 1980s was electrifying. Sixteenth and Valencia was a hub of activity. A.R.E. (Artists for Revolution in the Eighties) occupied the upper floors of a three-story apartment building across the street from the Gartland Pit, where artists and housing activists, called the Urban Rats, regularly held vigils and demonstrations to protest the fire there that had killed an estimated fourteen people (the final number is still unknown) in 1975. Down the street was the Eye Gallery, a collective of social-documentary photographers, and the Crystal Pistol, a nightclub with pool tables, dancing, and local punk bands. On 16th Street, near the historic art cinema the Roxie Theater, a tiny shopping mall, the Compound, opened with the latest street zines and T-shirts. Telephone poles were blanketed with flyers announcing music and events such as Night of Mayhem, an all-night performance in an abandoned factory, or the latest happening by Mark Pauline, the Mad Max of performance art.

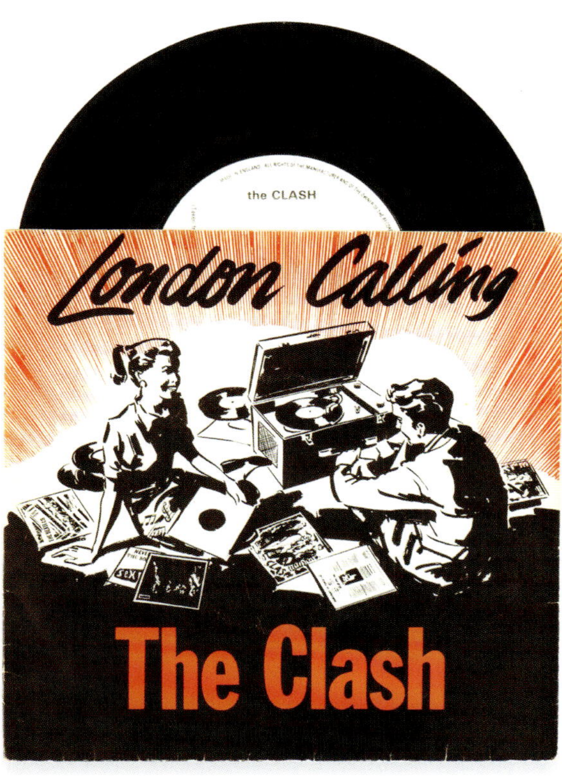



## The Clash

Hearing *London Calling* (1979) by the British punk band the Clash in early 1980 was thrilling. The title song, written in response to global catastrophes, including the meltdown at Three Mile Island the previous spring, entered my bloodstream with an adrenaline rush and was a welcome reminder of the rebellious music of the 1960s that inspired me to take up photography as a teenager. The Clash's music heralded the type of images I would make throughout the 1980s.

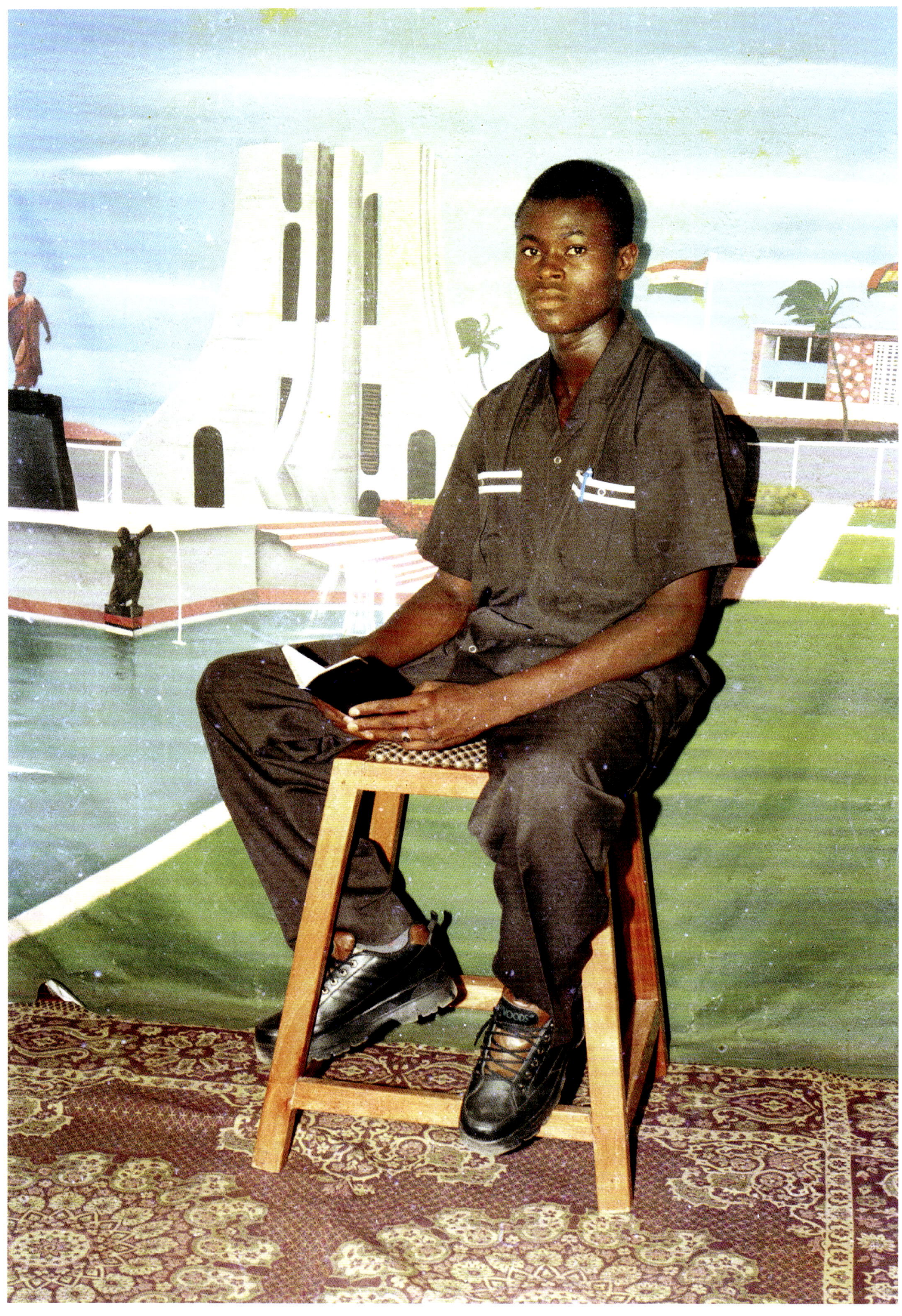

# Accra

## Guest edited by Lyle Ashton Harris and Nii Obodai

Since winning its independence from British colonial rule in 1957, Ghana has been a beacon for liberation and civil rights movements around the globe. During the leadership of Kwame Nkrumah, Ghana's first president, the country became a storied center of Pan-African thought, political activism, and spiritual connection for artists and intellectuals. That role has been sustained throughout the decades. In 2019, the Venice Biennale presented the first-ever Ghana Pavilion, designed by the celebrated architect David Adjaye and featuring an array of participants, including the filmmaker John Akomfrah and the photographer Felicia Abban. Earlier this year, the Scottish Ghanaian architect Lesley Lokko became the first curator of African descent to direct the Venice Architecture Biennale, turning the spotlight on creative production across the continent. Today, Accra continues to capture the global imagination as a vital cultural center and a site of return for people throughout the diaspora.

The New York–based artist Lyle Ashton Harris found himself drawn to the country well before he decided to relocate, in 2005, to Accra, where he was a professor at New York University's Ghana campus for seven years. During this time, he met Nii Obodai, an enterprising photographer and revered mentor to a younger generation. Together, they are the guest editors of this issue of *Aperture*. "I wanted to collaborate with Nii to produce a conduit that would bring viewers into the fertile intellectual history and contemporary social landscape of Accra," Harris explains.

Ghana has been a center of compelling photography since the late nineteenth century onward, from the output of the hundred-year-old Deo Gratias photo studio to the stylish midcentury visions of James Barnor. As a curator, educator, and founder of Nuku Studio, an essential workshop for photographers, Obodai builds on these precedents. "Younger photographers are using photography not just for self-expression but to carry the stories of our time," he says. "How do we push photography from our point of view, beyond our own comfort zones?" A new generation does just that. Eric Gyamfi documents the city's queer community. Fibi Afloe highlights the energetic sartorial expression of one Accra neighborhood. Misper Apawu trains her eye on women's entrepreneurialism.

"Photography is a potent medium for situating history," Obodai states. That history is held in the many physical photography archives within the city—and also in the collaborative archives assembled by artists on social media platforms. Works from Zohra Opoku's and Lloyd Foster's multimedia projects about the diaspora to Carlos Idun-Tawiah's profiles of subcultures and fashion trends, which frequently reference legendary West African image makers of the 1960s and 1970s, show how artists are often the link between the past and the present.

"This issue lays bare the current complexities around representation, not only through photography but also film, architecture, and spaces for gathering," Harris says. "What does it mean to bring a multiplicity of identities into one sphere? In what ways do conflicting ideas rub up against each other?" In Accra, artists are connecting local visual culture to global conversations. Their dynamic work engages history and meets the contemporary moment.  —**The Editors**

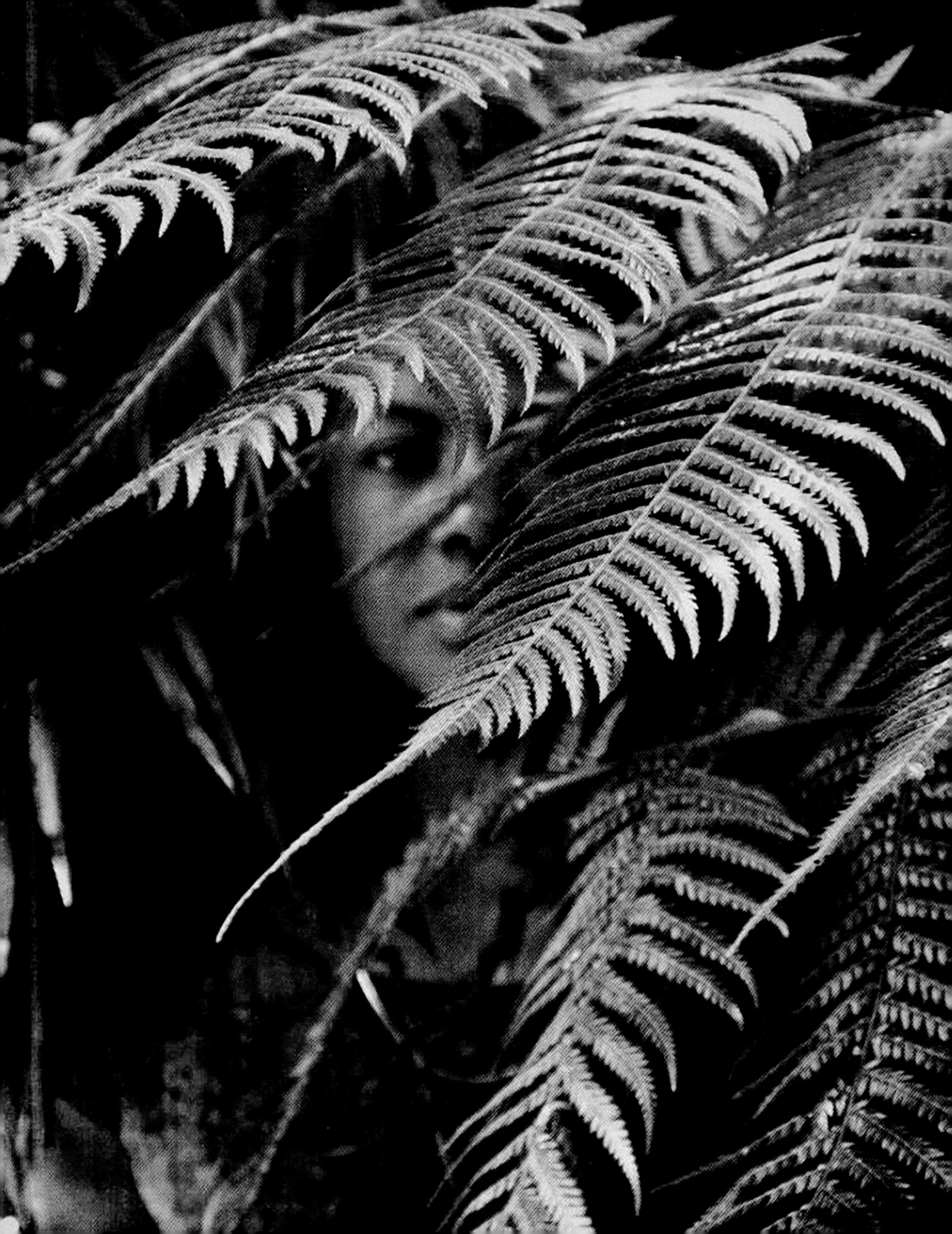

# Zohra Opoku
# Ghana Becomes You

**A Conversation with Ekow Eshun**

The German Ghanaian artist Zohra Opoku first visited Ghana in 2003, having grown up in East Germany. In 2011, she relocated to Accra, where the emotional and aesthetic inspiration she finds in the city has become a prevailing element in her art. As Opoku says, "Once you are in Ghana, Ghana becomes you and you become Ghana."

Through a practice centered on textiles and photography, Opoku explores nuanced themes of cultural identity. She prints directly onto textiles, weaving together archival images, family photographs, and self-portraiture to create lyrical composites that marry personal experience and collective memory.

In 2019, Opoku received a diagnosis of breast cancer. She began her most recent body of work while receiving treatment in Berlin and continued its development during an artist residency in Dakar, Senegal, at Kehinde Wiley's Black Rock Senegal program. The resulting series, *The Myths of Eternal Life* (2020–22), takes its structure and inspiration from the Egyptian Book of the Dead, an ancient text that provides instruction on preparation for the afterlife. Opoku's art offers lyrical reflections on questions of mortality and resilience she found herself addressing during and after her illness.

Ekow Eshun: **Let's start at the beginning, with you growing up in East Germany. In what ways does that play a part in the work you do today?**

**Zohra Opoku**: The GDR (German Democratic Republic) is now just a subject in school, it's part of history, something children have been taught. Childhood was amazing, but looking back, I understand how, for my mom, it was an upsetting story, while for my dad it was a devastating story. My father did his PhD in economics in the GDR, and after he had to return to Ghana I was born in Germany. He could write us, come back, try to connect. But then, also, it was a time of no internet and not having phones in the home. When he started studying abroad, it was part of the exchange program developing in East Germany, because for the GDR, Ghana was kind of a neutral country.

EE: **Part of the socialist states reaching out to the so-called third world at that time.**



# How can I relate to the place I'm dealing with? How do I connect?

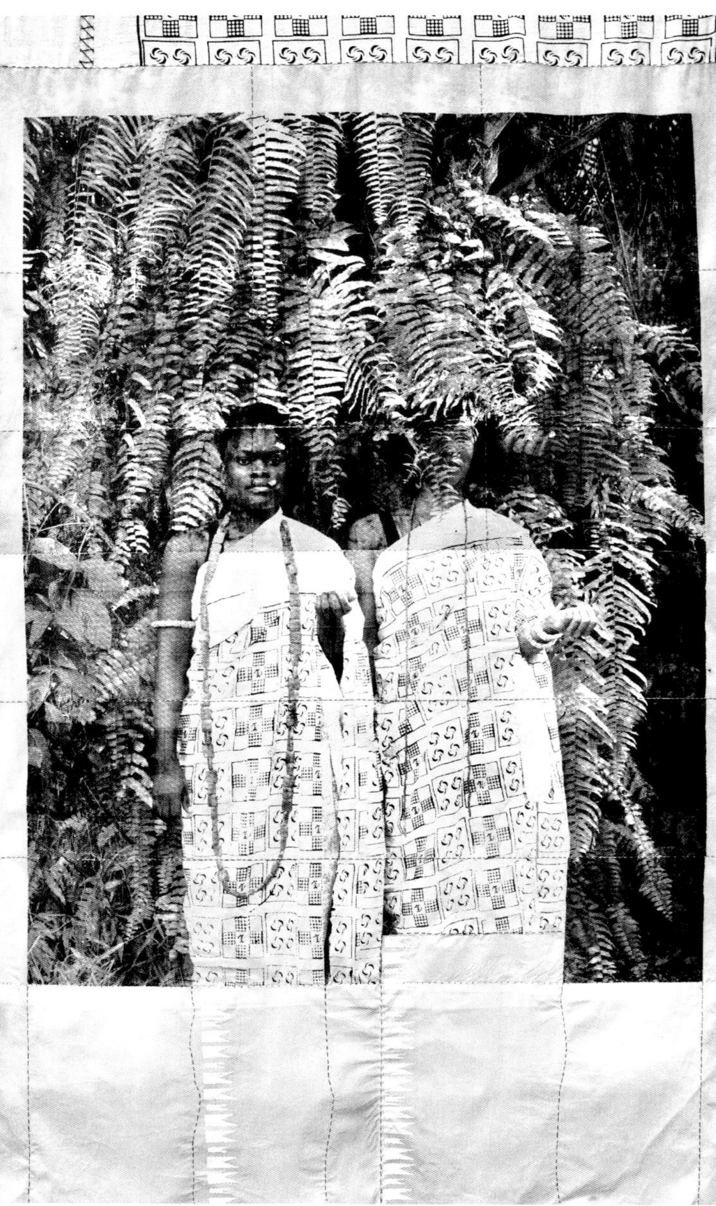

Left:
*Debie*, 2017. Screenprint on canvas and cotton, black tea dye, thread, acrylic

Opposite:
*In Bob's Footsteps*, 2017. Screenprint on cotton, tea dye, denim, thread

**ZO**: Right. My parents tried to stay connected with letters. My dad could have taken me to Ghana, but not my mom. That was the really sad part. I grew up with a stepdad, and then a single mom, because she and my stepdad got divorced. It was an environment of Caucasian people around me. I tried to explain to myself why I looked different. I made up stories. I was very young, around five. I told my friends that there was something wrong with my baby milk.

Later, when the wall came down and I was able to travel to West Germany, my auntie, who was kind of my mentor, started traveling with me. She took me to London, and it was so liberating because finally nobody stared at me. I felt like I could just disappear. I think that's where I started to realize that what was missing for me in my upbringing was a connection to my African background. It is always the driving force, this question of identity. How can I relate to the place I'm dealing with? How do I connect? What is familiar? And what do I have to bring to reconnect to the new environment? That's how my self-portraits actually came out, because it was always a question: What is myself here?

EE: **You studied fashion in Hamburg. But with the materials you use, there is a merging of vintage fabrics, photography, and imagery as a way to explore large questions of history and memory, of place and identity. How did you come to this as a way of working?**

**ZO**: Today, it looks like such an organic process. When I grew up, my mom was always sitting at the sewing machine or knitting; my grandmother was doing embroidery and knitting as well. The handcraft was present in my upbringing. And painting and drawing came naturally to me. Textiles were always around. Later, when I studied fashion, I realized I was already done with it; I spent more time in the photo department than in the fashion department. I was exploring black-and-white photography, especially because it always connected me to my childhood, because all the archival photographs of my mom and my grandparents, and the pictures in our photo-albums, everything that I found was black and white. Even later, when color photography became a modern thing, it was still cheaper to do it in black and white.

EE: **When did drawing and painting become part of the process?**

**ZO**: Drawing and painting were always part of it. But I would never actually see myself

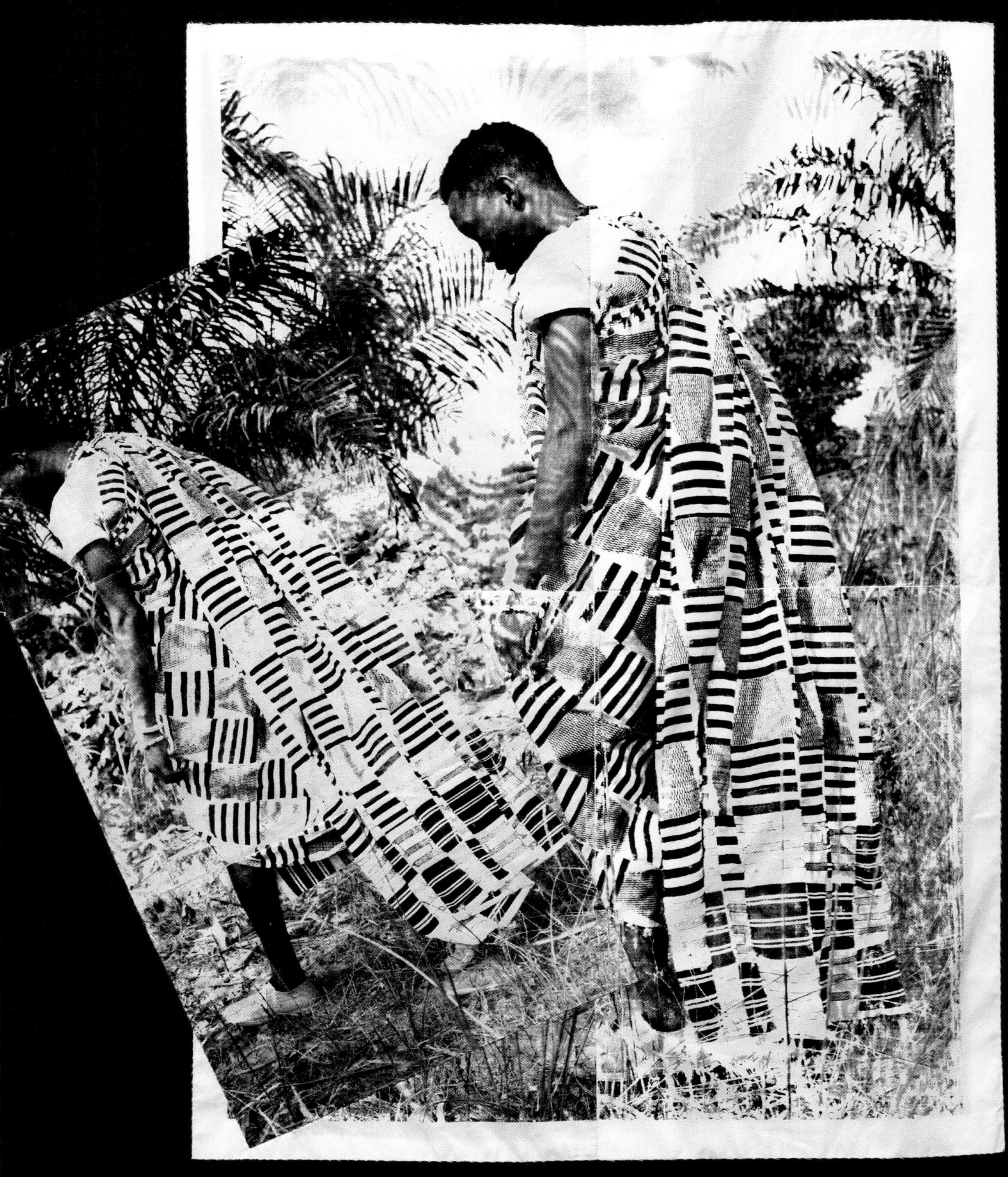

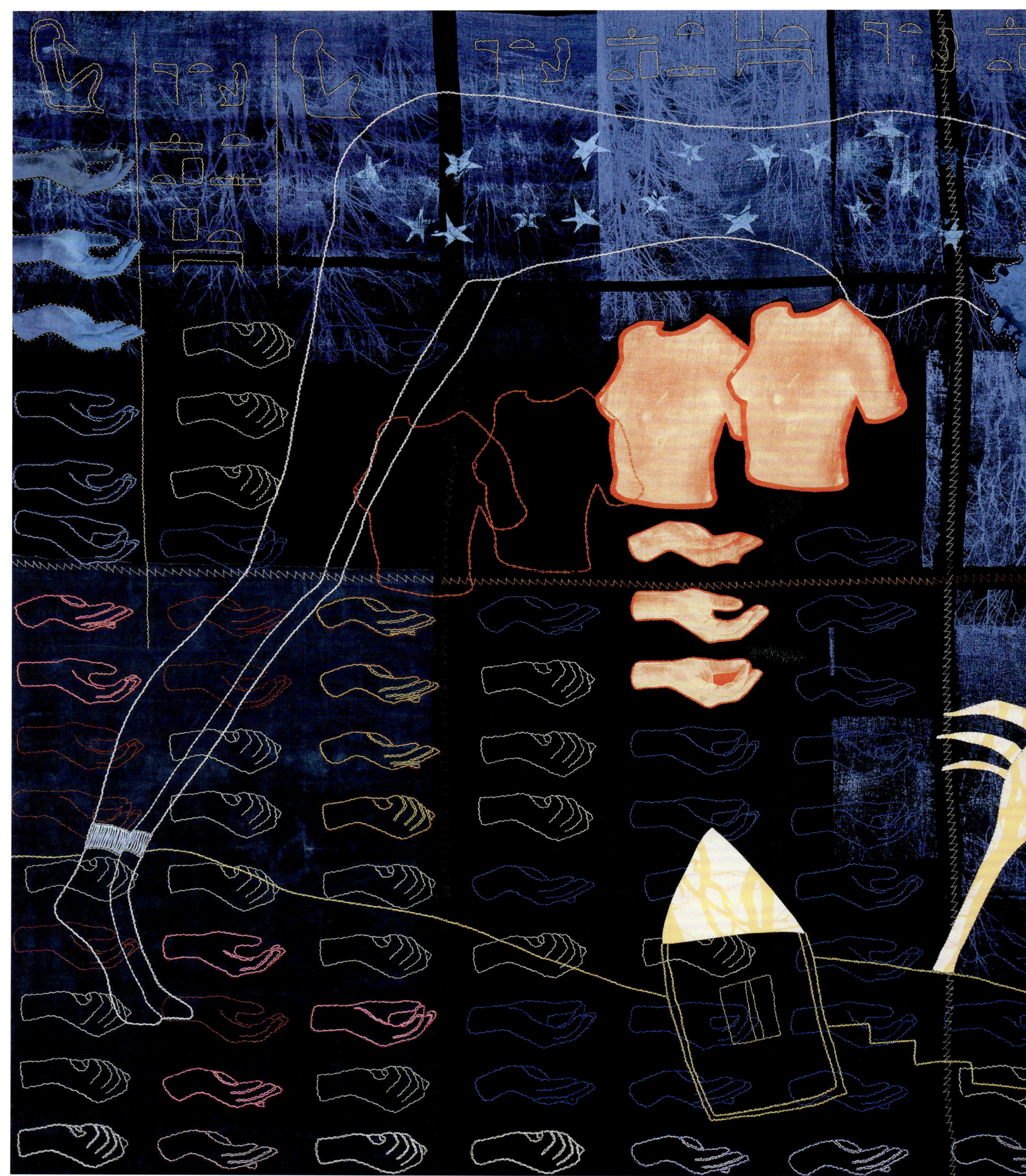

*"I have opened the doors of truth. I have passed the waters of heaven. I have raised up a ladder to heaven among the gods. I am one who is with you,"* 2023. Screenprint on dyed vintage linen with embroidery

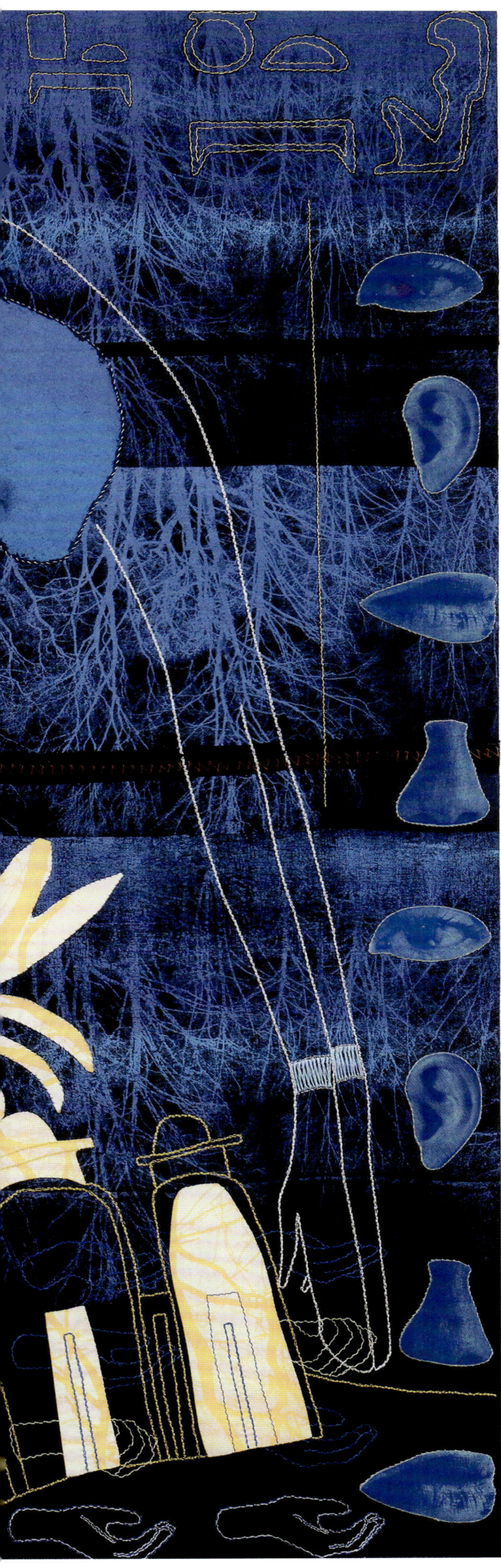

as an artist. I've always thought, I'm a fashion designer. I'm going to be big in fashion. I kept going for many years, doing styling, working for fashion brands, doing window installation, working in design, traveling in Europe, living in Copenhagen and Paris. But I always felt like my soul couldn't expand; it couldn't really explore and understand a lot of things. I realized that with fashion, it's so fast, and too beautiful to seek the truth. As an artist, you always want to excavate the truth of something.

**EE: How long have you lived in Ghana now?**

**ZO:** For twelve years.

**EE: Why did you move to Accra?**

**ZO:** It has the energy I was seeking. Since 2003, I came to Ghana maybe every other year. Every time I returned to Germany and arrived at the airport, I felt so empty—something was missing. I just knew I had to find a way to turn it around and visit Germany from time to time.

**EE: There's so much emphasis in your art on embroidery and weaving and a handmade sensibility. It seems to me it makes everything very personal—that there's *you* in the fabric of all the work.**

**ZO:** I think the textiles were coming back to me strongly when I started living in Ghana. Everything is textile for me in Ghana. It has so many meanings, histories, and backgrounds that I wouldn't really feel or be able to touch on in Germany—or understand. Even if I would want to dive into the same topics I'm touching on in Ghana, it's just not the same energy. It's like once you are in Ghana, Ghana becomes you and you become Ghana. I was also able to articulate my family heritage, my emotions within my identity, using Ghanaian symbolism and traditions.

And I insist now, when we are describing the works, that people actually understand that everything is handmade. I don't want to have any machines involved. Today, everything is ultradigital. I wanted to stay within that kind of analog space, similar to how I grew up.

**EE: You've talked before about having an affinity with West African studio photographers such as Malick Sidibé and Seydou Keïta—the ways they used fabric as backdrops but also as part of the self-fashioning of their subjects.**

**ZO:** Absolutely. I have all the books of these masters. In the very beginning, I was even more interested in photographing or portraying other artists or other people, and I used their clothes as a sort of tool to drape around the body, to actually capture an energy. It's like taking your time and carefully thinking through the process: What does the material say? What does the print say? How does it look in black and white, for instance? Because photographing in color or black and white are two different thought processes. This kind of style, expressing swag, expressing a kind of African soul, being in that space of coolness—that's something I was seeking.

**EE: With the family photographs and family fabrics, do you consider these an archive that you're drawing from?**

**ZO:** I started to really appreciate this idea of an archive when my dad passed, because he was also a traditional leader. When I created the series, I was working with the old photographs and the textiles from my father. They don't only give you a material thing—so many memories are burned into that fabric. I realized how heavy the fabrics are, how difficult they are to handle and actually wear, and how my father could walk in them and move in them the whole day. It's not just a piece of fabric or a cloth. You have to be able to carry them, especially these old, traditional kente; when they are made from silk, they are much heavier than the new ones. In Ghana, a lot of things are not archived, and so, for me, it's very important to make sure we preserve and take care of them.

**EE: In your series *Self Portraits* (2016–ongoing), you are there but not there. Your face is obscured by foliage. What are you exploring in those works?**

**ZO:** I explore a version of the self, right? I want to look into a social environment, geographical environment, a dialogue with a surrounding. I was at an artist residency in Berkeley at the Kala Institute, and I ended up having more conversations with the landscapes around there, and looking at myself. I was very intrigued by the fact that most of the plants are actually not from that area. They were immigrants, like me. Plants from Middle Europe to the Mediterranean to desert to grassland. There's this wide range. It was impressive to me how everything could grow in California. And since I have a very strong background of farming and being in nature—my father was also very strongly

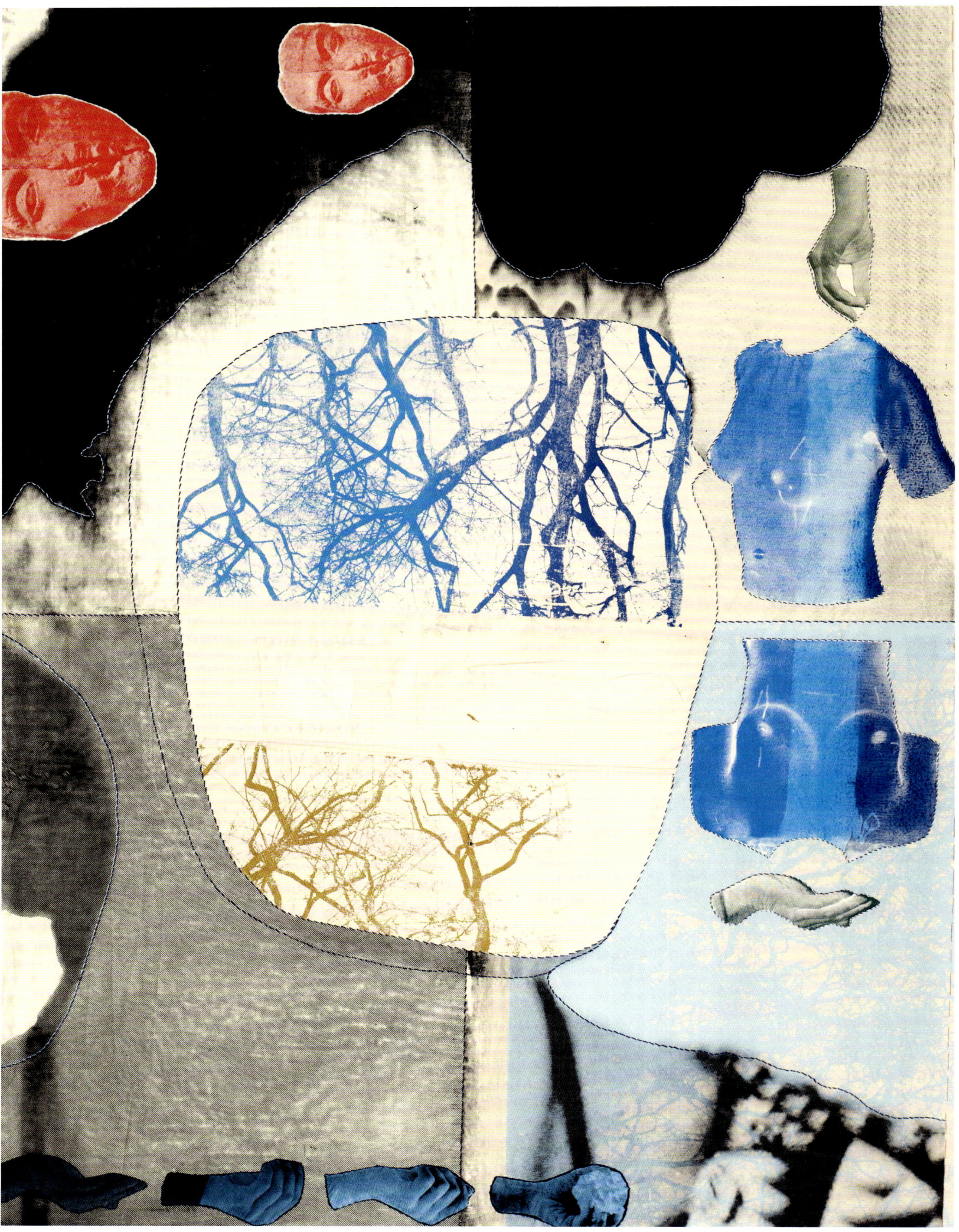

connected to greenery—nature really represents home to me.

**EE: In 2019, you were diagnosed with breast cancer, which must have been very difficult. When you started making work in relation to that, you looked to the Egyptian Book of the Dead. What did you find in that book?**

**ZO:** In the beginning, I was just trying to figure out how to survive, how to get through all these treatments. I ended up in Berlin. I had a bicycle and would ride through parks and go to museums, where I fell in love with ancient Egyptian mythology. That's how I decided to work with the tomb paintings, the colors, the hieroglyphs. To understand their meanings and the concept of afterlife— and that I can create my own narrative around this.

**EE: Let's talk about those trees, because they are present throughout the series *The Myths of Eternal Life*. You started photographing these trees while you were receiving treatment. They're in a park in Berlin, but all the trees are bare because it's winter. They're yet to blossom and produce new life.**

**ZO:** What I found interesting is how trees are a metaphor for life and death. I thought, Okay, they can become my protagonist, something that reappears in all the works. By my printing them in so many colors, they morphed into things we can feel or imagine, like veins, or streams of rivers, or greenery, or a kind of energy.

**EE: They are another form of self-portrait, in a way. We see you with nature again, but it's a different form of nature now, compared to the *Self Portraits* series. It's empty branches and so on. But also, your body is dismembered, as it were, in separate pieces—your head, your arms, your legs. How much is this speaking of your mental state or your physical state at that time?**

**ZO:** I feel like the body is just existing in a particular time of the life span, but our soul, our being, is continuing. What represents that? And, on the other hand, I found it interesting how hieroglyphs have elements of body parts as a sign language. Now, my pieces are becoming more complex, because I print and cut and apply, then I have the embroidery, and then I have all kinds of practical stitching. There are so many different layers that create the narrative.

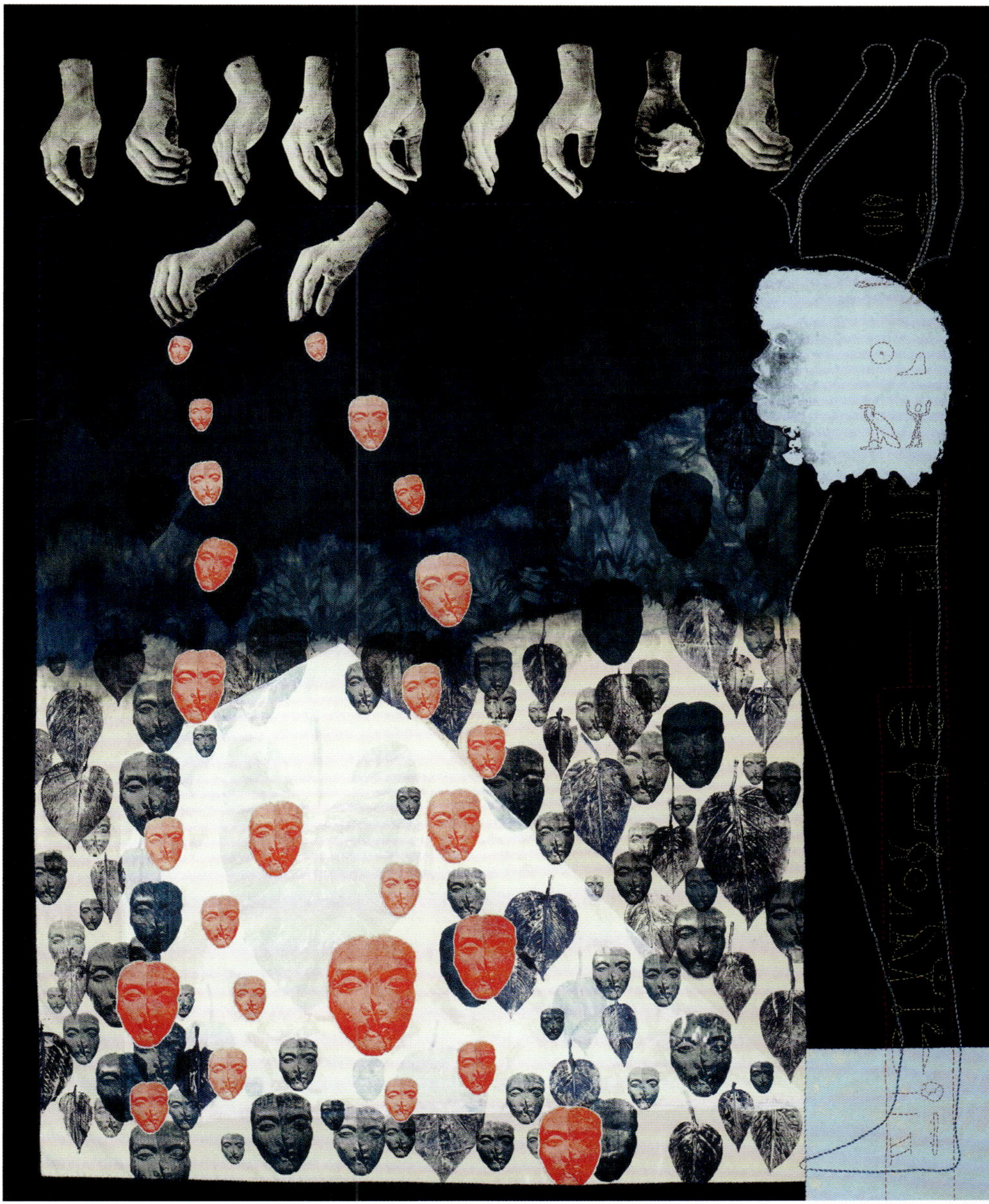

Opposite:
*"I have arisen from my egg which is in the lands of the secrets . . .,"* 2020. Screenprint on linen

This page:
*"To me belongs mankind, given wholly to me . . .,"* 2021. Indigo-dyed linen, monotype print, screenprint, thread

# Trees are a metaphor for life and death. I thought, Okay, they can become my protagonist.

**EE: Did you have in your mind an aesthetic goal for these pieces?**

**ZO:** The first night after I had the diagnosis, I started dreaming. I never wrote the dreams down but they were present in my thoughts. I realized that something in my work has to reflect that very surreal feeling.

**EE: What kind of dreams were they?**

**ZO:** I was dreaming of dying. Dreaming of being buried. Very weird constellations of people around me, who don't know each other, talking to me about my decisions. Because I decided against the chemotherapy and against hormone therapy. With this, I took a risk but wanted to engage in holistic healing. It's hard to actually put in pictures. But what I always saw was the sun. That was also something that I always missed in Berlin. That's why I chose the sun god Re in one of the works. The hands coming from his sun disk are standing for sunrays shining in my face.

I didn't make a sketch and say, This is how I want it to look. It was like putting it together, step by step, with those elements I had, knowing that in every chapter of the series, I focus on a particular stage of my healing. The last stage, which is the afterlife, was definitely becoming focused on indigo dye, which I was exploring in Senegal, along with darker colors, bluish colors. And in another chapter, dealing with the dead, I was looking into the symbolism of dying. For instance, I learned about the Serer culture, the third-largest religion in Senegal, who used to bury their griots in a baobab tree, which is also known as the Tree of Life. I have two works reflecting on this. I used for the textile piece dead leaves, to print the background as well as to use something that we would actually throw away, but I put some life back in and printed with it. The other work is a brass sculpture of my leg turning into the trunk, and imprints from original baobab leaves are attached to it.



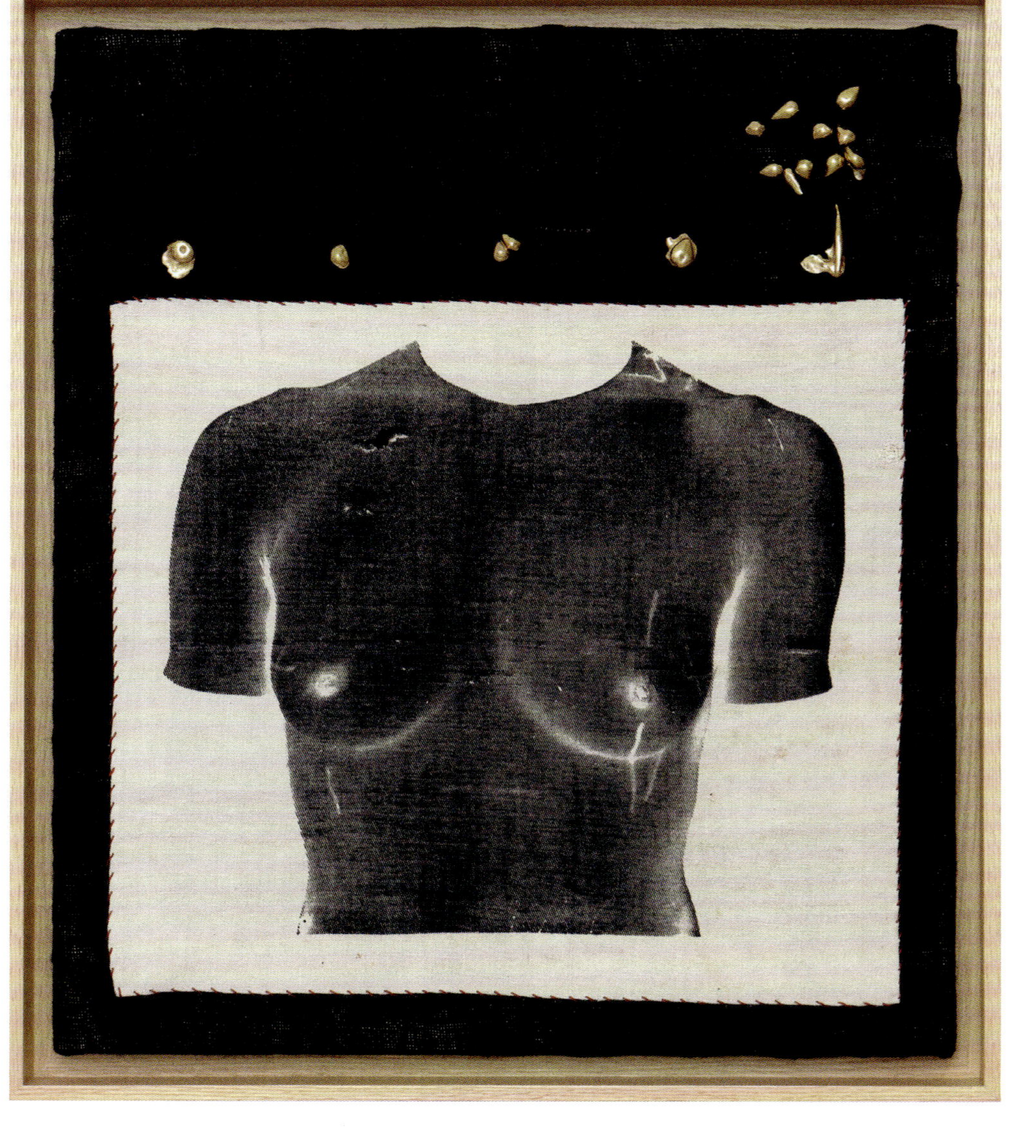

**EE: I've never read the Book of the Dead. What's in it that's captivating for you?**

ZO: What I love is that you insist on your own truth. You insist on your own authentic being. While you're entering the afterlife, you have to be honest in front of the council of deities, that you have not done anything wrong, let's say, which would harm your path into the afterlife on the journey to a new existence.

The translation is so poetic, so beautiful. Then I realized that the tomb paintings, or the drawings in the papyrus, have a lot of poetic elements, corresponding with the words I was reading. That's why I was very interested in bringing what I liked most in the text into the titles. I'm not very good in doing titles myself, so it was great to have the opportunity to use something that sounds so imaginative and captured the energy of a work. It also took, of course, a lot of reading and understanding what goes well with the piece I wanted to give a title to. That was probably the most important part—that it reads almost like a poem.

**EE: That's absolutely the case. The titles are brilliant, such as this one: _"I am the terror in the storm who guards the great one [in] the conflict. Sharp Knife strikes for me. Ash god provides coolness for me."_ They are mysterious and poetic. But also, the works aren't illustrative, they are in conversation with these words from thousands of years ago. It seems an extraordinary connection you've made with, I suppose, a way of looking at life and a way of looking at death that are contained within that book.**

ZO: When you really digest something, whether positive or negative, something comes out of it. You don't see it when you start the process, but sometimes, I'm impressed with the result. It's probably for the best, what happened to me, because I had to go through it, and I had to actually work out a lot in my life. I think by taking time, so much more depth can be achieved, more knowledge and connection. That's what I appreciate about this body of work— it gave me space to develop my being within a progression.

Ekow Eshun is a curator and writer based in London. His latest book is _In the Black Fantastic_ (2022).

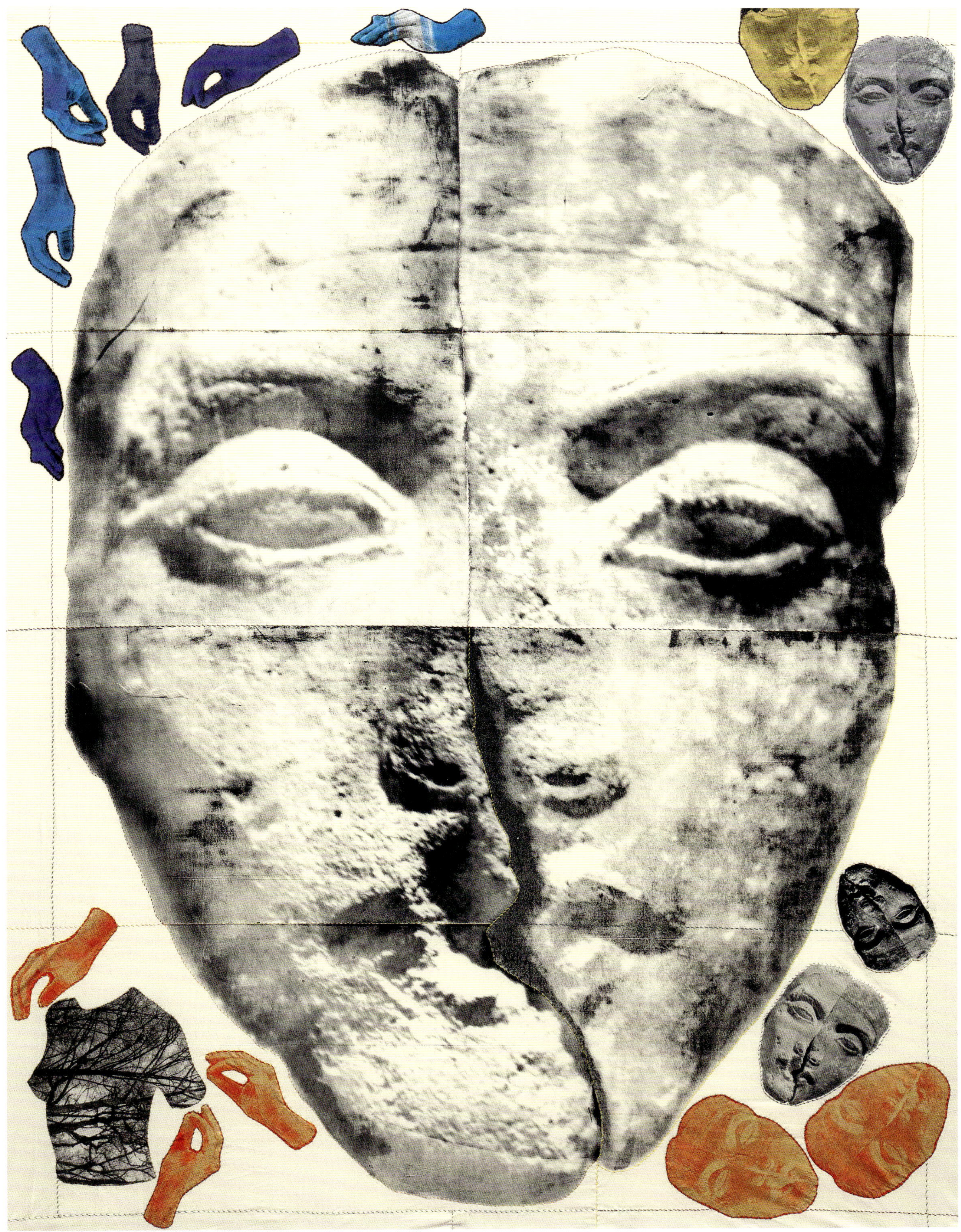

Lyle Ashton Harris arrived in Ghana in 2005 to teach at NYU Accra, a study-abroad campus of New York University. Not entirely by chance, his entrée into the company of a select branch of Ghana's political community was facilitated partly through introductions made by myself and my family, and partly because of the status accorded professors, since education is a strong marker of class in Ghana. I immediately secured him housing at Scott House, a celebrated modernist home, bringing Harris to the epicenter of Accra's established patrician society. In September of that year, I invited him to join us at the Brazilian Embassy Residence in Accra, where he photographed a charitable fundraiser for the Infanta Malaria Prevention Foundation, which had been established by a group of society women that the Ghanaian tabloids satirically called "the Hollywood Wives," several of whom appear in Harris's previously unpublished series *Ghana Society* (2005).

Harris's portraits reflect a cosmopolitan elite, many of mixed African and European heritage who, nonetheless, identify strongly as Ghanaian. But these photographs show more than a privileged set. They present a rare grouping of individuals, including those who had known political exile at one point or another, who had campaigned for human rights in Ghana and abroad, and who, in spite of working in the field of development, would be seen as especially elite, being direct descendants of the "Big Six"—the men known as Ghana's founding fathers—and their immediate peers.

That being said, this description might be read as controversial in Ghana, as it is often joked that no one in the Ghanaian upper echelons will claim to be anything other than middle class. Too often in recent memory, appearing as anything more could cost you your life. Privilege is a tricky thing in a country that has seen numerous socialist revolutions, military coups, and upheavals, and in which, at the most radical point in the 1980s—the years after Flight Lieutenant Jerry Rawlings assumed power after a coup and attempted to stamp out corruption—bourgeois citizens could be imprisoned for having not just two homes but two toilets in a home, which were indicators of immense wealth.

So how do we land in this gathering of clearly distinguished guests, who appear so at home with their photographer? In 2005, President John Kufuor, celebrated for peacefully transitioning the country, in wholly transparent democratic elections, from the Rawlings government, was in his second term, a clear marker of the end of the political instability that brought three decades of military rule. This was a time when members of Ghana's educated and social elite returned from decades of economic and political exile. The country was beginning to experience a relative economic turn, with rapid expansions of business, services, and culture. It was a period of immense optimism, as the country busily planned its 2007 celebrations marking fifty years of independence from European colonialism.

*Ghana Society* includes ambassadors, diplomats, politicians, and businesspeople, many of them related or friends—an interconnected assembly. The predominance of African clothing (modern versions of traditional dress), in combination with black-and-white photography, gives Harris's images a sense of a bygone era. I was photographed that night, too, as I was acting as auctioneer for the charity event, which my mother had organized. It was a casually elegant but relaxed evening by Ghanaian standards. Harris took advantage of this atmosphere to create remarkably intimate portraits of a group of figures united by the business of postcolonial nation-building, at a rare moment of total ease with themselves and the world.

# Lyle Ashton Harris
## *The Society*

**Senam Okudzeto**

Opposite:
First Lady Rebecca Naa Okaikor Akufo-Addo, the wife of Ghanaian President Nana Addo Dankwa Akufo-Addo and Chairperson of the Infanta Malaria Prevention Foundation, who was then Minister for Foreign Affairs. Her father, Judge Jacob Hackenburg Griffiths-Randolph, was Speaker of the Parliament of Ghana. Her husband is a son of one, and closely related to two other members, of the Big Six, the founding fathers of Ghana.

Senam Okudzeto, PhD, is an artist and educator who lives and works in Basel, Switzerland.

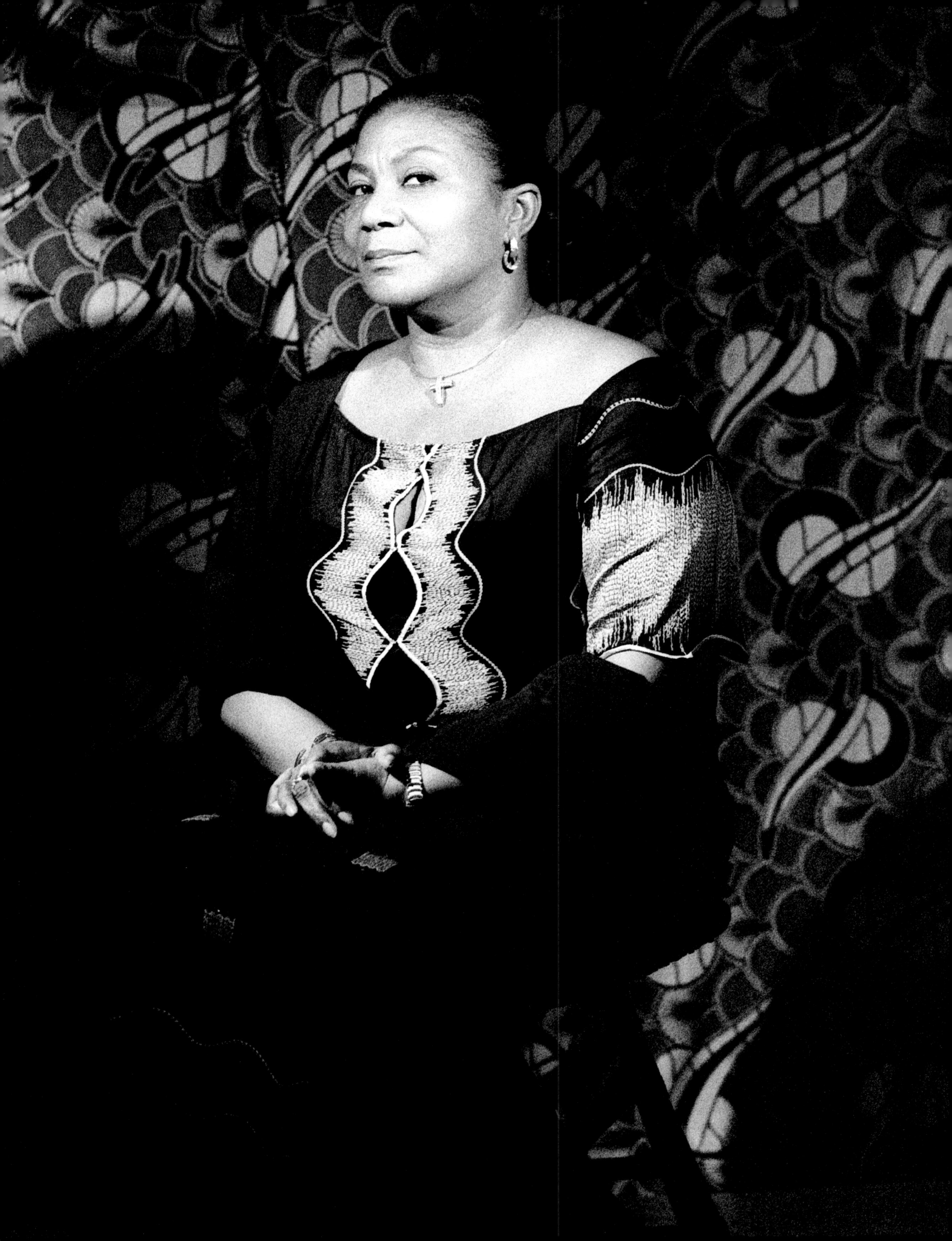

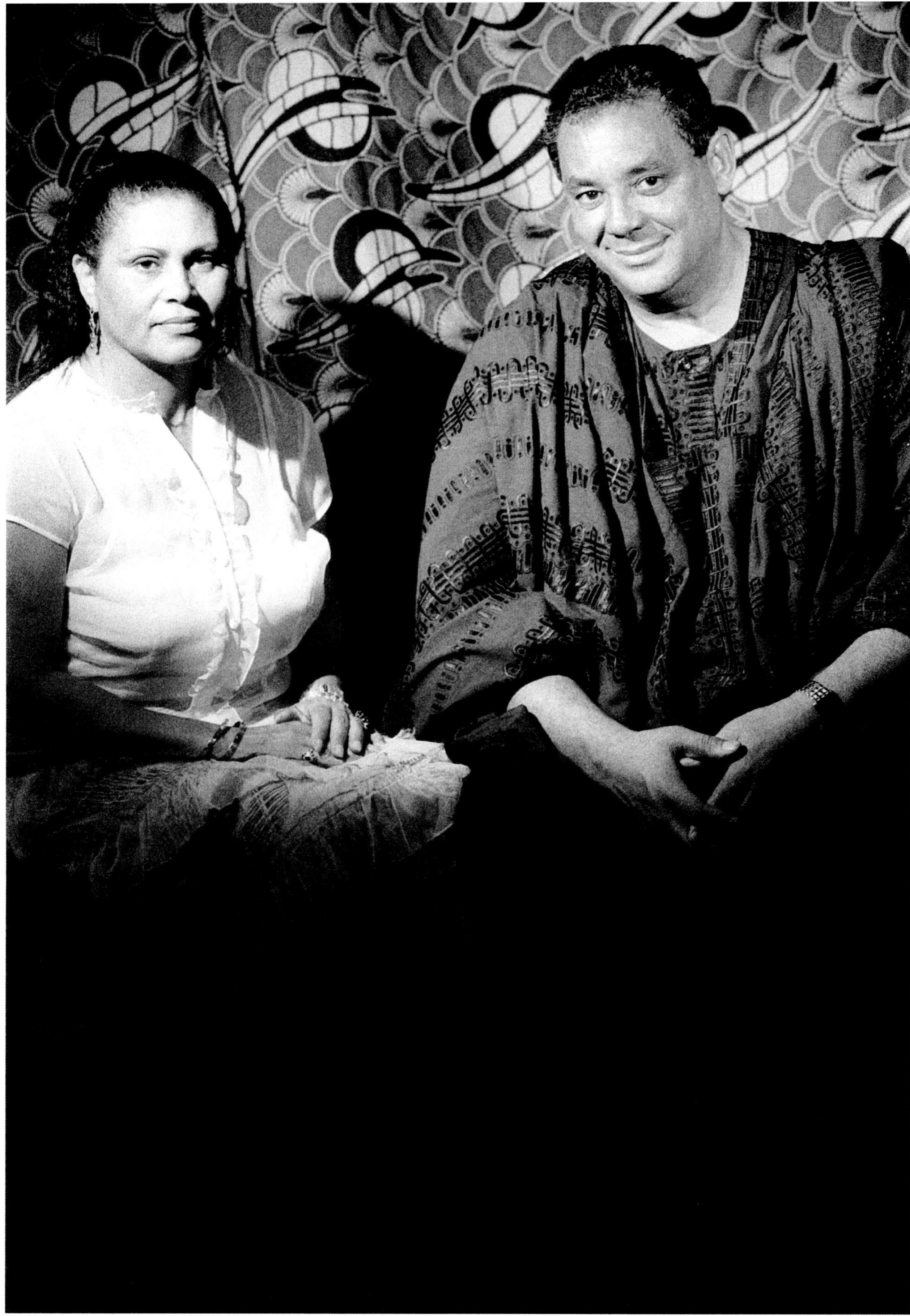

This page:
Esther Obetsebi-Lamptey and her husband, the Hon.
Minister Jacob "Jake" Lantei Otanka Obetsebi-Lamptey,
a politician and later Minister of Tourism and Diaspora
Relations, who died in 2016. His father, Emmanuel
Odarkwei Obetsebi-Lamptey, was one of the Big Six.

Opposite:
Haifa Laba, a businesswoman, publicist for the Infanta
Malaria Prevention Foundation, and a member of
Ghana's Lebanese community, which dates to the
nineteenth century.

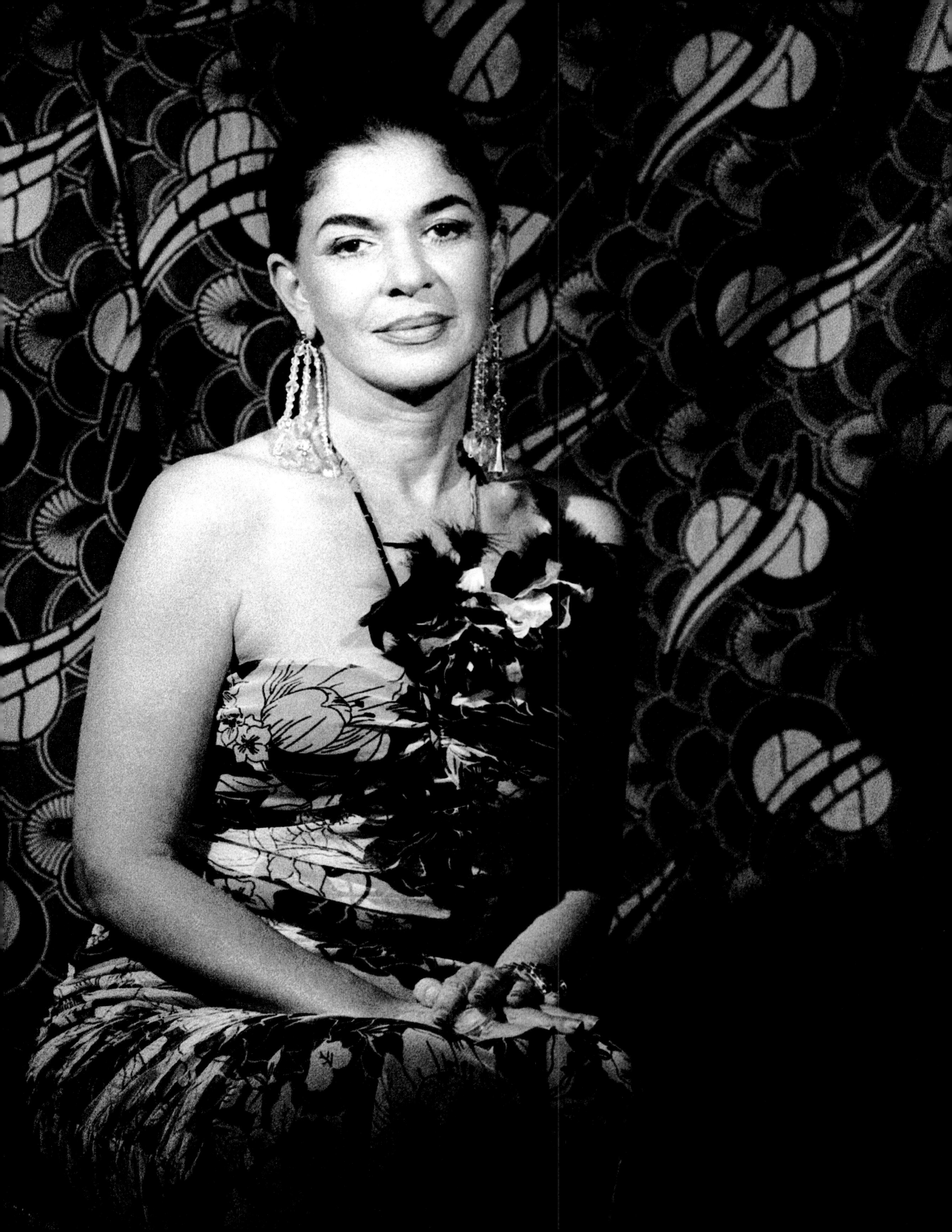

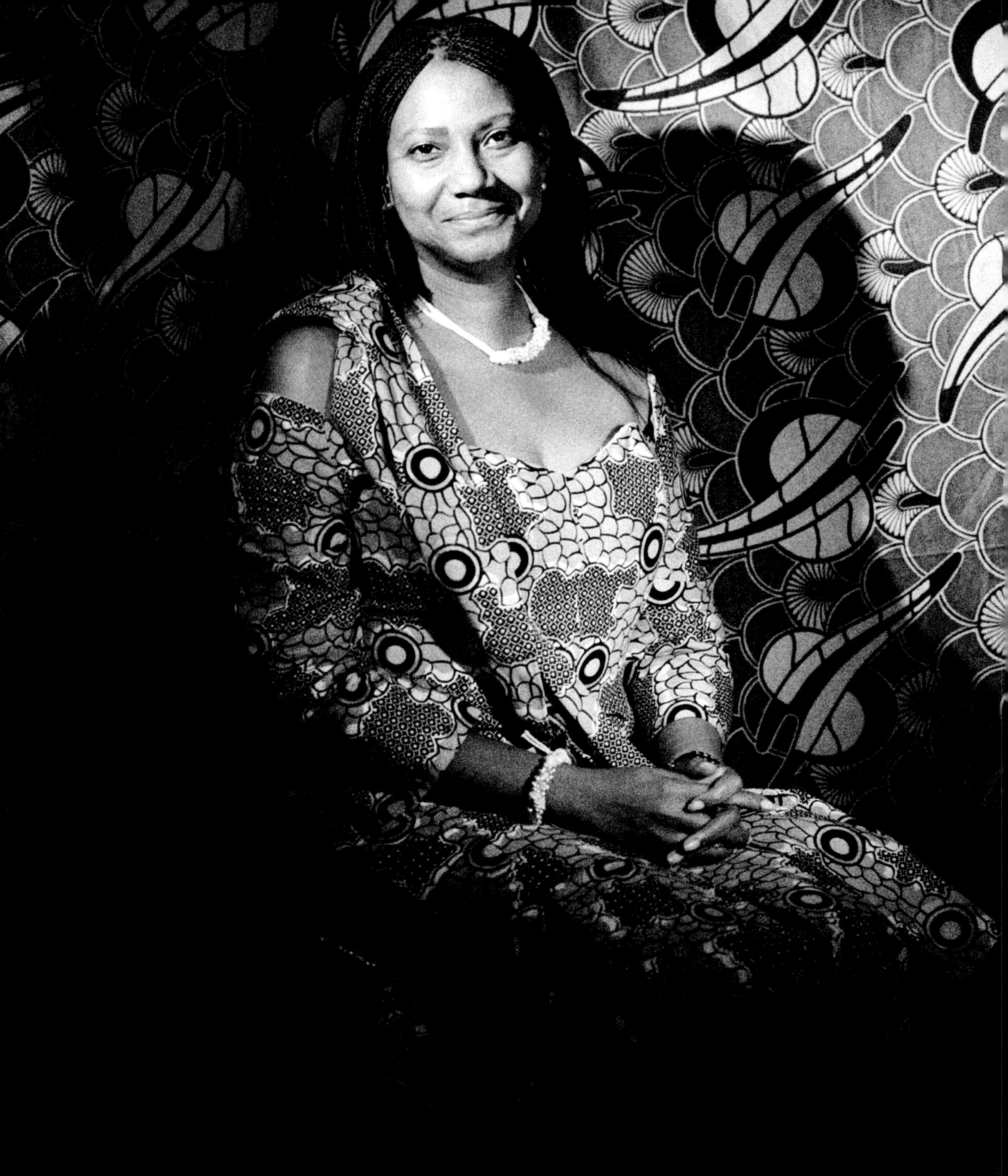

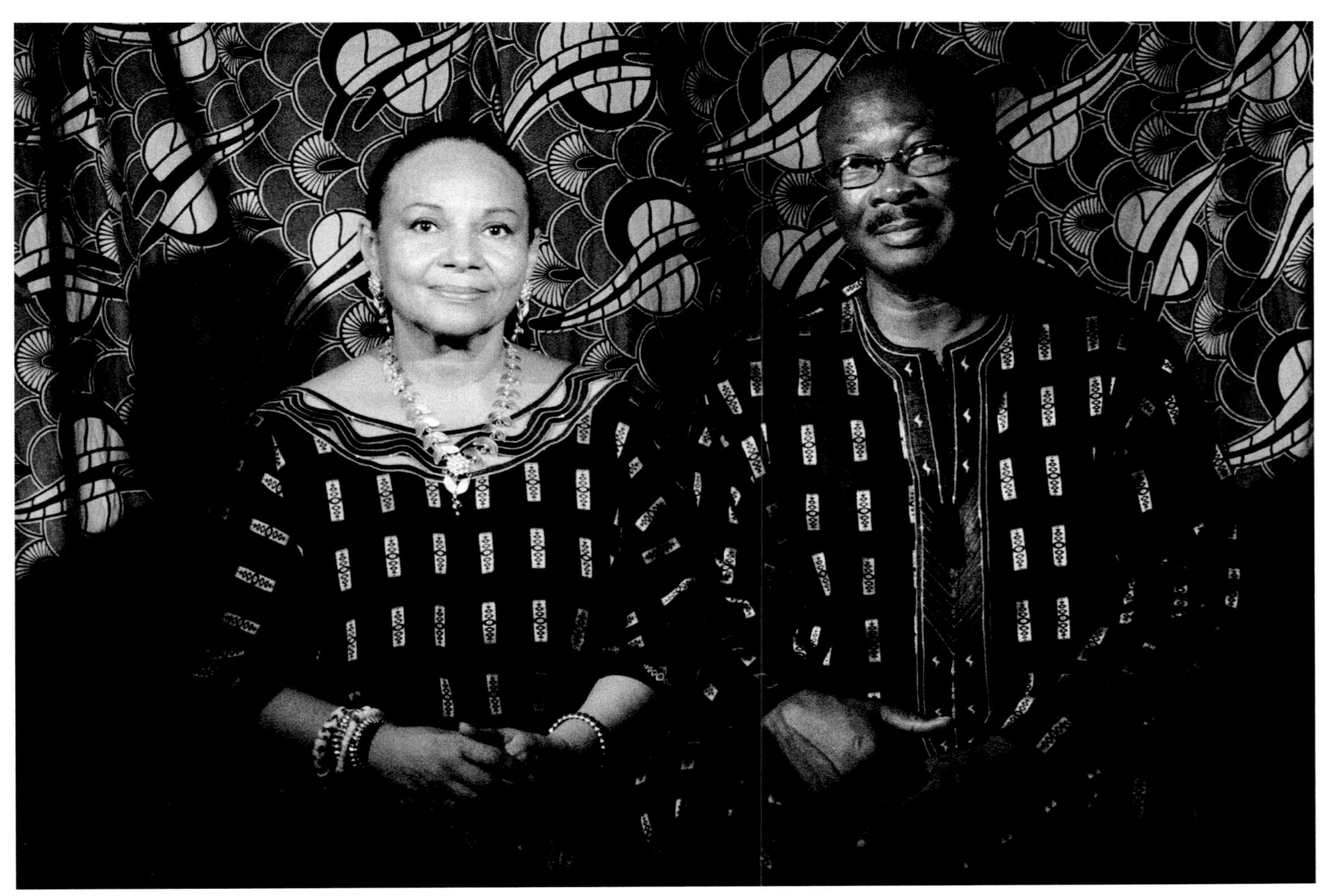

Opposite:
Regina Nynantaky-Owusu, sister of First Lady Rebecca
Naa Okaikor Akufo-Addo.

This page:
Lois Okudzeto, an American originally from Chicago,
is Queen Mother Amexleti II Dunyeno II of Atorkor and
director of the Infanta Malaria Prevention Foundation.
Her husband, Raymond Okudzeto, Dumega of Anlo State,
was a political figure from Ewe and Ada royal families;
he died in 2017. He is the brother of Sam Awuku Okudzeto,
a prominent lawyer and human rights campaigner who
was one of the drafters of the constitution of Ghana.

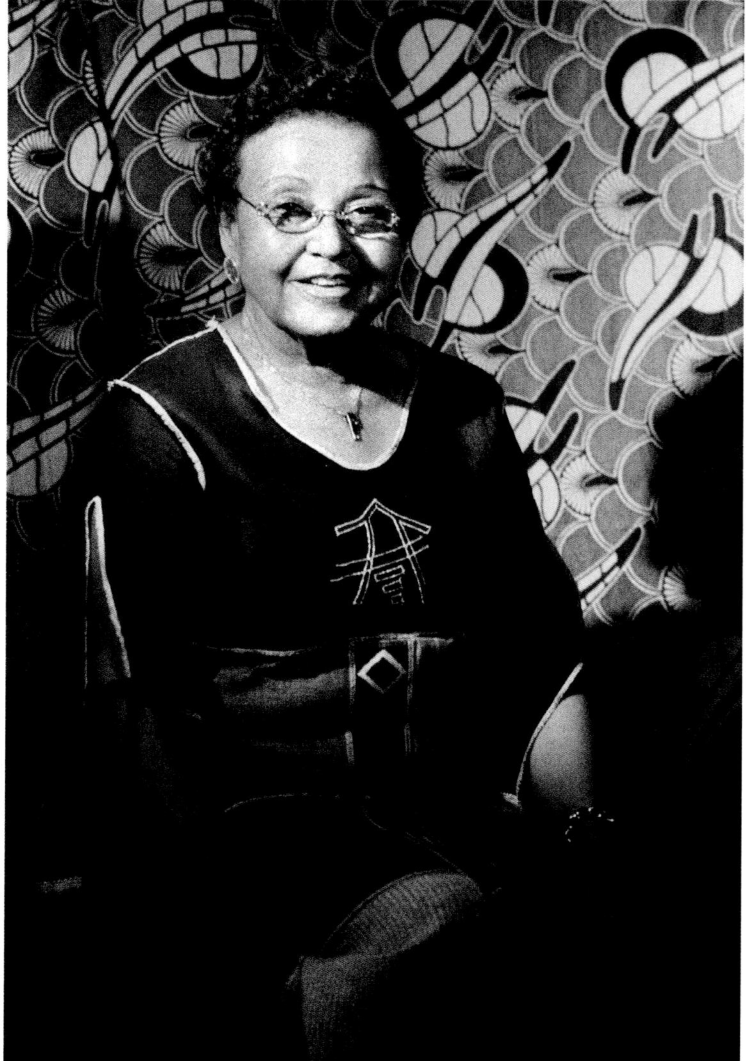

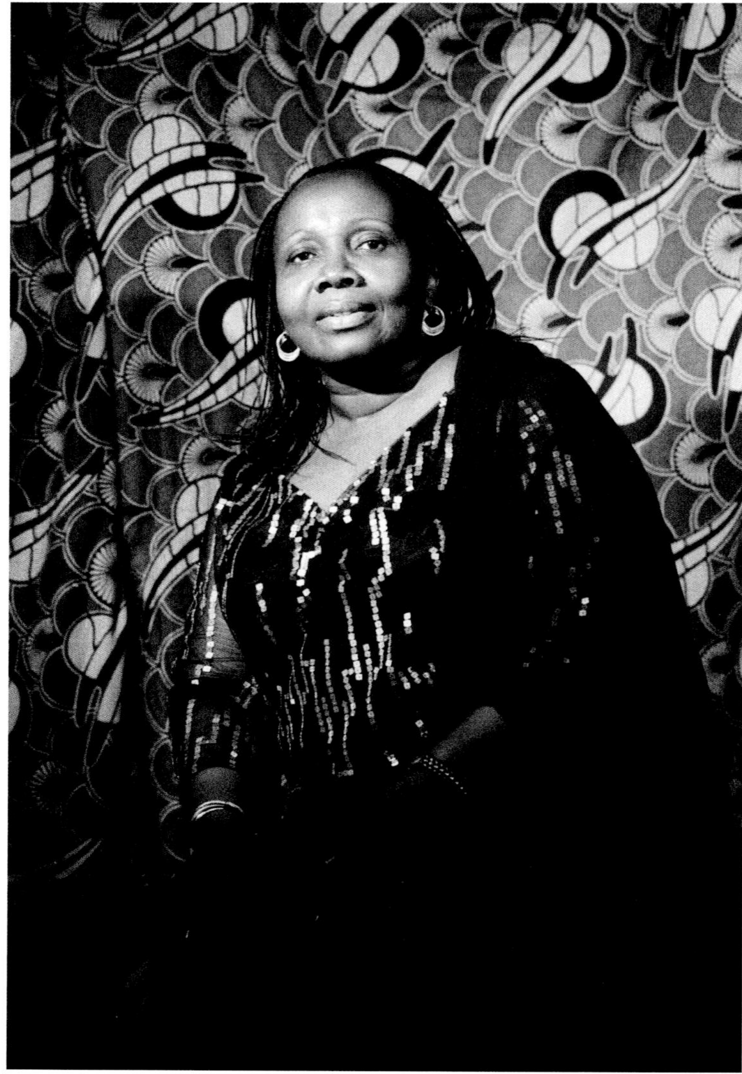

This page, left:
Ambassador Justice Thérèse Striggner Scott, a former
Chief Justice, chair of the Ghana Law Reform Commission,
UNESCO Board Member, and member of the United
Nations International Commission of Inquiry on Darfur.
She died in 2021.

This page, right:
Dr. Henrietta Asare, a senior medical doctor and niece
of First Lady Rebecca Naa Okaikor Akufo-Addo.

Opposite:
Ophelia Akiwumi, a renowned furniture designer and
restauranteur, and her husband, Ambassador "Nini"
Akilaja Olufemi Akiwumi. Akilaja is from a prominent
Nigerian Ghanaian political family and Ophelia's father
and grandfather were famous medical doctors who started
the first African-run hospital in Accra.
All photographs from the series *Ghana Society*,
Brazilian Embassy Residence, Accra, 2005
Courtesy the artist

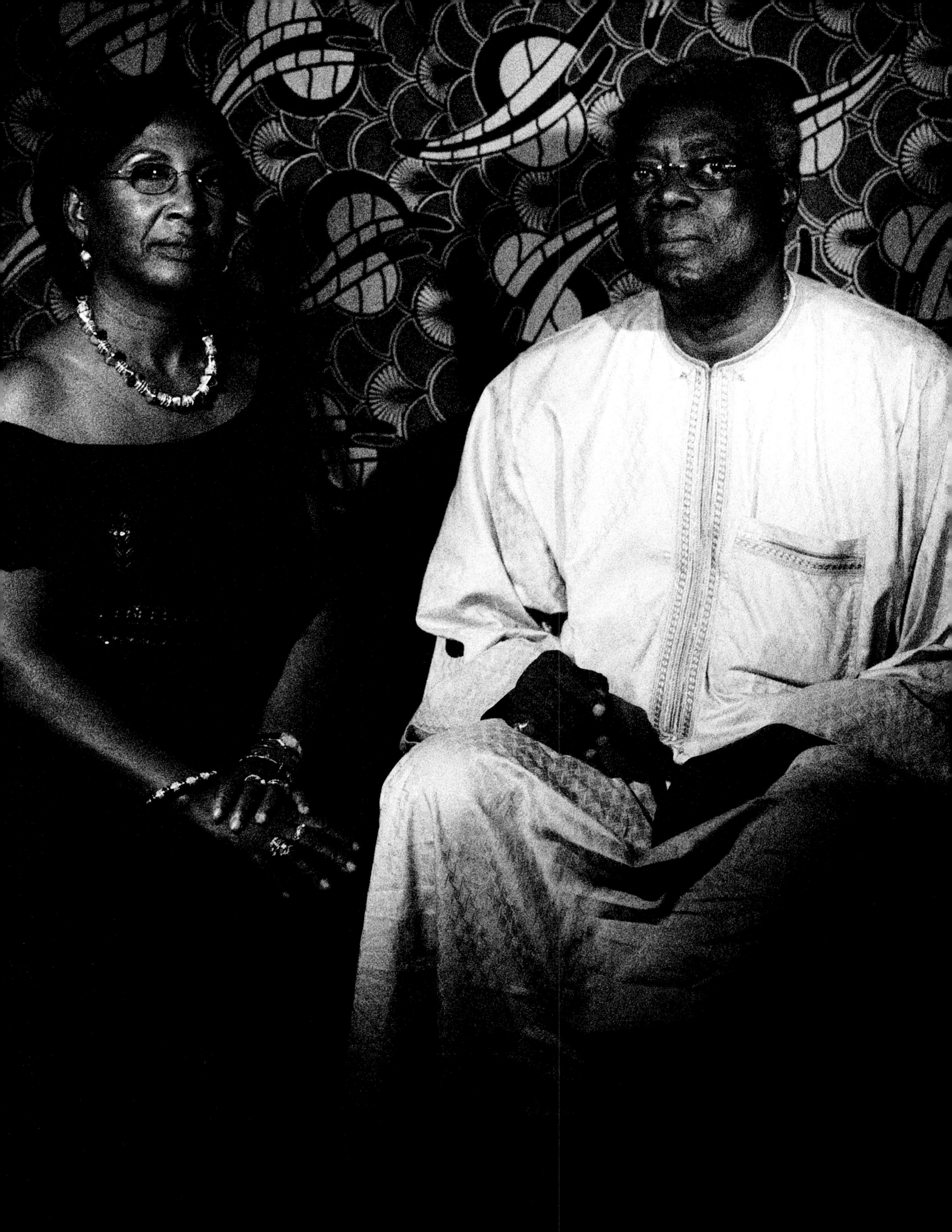

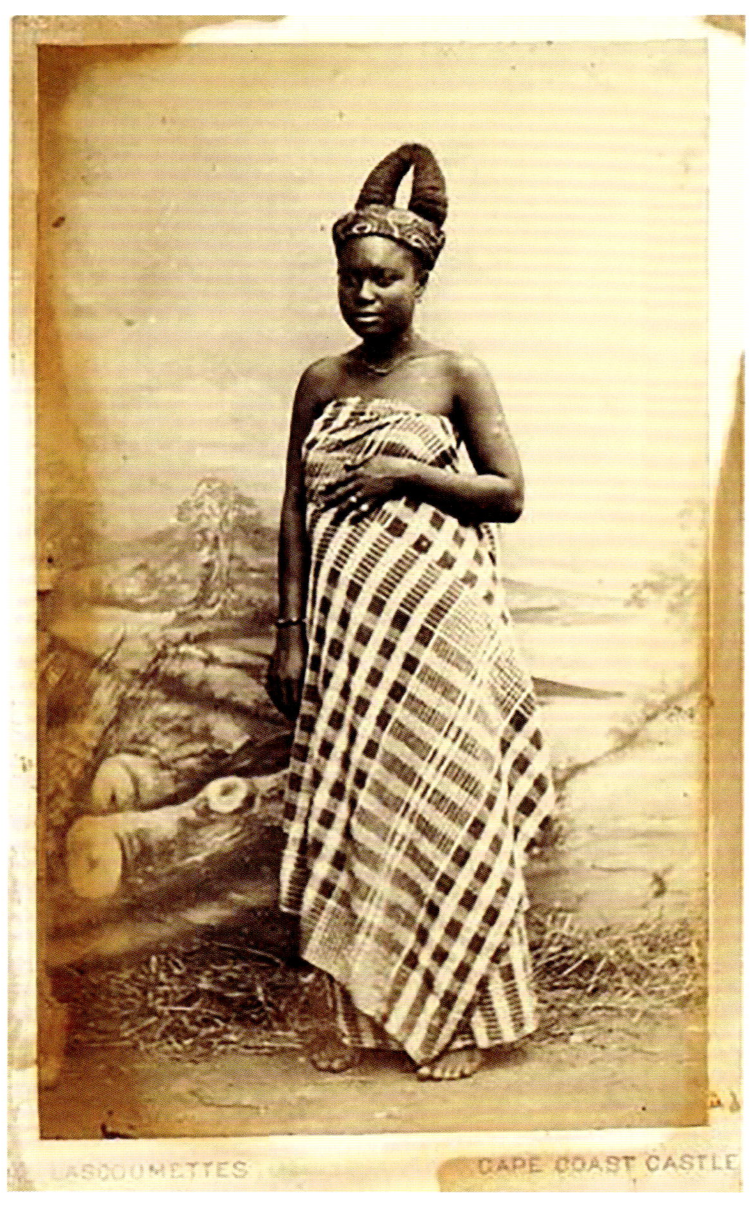

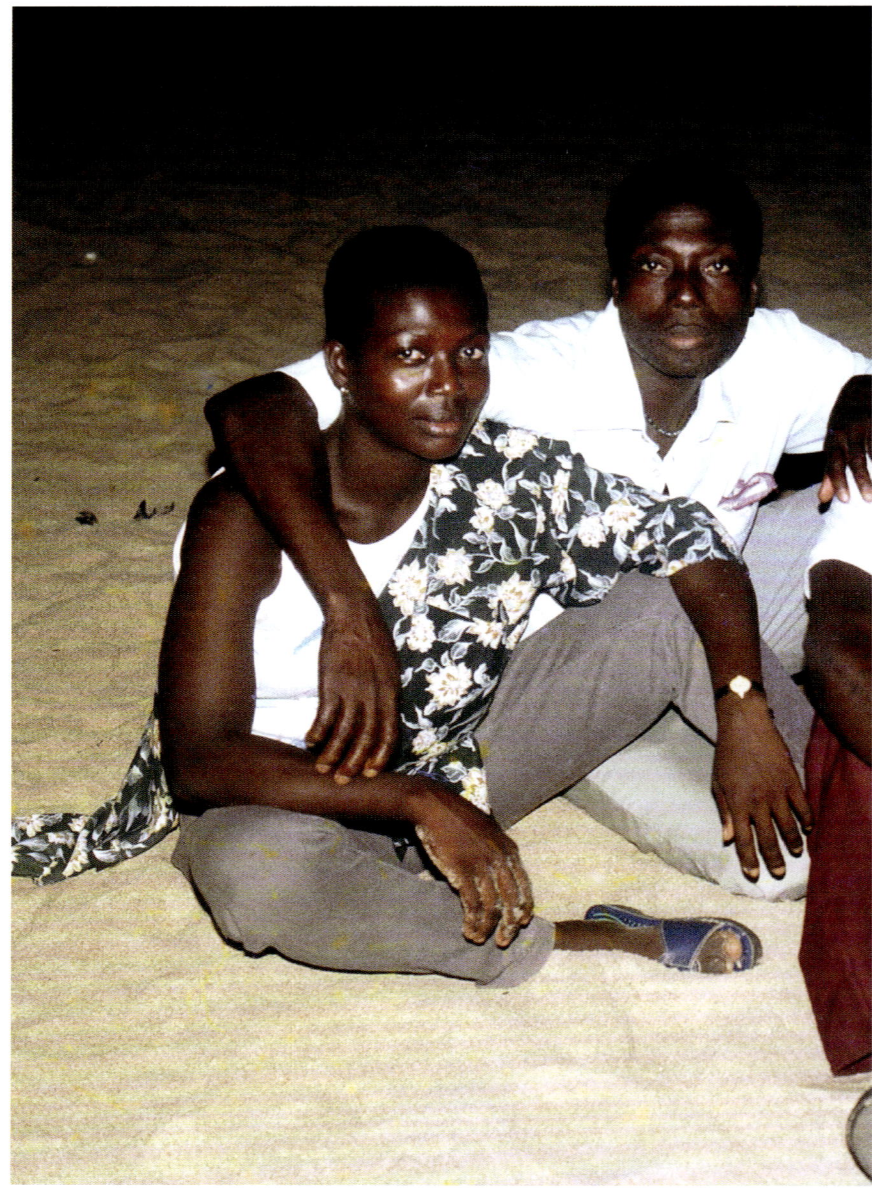

Clockwise from top left:
J. Lascoumettes, *Fante Woman from Cape Coast*, ca. 1880; Photographic City, Agbozume, *Group of friends photographed at the beach*, Volta Region, 2000s; Deo Gratias studio, Accra, 2023; Album cover for King Kwabena Onyina, *Evergreen Tunes*, 1970
Lascoumettes: © National Museum of African Art, Washington, D.C., and courtesy Si Hene; Photographic City: © and courtesy the artist and Saman Archive; Deo Gratias studio: Photograph by Francis Kokoroko for *Aperture*; Onyina: courtesy Bokoor African Popular Music Archives Foundation (BAPMAF) and J. H. Kwabena Nketia Archives

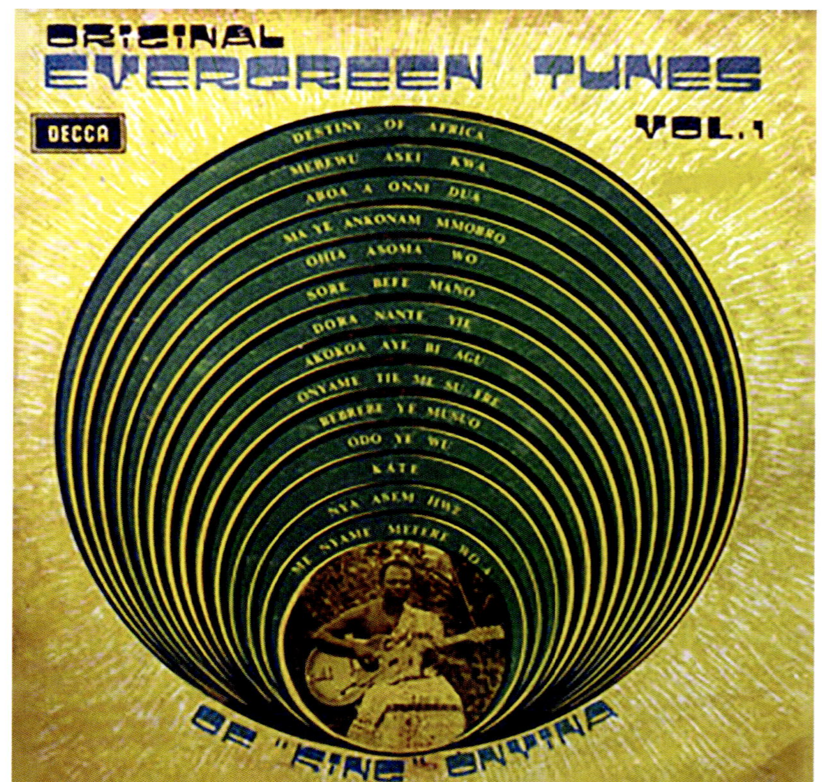


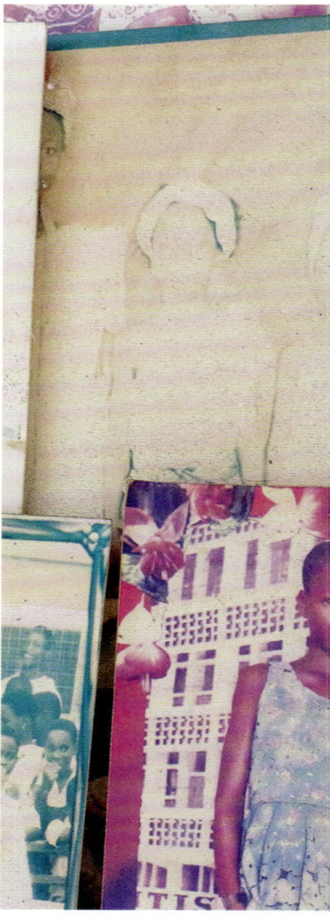

# Image Bank

Illuminating history, culture, and lifestyle, archives in Ghana are living catalogs of the nation's past.
**Kobby Ankomah Graham**

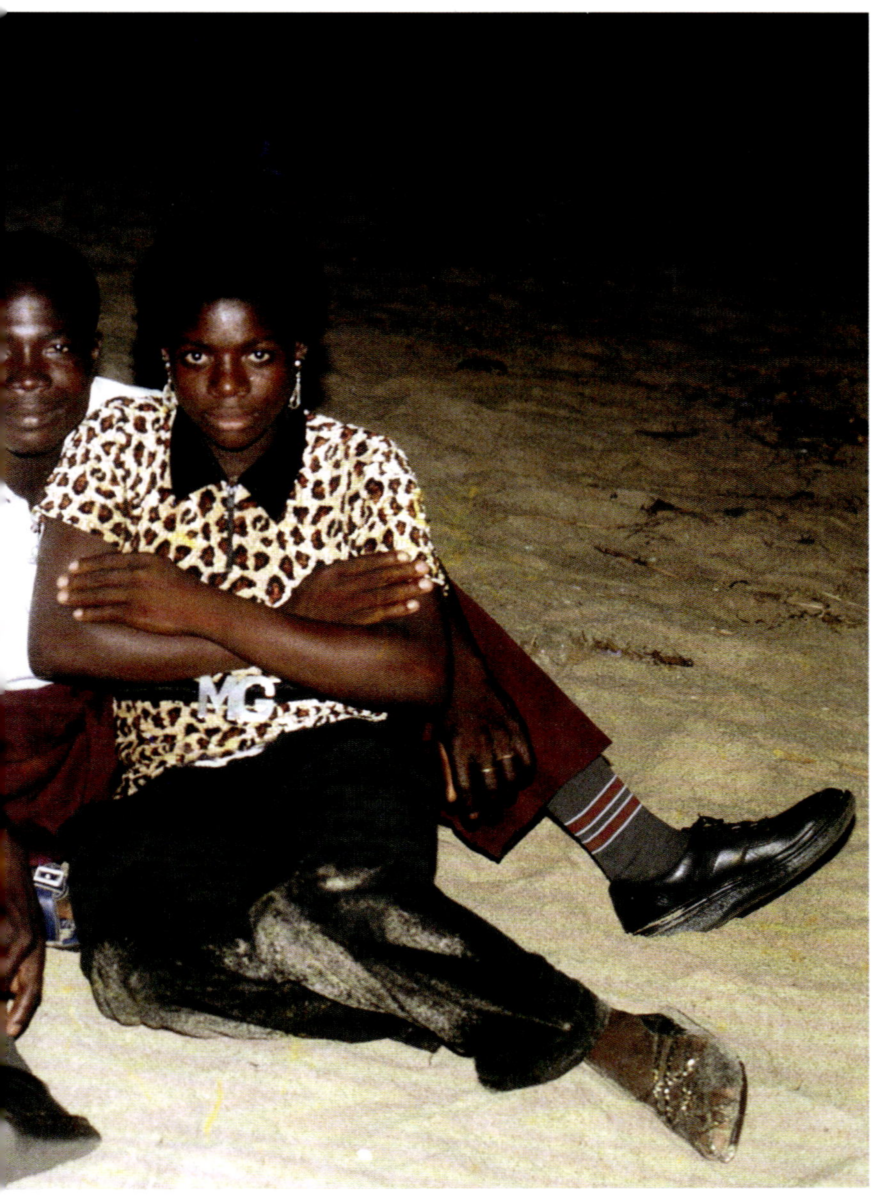

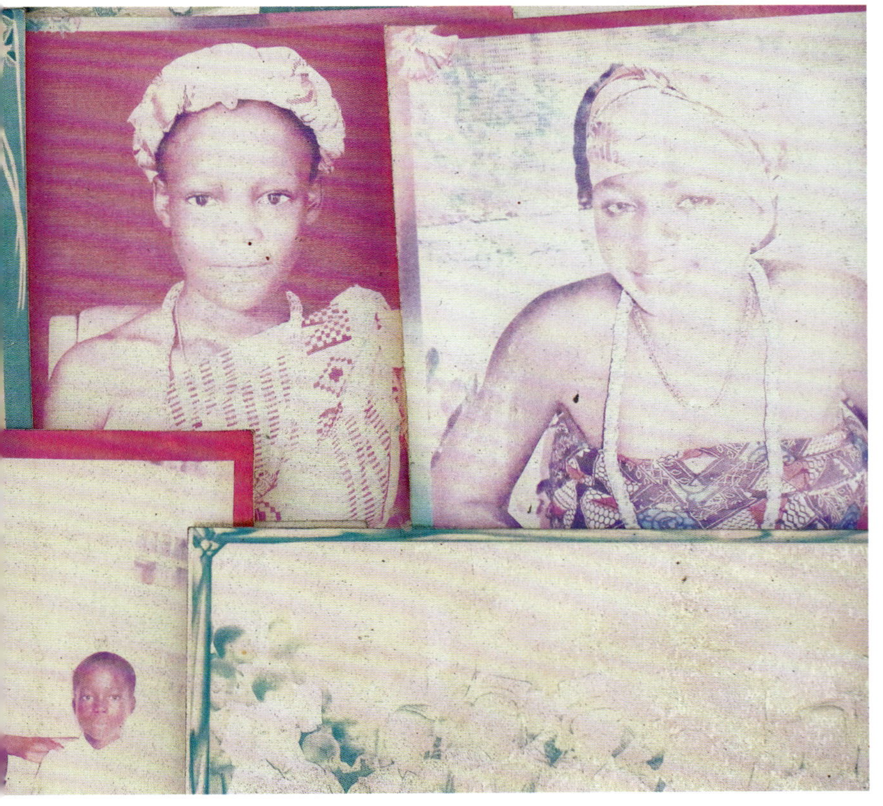

The first time I heard of a photographic archive in Ghana was in 2009 after returning to Accra following studies in London. I was the editor of *Dust*, a quarterly love letter to Accra that documented the city's (then) nascent cultural scene. We were drafting an article about one of our inspirations—the iconic South African magazine *Drum* (which published photography by the likes of Ernest Cole and James Barnor in the 1950s and 1960s)—when my photo-editor, Seton Nicholas, mentioned the Willis Bell Archive.

Bell, an American photographer who died in 1999, snapped thousands of images during a long residence in postindependence Ghana, including commissioned photographs of Ghana's first leader, Kwame Nkrumah. Those photographs are currently being restored and digitized by the Mmofra Foundation, a nonprofit organization continuing the work of Bell's close friend Efua Sutherland, a playwright who was one of Ghana's first and most prominent cultural activists and advocates for children. Mmofra (which means "children" in Akan) runs a beautiful park on the Sutherland compound, where Bell once lived, and is dedicated to the cultural and intellectual enrichment of Ghana's children.

There are, of course, other archives in a land as visually compelling as Ghana. Photographs were once a marker of social status here, and many elite Ghanaian families have flocked

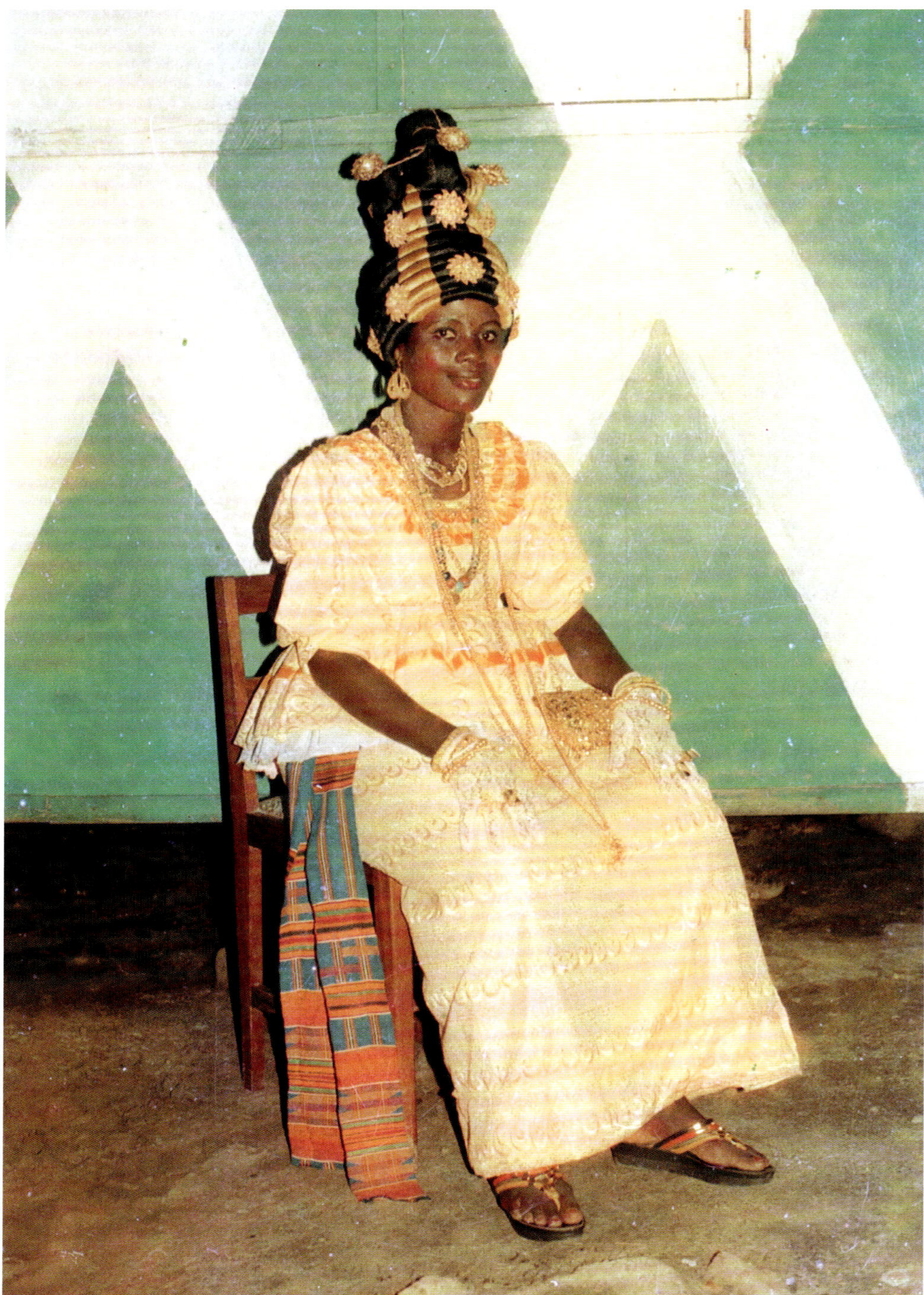



**Photographs were once a marker of social status, and many elite Ghanaian families have flocked to studios to immortalize themselves.**

to places such as Accra's Deo Gratias, one of Ghana's oldest photographic studios, to immortalize themselves. Deo Gratias (Latin for "thanks to God") was founded by the photographer J. K. Bruce-Vanderpuije in 1922. Born to a wealthy family in 1899, he opened the studio after a three-year apprenticeship under the photographer J. A. C. Holm. The firm made portraits of British and Indian families as well as Black professionals, then expanded to cover corporate events. Bruce-Vanderpuije was later joined by one of his sons, Isaac, also a gifted photographer. Deo Gratias, situated in a graceful old building in the heart of Jamestown, one of the city's first districts, is surrounded by history: it is walking distance from a lighthouse, two colonial-era forts, and a palace. It is run today by Kate Tamakloe, who builds on her father's and grandfather's work by scanning and digitizing pictures from old film and glass plates.

Tamakloe considers archives such as Deo Gratias to be vitally important in Africa, where history is often ignored, forgotten, or

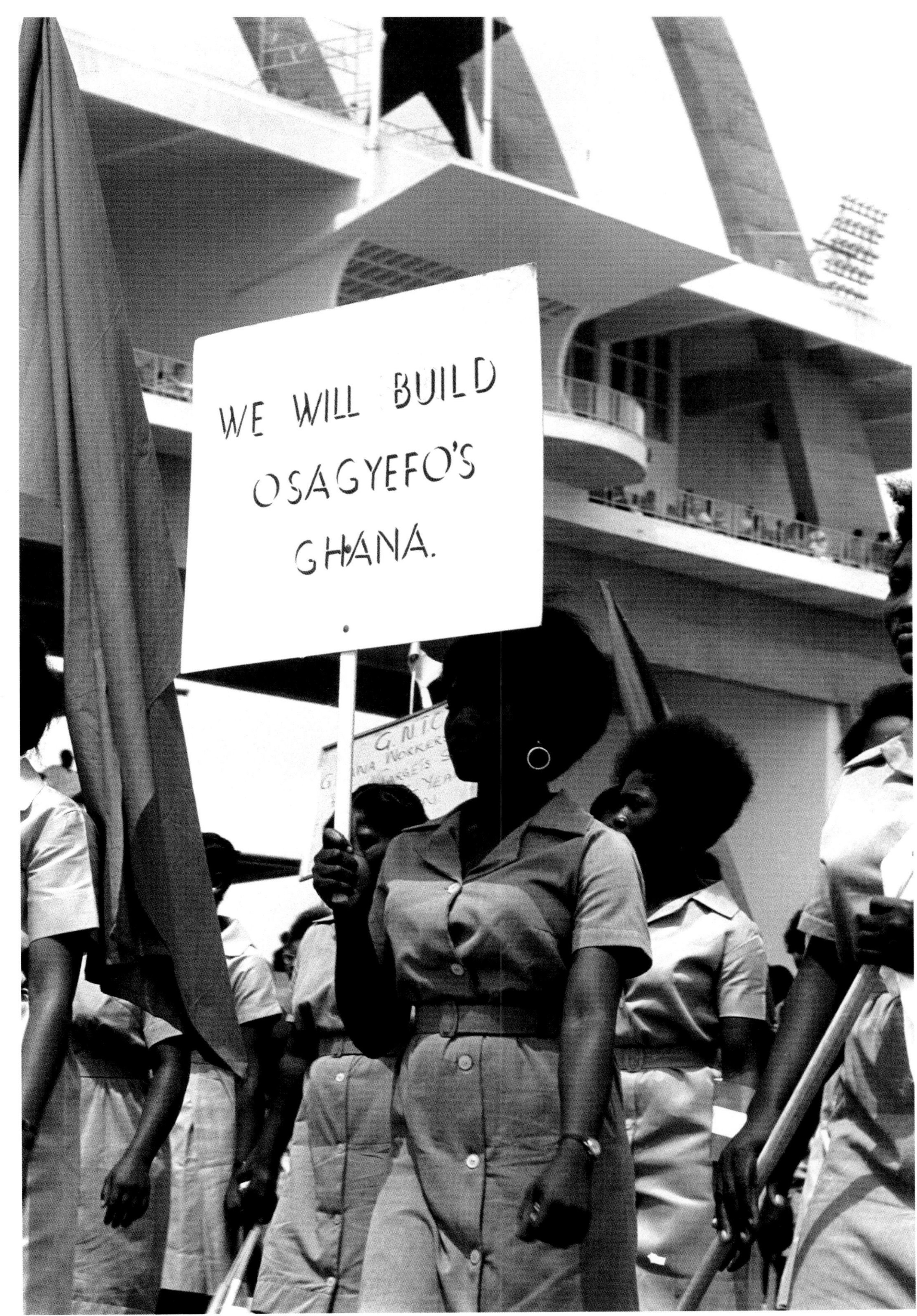

WE WILL BUILD OSAGYEFO'S GHANA.
G.N.T.C
GHANA WORKERS

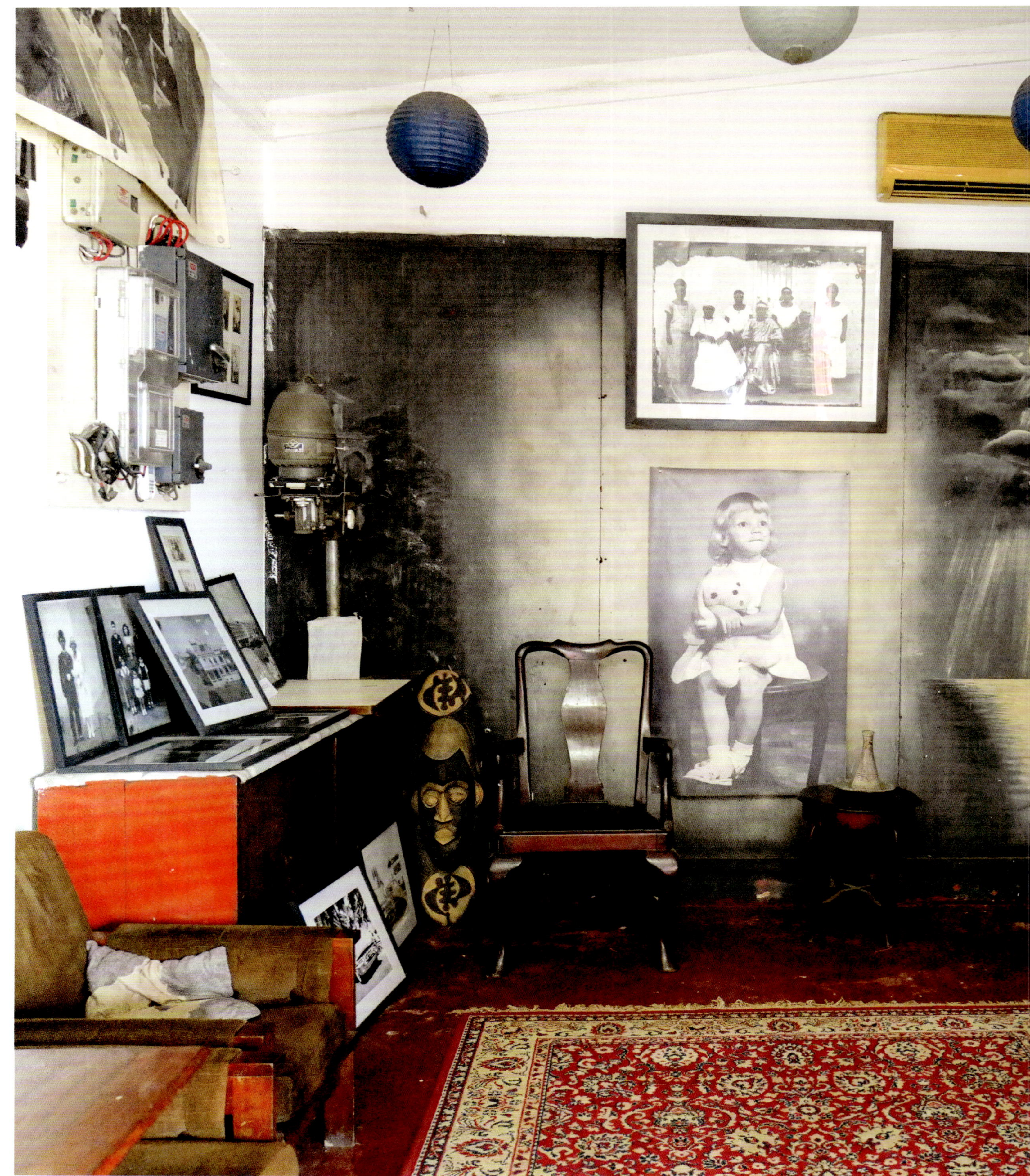

**Deo Gratias studio,
Accra, 2023**
Photograph by Francis
Kokoroko for *Aperture*

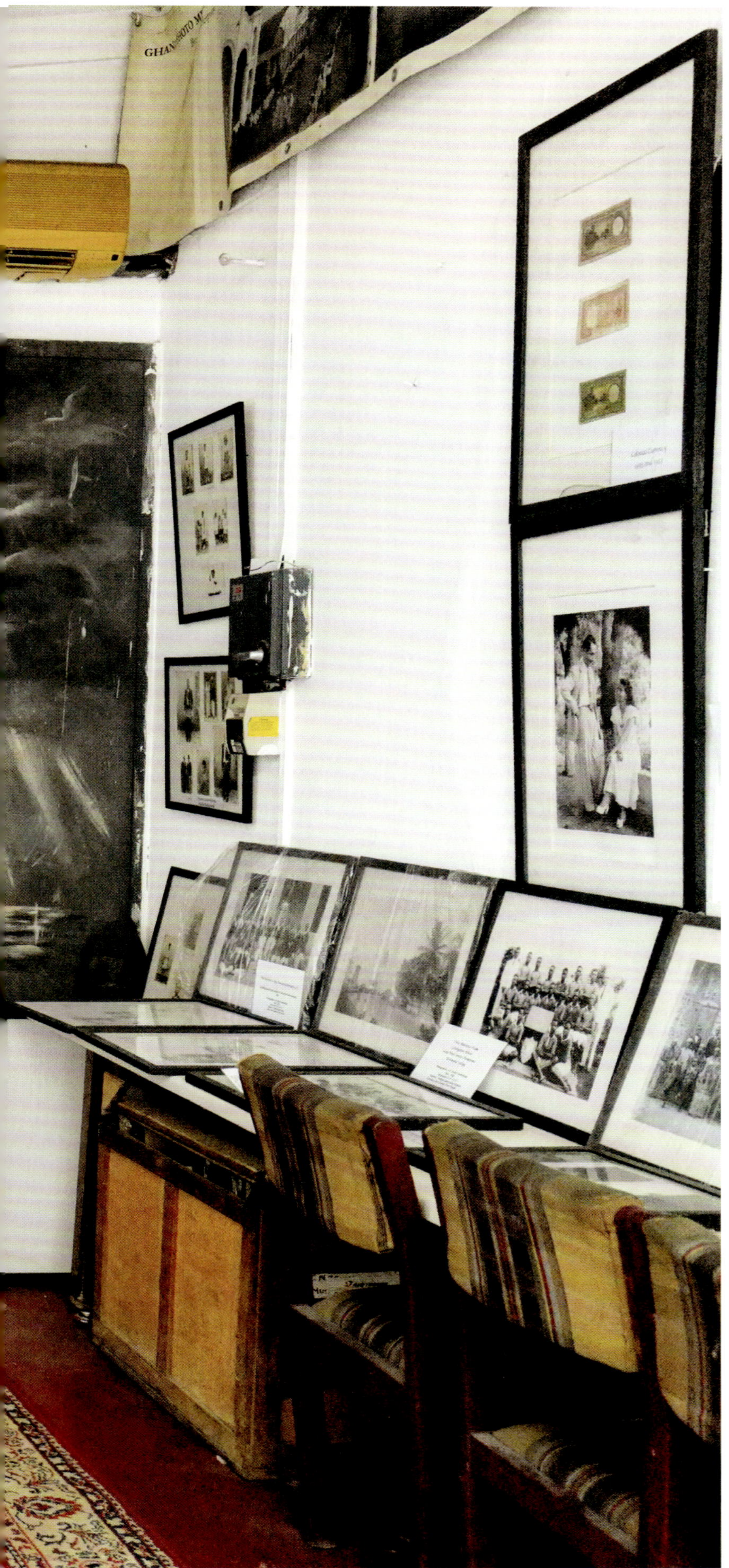

obscured. The introduction of photography in West Africa in the mid-nineteenth century would ultimately give Ghanaians a better appreciation of the landmark events of independence a hundred years later. The photographs housed at Deo Gratias "prove history, occasion, and even lifestyle," she says, and, in turn, inspire books, films, and documentaries. One might think that this would make the archiving of photography a national priority, but Tamakloe explains that individual Ghanaians have always been more supportive of photography than any of Ghana's myriad political administrations.

That said, one of Ghana's most important repositories, the J. H. Kwabena Nketia Archives, part of the University of Ghana, benefits, at least indirectly, from government support. Currently run by Judith Opoku-Boateng, the archive is named after Joseph Hanson Nketia, Africa's foremost ethnomusicologist until his passing in 2019, at the age of ninety-seven. Its contents include music from all over Africa—priceless recordings of vanishing traditions—as well as the Institute of African Studies' historical records dating as far back as the 1960s, and a large photographic collection of postcolonial Ghana. It is the largest and most systematic set of recordings of any African ethnomusicologist, initially spanning forty years of field research by Nketia and his colleagues, and documents sounds, stories, and songs across the length and breadth of Ghana, along with oral and performance traditions of the numerous peoples within (and sometimes beyond) its borders. Recent initiatives to grow the collection have included the gathering of special historical papers, photographs, and other audiovisual materials from the families of other deceased scholars. Nketia was the first to capture practices passed down for generations through oral tradition. While his association with music means that the archive may be known primarily for its traditional and highlife recordings, it also houses thousands of negatives and prints that capture the lives of Ghanaians of all walks of life at a crucial time in our history.

Although it feeds from the budget allocated to the Institute of African Studies by the University of Ghana, Opoku-Boateng explains that funding is still barely sufficient for the smooth running of the complex equipment and logistics required by the archive. Another challenge is understaffing: besides Opoku-Boateng and two senior research assistants, one of whom is part-time, the archive relies on interns. There is also the problem of obsolescence, with much of the information being stored on analog media formats and requiring playback equipment unavailable in Ghana, "leaving the value of these materials totally locked up."

Photographs are no longer exclusive to high Ghanaian society. I remember how hard it was to get one's photograph taken while growing up in 1990s Cape Coast, Ghana's former capital. My boarding-school mates and I would pool together pocket money, and one of us would make a beeline to the nearby photo studio to book an appointment for the following weekend, when we would pose in our best school uniforms. Then we would wait—for as long as a month—for our pictures to be developed and printed. Unlike for today's middle-class Ghanaians, who grow up capturing their entire lives on mobile phones to share on social media, there are reasons why many in my generation lack the millennial impulse to document the mundane.

Tamakloe expresses skepticism for online platforms such as Instagram and the dominance of digital. "We have lost all the technicalities of a beautiful photograph, even knowledge of the long process of using chemicals in the darkroom," she says. "Today, it's plug and play. Once the photo is not blurry, it's considered 'a good shot.'" Nevertheless, some do attempt to harness the power of these platforms for the greater good. One such entity is Si Hene— a reference in Akan to the enstoolment of royalty—which was founded in 2020 as a website and Instagram account by Rita

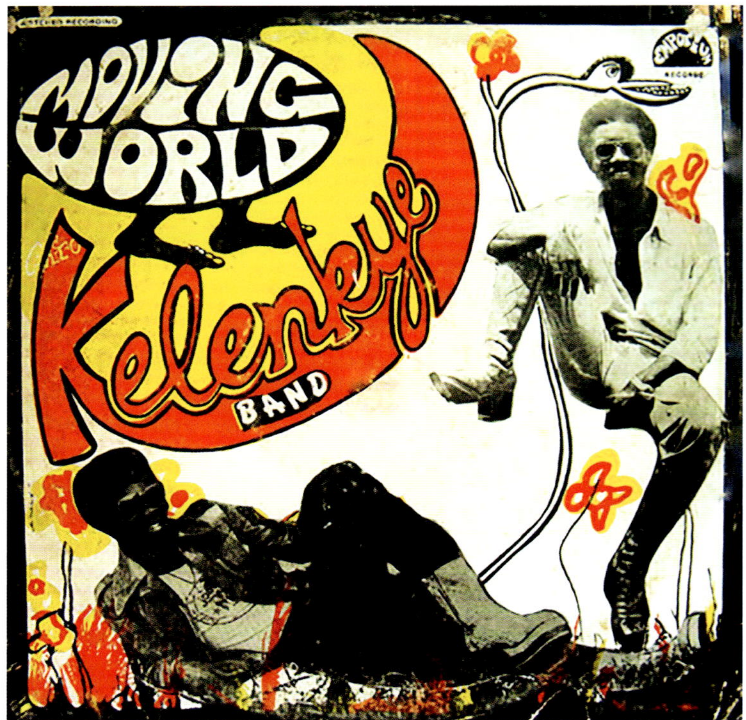


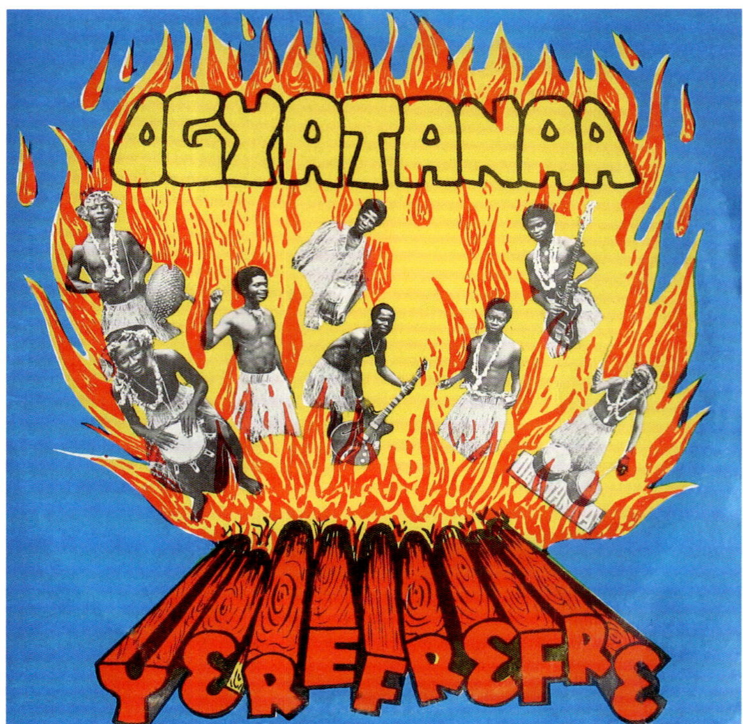


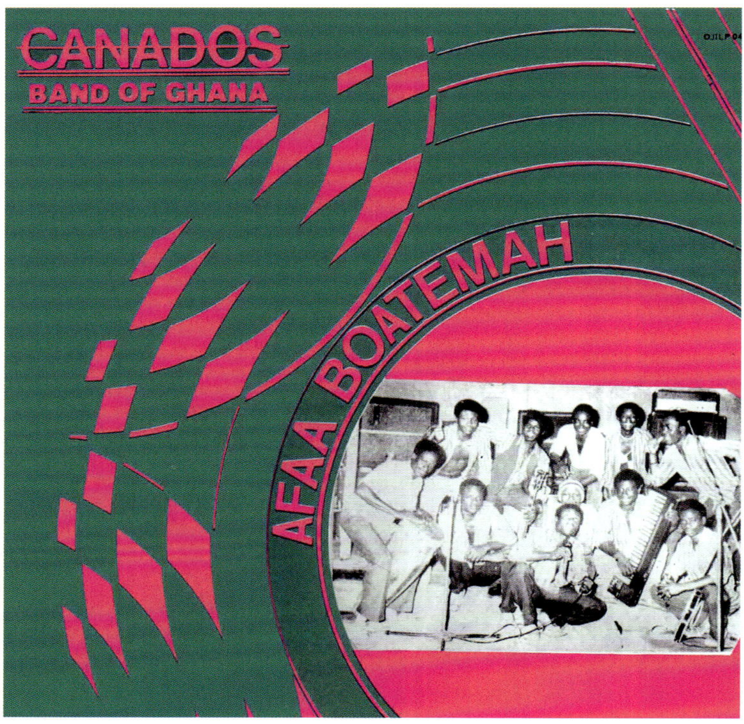


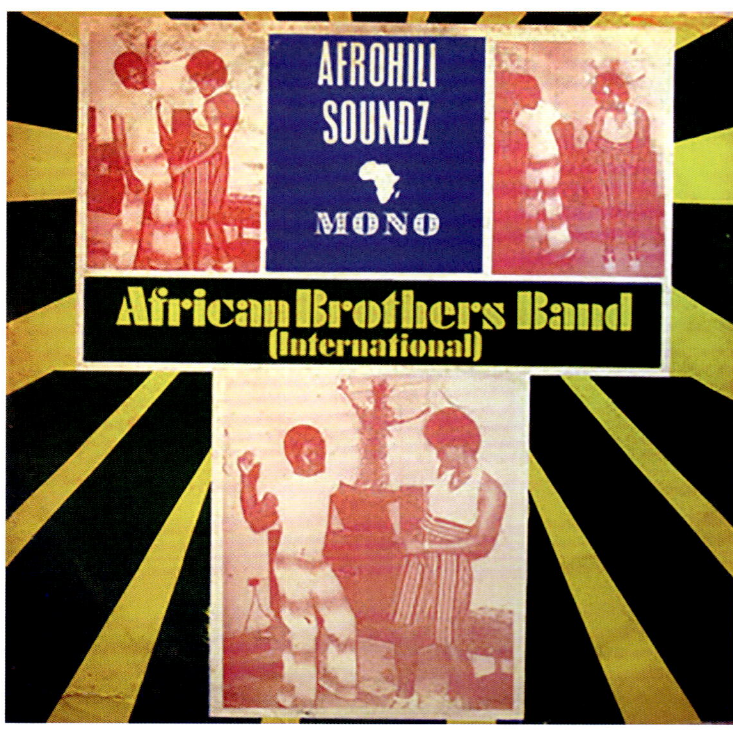


**This page, album covers, clockwise from top left: Kelenkye Band, *Moving World*, 1974; Ogyatanaa Show Band, *Yerefrefre*, 1975; African Brothers Band (International), *Afrohili Soundz*, 1973; Canadoes Super Stars of Ghana led by Big Boy Dansoh, *Afaa Boatemah*, 1985**
All images courtesy Bokoor African Popular Music Archives Foundation (BAPMAF) and J. H. Kwabena Nketia Archives

Mawuena Benissan, a Ghanaian American interdisciplinary artist who describes Si Hene as "an archive-based collection of images of Ghanaian chieftaincy." Such work is important in the context of a continent whose royals were reduced from kings and queens to "chiefs" by colonizers whose worldview stopped them from seeing Africans as equals.

When I visited Benissan at Gallery 1957, a contemporary art space and commercial gallery housed in Accra's Kempinski Hotel, she was preparing for an exhibition at the gallery on the elaborately designed umbrellas that provide more than mere cover from sun and rain to Ghanaian chiefs during royal durbars and festivals. (In Ghana, such umbrellas, as much symbols of royalty as any crown or scepter, are used during sacred traditional ceremonies and festivals.) Benissan tells me that she sees her exhibition and online archiving as extensions of the same work. "People say 'chieftaincy is dead,' but it's not. Literally everything we do is derived from chieftaincy: from our stools to our names to the kente we wear to how we style our hair and present ourselves. It all comes from the chieftaincy. The photos are a way to bridge that heritage."

She has been inspired by others including Amy Sall, founder of *SUNU Journal*—an independent, Pan-African, postdisciplinary multimedia platform that publishes works dealing with Africa and its diaspora—as well as by Nana Oforiatta Ayim, a Ghanaian art historian, and Deborah Willis, the African American historian of photography who once invited Benissan to a "life-changing" conference on Black portraiture at New York University. Benissan was struggling to find images of royal umbrellas for her US graduate-school research. Out of this frustration Si Hene was born. "Even though I had a lot of books," Benissan explains, "there were no old images, only pictures of recent chiefs, or images from Benin and Nigeria but not Ghana." Wanting to find out more about how these umbrellas were designed in the early 1800s and 1900s, she scoured archives at museums, institutions, and universities; family albums; and YouTube and internet resources, including Tumblr, to find the answer. It was hard work. "Sometimes, I could spend five hours looking for a photo and not find anything. But then you change a keyword, an image pops up, and you spend six more hours from that one connection," Benissan tells me.

After the COVID lockdowns lifted, Benissan returned to Ghana and gained access to chieftaincy meetings, where she was guided toward reference materials and archival collections that included pictures, postcards, stamps, and stills. She is seeing a slow rise of chiefs building their own museums, but she wonders whether these are aimed at Ghanaians or visitors from Africa's diaspora trying to better understand the ancient nations and cultures out of which their ancestors were stolen. It is an important question: Africans in the diaspora have access to museums, universities, and other institutions their cousins in Africa lack. In Ghana, Benissan explains, you have to ask "a hundred people" for that kind of information, you have to wait and seek approval. Accessibility afforded by social media is key, but Benissan also notes that many parents, grandparents, and chiefs are not on Instagram. She describes being introduced to chiefs who appreciate her idea but ask an important question: "How do I see it?" She also faces copyright issues, as Si Hene does not own any of these images. She nevertheless tries to contact as many institutions, curators, and families as she can. Even if some do not respond, others, Benissan says, "seem happy we are providing another accessible way to see their collections."

Similar in digital form to Si Hene stands Saman Archive, named after an Akan word that simultaneously means "ghost" and "photographic negative." Founded in 2015 by the artist and writer Adjoa Armah, Saman began as a repository for the thirty thousand negatives dating from 1963 to 2010 that Armah collected from studios and photographers across Ghana as part of her practice-led doctoral research at the University of Oxford. She considers Saman to be more than just a collection of negatives, stating that the project is a place for "my own photographs and those of my collaborators across the country, recorded conversations with photographers, ephemera, and the research conducted as negatives are being collected."

Saman stands on the shoulders of giants. As Armah explains, "We never start from zero. The best we can do is honor those who came before us." She values Deo Gratias and holds particular appreciation for the Nketia Archives' custodianship of Ghanaian sonic histories, saying, "It's their work and the work that families do, in which the stories around photographs are central, that really influence me." In contrast to Si Hene, Saman's areas of collecting go beyond chieftaincy, and its public face is a website. Noting the



Perseverance Photo Studio, Teenage boy photographed with studio backdrop, Anloga, Ghana, 2000s
© the artist and courtesy Saman Archive

**Photography has changed from focusing on members of high society to becoming a people's visual history.**

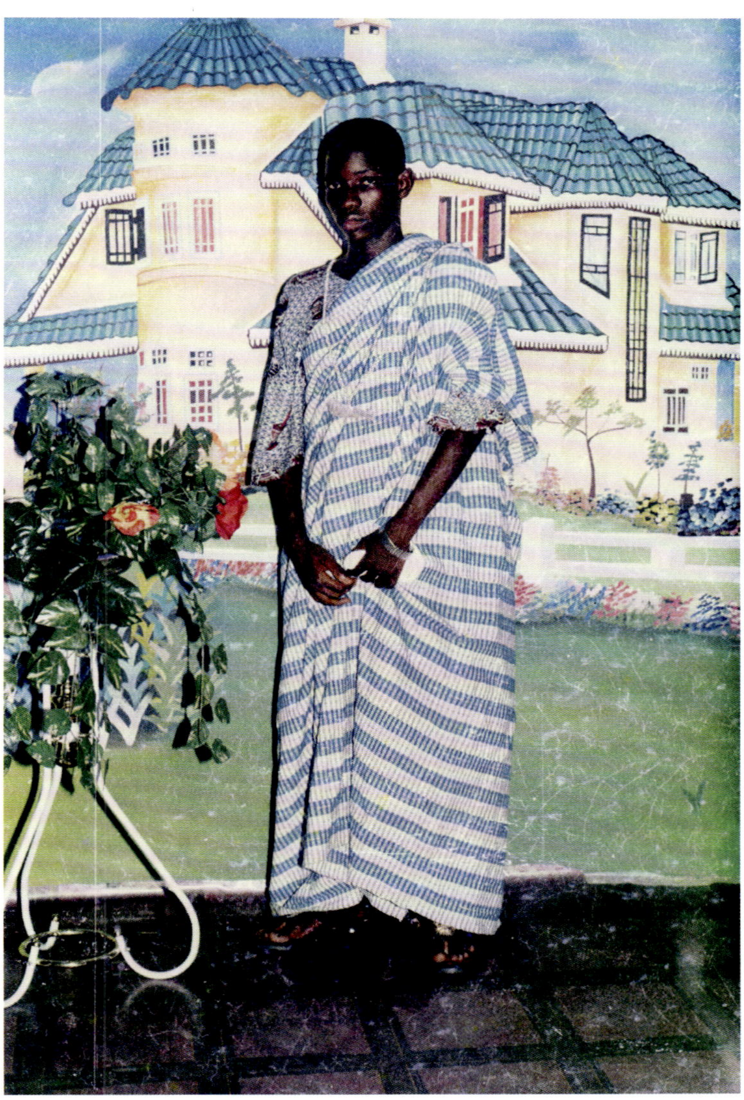

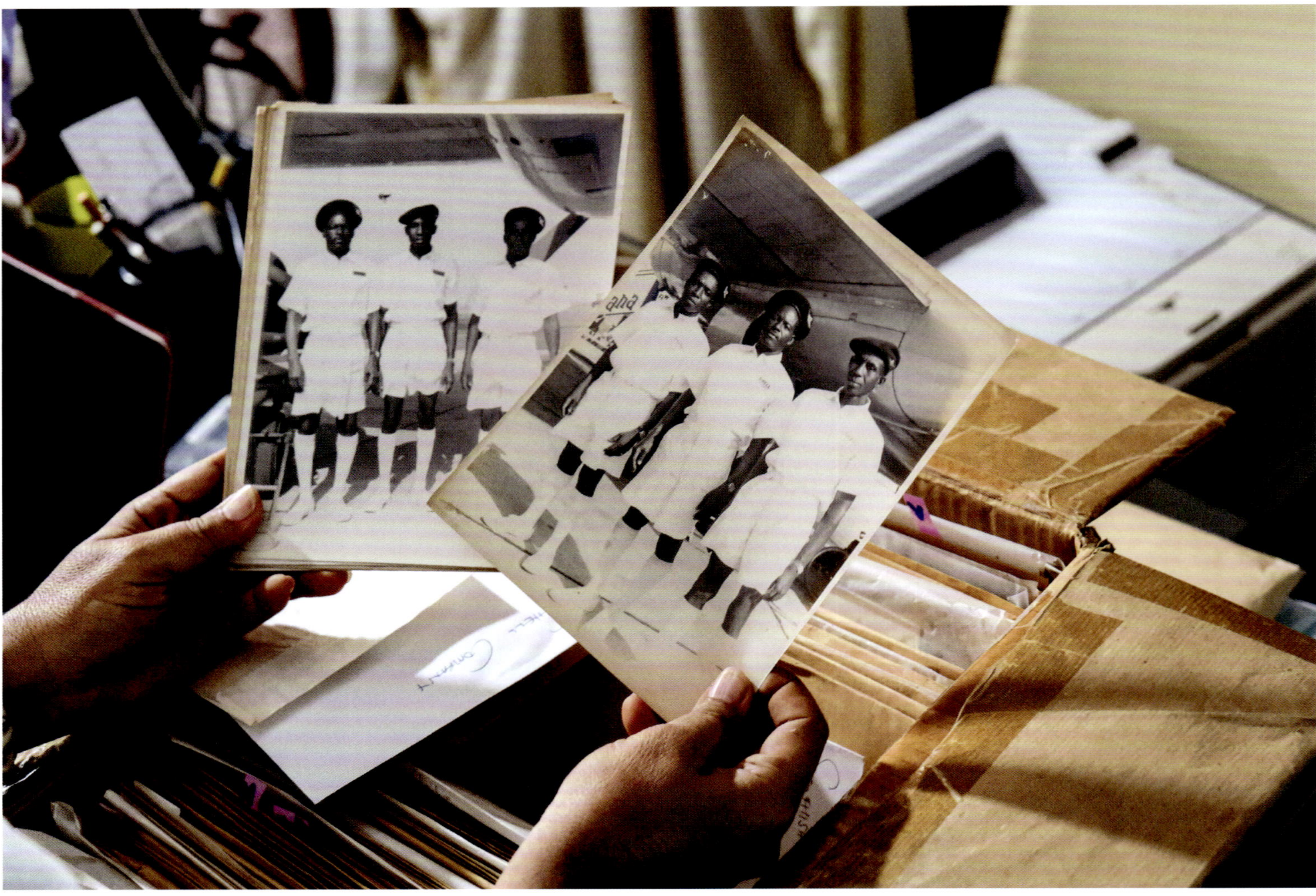



way photography has changed from focusing on members of high society to becoming a people's visual history, Saman is, she says, "interested in what lives looked like beyond the grand narratives that cater toward middle-to-upper-class people."

Armah surprises me with a "two-hundred-year plan" that includes eventually housing Saman in a physical space. Benissan also dreams of museum and research institutions, where physical images can be better preserved, in all sixteen regions of Ghana. She points out that chieftaincy palaces are ultimately homes and, as such, cannot offer visitors the same levels of exposure as museums. The goal is to balance access to the physical images housed in these spaces with respect for royal privacy. While Deo Gratias already serves as a physical museum, it, too, encounters problems of scaling up, a process that involves, as Tamakloe explains to me, "maintaining the glass plates, digitizing them totally, and making it available virtually to the world to tell the Ghanaian story."

Ghana's archives are invaluable resources for understanding the nation's past. Ongoing efforts to preserve and digitize such records—both physical objects and data—are essential for future generations. This work is shaping a collective understanding of history and identity that may otherwise be lost in the maelstrom of modern culture: a thing that is never static.

Kobby Ankomah Graham is a writer, DJ, lecturer, and cultural activist who lives in Accra.

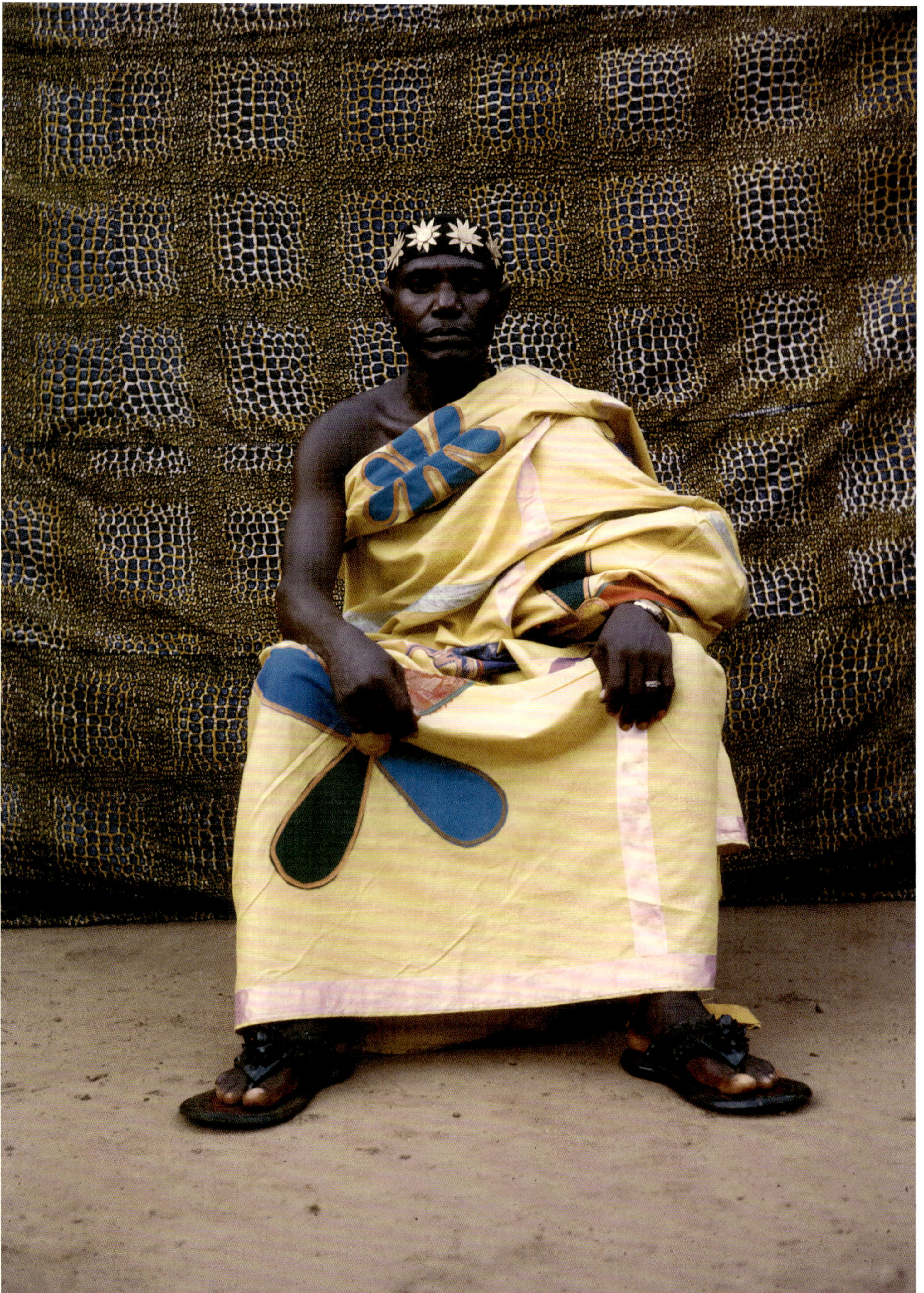

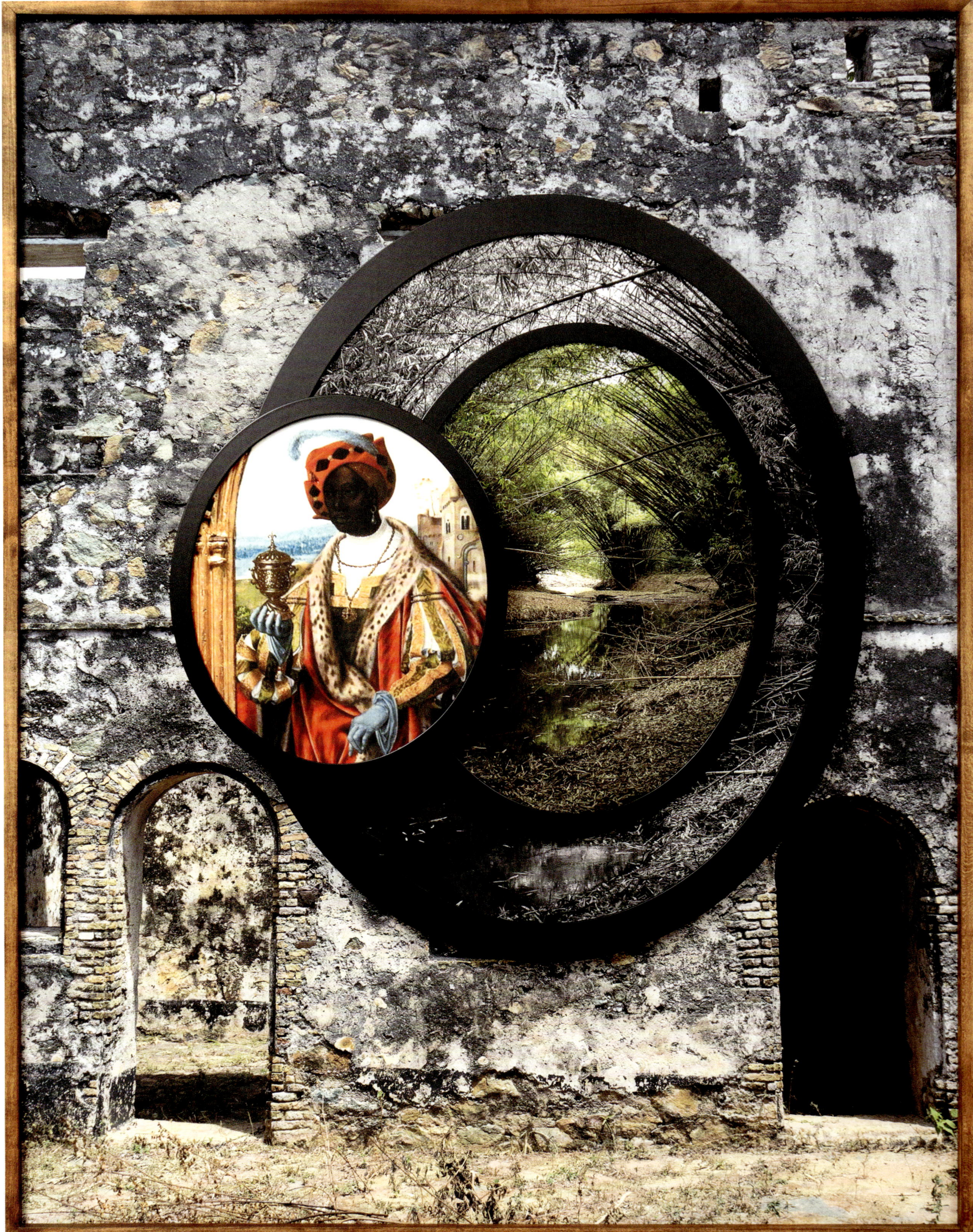

In the decades since independence, writers and artists from the diaspora have returned to Ghana. What are they looking for?

# Ghana Obscura

**Anakwa Dwamena**

"Small Rally, Accra." 1964. Townspeople, watching and listening with rapt attention, sit in a semicircle, oriented toward a speaker just outside the frame. It's a mixed group: uniformed high-school girls in sleeveless white dresses, men in traditional woven cotton cloth worn toga-style, others in long sleeves and slacks with a cigarette clasped between their lips. Children of all ages sit, squat, and crouch on the swept-dust floor. A juvenile rebel stares at the photographer—Paul Strand. A group of women sit on a bench in front. Signs pinned to their headscarves say "C.P.P.": Kwame Nkrumah's Convention People's Party.

The scene is an early glimpse at Nkrumah's ongoing project of building a modern Ghana, a new country that piqued the attention of seemingly the whole world. Where the Cold War thinking held countries hostage to the narrow interest of Western white powers, Nkrumah and his peers in the so-called third world were putting forward an alternative global vision. Where Western leaders and their security details were cracking down on political protest and minority rights, Nkrumah himself embodied a continuation of the Pan-African struggle forged in the streets of Harlem, Philadelphia, and London.

It was easy, then, for many Black people in the diaspora to imagine Ghana as a home. Its name harkens back to the idea of a great African empire; its invitation to create a new African presence was compelling. This was the chance for people to go "back" to the motherland, roll up their sleeves, and help build the future. From Richard Wright's *Black Power* (1954) and Maya Angelou's *All God's Children Need Traveling Shoes* (1986) to Ekow Eshun's *Black Gold of the Sun* (2005) and Saidiya Hartman's *Lose Your Mother* (2007), writers and artists from the diaspora, having made journeys to Ghana, have composed distinctive travelogues about this possibility of a different world. They came to explore and see where they might fit in. This place of ideal perfection would provide a familial embrace. "We had come to Africa from our varying starting places and with myriad motives, gaping with hungers, some more ravenous than others," Angelou writes in *All God's Children*, "and we had little tolerance for understanding being ignored."

The potential of a shared political and spiritual struggle stoked the impulse for homecoming, for healing and renewal. This was a society in transition. A society that brought together elements of

# The people in Strand's photographs appear determined to be exemplars of the "African personality."

the traditional and the contemporary, the old and the young, the spiritual and the scientific—all to fashion a modern technological behemoth. This is what Strand would spend four months and ten thousand miles attempting to capture in *Ghana: An African Portrait* (1976). It's there in the cold power of the overwhelming metal structures, pipes, and concrete of the Tema Oil Refinery. And in the massive ships docked at the Tema harbor, promising the possibility of benefiting from a coastal proximity that had been a curse not long ago. Deeper inland, Strand preserves the mystery and majesty of ritual dance and incantations in Larteh, and with it, the timeless connection to the ancestors, land, and life force the people have always subsisted on.

Strand, with the blessing of the president, showed the world what Africa looked like. Ghana, he decided, was the best case study. I imagine the project as the first half of a before-and-after comparison, which meant to serve as evidence for awe-inspiring transformation to come. The country's diversity, economic patterns, and environmental resources at the time adequately reflected conditions in other parts of the continent. But its more recent history—its complicity in the slave trade, supply of materials for the Industrial Revolution, and invaluable role in both world wars—linked it to the modern world. The people in Strand's photographs appear determined to be exemplars of the "African personality," demonstrating autochthonous values and characteristics in all their complexities, which would counter long-held racist ideas of the continent's being a backward place.

"I was black and they were black," Wright wrote of his experience in Ghana, "but my blackness did not help me." Many returnees do not know the specific location of their roots on the continent, and their choice of Ghana is often attributable to a sense of ease: the use of English, and the relatively high quality of infrastructure and amenities. Rather than Ghanaians ready to welcome long-lost siblings, seekers met locals who knew little of their plight. The years apart and differing histories had made lasting

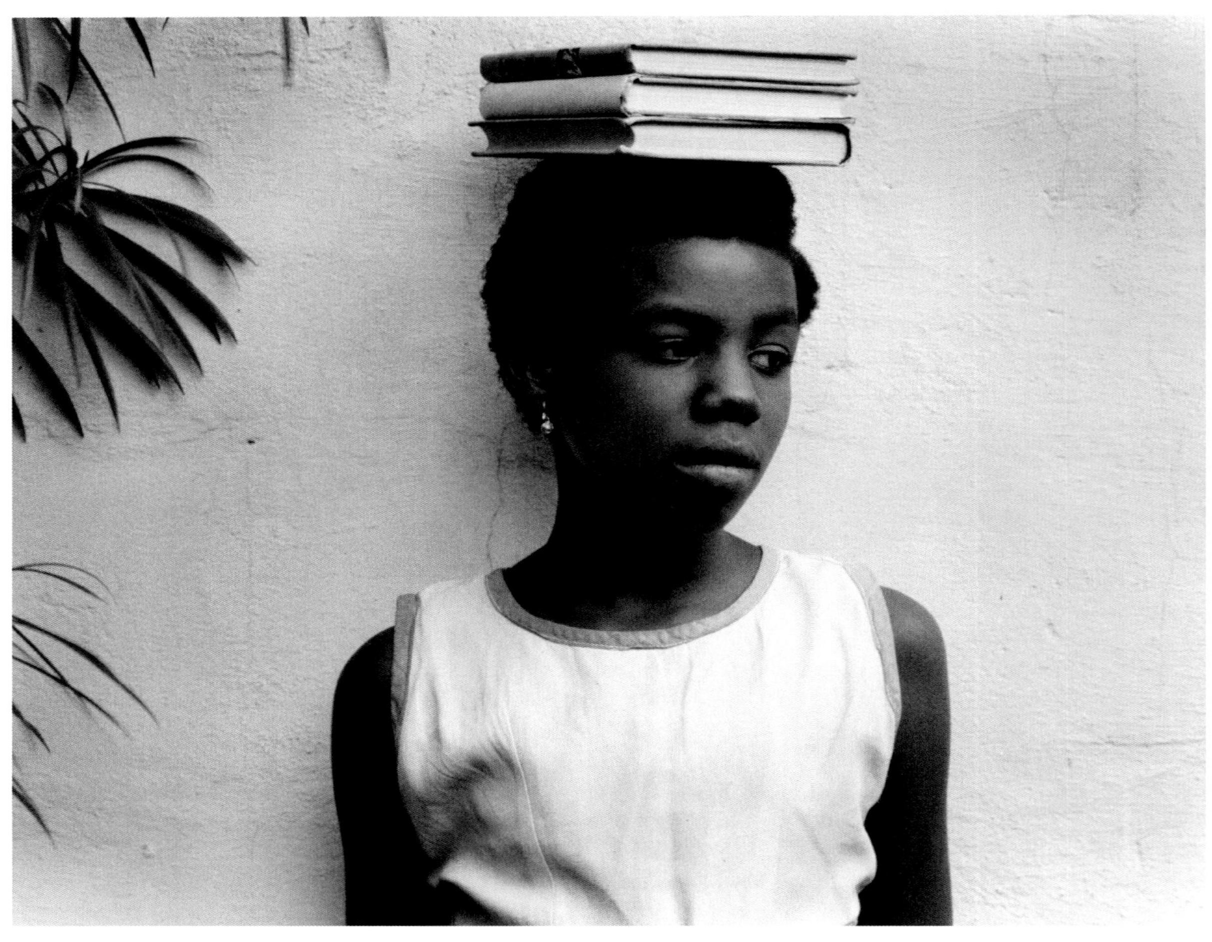

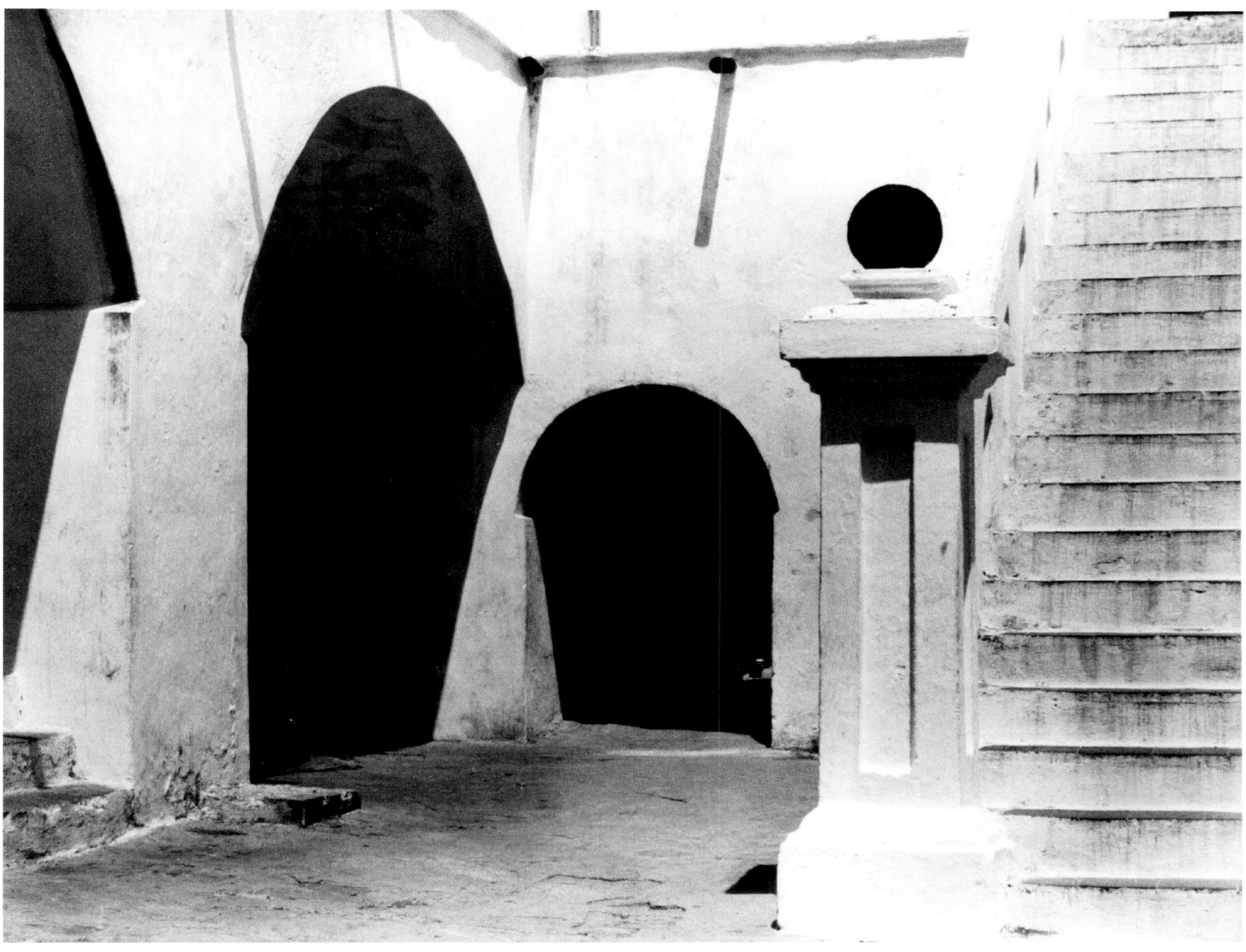

marks. Culturally, Ghanaians found little in common with the goals of the Black American and British arrivals. Where children of the diaspora sought remnants and an understanding of their historical roots—hopefully untouched by Western elements—they discovered a Ghana detached from a meaningful engagement with the darker elements of its own history, betraying a narrower conception of what connected them. The wound of belonging festered, and as Angelou points out, the disappointed returnees "didn't want to know that they had not come home, but had left one familiar place of painful memory for another strange place."

What made the place strange was the apparent amnesia on the part of Ghanaians about the slave trade. The elephant in the room was the human in the barracoon. At the peak of the slave trade, in the eighteenth century, nearly a million slaves were shipped to the New World from Ghana alone. To Ghanaians like me, the slave trade is often thought of as a tragedy from outside that happened to us. Ghanaian schoolchildren took excursions to the castles at Cape Coast and Elmina to learn about how the white man tricked our ancestors. But, as Hartman points out, the largest slave market feeding the ravenous appetite of the trans-Saharan, transatlantic, and African slave trades was located not in the castles (the domain of Europeans, where returnees and tourists are shepherded to reflect) but, instead, in the town of Salaga, some 250 miles from the coast.

Ghanaian history has always felt to me like a black box. My elementary-school curriculum focused on how Ghana got its colonial name, the Gold Coast (skirting the fact that it exported far more slaves than gold), and extolled the achievements of select individuals, then covered the arrival of Europeans, debating the pros and cons of colonialism. Despite Ghanaians' repeated citing of the Sankofa ethic to remember the past, it seems our desire has been to look forward, and to silence the sordid history. It is in the work of our artists, and Black artists from the diaspora, that a fuller sense of who we are, and who we have been, remains preserved.

In this vein, thinking "early Ghana" brings up images of Accra in the 1960s and 1970s. Of bell-bottoms, high-heeled shoes, and Afros. The smell of Ghanaian printed cloth and heat. No one quite captured the feeling of optimism lighting up Ghanaians like the photographer James Barnor. Beginning in the 1950s, Barnor pictured the sense that everyone had a role to play in building not just the country of Ghana but a free, self-sufficient, and productive Black society. The era is, perhaps, embodied best by the dashing, modern women who stopped by his Ever Young studio, located in the Jamestown area of Accra, adorned in their Sunday finery—hair curled out or flattened and swept into a bun with perfect sheen, opera gloves caressing their arms, their most prized earrings dangling over their shoulders. Following a sojourn in the United Kingdom, where he made fashion portraits and covers for South Africa's *Drum* magazine, Barnor returned to Ghana in the late 1960s and set up the country's first color photography lab.

Where Barnor's previous work had been in the studio, the scenes from his return to Ghana portray the breadth of urban

# Barnor's scenes from his return to Ghana portray the breadth of urban experiences.

experiences. The aspirational images with fanciful, extravagant backdrops are replaced with energetic, unvarnished landscapes of a young nation: the loneliness of an empty bus stop illuminated by a trenchant sun, the vibrancy of a troupe of traditional dancers and drummers performing for a mesmerized crowd, the overjoyed demeanor and gaiety of revelers.

Not long after, the country would fall on hard times. Following a succession of coups and countercoups, Ghana's economy crashed. The party ended. The state's attention would turn from the dream of building a Black global capital. Some claim that Ghana was broke because Nkrumah spent all its money trying to help other African countries fight for their independence. Yet a connection to Black culture in the arts worldwide, particularly music and the resilient blues ethos, would in times of desperation serve as a balm for many Ghanaians. Jazz and reggae would inform highlife and hiplife, and Black comedies would inspire the concert parties staged in towns and villages across the country.

Throughout difficult economic times and military dictatorships, the natural charisma of the country and this sense of hope and possibility remained. This atmosphere creates for a mysterious, organic feeling that has continued to draw the children of Ghana to itself, over and over again. This is the experience the British Ghanaian writer and curator Ekow Eshun describes in *Black Gold of the Sun*. In 2002, he decides to visit Ghana, in the hope that it might help him "become whole again." In London, at the age of thirty-three, he has been experiencing nightmares of lynch mobs chasing him. He wonders if it is the separation from Ghana—the

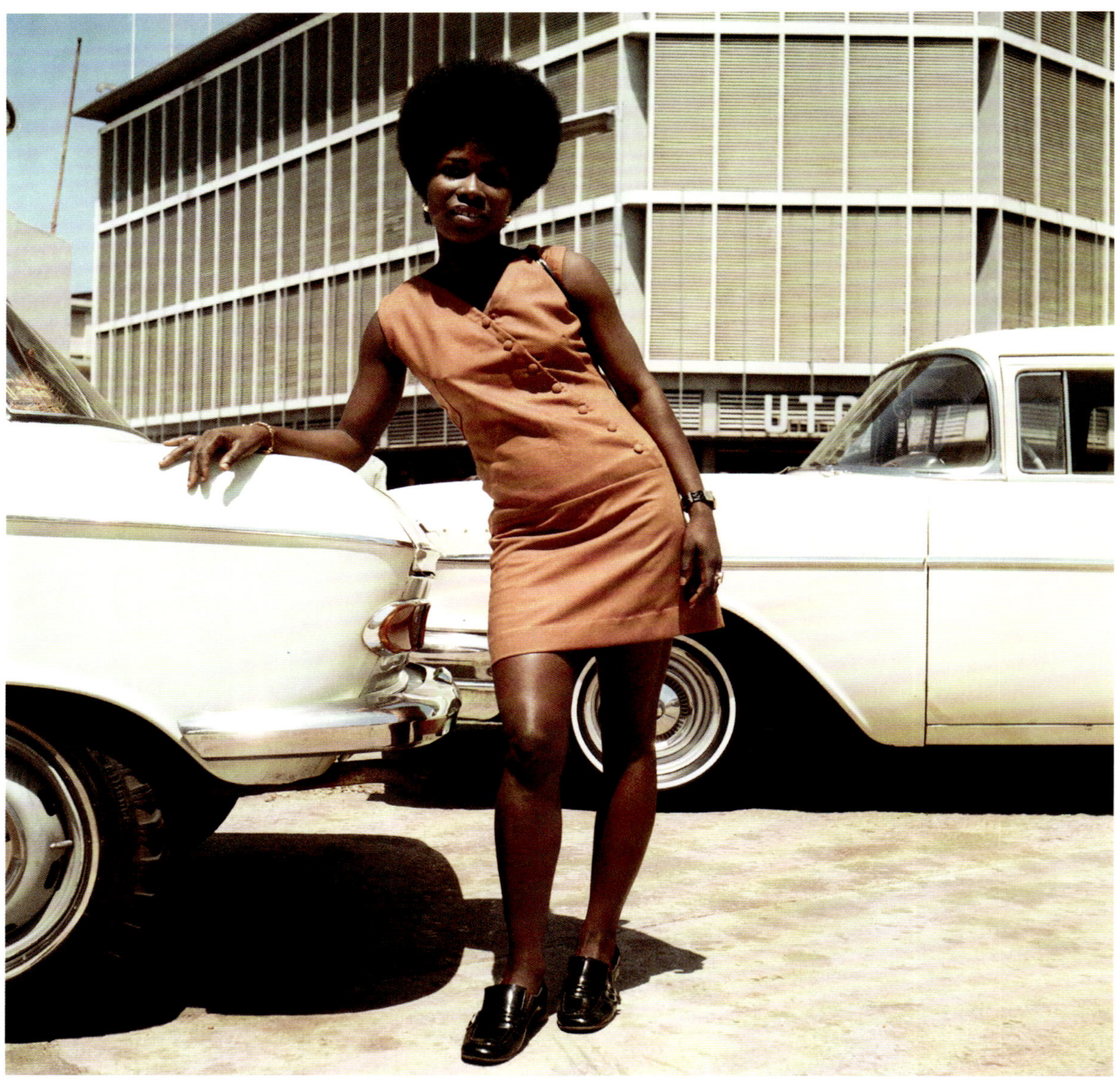

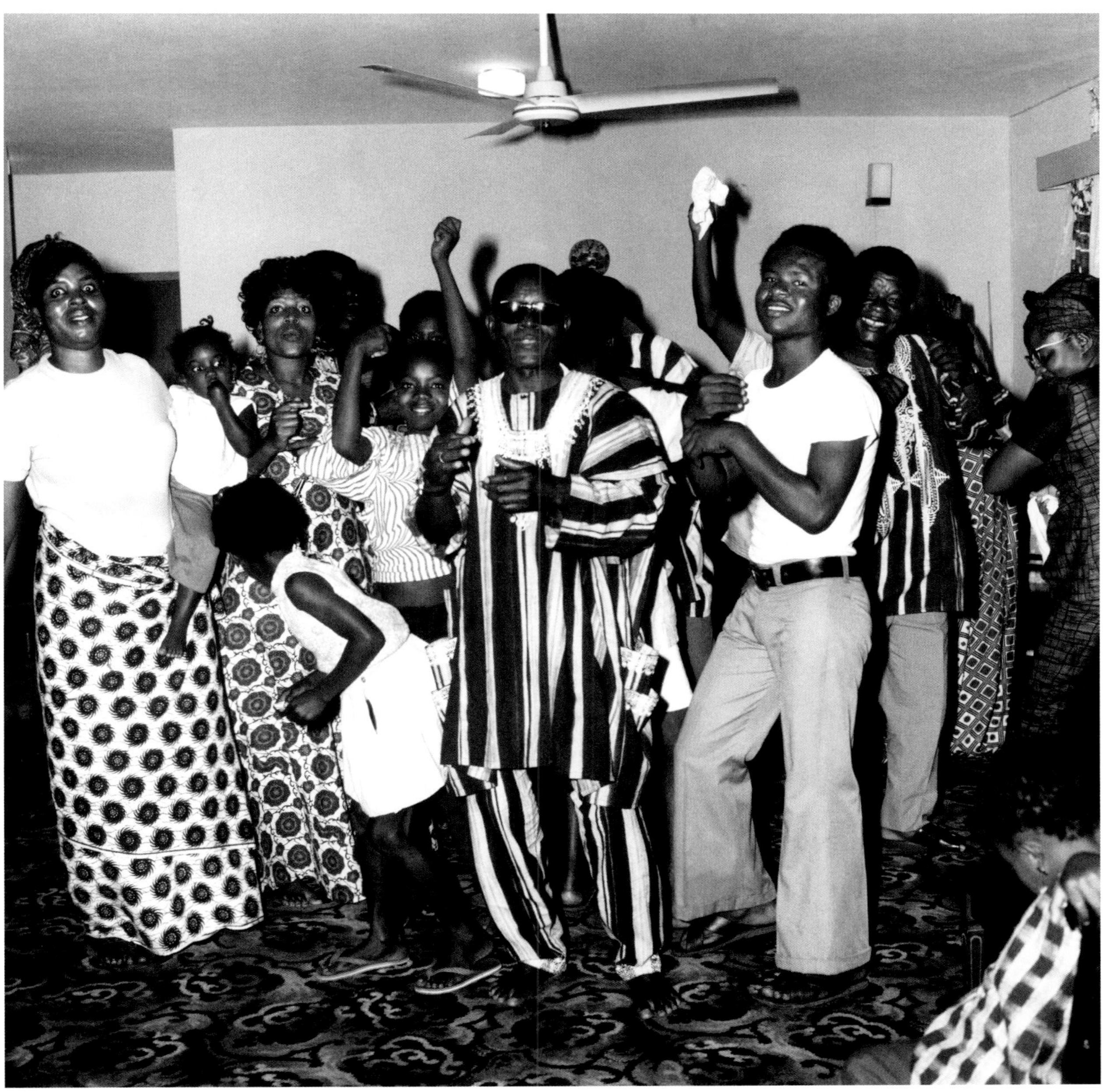

land of his parents, and a place where he lived for part of his childhood—that is causing this pain.

Wherever he looks in Ghana, however, he finds the world from which he is ostensibly escaping. At the cool bars, the songs he hears are the same ones topping the pop charts in London and the United States. The way hip young people dress mirrors the images they see of hip-hop acts and vixens in Western music videos. Far from being a reprieve from the vagaries of the West, he finds that Ghana is actually an integral and key hub in the global exchange of materials and culture. And also history. Eshun's trip to Ghana is soured when he learns that his great-great-great-great-great-grandfather had, around the 1750s, arrived from the Netherlands as a slaver. Worse still, the man's son, whose mother was a Black local, also became a slave trader when his father returned to Europe. What is this discovery like? "The disgust is overpowering," he writes. "You wonder what kind of temperament it took to be a slave trader. And whether the responsibility for his actions runs through your blood."

The loss and the survival, the mourning and the celebration, the local and the global—how can it all be held together? This is one of the central questions posed by the American artist Todd Gray. For the last seventeen years, Gray has lived between Ghana and the United States, meditating on the painful but strong poetic connection that exists between these places. Gray first visited

Ghana as a photographer working with Stevie Wonder. When Wonder suggested that Ghana was their shared homeland, Gray responded that he didn't even know who his great-grandfather was, so he couldn't say. And yet, he told me recently, "Stevie made a strong case in the poetic sense that because of the Atlantic passage, and the route from the Gold Coast to the Americas, this was the point of departure for many of us." He returned on his own and enjoyed the tranquility of being "invisible" in a Black-majority culture. "The vibe and the relationships were different," Gray says. "When you walk into a place, you are just who you are. I felt at ease."

Today, as in the late 1960s, there are initiatives from the Ghanaian state promoting return and efforts to encourage people in the diaspora to engage with the country's history once again. Unfortunately, it all feels like a gimmick—a McKinsey consulting deck estimating how much money the state of Ghana could generate from its "heritage" rather than a meaningful attempt to rebuild and strengthen relationships. Wright or Angelou might be discouraged from making it past the fancy bars and restaurants of contemporary Accra's Osu neighborhood, where photographs of encounters with celebrities go viral.

Projects such as the new Pan African Heritage Museum are thriving. The long-standing Institute of African Studies at the University of Ghana, and other academic spaces that welcome thinkers from the larger Black world, continues to churn out

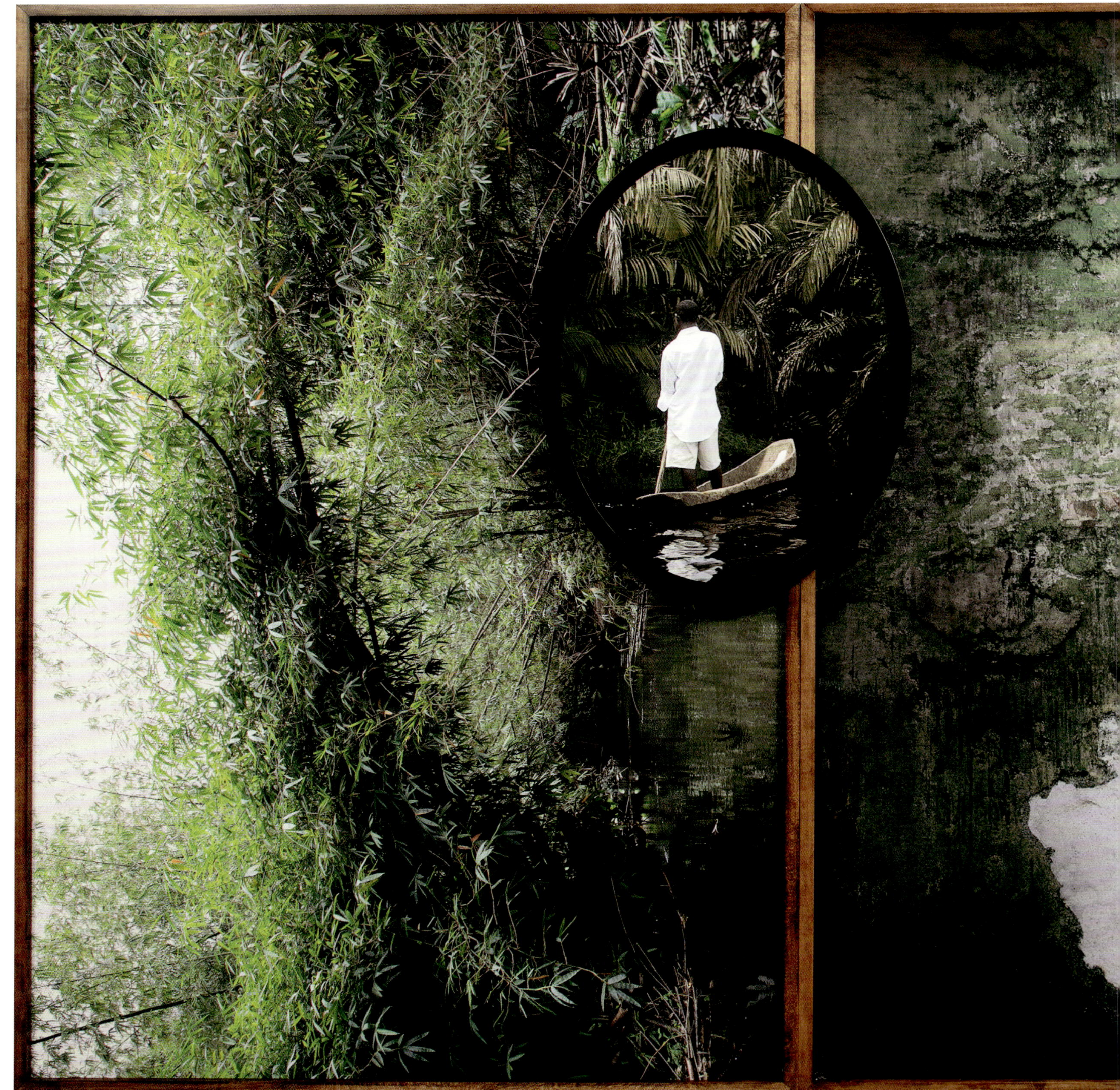

**Todd Gray,** *Green Green,*
**2023**
Courtesy the artist and
Lehmann Maupin, New York

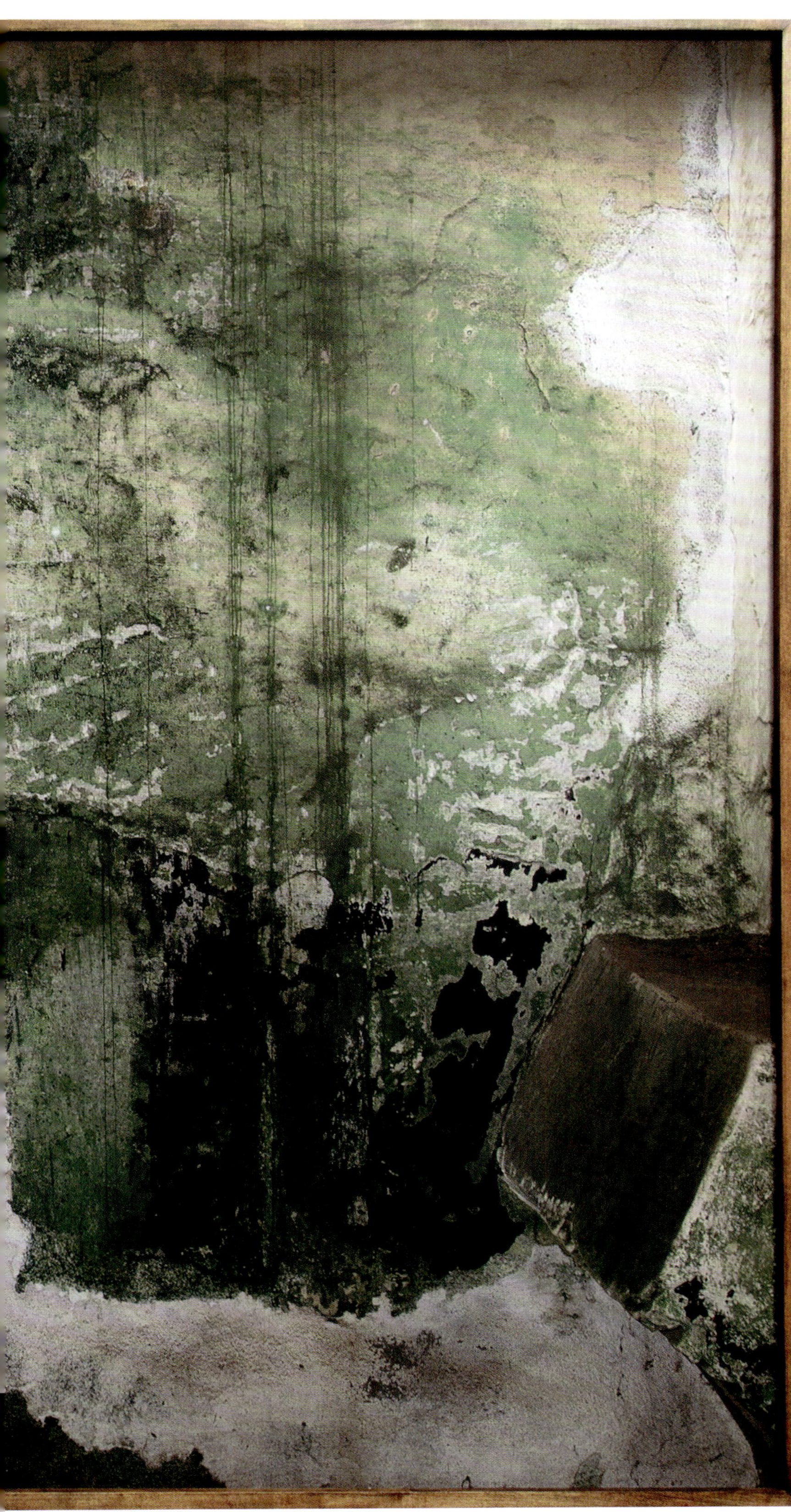

thought-provoking scholarship on Black futures. Starry-eyed students from historically Black colleges and universities, Black Peace Corps volunteers, and Fulbright participants arrive at Kotoka Airport in steady supply. Courageous and idealistic individuals land on the shores of the country each day with little but the embers of that moment of promise—of an escape from a racist world that holds no hope for them; of a land still entwined with ancient African ways and practices that can nourish the soul. Many have set up charities, schools, or other beneficial initiatives and go on with their quiet presence and enduring work.

From the inside looking out, it's the return to this vision of what can be that is most important. It's the reminder from Wright and Angelou, Eshun and Hartman of the dream and what could be possible if we are open to new perspectives. Todd Gray's photographic sculpture *Green Green* (2023) provokes such wonderings about envisioning that future with the turbulent present as a starting point. In it, an image on the left of marshy waterways abuts one on the right showing a segment of a wall. The first is along a slave trail leading down to a slave castle. The second is from Elmina Castle. Nevertheless, there is a calming, meditative beauty to the waterway. You imagine the water gliding along in tranquility, and the multitude of creatures put at ease by serene birdsong. In the scene, illuminated as it is by the sun, one senses the fecundity of life, the possibility of a welcome, an Edenic embrace, an opportunity for new beginnings.

You can't get a sense of Gray's work if you see it from only one place. "I do that to make the viewer always have to move, to always be making meaning, and to constantly have to appraise," he says. What does it mean to leave and to return? To change and to see change? At the center of *Green Green* is a man on a boat, rowing into a grove. He's going into the past. He's going into the future. He recalls the ancient African idea of a ferryman taking the dead across to the other side. In *Green Green*, is this other side a point of arrival or departure? No matter. The vision and hope of the Black Atlantic Future is an undying one. And as Ekow Eshun realizes toward the end of his travels in Ghana, "You never truly leave home. It stays with you even in the worst of times."

Anakwa Dwamena is a writer based in Accra.

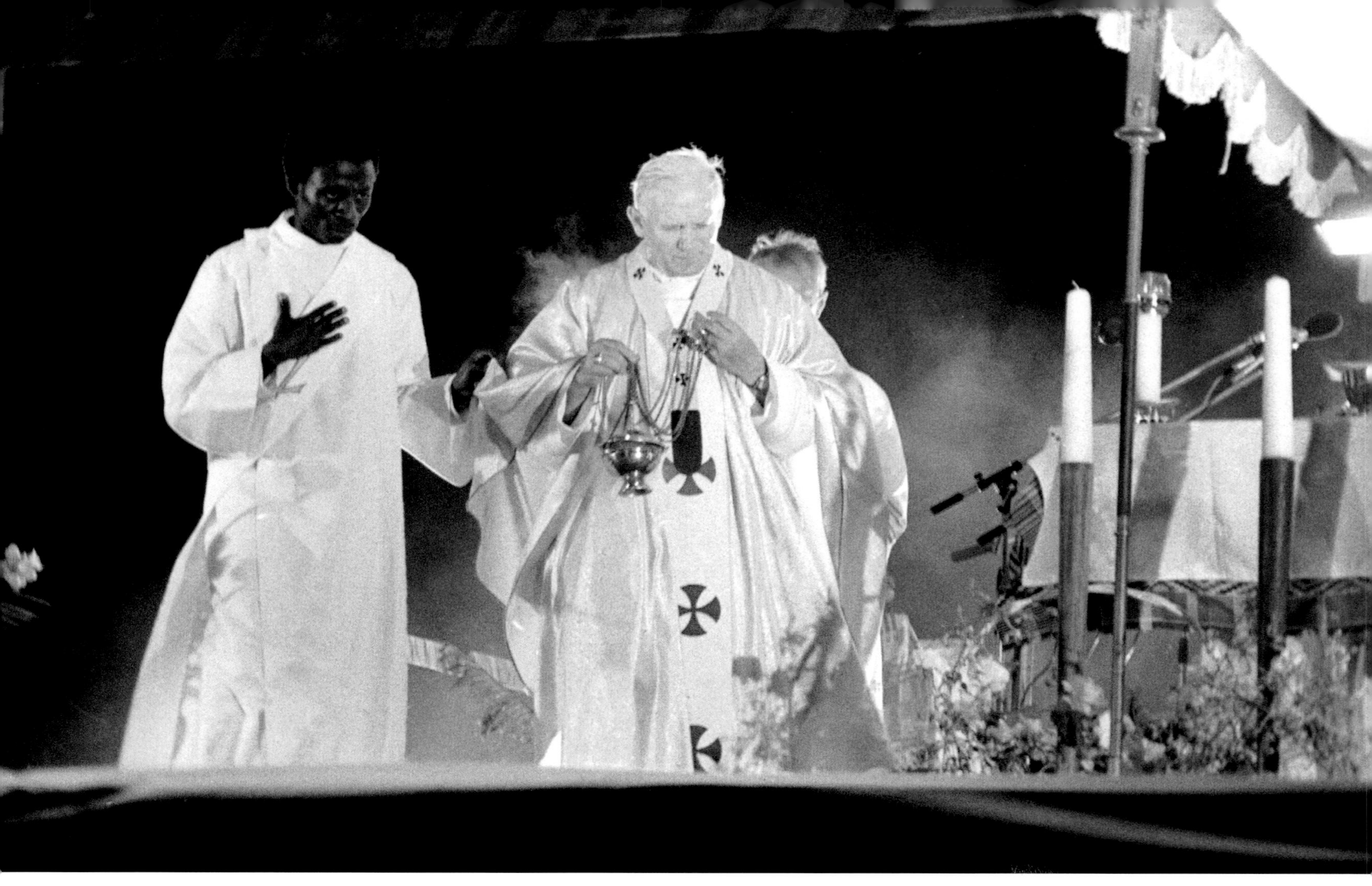

# The Correspondent

Gerald Annan-Forson documented the transformations of postindependence Ghana from an intimate perspective, telling a spectacular story of political and social change.
**Jesse Weaver Shipley**

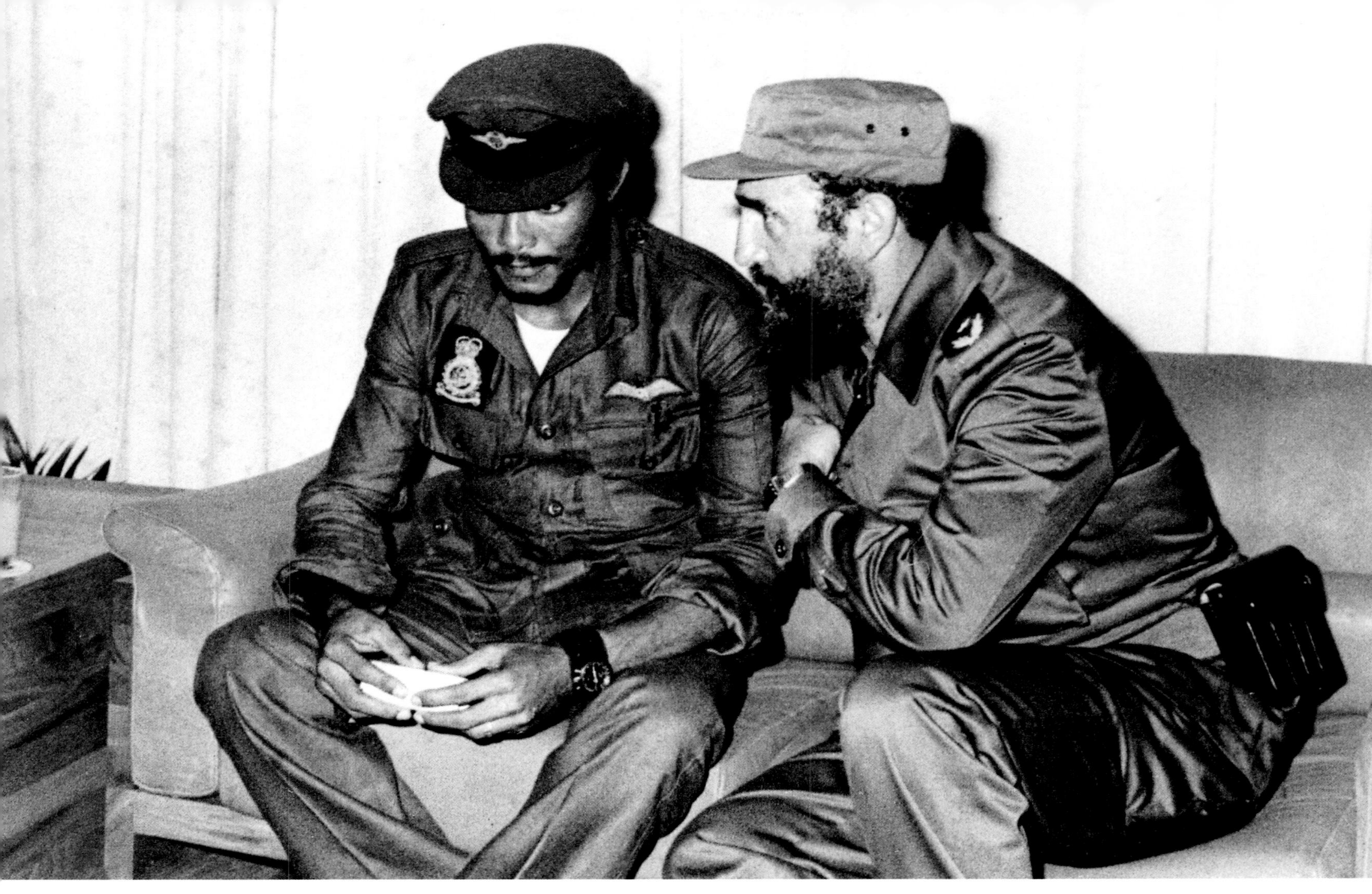



Gerald Annan-Forson seeks offbeat images in routine social scenes and during spectacular events. His first job as a professional photographer was taking secret pictures for a private investigator, capturing evidence of cheating spouses and people faking injuries for insurance scams in 1970s California. This required technical precision and a bold eye for visual reportage. Traces of his reflex for catching people in the act, for freezing a moment in time to tell a complex story, permeate his photographic practice, lending it both a narrative sensibility and an ethereal character.

Annan-Forson was born in London in 1947, to a mother from Kildare, Ireland, and a Fante father from the Gold Coast, an officer with the British West African Frontier Force stationed in the UK during World War II. In London, to hide his color and avoid racist attacks, Annan-Forson's mother had to wrap him in a blanket when they traveled. The family moved to Accra in 1954 to be a part of the Gold Coast's fight for freedom from British colonial rule. But in the passionate racial and national struggle, the young Annan-Forson was often confronted for being a foreigner, due to his mixed ancestry. In 1957, the new nation of Ghana won independence under the leadership of the Pan-African politician Kwame Nkrumah, and the capital of Accra became a cosmopolitan global center of Pan-African artistic expression and political thought.

Annan-Forson learned photography and image developing with a pinhole camera at a central Accra studio. The experience of being seen as Black and foreign in Britain and white and foreign in Ghana shaped his desire to challenge the idea that identities are singular. Like that of many artists who have multiple sociocultural fluencies, his aesthetic practice has been a response to his status as a constant outsider. Photography became his way to grapple with this double form of exclusion and seek refuge from racial

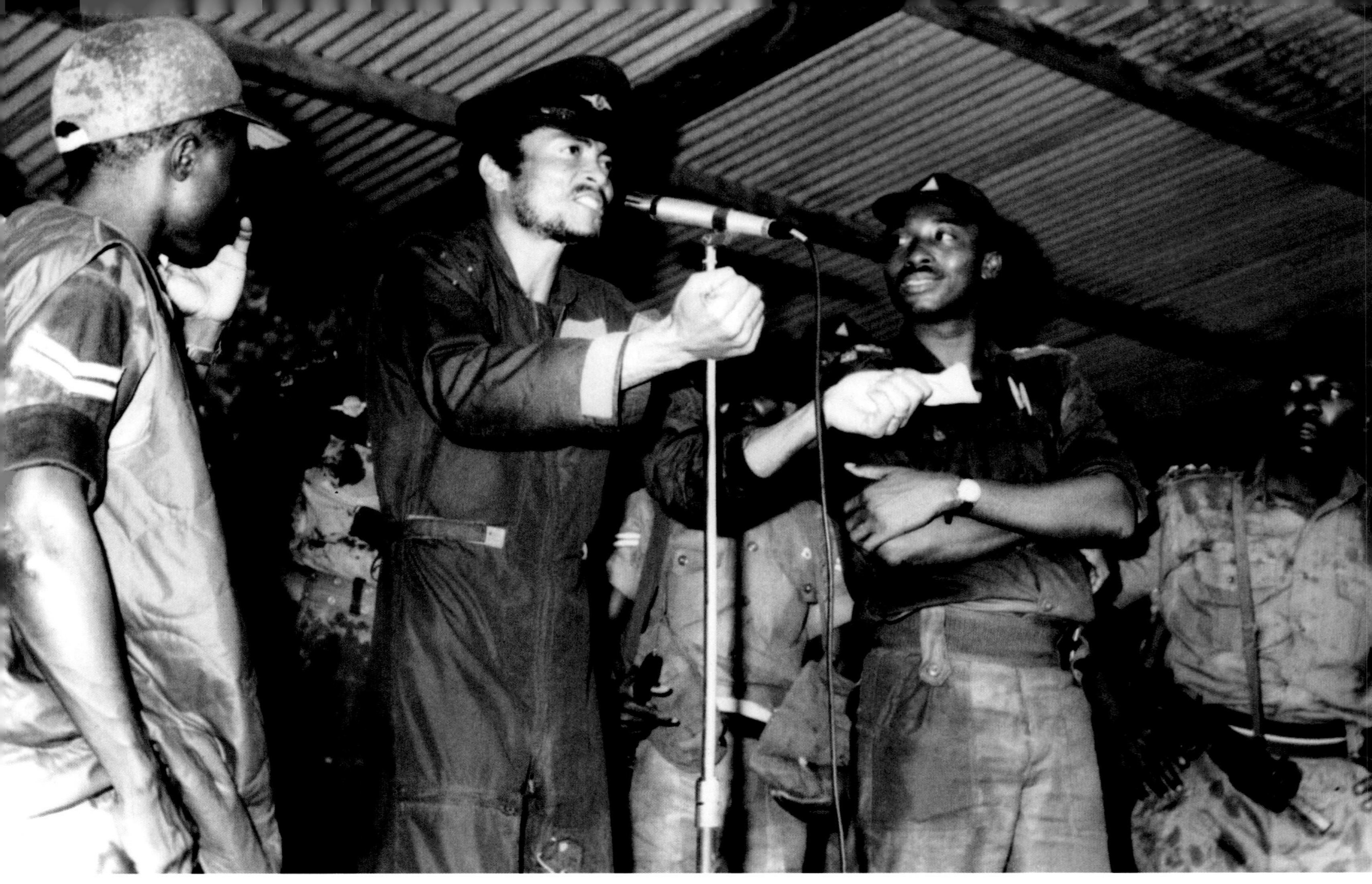

After the coup d'état on June 4, 1979, Rawlings, Chairman of the Armed Forces Revolutionary Council, speaks to soldiers while Captain Boakye Djan watches, Burma Camp, Accra, 1979

violence. Taking pictures allowed him to move through the world while hiding in plain sight and sidestepping simplistic facades of public belonging by telling multilayered tales.

His photographic journey reflects the variegated political history of Ghana more than other image makers who have covered the same terrain. He grew up during the renaissance decade of independence-era Accra, when it became a magnetic hub for radical Black thinkers, musicians, and artists from around the world. The city evolved rapidly as Nkrumah sought to modernize the country and create a strong Pan-African socialist state. But in 1966, this revolutionary experiment ended when the government was overthrown by senior military and police officers in a US- and British-backed coup d'état. Ghana was restructured under a neoliberal capitalist regime, which in 1972 was also overthrown in a coup. Over two decades, as Ghana alternated between civilian and military regimes, the rising generation of artists and intellectuals blended Pan-Africanism, futurist aspiration, and myriad local expressive styles into a uniquely West African modernist aesthetic.

Annan-Forson returned to Accra from California in the mid-1970s and began to develop his visual approach by documenting the changing city and its eclectic, diverse inhabitants. He worked across genres and styles as a freelancer, photographing heads of state and national events and selling pictures to *New African*, *African Business*, *West Africa*, *Essence*, and international magazines and newspapers. Even as radical ideas of Pan-African political unity were diluted, Accra was alive with highlife and Afrobeat music and celebrations of global Black styles. A rising generation sought new dreams and hustles that were at once locally grounded and cosmopolitan. Two of his early major assignments were to capture the visit of Charles, the Prince

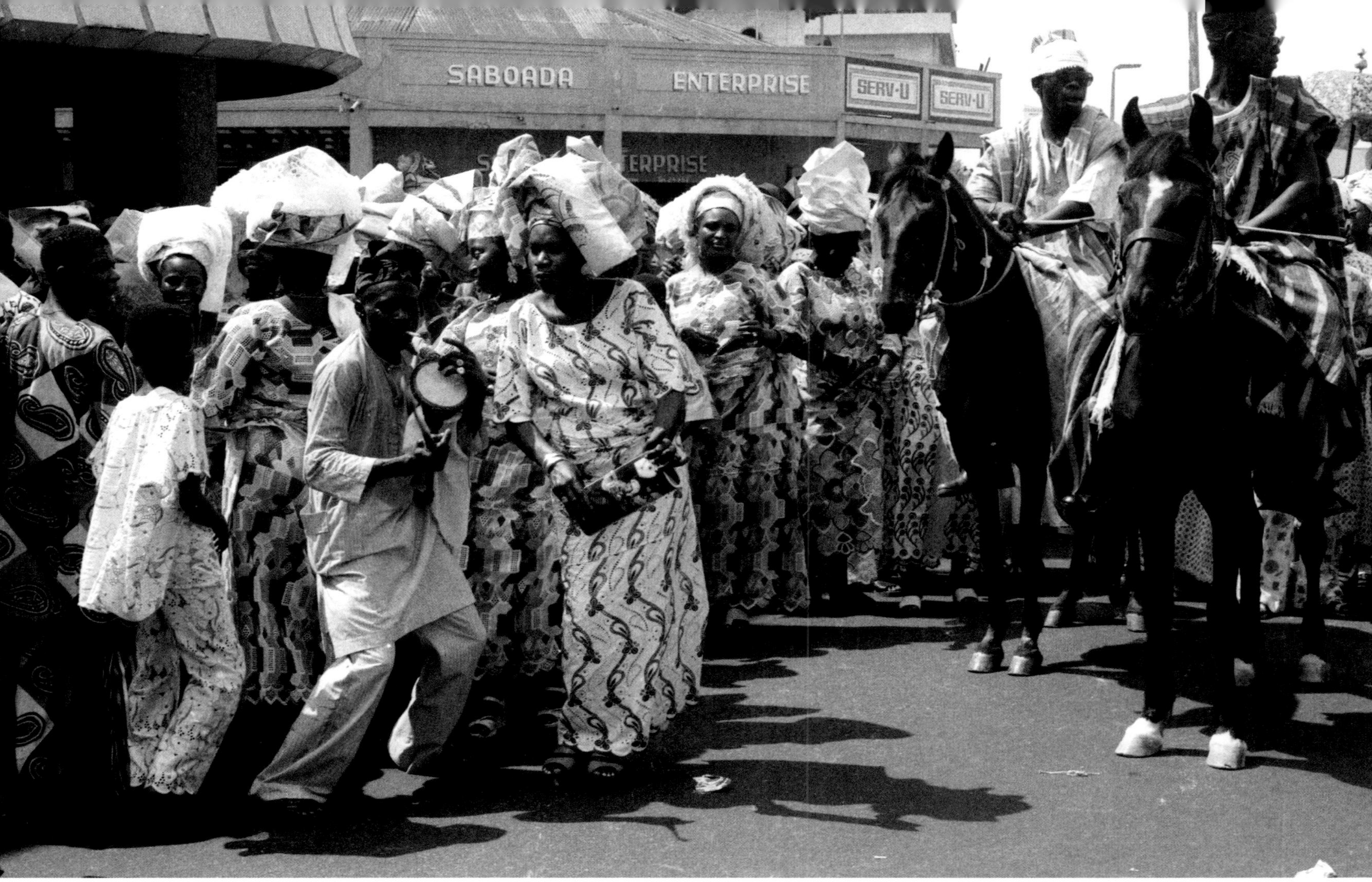

Celebrations after the last prayers of Ramadan in central Accra. Nobles on horseback are protected by umbrellas, 1981

**Annan-Forson's images challenge colonial modes for organizing a visual language of African urban social and political life.**

of Wales, with the head of state General I. K. Acheampong, in 1977—an unusual pairing of old imperial ruler with young defiant military officer—and, in 1980, to photograph the arrival in Ghana of the pope, not long after another coup. Annan-Forson's camera witnessed the mix of political ideologies, social pleasures, and economic struggles of 1970s and 1980s Accra, a city characterized by its easy intimacies and stark contrasts. His images highlight juxtapositions that express the contradictions of life in the coastal capital after the celebrations of independence faded.

Annan-Forson's photographs are hard to categorize. They encompass street photography, documentary, portraiture, landscape, and abstraction. His archive organically challenges colonial modes for organizing a visual language of African urban social and political life. In his relationships with his subjects, he implicitly counters pervasive orientalist image-making practices, creating what the curator Okwui Enwezor has described in relation to postindependence African photography as a "different iconography of the African self." In the colonial lexicon, photographs of Africa were means of objectification drawing on tourism and travel, ethnography and documentation, administrative fixity and exoticizing obsession. Instead, Annan-Forson finds vibrant, quirky uncertainties and moments of personal recognition within public events and spaces. He often uses compositional doubling, pairing contrasting figures he finds in a social scene. Annan-Forson's image making reflects the ways Accra's citizenry navigates the multiplicity of its dynamic landscape and shows how life in the city requires people to be many things in rapid succession.

Annan-Forson was thrown into political change when a coup d'état on June 4, 1979, elevated Flight Lieutenant Jerry John Rawlings as chairman of the new ruling Armed Forces Revolutionary Council. Annan-Forson had been schoolmates with Rawlings and suddenly found himself with insider access to a revolution. Rawlings, like Annan-Forson, was of mixed European and Ghanaian ancestry, and at times the photographer was mistaken for the head of state. Annan-Forson documented key national transformations from an intimate perspective, telling the spectacular story of change through the candid eyes of major players as well as common people caught in unexpected moments of terror, joy, contemplation, and frustration. He was an observer at the center of power. As a photographer among soldiers he documented the tenuous ways power was formulated.

But the pressure of taking pictures in the midst of political upheaval took its toll, as he was constantly on call to capture everything from executions to trials to clandestine meetings. Soldiers woke him up at all hours to record secret military maneuvers and meetings, the whipping of market traders accused of hoarding commodities, and surreptitious images of the country from a military fighter jet re-creating the experience of an aerial battle. His camera followed Rawlings over several decades of transformations: rebel, populist revolutionary, authoritarian leader, and democratic president.

On one level, Annan-Forson's work is engaged in a grand scheme of mythmaking, reimagining an African urban future. On another, his images expose cracks in the edifice of the normative and the powerful, and how they are challenged by contradiction, humor, pleasure, and pain. His work often focuses on the aesthetics and rituals of power, revealing how authority is conferred through ceremony. But his ability to find the intimate within formal portraits of leaders shows how authority is always partial, temporary, and unstable. He seizes on signs that disrupt expectations, revealing the inner lives of his subjects through unexpected downcast eyes, hidden glances, and quirky gestures. When public figures are caught off guard, we see another side of power. At its core, Annan-Forson's work illustrates the contradictions that emerge in periods and spaces of transformation. His visual grammar, refined over a lifetime of taking pictures, provokes observers to ask what kind of mythic landscape the contemporary decolonizing city constitutes.

Jesse Weaver Shipley is the author of *Living the Hiplife: Celebrity and Entrepreneurship in Ghanaian Popular Music* (2013) and *Trickster Theatre: The Poetics of Freedom in Urban Africa* (2015).

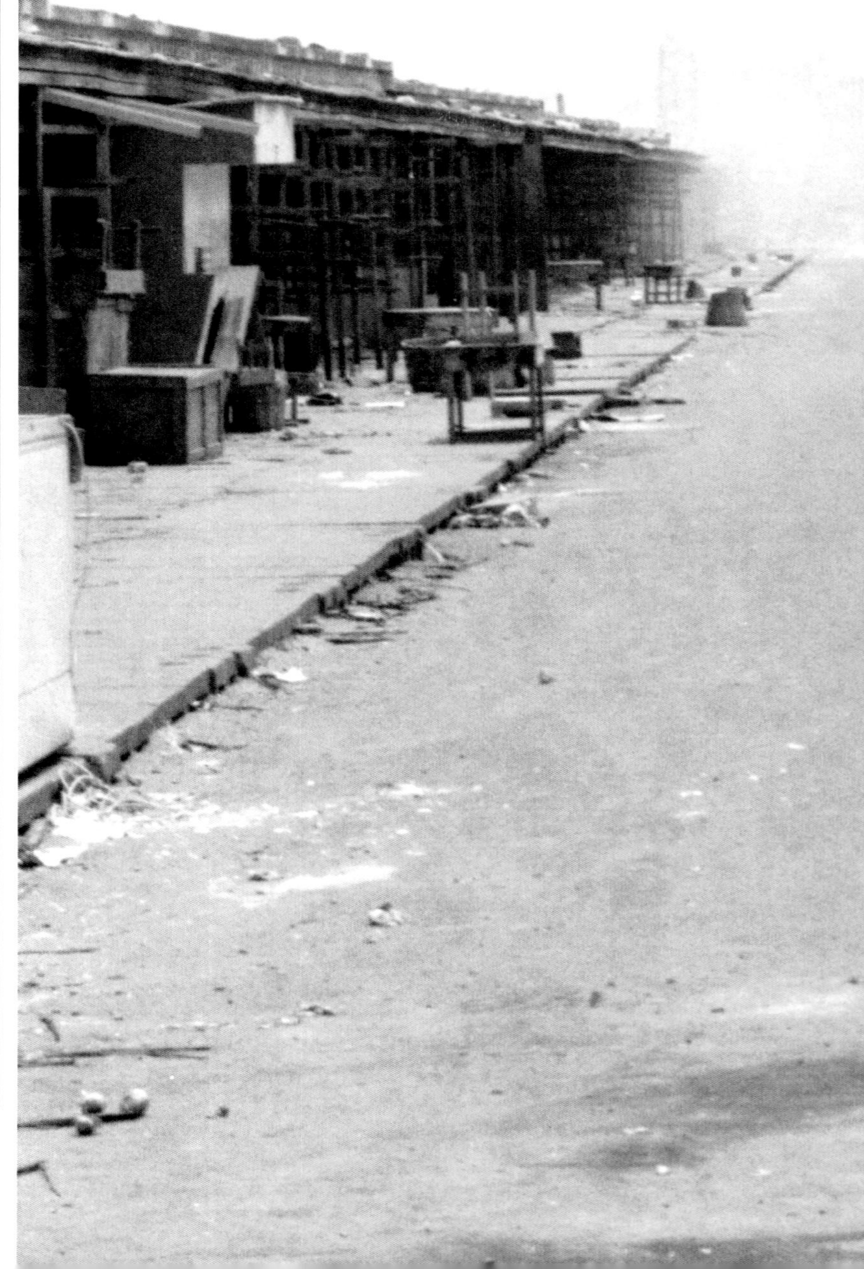

A soldier keeps guard after the military regime dynamited and bulldozed Makola Market in central Accra, 1979
All photographs courtesy the artist

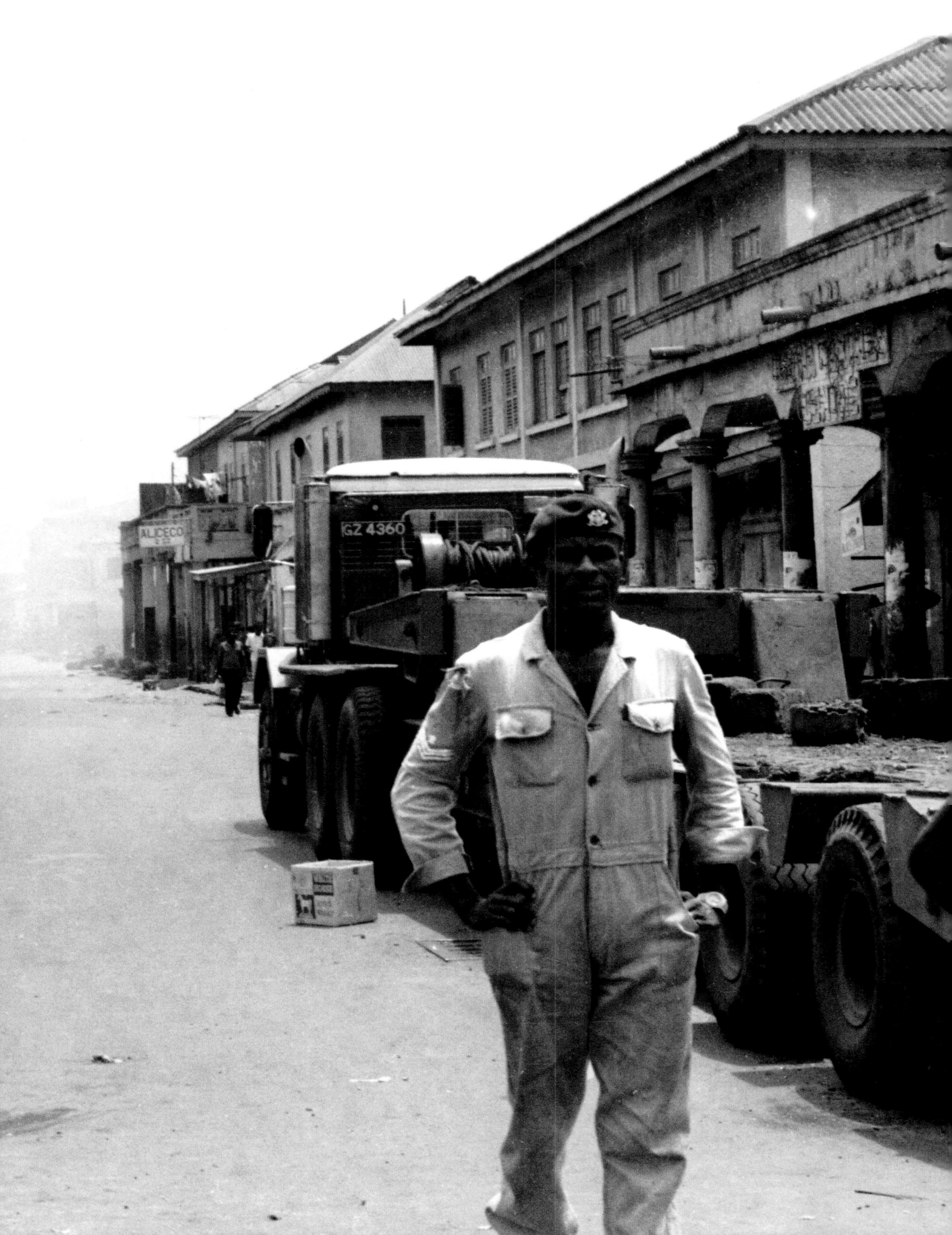

GZ 4360
ALICE CO

Images of what are widely considered the golden years of Ghana's modern history—the independence era, from the mid-1950s to the mid-1960s—have a powerful nostalgic allure. I read this as not only nostalgia for the past but desire for an alternate reality. Photographs of pristine, modernist architecture and infrastructure are especially popular because, more than most types of imagery, they illustrate physical manifestations of the power and promise of that era. Older generations that witnessed and lived through the scenes depicted as well as younger Ghanaians guided by historical accounts, fragmented archival records, and their imaginations are united in a shared nostalgia for what could have been.

Today's artists, scholars, and creators in Ghana and across the wider diaspora have, especially in recent years, been inspired by this nostalgia to carry out memory, archiving, and history-inspired projects. Ibrahim Mahama's art based on defunct modernist silos, Adjoa Armah's Saman Archive repository of photographic negatives, Joewackle J. Kusi and Fui Can-Tamakloe's audio drama *Goodbye, Gold Coast,* and my own Accra Archive project digitizing historical architectural materials are a few examples. Images by Felicia Abban, a photographer of Ghana's first president, Kwame Nkrumah, and by James Barnor, with his extensive and wide range of pictures from that era, have found resonance with a new generation of Ghanaians.

Courage Dzidula Kpodo, an architect currently studying at the Massachusetts Institute of Technology, worked with the art directors Manuela Nebuloni and Nana Ofosu Adjei to create Postbox Ghana. Their project seeks to "collect, research, and share" Ghanaian historical documents, particularly postcards showing pictures of buildings and scenes from Accra's modern history. (The group posts to Instagram with the handle @postbox. ghana and was recently featured in the Venice Architecture Biennale, curated by the Ghanaian Scottish architect Lesley Lokko.) Some of the postcards were circulated—they bear stamps and notes from residents or by visitors on holiday in Accra—providing small glimpses into the city at the time. The photographers' names were occasionally included, and Postbox Ghana highlights and celebrates this indigenous authorship.

The postcards, along with the stamps appearing on them, were deliberately produced and promoted to highlight Ghana's independence. As the first Black African leader of the former British colony, Nkrumah was a strong believer in the power of visual symbolism and imagery, using statues, currency, and other items bearing his portrait to demonstrate the fact that he was now in charge. These were important statements because the people of Ghana would previously have seen likenesses of the white queens and kings of England who had ruled them. Nkrumah employed photography, radio, and video to broadcast infrastructural, architectural, and cultural achievements across the nation, with mobile vans distributing films to remote villages. Through postcards and stamps, Nkrumah reached a wider global audience, and he utilized these promotional materials to great effect.

Ordinary Ghanaians, proud of their fledgling nation and excited by its rapid transformations, also contributed to this visual culture. Photographers such as Kwaku Bonsu, D. K. Acheampong, and J. Halifax Ashrifie took stunning images for postcards and, in doing so, documented a remarkable era in Ghana's history. Although the photographs on the postcards were intended primarily for recipients outside of Accra and Ghana, the choice of subjects and the compositions can tell us about the ideas, thoughts, and visions of the people who created and sent them.

In present-day Accra, not many of the sites and spaces documented on the postcards remain as pristine as they were in the 1950s and '60s. But more disconcerting than that, the photographs represent a moment of great promise that now seems lost forever. With worsening economic conditions, looking at images from the independence era evokes the longing for a different, better future that could have emerged from our not-so-distant past. Yet there is a thread of hopefulness in projects such as Postbox Ghana, which seek to show what was done in the past, and what can still be done in the present and the future.

# Postbox Ghana

## Kuukuwa O. Manful

Kuukuwa O. Manful is an architect and researcher who creates, teaches, and documents histories and politics of architecture in Africa.

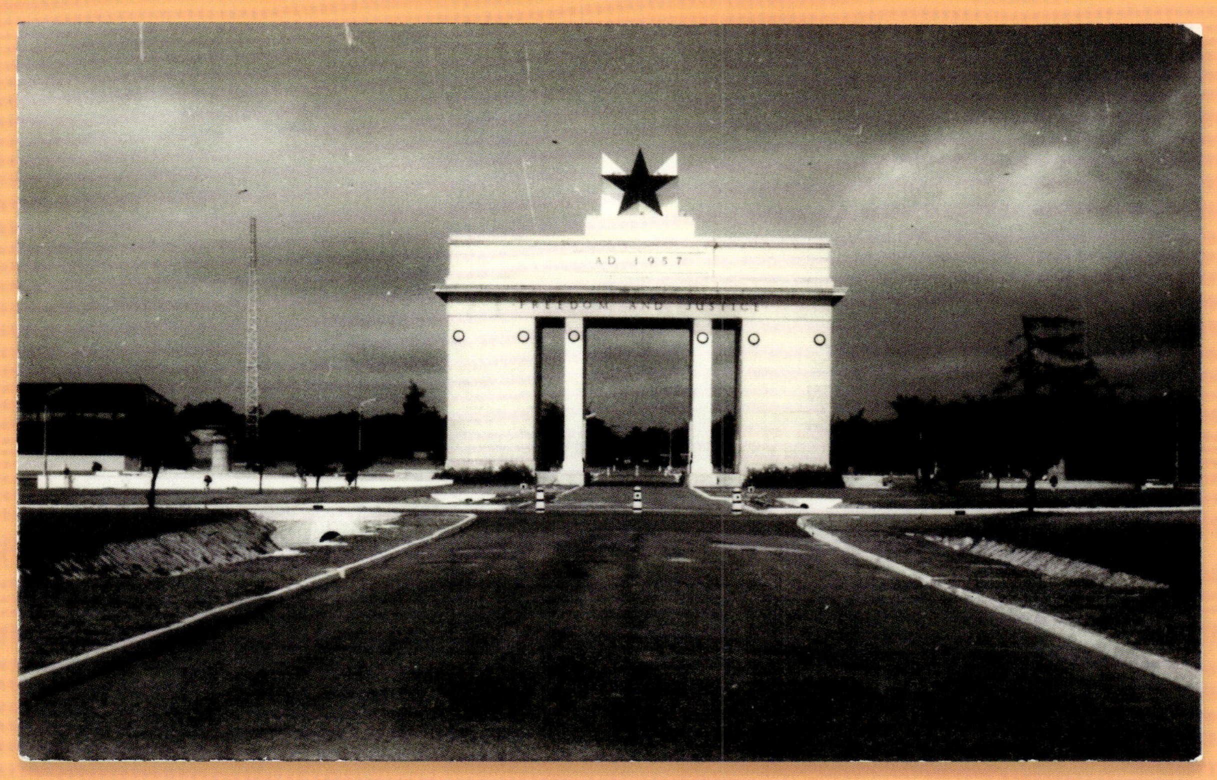



Independence Arch at Black Star Square, 28th February Road, Accra, ca. 1965. Photograph by Kwaku Bonsu

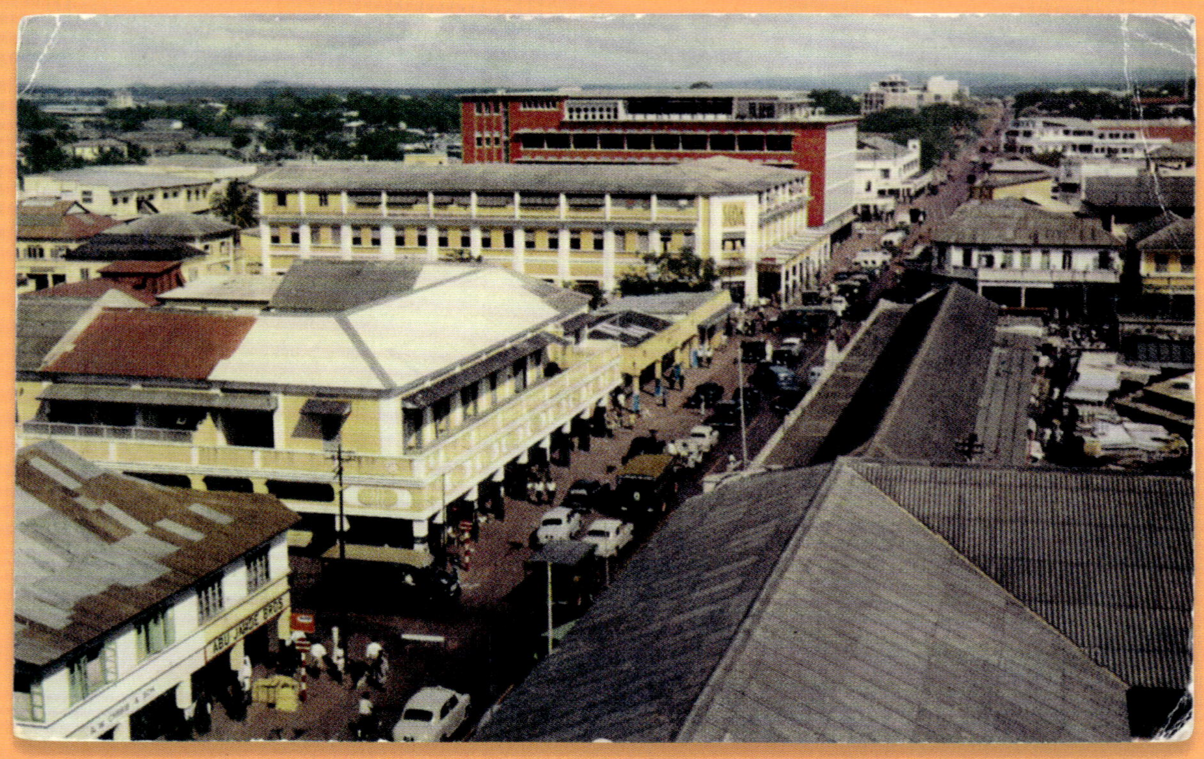

BX 36242

# POST CARD

CORRESPONDENCE

ADDRESS ONLY

POSTAGE
Surface :
Ghana — 1d.
Commonwealth — 1d.
Foreign — 2½d.
Airmail :
West Africa — 3d.
U.K., Europe, Middle East, East and South Africa — 8d.
Americas, Far East, India — 1/-

Enjoying a very nice holiday in the sun. The flight out was very good, and was a wonderful experience. Arthur & Am met me at the airport and we motored back to their bungalow. Will tell you all about it on my return. The temperature runs at around 100 to 120 in the shade, but it's lovely. Space doesn't permit any more. Thinking of you, and wishing you were here. Love. J.H.

Mr & Mrs A. V. Burgess
27 Stanhope Road
Darlington
Co Durham
England
U.K.

Station Road, Accra, Ghana.
Colour photograph by Ghana Information Services.
Printed in England by Brown Knight & Truscott Ltd., 11/12 Bury Street, London, E.C.3.

Station Road, Accra,
ca. late 1950s. Photograph
by Ghana Information
Services

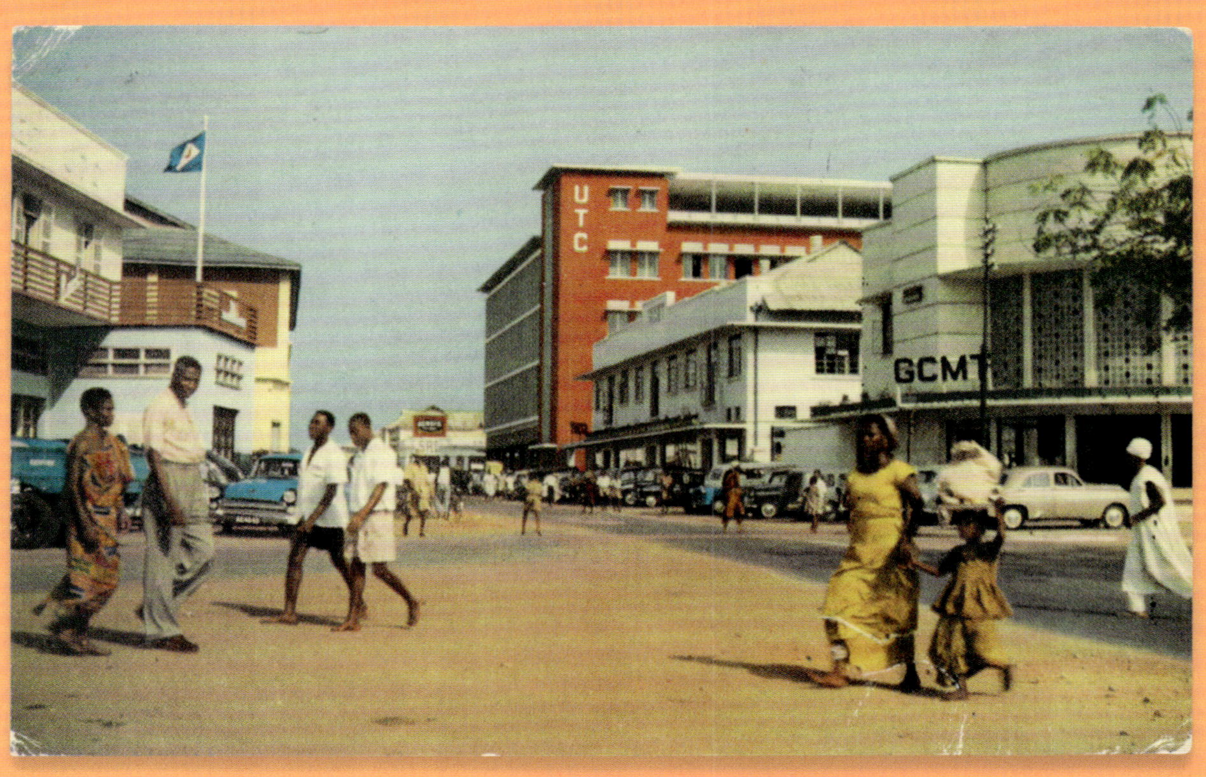

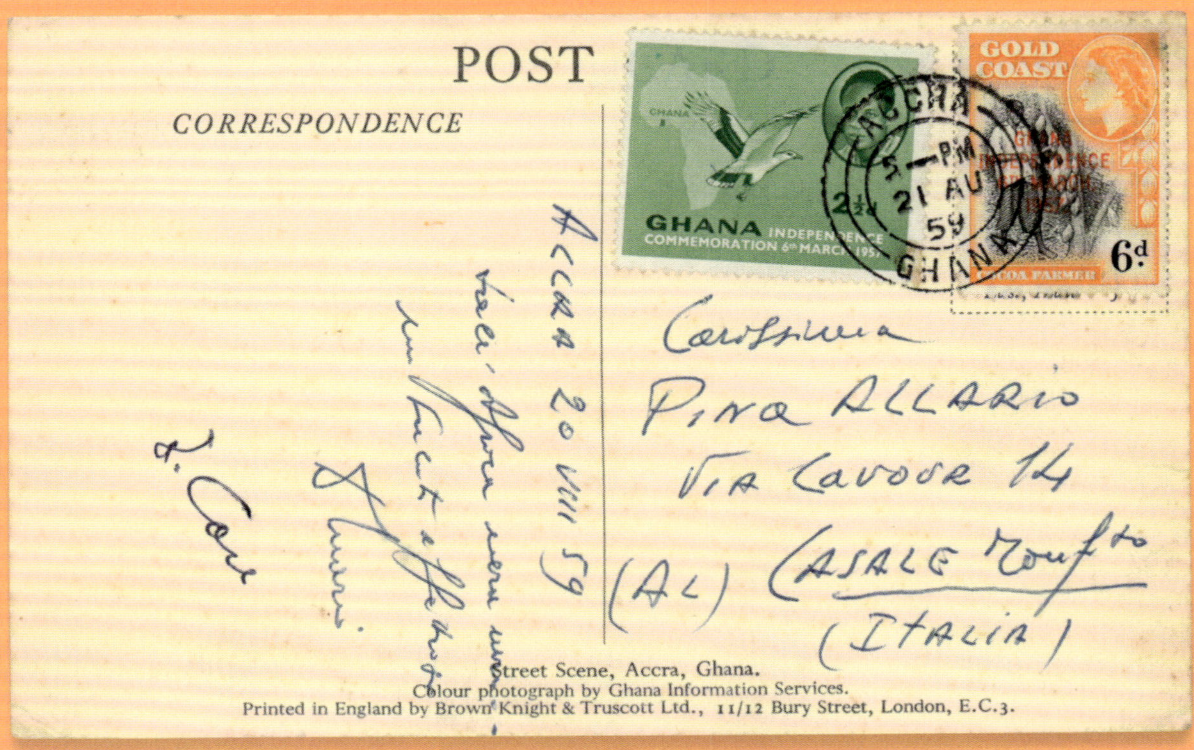



Street scene showing Union Trade Company building, Commercial Road, Accra, ca. late 1950s. Photograph by Ghana Information Services

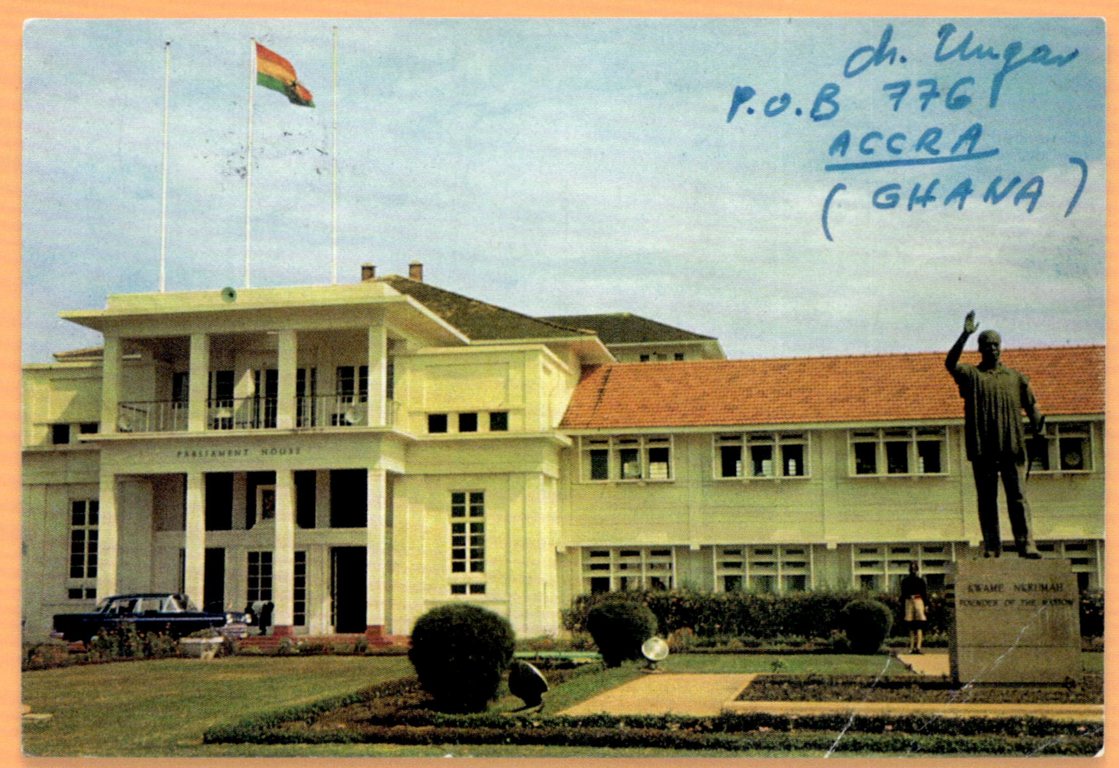
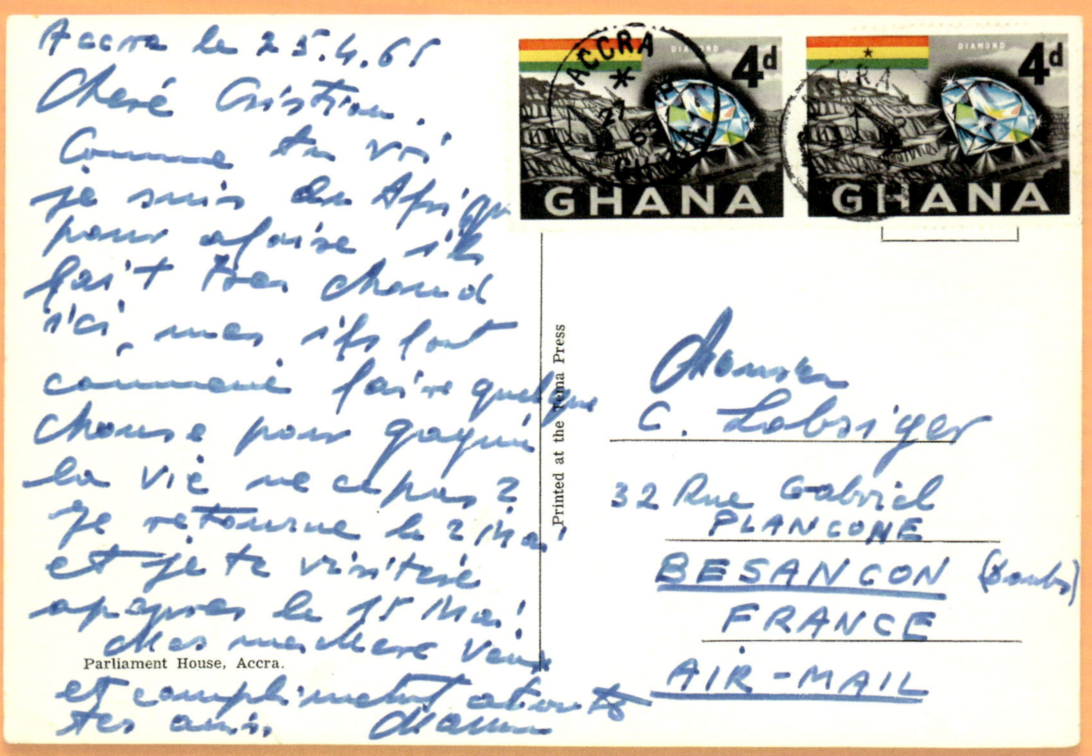

Parliament House
(now the Commission
on Human Rights and
Administrative Justice),
Accra, ca. mid-1960s

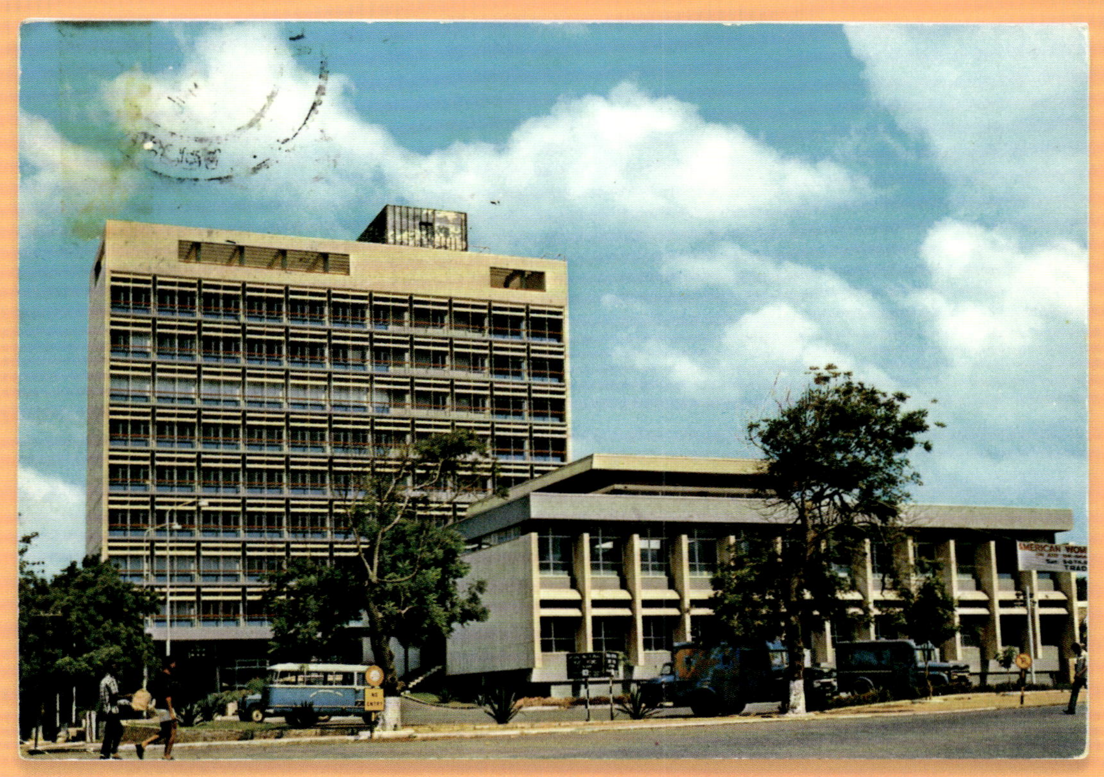

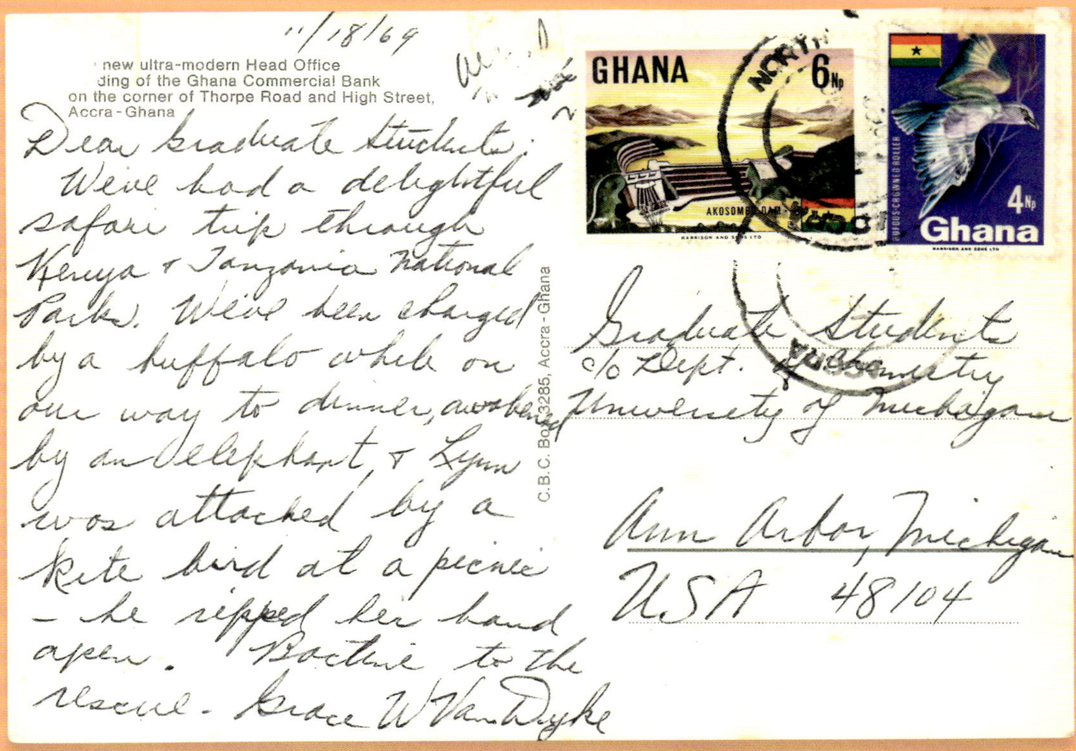

**Head office of the Ghana Commercial Bank, Thorpe Road and High Street (now John Evans Atta Mills High Street), Accra, ca. late 1960s**
All works courtesy Courage Dzidula Kpodo/Postbox Ghana

# Carlos Idun-Tawiah
## *Sunday Special*

**Nana Oforiatta Ayim**

Family albums are the starting point of the series *Sunday Special* (2022) by Carlos Idun-Tawiah, who draws on the semiotics of earlier Ghanaian photographers' work to create his own visual language. It's a language that resonates with a bygone time but is also deeply contemporary. Incorporating his experience with fashion photography, from *Vogue* to *GQ* to *Harper's Bazaar*, Idun-Tawiah's photographs emit the highly stylized tone of editorial spreads and, at the same time, the intimacy of personal pictures of friends and loved ones.

Idun-Tawiah who is based in Accra, was born in 1997, exactly forty years after Ghana's independence. His vision is steeped in nostalgia—both personal (depictions of young people attending school, visiting the barber, playing soccer, or going to church) and collective (poses, fashions, and hairstyles). He conjures visceral recollections held in his memory yet out of reach. The photographer does this not just through his aesthetic approach but by constructing whole stories, biographies, and characters, by bringing in costumes and sets, and by having his subjects freely inhabit the roles they are playing. These scenes have, both in composition and intent, a multilayered and multifaceted resonance.

While images by Ghana's twentieth-century photography pioneers typically served one purpose—documentation or representation—Idun-Tawiah's pictures, with their self-conscious referencing and intentionality, go beyond that singular role. He describes his new work as a requiem to moments of his past, inspired by photographers from Africa's visually rich history, such as James Barnor, Malick Sidibé, Seydou Keïta, and Felicia Abban—Ghana's first female professional photographer— along with US photographers including Roy DeCarava, Gordon Parks, Alex Webb, and Alec Soth. He is especially interested in vernacular portraiture, and aims, he says, to put the "emotion-forward" quality of films into his pictures, using style and scenery to establish settings in which his subjects act and move freely in what he terms "photographic biopics."

In 2007, I curated an exhibition of Barnor's photographs at the Black Cultural Archives in London, one of the earliest shows of his work, and in 2017 I organized the first public presentation of Abban's images, at ANO Institute of Arts and Knowledge, in Accra. I also undertook the digitization of the archives of these two artists so that young photographers would be able to draw on their work and not constantly have to look outside our own stories for inspiration, for foundation. Idun-Tawiah's photography is not just a testament to his forebears but an expansion, a deepening. Through its beautifully drawn reflections of our being it reveals the evolution of our modernity.

Nana Oforiatta Ayim is a writer, filmmaker, and art historian based in Accra.

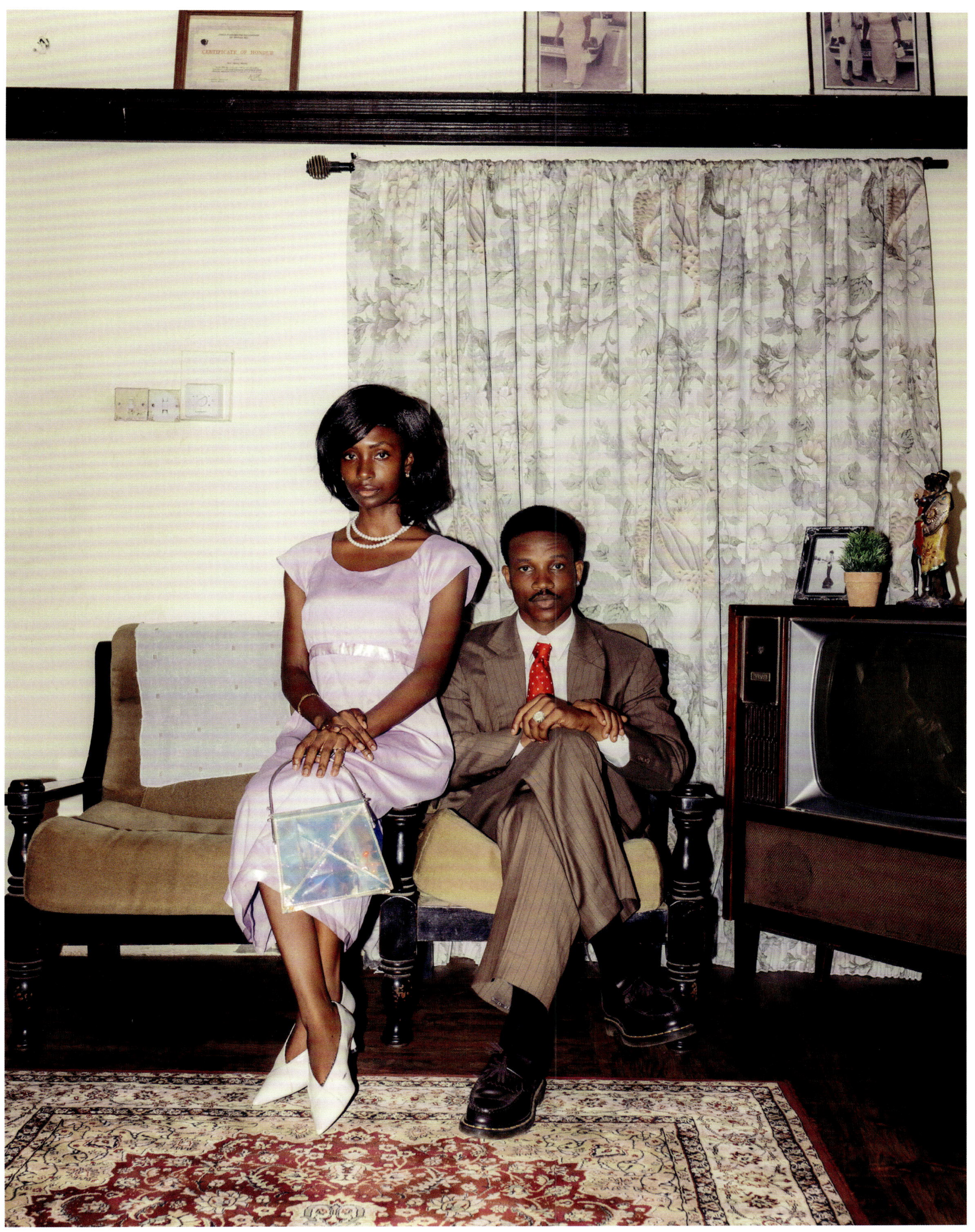

*Daddy's Polaroid*, 2022,
from the series *Sunday
Special*

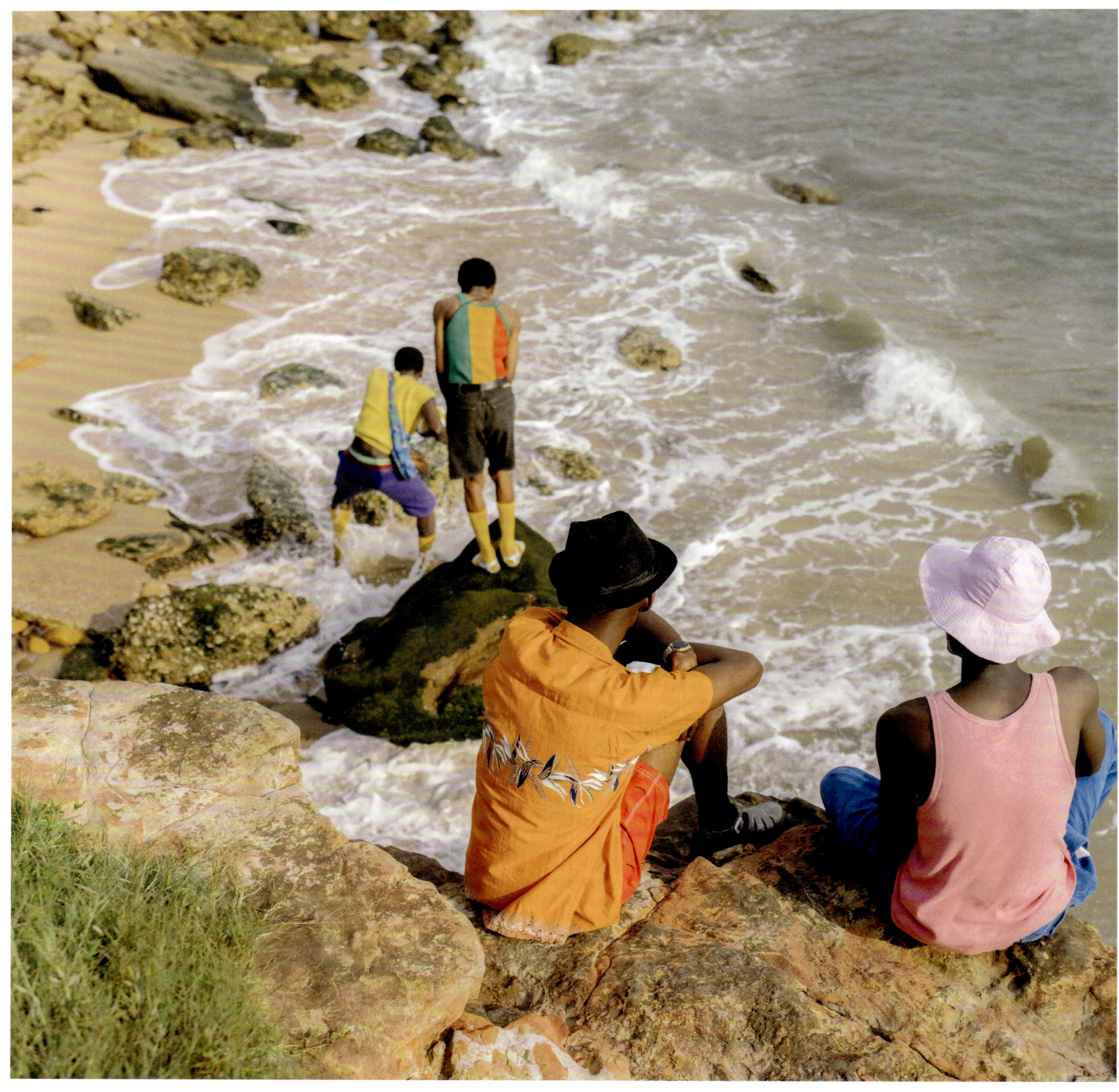

*Hide and Seek*, 2023, from
the series *Boys Will Always
Be Boys*

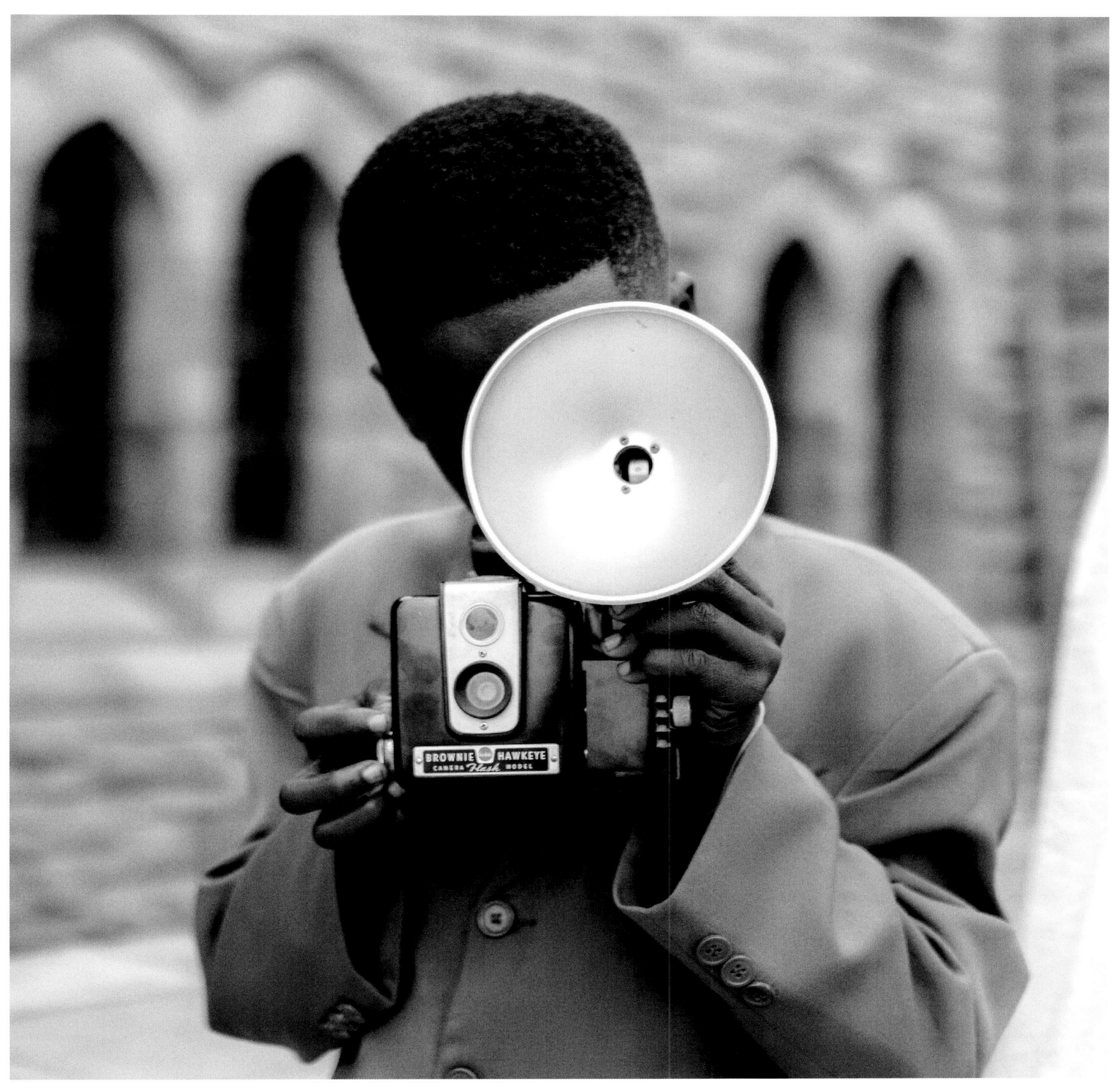

*Mommy, Smile*, 2022, from the series *Sunday Special*

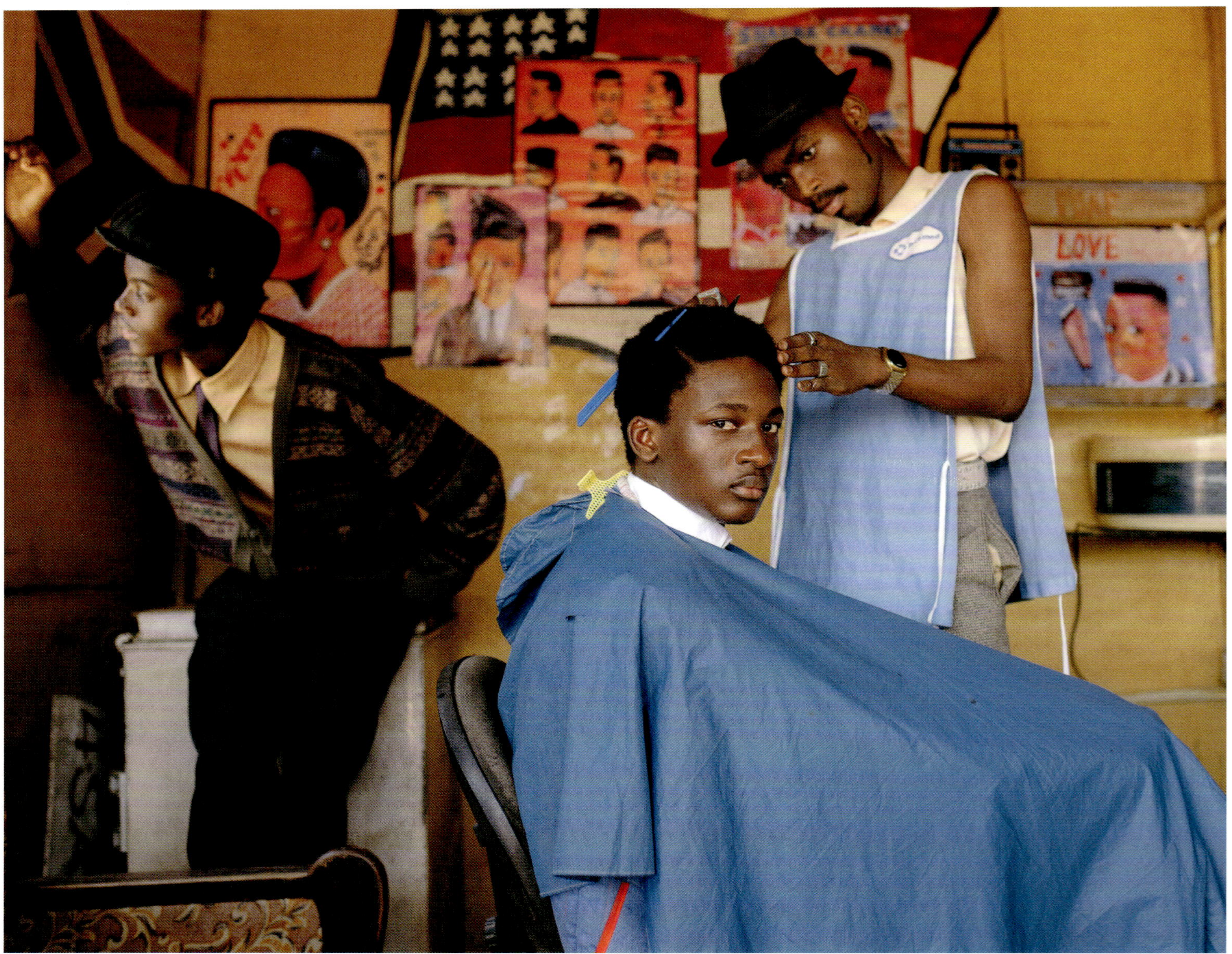


This page:
*The Barbershop*, 2023,
from the series *Boys Will
Always Be Boys*

Opposite:
*Uncle Adu's Studio*, 2022,
from the series *Sunday
Special*
All photographs courtesy
the artist

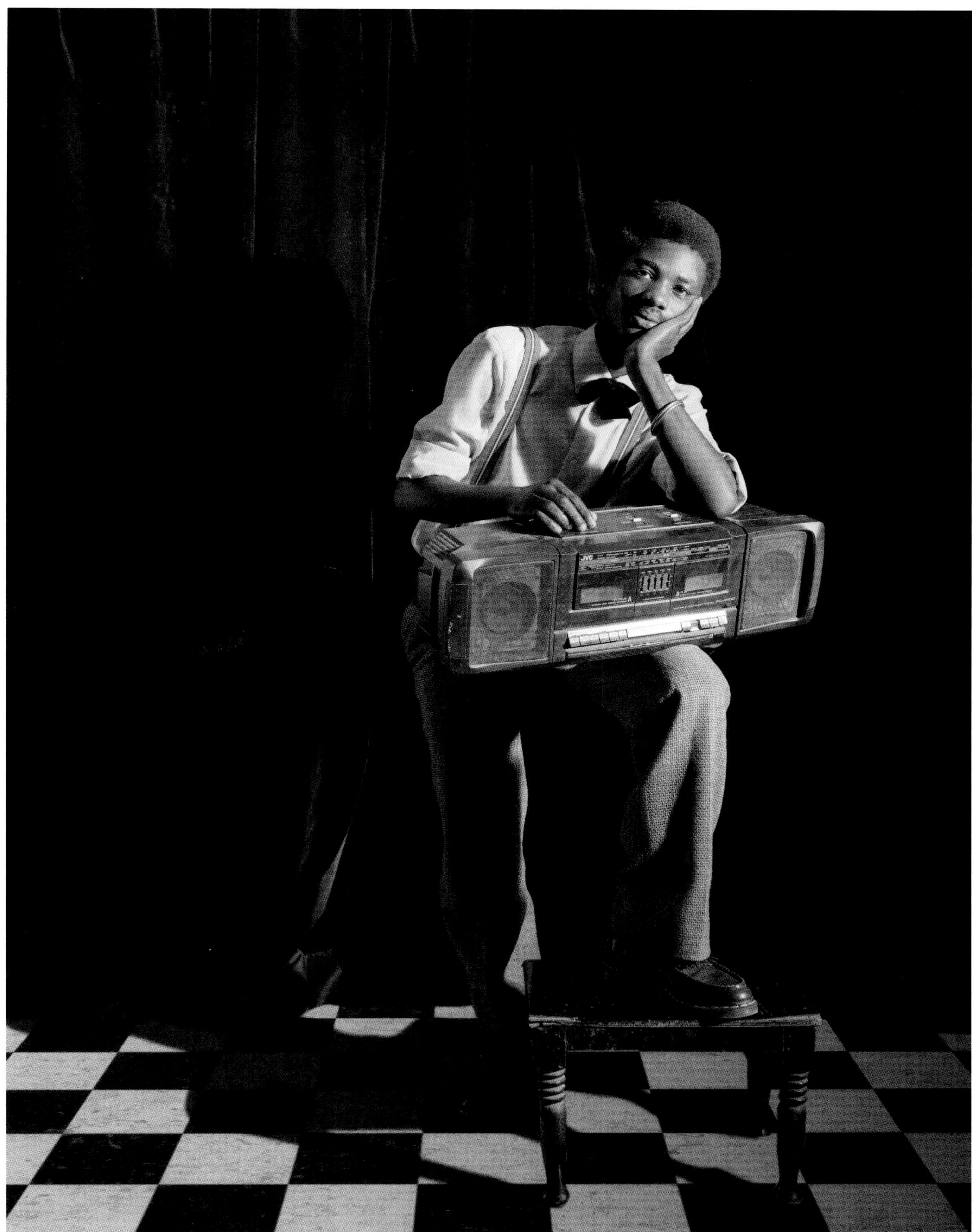

# Kay Kwabia
## *Early Risers*

**Lovia Gyarkye**

The warm orange glow of the streetlight in *Early Risers I* (2021), the photographer Kay Kwabia's atmospheric image of daybreak in Sekondi-Takoradi, tipped me off. Its soft emission fused with the incandescent car headlights to illuminate a corner of the dimly lit street. That light, spilling onto the cream-colored building, prompted me to sift through my bookshelves, where I pulled Ayi Kwei Armah's 1968 novel *The Beautyful Ones Are Not Yet Born*. In the first scene of the Ghanaian writer's sharp and cynical debut about a fledgling postcolonial nation, a driver disembarks from a bus and tries to light a cigarette: "The head refused to catch, however; there was only the humid orange glow as the driver resignedly threw away the stick and took out another."

Is it a coincidence that Armah and Kwabia, whose image wrested my attention, share not only a home country but a city? Maybe. Still, it feels apt that Armah was born in Sekondi-Takoradi, the twin metropolis where Kwabia, who now lives in Accra, spent his formative years and credits with shaping his visual language. The blues and greens of the port city can be found throughout Kwabia's mellow representations of Ghana. They are in the awning and trash bins of *Early Risers II* (2021), taken during a morning stroll. In two pictures titled *Play with Your Food* (2020), green vibrates from kontomire leaves, which hold drying dandelions resting against a sliced mango in one image and serves as the background for Kwabia's aunt's gold earrings in the other.

Kwabia does not live in Armah's Ghana, which was a transitory space between colonial rule and democratic promise, but his images operate on a similar poetic register as the author's writing. Compared to Armah, the photographer has a more optimistic view of the nation, now sixty-six years independent. Kwabia focuses on the beauty of quotidian living in Accra and its nearby cities, finding dreamscapes where others might see only harsh realities. In *Early Risers II*, Kwabia highlights a pair of trees in Sekondi-Takoradi. Backdropped by the water, the woody plants watch the city shake off its slumber.

Kwabia's way of seeing might have something to do with his early childhood in Kwahu Plateau, where he was surrounded by the natural world. When he started taking photographs on a smartphone in 2013, he was drawn to capturing insects and plants. The switch to more sophisticated digital cameras only clarified his desire to seek out peacefulness and follow his aesthetic sensibilities. Ghana, to Kwabia, is synonymous with beauty, and his relatively young practice makes that clear. Projects are guided by instinct, boredom, and fancy. Earlier pictures experiment with the earth and its tones, while later ones proudly gamble with more vibrant colors. The results, whether staged still lifes, fashion portraits, or landscapes, are always refreshing: they tickle the senses, activate the imagination, and soothe the soul.



Lovia Gyarkye is a writer based in New York.

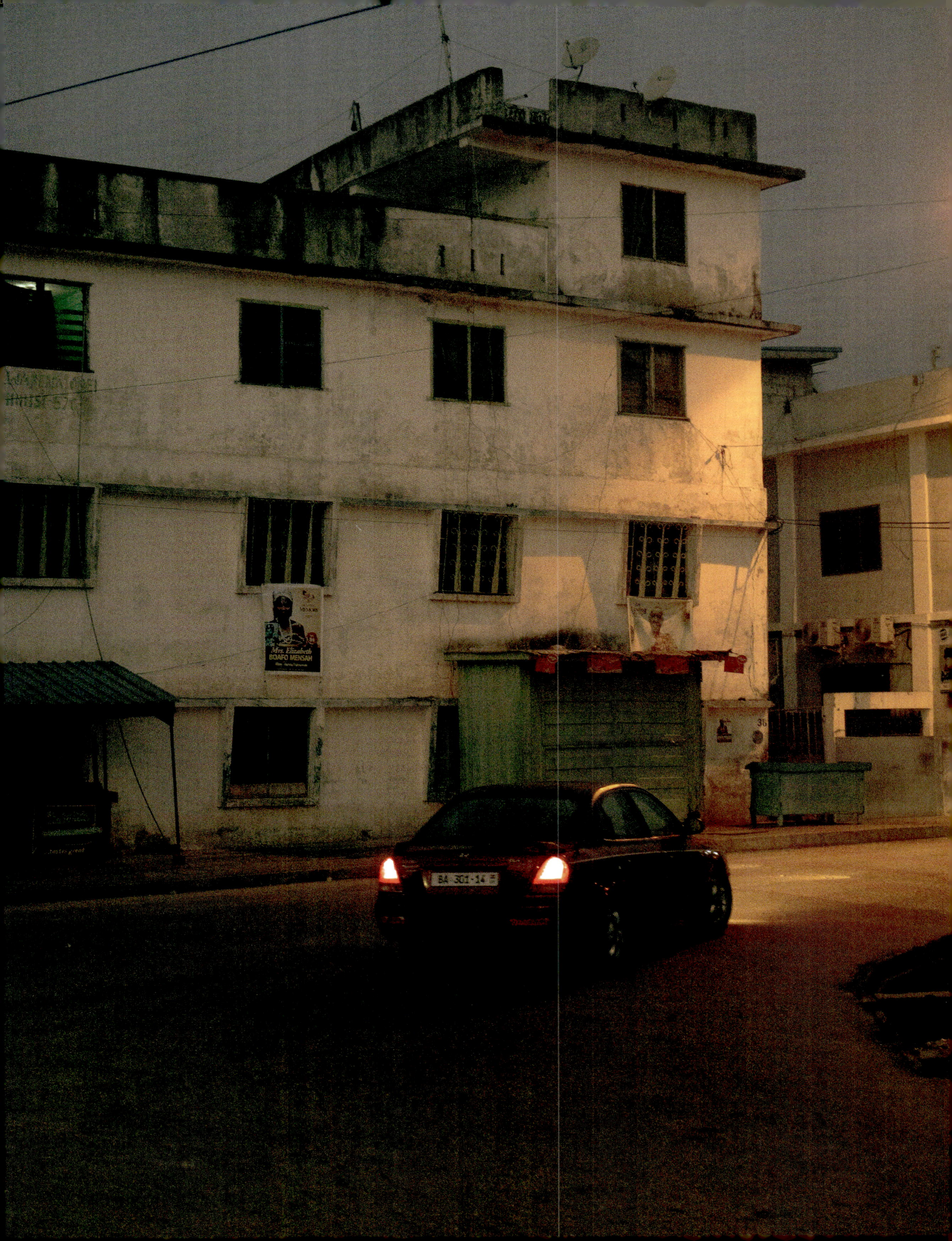

Mrs. Elizabeth
BOAFO MENSAH
BA-301-14

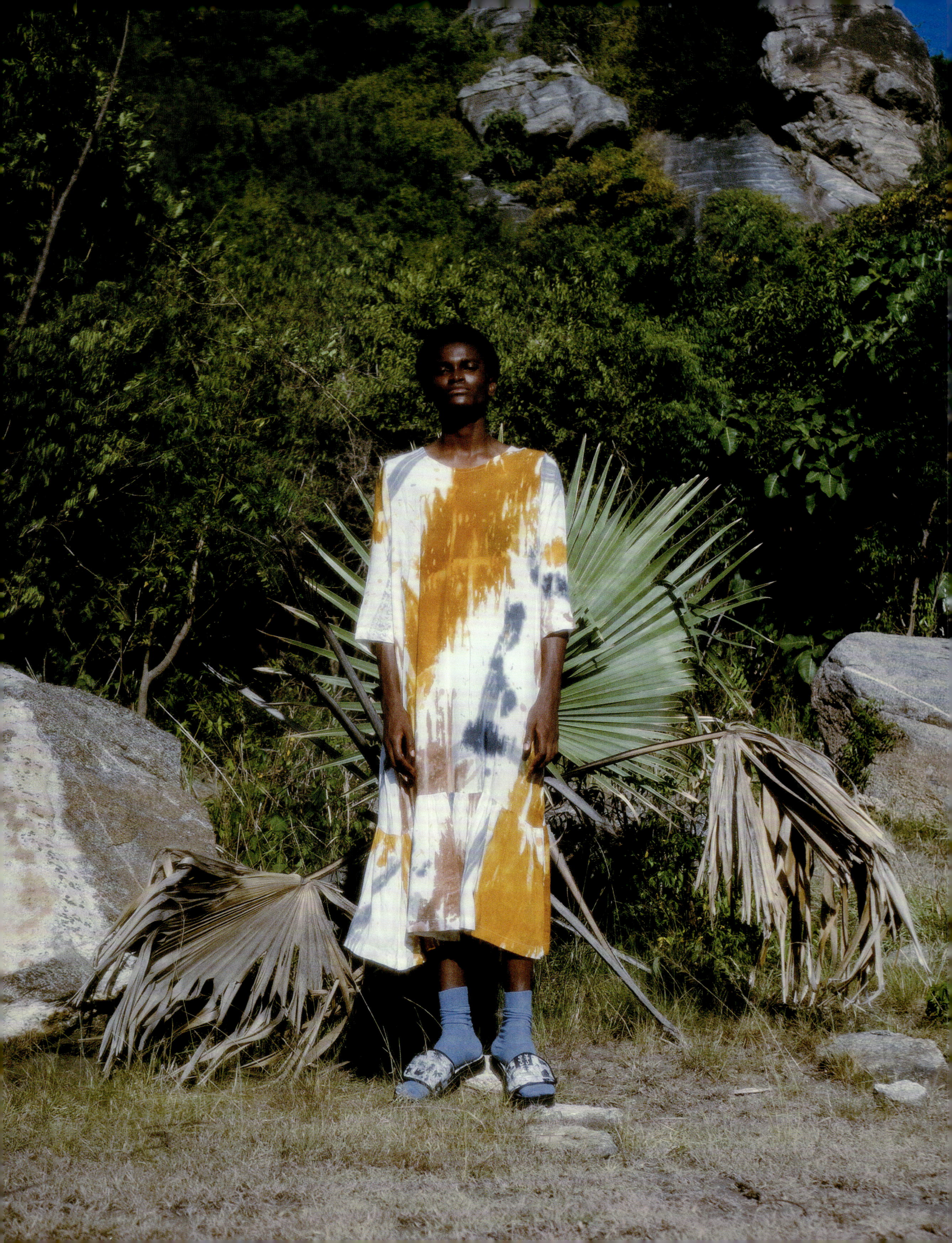

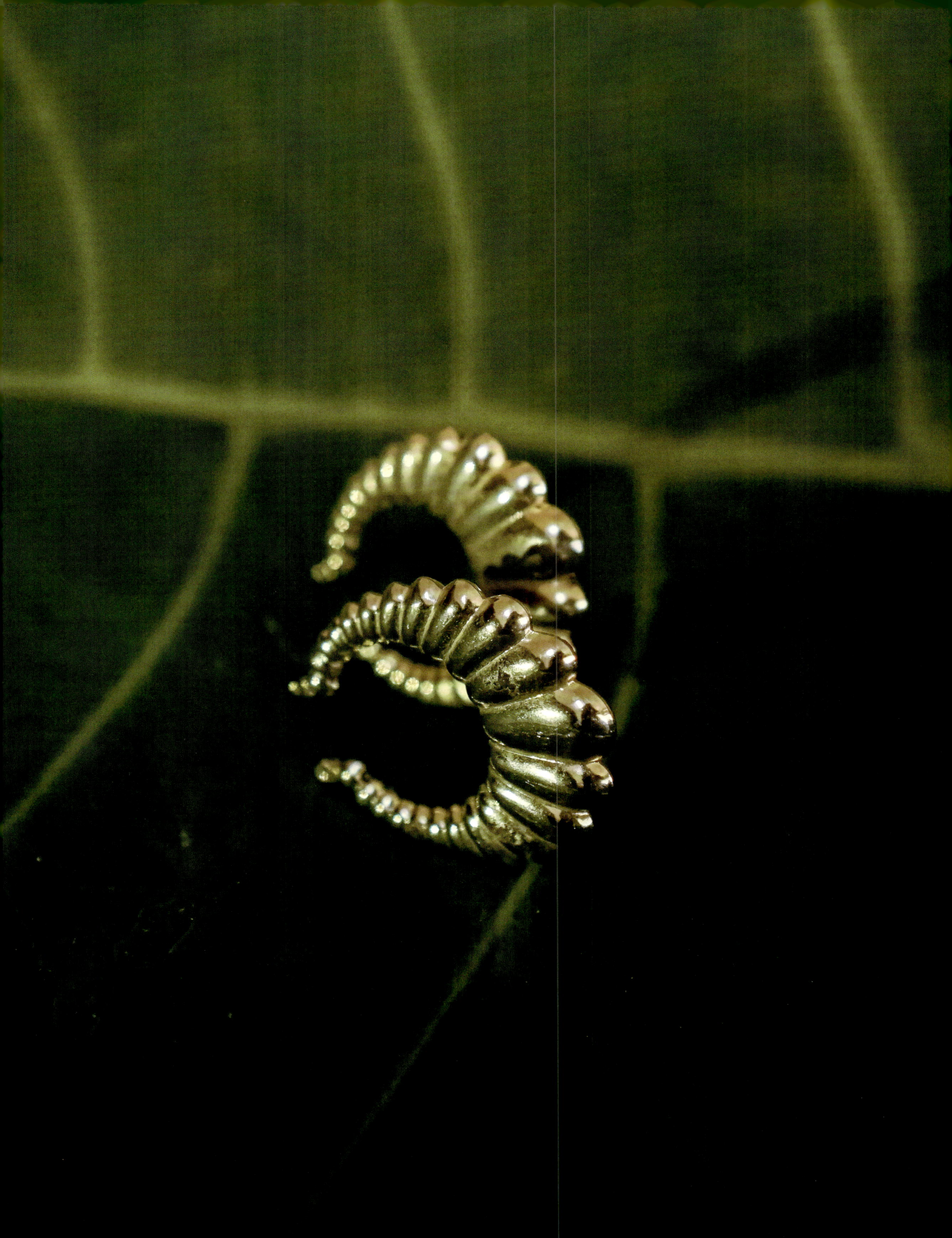

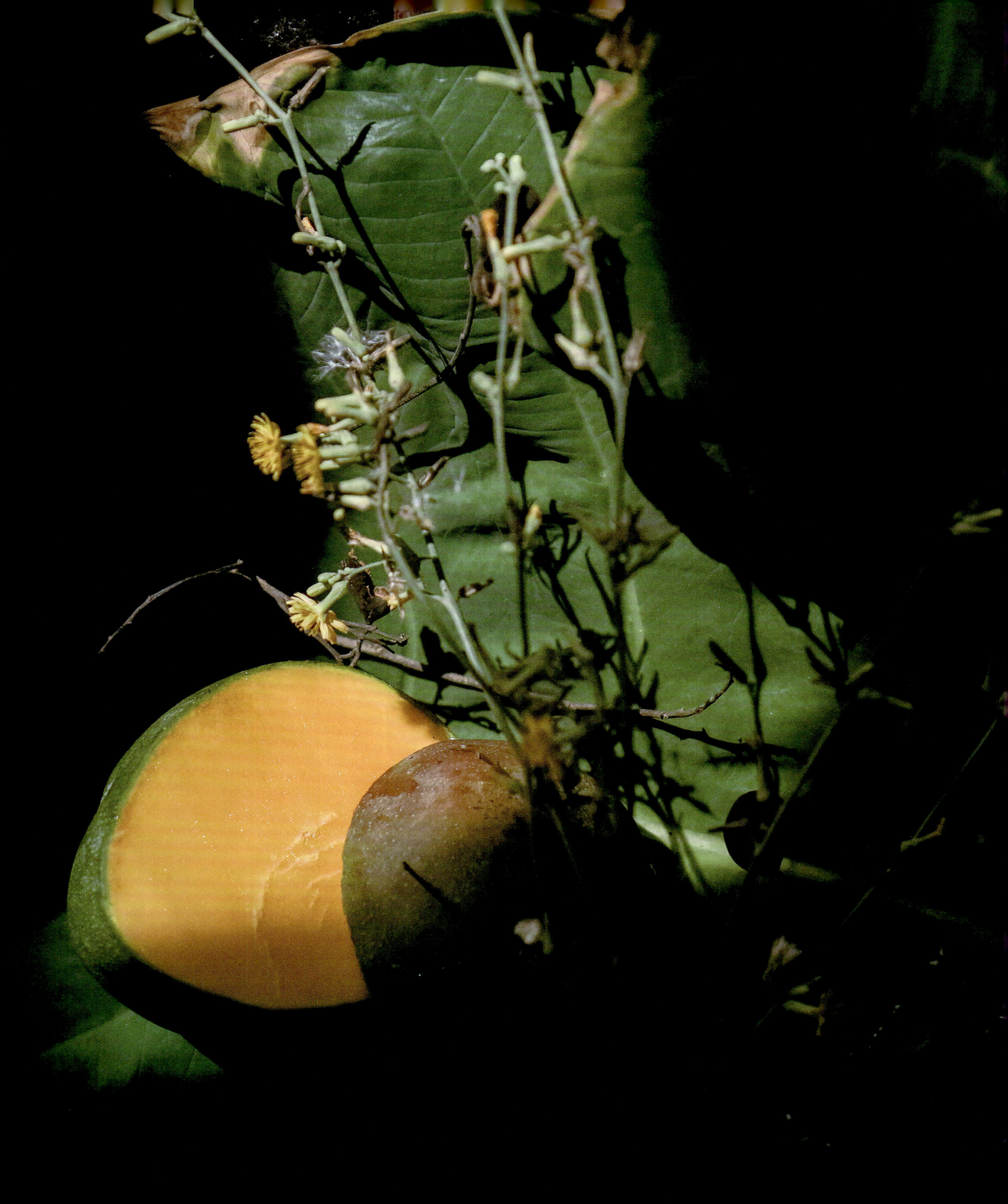

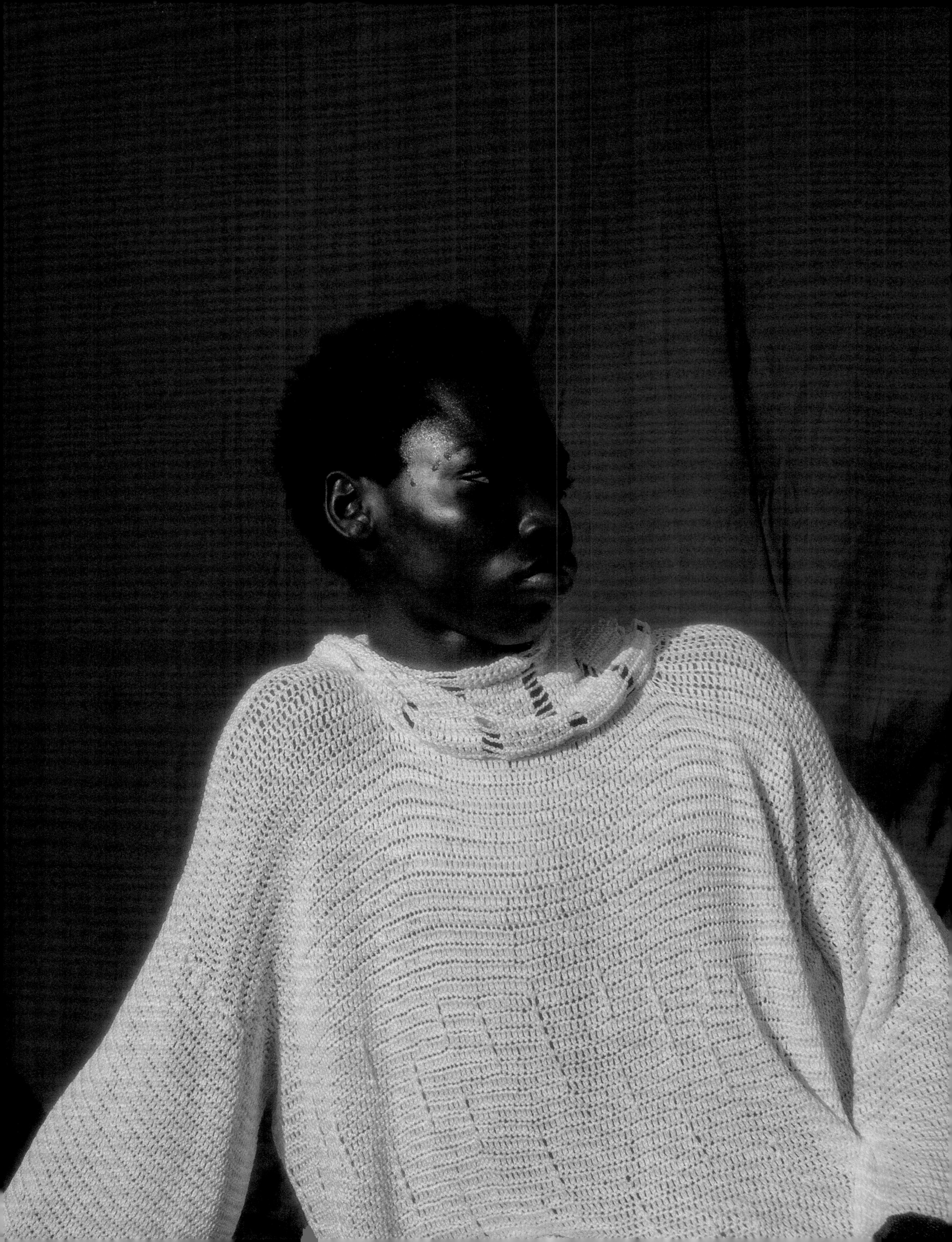

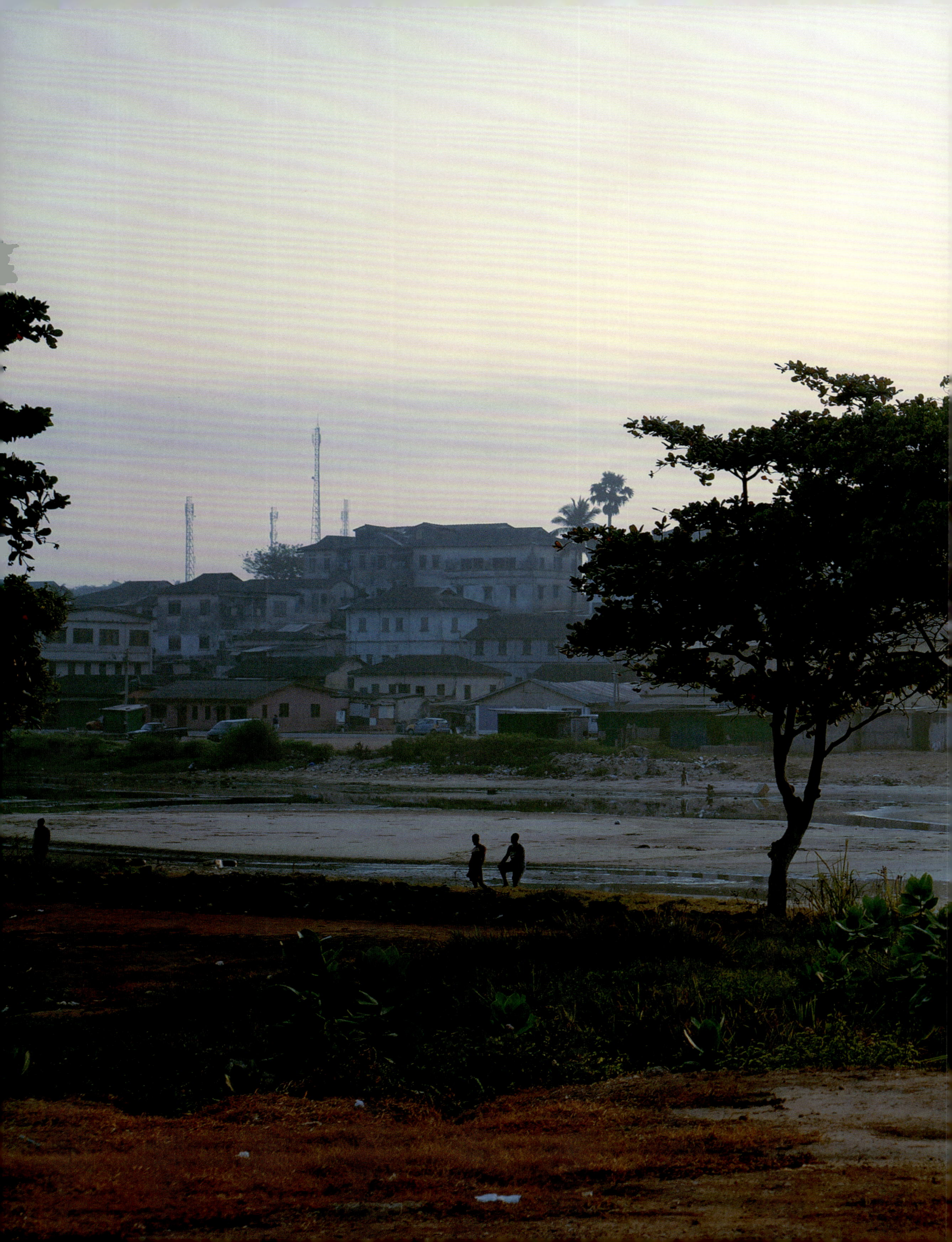

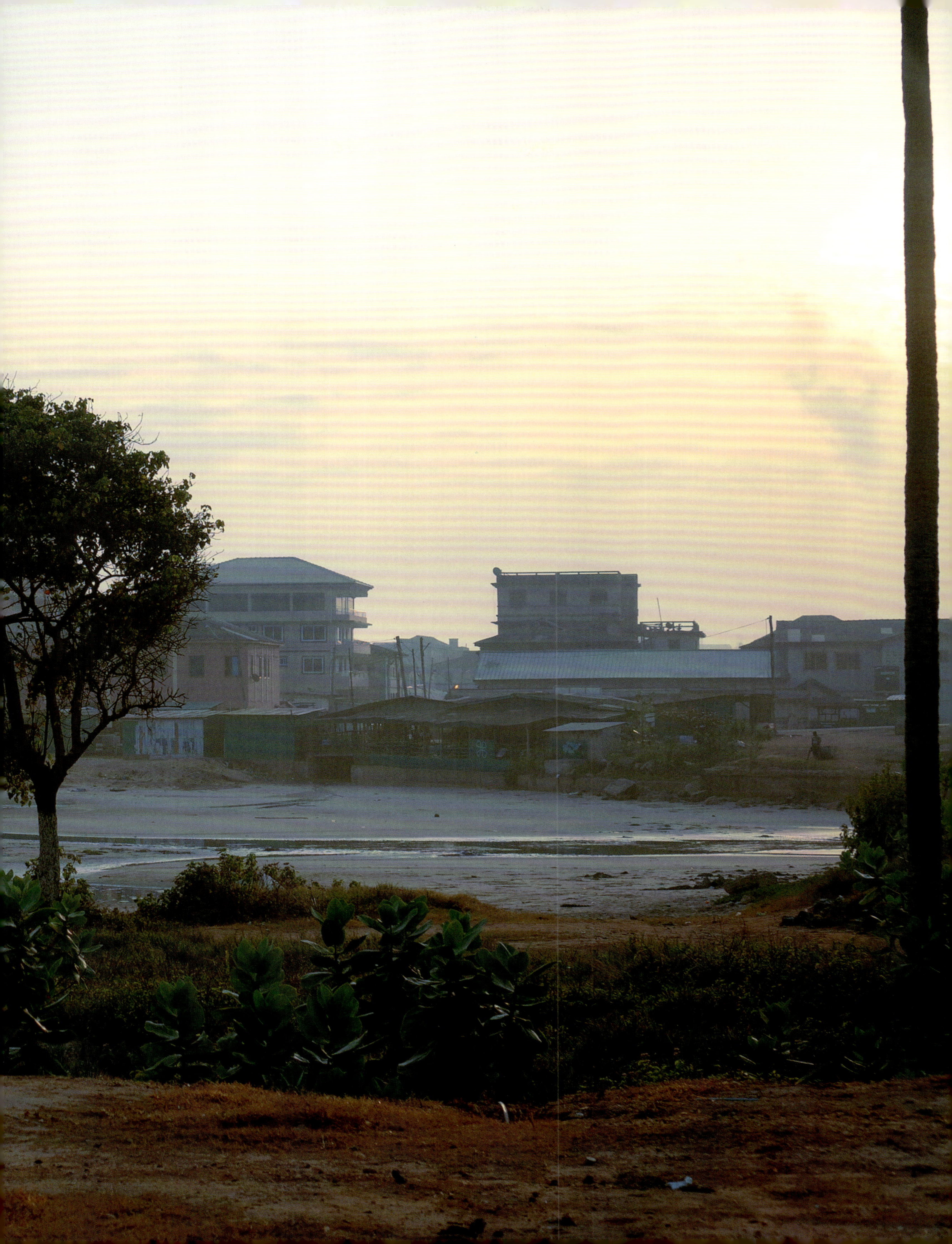

Located in Ghana's capital, Accra, Nima is a predominantly Muslim urban settlement, considered to be one of the country's oldest and largest *zongo* communities. Common throughout West African cities, *zongos* have roots in Hausa culture, and are linked historically to Muslim Hausa traders who traveled throughout West Africa and settled in various cities in the region. Over time, *zongo* communities came into being largely through the influx of immigrants of various ethnic groups from neighboring countries and the influence of Islam. In Nima, residents come from northern Ghana and countries such as Mali, Guinea, Nigeria, and Burkina Faso.

As a result of rural-to-urban migration, and the socioeconomic conditions and inequities attributed to rapid urbanization in the Greater Accra region, Nima is often described as an impoverished area. The photographer Fibi Afloe challenges the harsh narratives that are often associated with such categorizations and highlights the multiple forms of beauty that permeate her hometown, as reflected in the community's sartorial sensibilities and traditions.

Born and raised in Nima, Afloe began learning photography in 2017, at the organization Lensational, under the tutelage of her mentor, the Ghanaian photographer Francis Kokoroko. Afloe's photographic approach strikes a stunning balance between documentary and classic portraiture. Her photographs of elegantly dressed and posed people on the streets of Nima during cultural and religious festivities are reminiscent of the vernacular photographs produced by known and loved African pioneers of the medium, echoing the work of those who captured the beauty, fashion, and style of their communities at midcentury.

Almost every weekend, Nima is bustling with festivities. Whether for a naming ceremony, an *awura* (Hausa for "wedding"), or the biannual Muslim celebration of Eid, the homes and streets of Nima become visual feasts. Men, women, and children dress in their best, donning vibrant outfits cut from colorful, printed African cloth and made to order by their local tailor. Afloe is out almost every weekend capturing the liveliness and grandeur of Nima during such occasions. Her reputation as a photographer and her closeness to the community very often grant her a *goro* or *tofi awura* (Hausa terms describing invitations extended by the family to a naming or wedding ceremony). Over a recent Zoom call, she described what Nima is like on any given weekend: "On Saturdays and Sundays, when you're in Nima, you can hear the sounds of music all around, and people are dressed up beautifully. Some even more than the brides themselves."

Afloe's subjects, who are predominantly women, pose proudly, gracefully, confidently. They stand poised, adorned with jewelry, dressed and draped in prints, lace, and embroidery. Their hands and arms are painted with intricate henna patterns. "Why do people really invest more—especially the women in Nima—to look beautiful?" Afloe says. "I started to ask myself, What does beauty mean to these women? With these photographs, it's me trying to understand." In fact, her portraits not only explore questions of beauty and individual aesthetic choices but also reveal how fashion can reflect values of togetherness and collective care. *Yayi* is a Hausa term that describes the tradition of people wearing the same fabric or cloth during a ceremony, so that the group looks uniform. The acquiring and wearing of *yayi* are demonstrations of support and shared effort, which illustrates how African clothing and fabrics hold and imbue meaning.

Afloe's work serves as a rumination on beauty and sartorial choice, and brings into consideration important pillars of African culture and society: the community and the collective. Beauty, as ritual and as virtue, is articulated through the town's stylish residents, through the honoring of transgenerational customs, and through care and mutual aid. It is evident from Afloe's photographs that beauty lives in Nima.

# Fibi Afloe
## *Beauty Lives in Nima*

**Amy Sall**



Amy Sall is a writer based in New York
and the founding editor of *SUNU: Journal
of African Affairs, Critical Thought +
Aesthetics*.

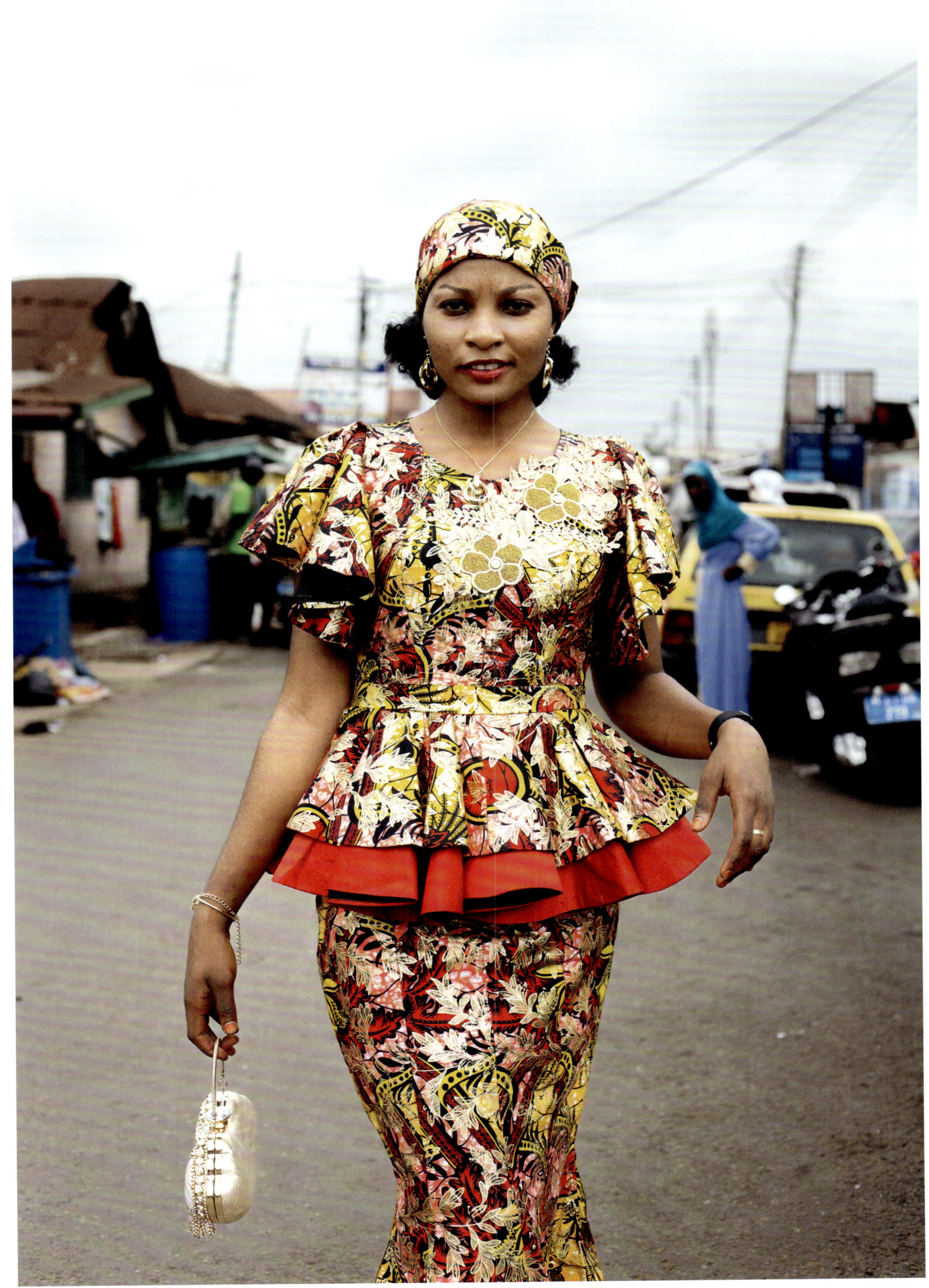

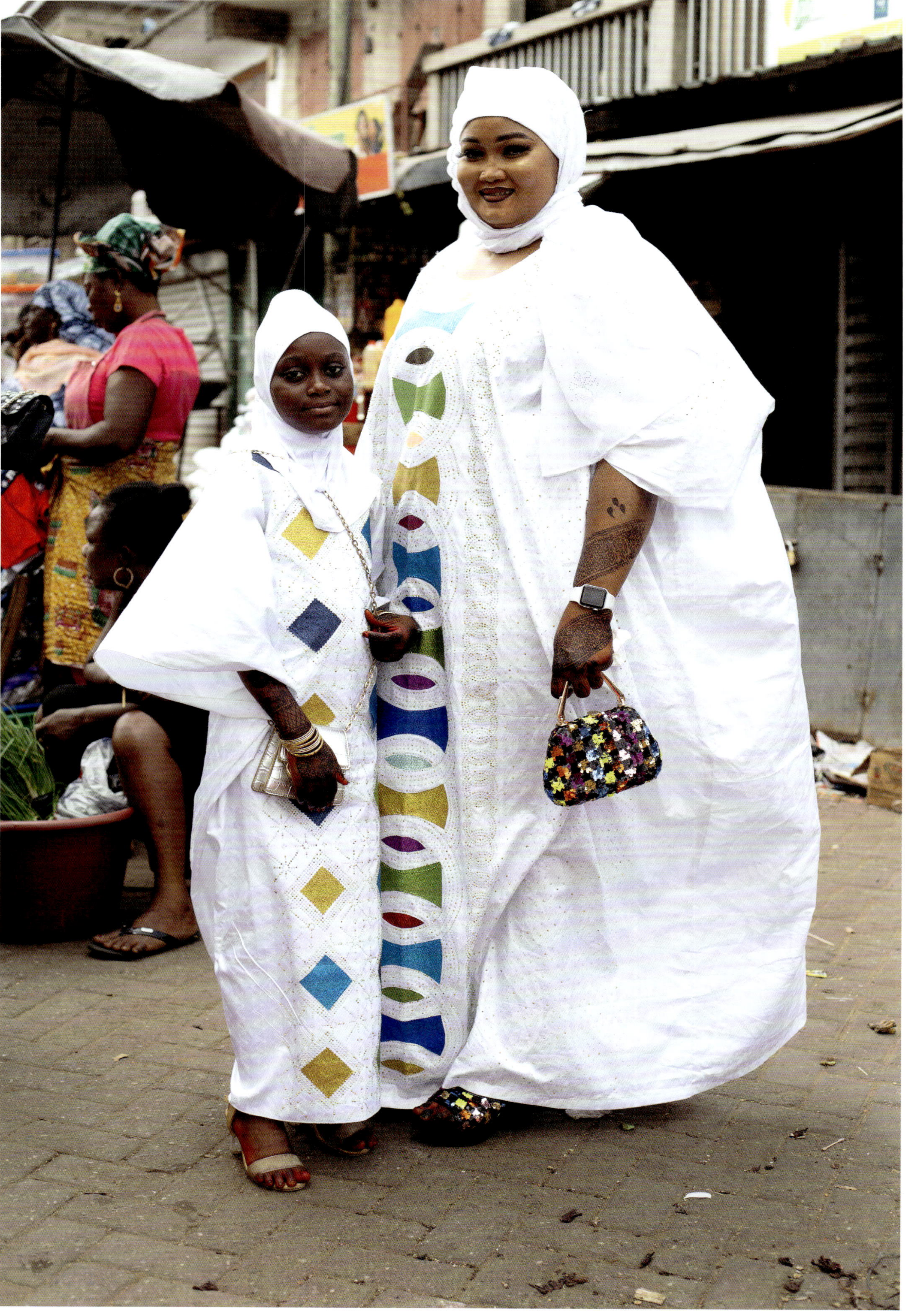

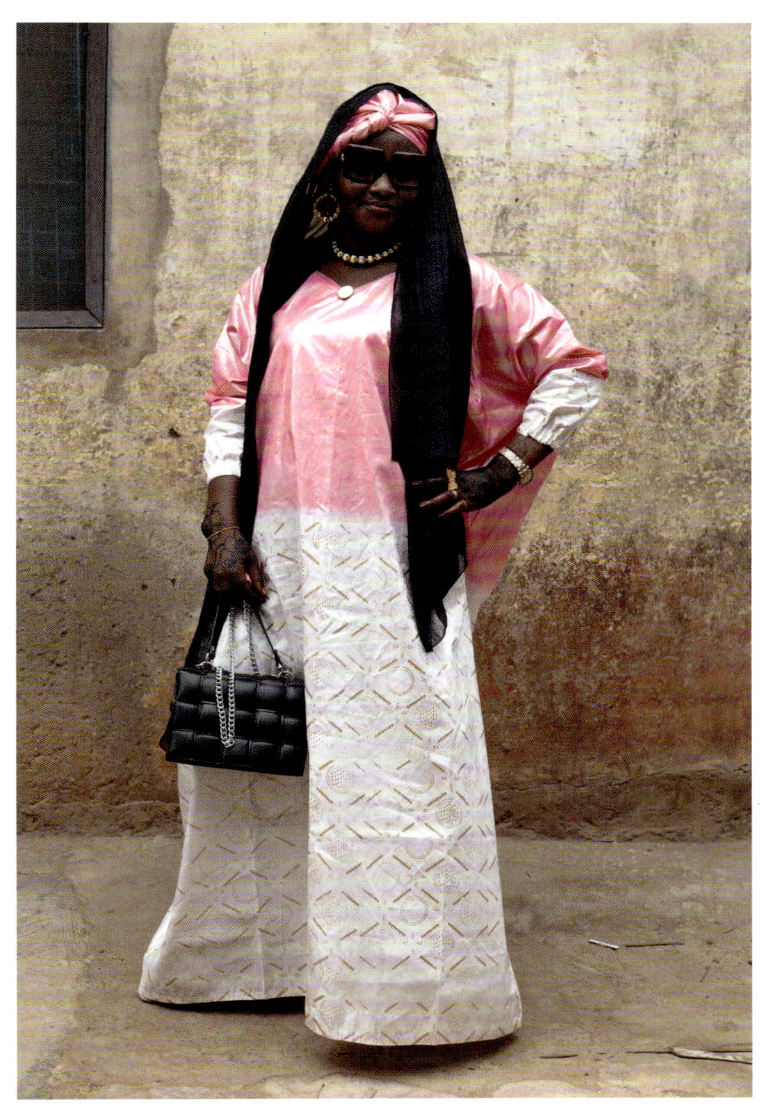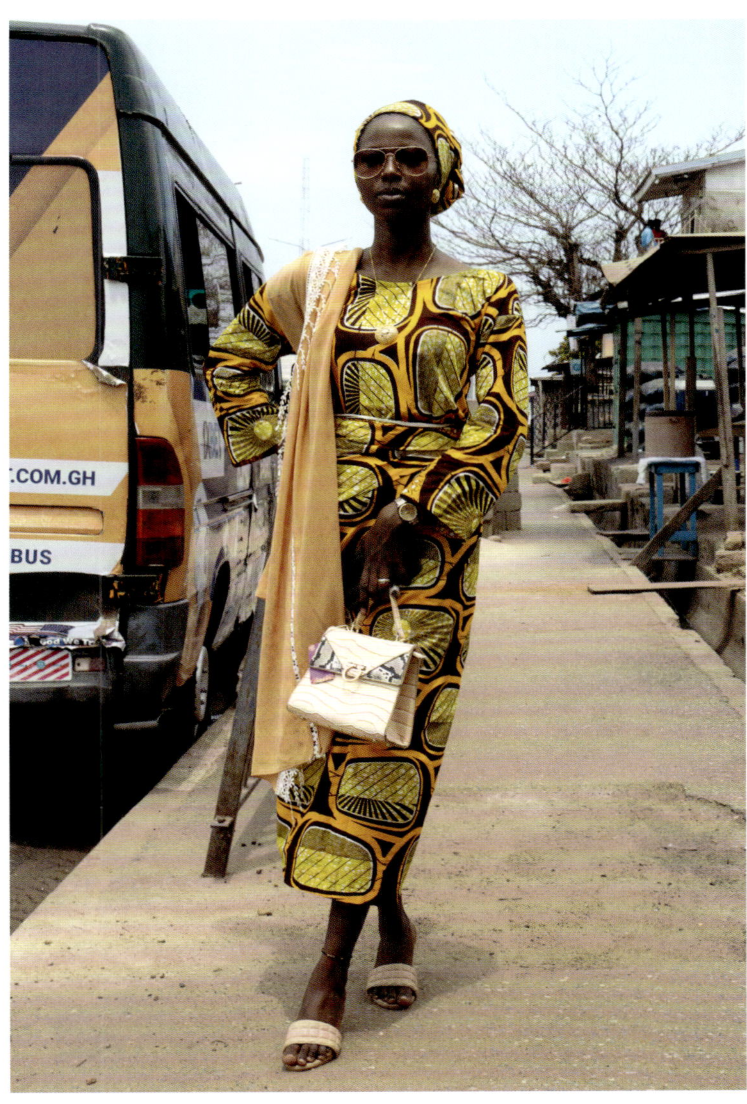

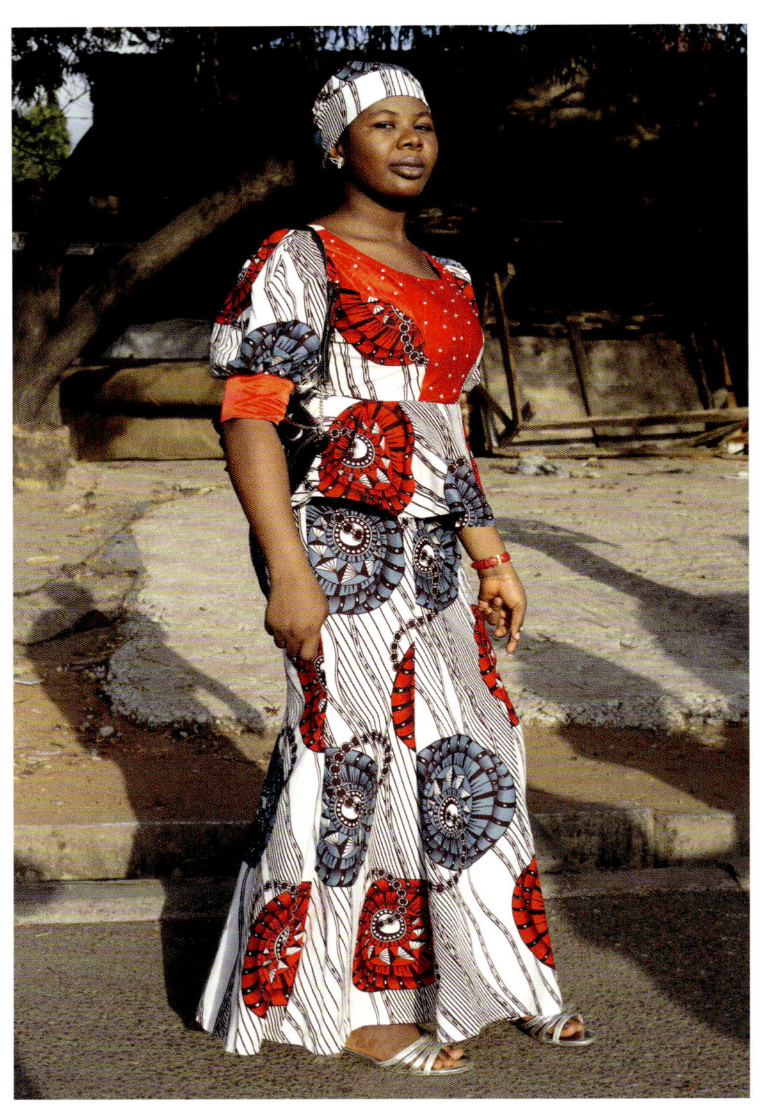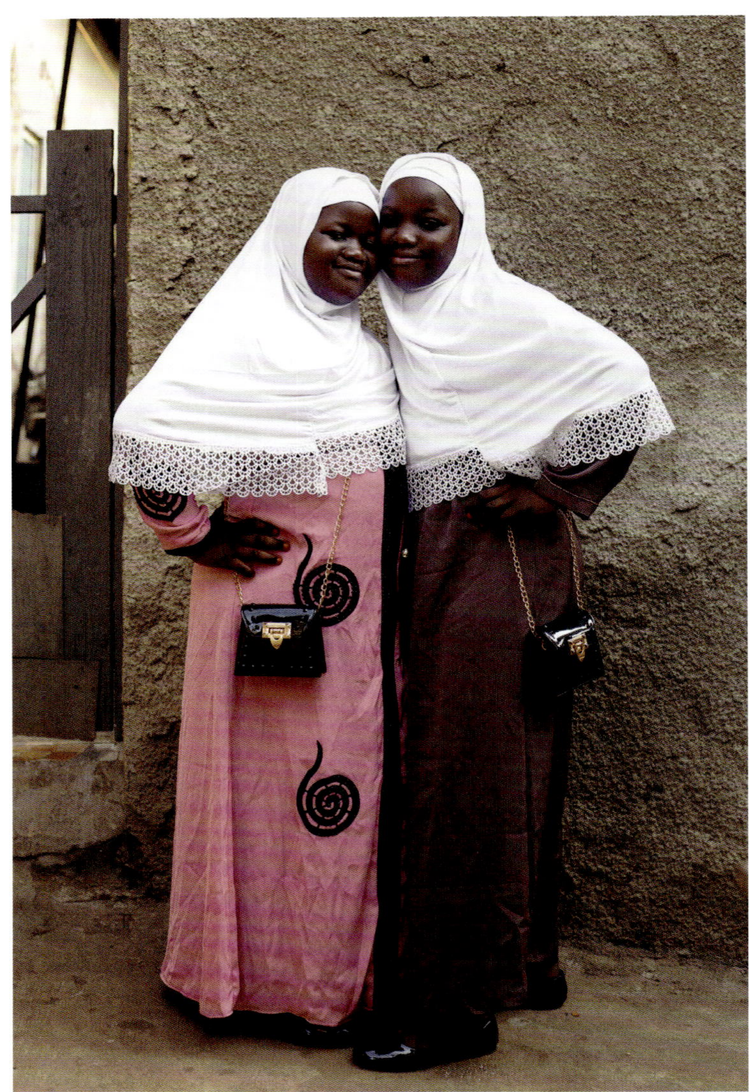

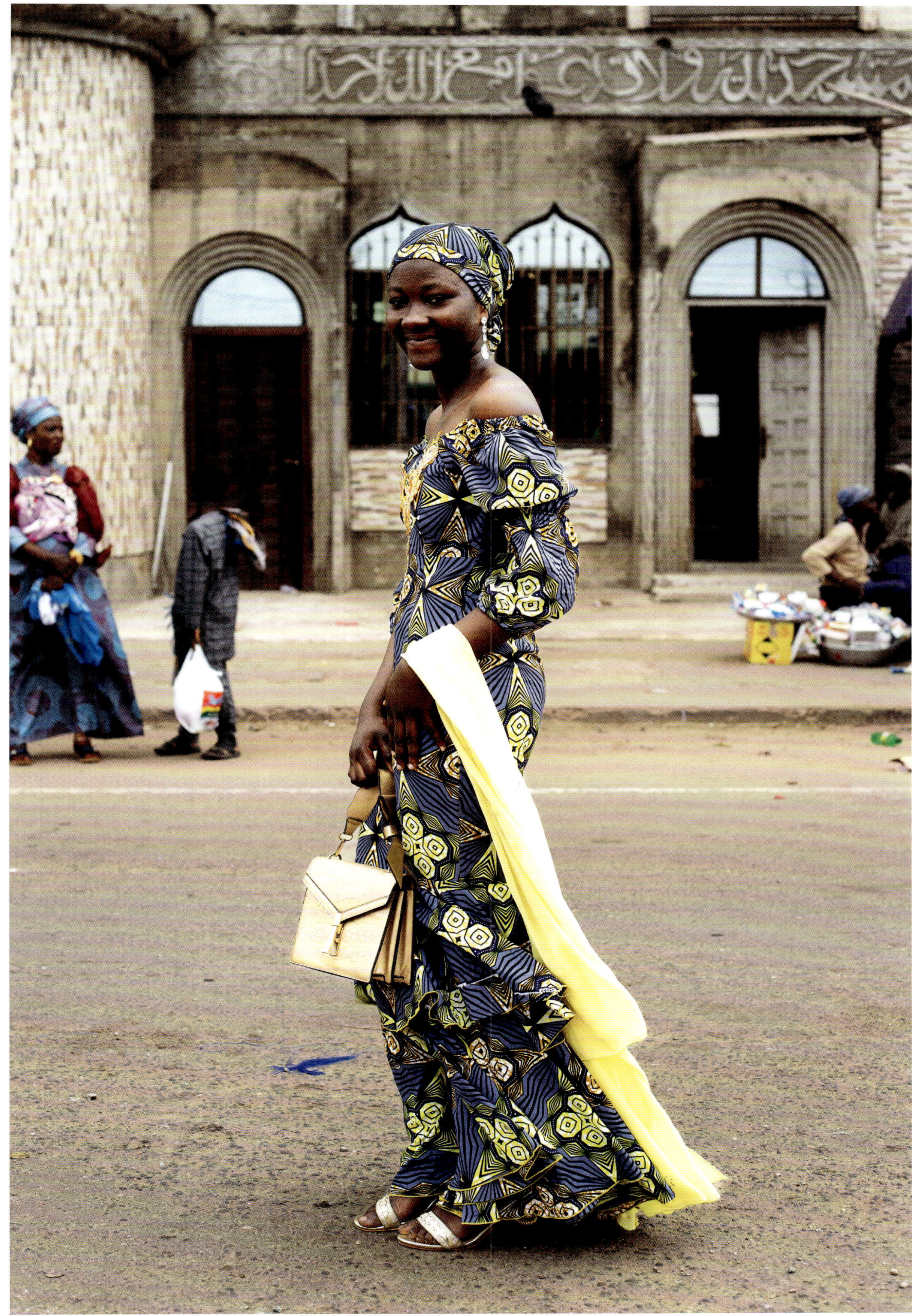

# DAILY GUIDE

NO. 1814  SATURDAY, SEPTEMBER 2, 2006  ¢4000

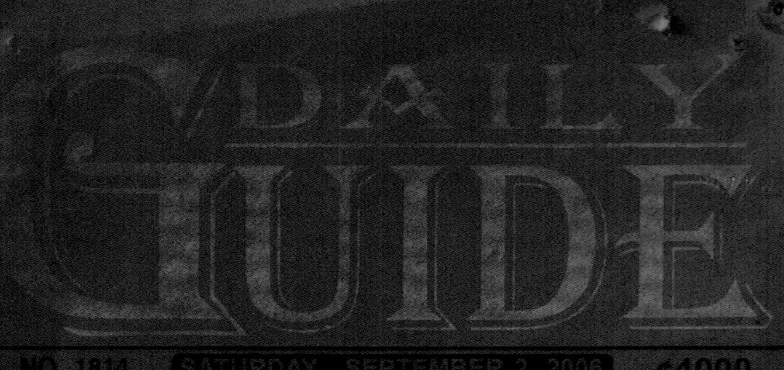


# GAYS LESBIANS ON FIRE

## •It's Animal Style

*By Mike Avickson*

THE DIRECTOR General of Ghana AIDS Commission, Prof Sakyi Awuku Amoa has stressed that homosexuality is one of the major contributors to the AIDS prevalence rate in the country.

According to him, the clandestine activities of homosexuals in the country pose an even greater risk in the transmission of the pandemic.

His remarks came in the wake of an intended international gay and lesbian conference to be held in Accra in the third week of September.

The conference was expected to have attracted several international gay rights activists as well as large numbers of their members who wanted to gain honour in the fight against what they perceived as discrimination against homosexuals in Ghana.

Cont'd on page 3

## Ghana Is Next Heaven
### •Says Spiritualist

*By Angela Otoo*

A 49-YEAR-OLD spiritualist, Akingre Amoah Akuoboe Aferpoaba from Bongo in the Upper East Region says God has revealed to him that the three Northern regions of Ghana would be the next heaven.

Cont'd on page 3

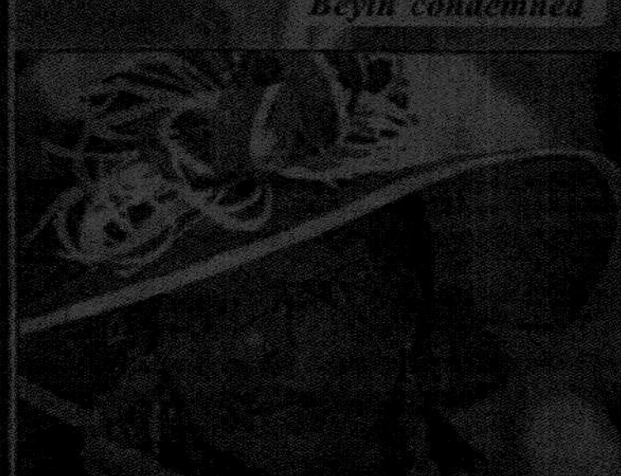
*Kojo Besia, Ama Beyin condemned*

# Pick Aliu Akufo Addo
## •Prez For NPP

A VETERAN UNITED Party (UP) man, Mr. Attoh Quarshie has called for the adoption of a win win strategy by the New Patriotic Party (NPP) towards the 2008 polls.

In the same breath, he condemned the incidence of over a dozen candidates gunning for the party's flagbearership, describing the situation as disgraceful and selfish.

According to him, "the NPP has a teeming 15 or so candidates, which is a disgrace, because it projects selfishness in the party. All of us cannot be presidents. That in itself is not a sign of democracy, it has no advantages," he said in a statement issued in Accra yesterday.

For him, the winning formula is an Aliu-Nana Akufo-Addo pairing, especially if it attracts the active support of President John Agyekum Kufuor.

According to him, there was no rea-

Cont'd on page 3

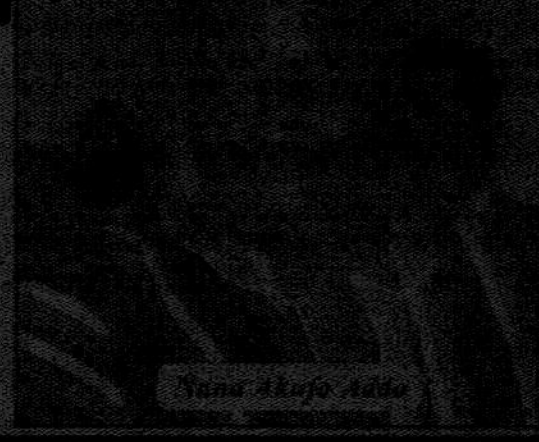
*Nana Akufo Addo*

# Why We Went Out

Although queer bars in Ghana are virtually nonexistent, Accra's LGBTQ community has always found places to drink and dance.
**Chiké Frankie Edozien**

It was a cool January afternoon in 2021. People walked down a quiet neighborhood street in an Accra suburb and passed through the nondescript brown gate into the walled-off compound to witness a bit of history. Inside, more than sixty guests were greeted with music, libations, and an explosion of color. Above them hung open, rainbow-colored umbrellas, and Ghanaian and pride flags unfurled from a window of the brick bungalow. It was the official opening of Ghana's first community center for LGBTQ people.

Organizers with the group known as LGBT+ Rights Ghana had worked and raised funds for years to create a place where queer people could find community. They told guests that this was a safe space for any queer person who needed shelter or just wanted a library with computer stations. In a time when being openly gay in Ghana is dangerous—bordering on criminal—the center also helped people hone life skills to work toward independence. Visitors could take lessons in computer literacy, résumé building, cooking, and more.

Most oohing and aahing in the crowd that day were Ghanaians, proud of this achievement and hoping that the community, by taking care of itself, could spur changes in the current discriminatory societal norms. Several of those present were West Africans, and three were foreign diplomats. The musical wunderkind Wanlov the Kubolor, a rare Ghanaian public ally of the LGBTQ community, gave a rousing performance in the evening.

But barely three weeks after the giant ceremonial ribbon was cut, a local chief threatened to burn the place down. And after a furor of media hit pieces riddled with salacious accusations and inaccuracies, police shut down the center in a dramatic predawn raid. The antigay rhetoric in Ghana ramped up even more, and queer people were forced to keep a low profile. "Not only was it a safe space, it was also a creative hub!" Wanlov laments. Spaces that protect and bring together the marginalized, he adds, should be supported by the state, as occurs elsewhere. "In this sad and wretched case, it was the state that unconstitutionally shut it down, sending the queer community and the creative community into hiding. A solid disgrace."

But it wasn't always this way. Queer people in recent years had been left alone, and were never seen as a threat to anyone, so there weren't big social proscriptions against them. "Every community could point out a few queer people and they never bothered anyone. And they were never bothered," Nat Amarteifio, the late mayor of Accra once told me.

Although explicitly queer bars in Ghana are nonexistent, the LGBTQ community has always found places to gather that are relatively free from harassment. The late 1990s and early 2000s saw the golden era of live and let live, with queer people hanging out in bars and nightclubs that welcomed them. In Accra, the hot spot in the '90s was an upstairs bar called White Bells, according to Ato Ofoli-Gakpo, a forty-year-old farmer who used to be a popular man-about-town—the "king of the streets," as he once put it. "And later Strawberry's opened about two hundred meters down the road," he says. "Strawberry's was on the roadside, and you could see who was coming and going. It was fun." Some bars often hosted nights specifically for queer folks.

For much of the 2000s, Chester's Place, still open in Accra's bucolic and tony Nyaniba Estates, was the place to be seen. Everyone was welcome, from expatriates and diplomats to young professionals and even off-duty women sex workers. The owner, Chester, is sixty, and has been running the business while practicing as an attorney. In 1994 he was visiting the city on a four-month break from his work in New York and wanted a place for music and camaraderie, with cool bistro vibes, away from the noisy bars and clubs that were commonplace. He created an Accra oasis where patrons could enjoy jazz, wine, and good conversation. A place without category.

"I was doing something that was accessible to ladies and gentlemen," Chester says. "People wanted to come out, listen to some Ella Fitzgerald, Diana Ross, and just hang out." And the queer people who flocked there went because Chester's was cool. "We didn't know they were queer. They were there for fun," he says. "It's a coded location. But my focus is, You come to a chilled zone. Ghanaians come in and have wine and conversation for three, four, five hours." And mingling next to them were other African professionals, European workers, and airline cabin crews from various countries around the world. "It is not an LGBT place, but I won't let anyone who was slovenly or drunk disrespect the next person."

On some nights he had a live band, and his team was known for top-notch hospitality that put everyone at ease. "Nobody cared," Chester says. "They were not crass. People came here because we are nonjudgmental. We don't give a shit." In its prime, the bar was upscale, and patrons dressed up for a night out. Even today, tourists who inquire about where to go for a drink with their queer friends are directed to Chester's.

Back in the day, Accra's queer community also frequented Champs, a sports bar at the Paloma Hotel. It was popular for its weekly karaoke with a vivacious host, Wilbert. "Wilbert was Liberian, and he brought a crowd every Friday night," Ofoli-Gakpo says. "He and the gay bartenders used to pull in all their friends, but he ended up in America after a few years." (Being a popular bartender wasn't a lifelong ambition, and he sought greener pastures.) Some queer people started the weekend revelry on Thursday evenings at a private home in the wealthy suburb of Tesano, where Wilbert and his pal Caldorf entertained them with their singing. When Wilbert left, others stopped going too, Ofoli-Gakpo says.

Folks then moved to a low-key place called Macumba, in Danquah Circle, where they let people dance on the stripper pole. Once a go-to club on Saturday nights, Macumba has long since closed. Beginning in the mid-'90s, Chester's was the place to go to be among a certain very mixed, middle-class crowd, but around 2001, Henri's Place, in the Kokomlemle neighborhood, had become a favorite for queer people of all stripes. The owner, Henri, had relocated from London in 2000 and invested in satellite-television service to create a sports bar where soccer fans and their dates could watch matches together. Henri was popular. His New Year's Eve parties were legendary. Once he opened a bar, crowds appeared.

"It was lovely and indoors and air-conditioned, and people had a place to dance inside," Ofoli-Gakpo says. "Lesbians were there, and you didn't see a lot of straight people."

After five years, Henri's Place moved to Adabraka, a gritty neighborhood, and the crowds followed. "It was a hundred percent gay," Ofoli-Gakpo says. He believes that because it was not far from a slum, those residents came around, too, so the crowd was fairly mixed. Everyone felt safe inside. Henri insists that this queer-friendly environment was pure happenstance: he didn't set out to open an LGBTQ bar. He had friends in the police and military, which at the time made people feel protected. "I'd phone them if there was any problem, and they would come around. It was a safe place," he says.

Henri's Place lasted until late 2008. A sensational article appeared in a local tabloid singling out the bar as a place to pick up male sex workers. Henri denies the claim, which had infuriated and hurt his family. "I closed because of the exposure," he says. "It was a bad experience for me." Today he runs two wholesale shops selling beer, wine, and spirits.

By 2009, Epos, a rollicking multilevel establishment with a rooftop terrace and cheap beers, was in vogue. It was and remains a destination for the hoi polloi to watch soccer or the sunset. One Wednesday evening in 2010 I went to its basement nightclub and marveled. The crowd that used to frequent Henri's had migrated there. As Afrobeats blared from the sound system, revelers were shaking it on the dance floor. Others flirted. It was your typical club scene, but women danced with women and men danced with men. Until then, many queer people remained hidden in plain sight, dancing in a corner on Friday nights at Rhapsody's, the restaurant that for a time was all the rage. There they danced close, but not too close, as they were typically surrounded by a sea of straight people. They had fun but worked hard to blend in.

"Epos was fun," Ofoli-Gakpo says. Epos was shut down temporarily due to an electrical fire, and when it reopened after renovations many queer people had discovered a new welcoming venue. Clubhouse was in Jamestown, a historic part of Accra that today has a functioning red lighthouse and grapples with abject income inequalities; it was primarily for residents of the area, but all were welcomed. The indigenous fishing community and other residents had lived with queer people for years. "Anywhere the gays go, the street boys will join," Ofoli-Gakpo says, referring to young men who roam certain neighborhoods at night. A pub called 10 Pounds opened next to Clubhouse in the late 2000s but closed during the pandemic.

Today, LGBTQ Ghanaians lack safe spaces. Even creative hot spots like a skate park can be targeted if they appear to attract queer folk. Recent attempts by a vocal few in Parliament to criminalize LGBTQ Ghanaians through legislation have been hailed by many. Very few have challenged the notion that queer Ghanaians can be illegal by virtue of their existing. Despite the harsh rhetoric and the frequent hectoring by the media, queer people are still socializing in public, although many choose to blend in and refrain from overt displays of their queerness. It's the way to survive in these times.

Henri believes that even with today's climate, there's a fifty-fifty chance that another entrepreneur will create a new venue for LGBTQ folks. Still, he adds: "I don't know if the next person would get it as smooth as I got it."

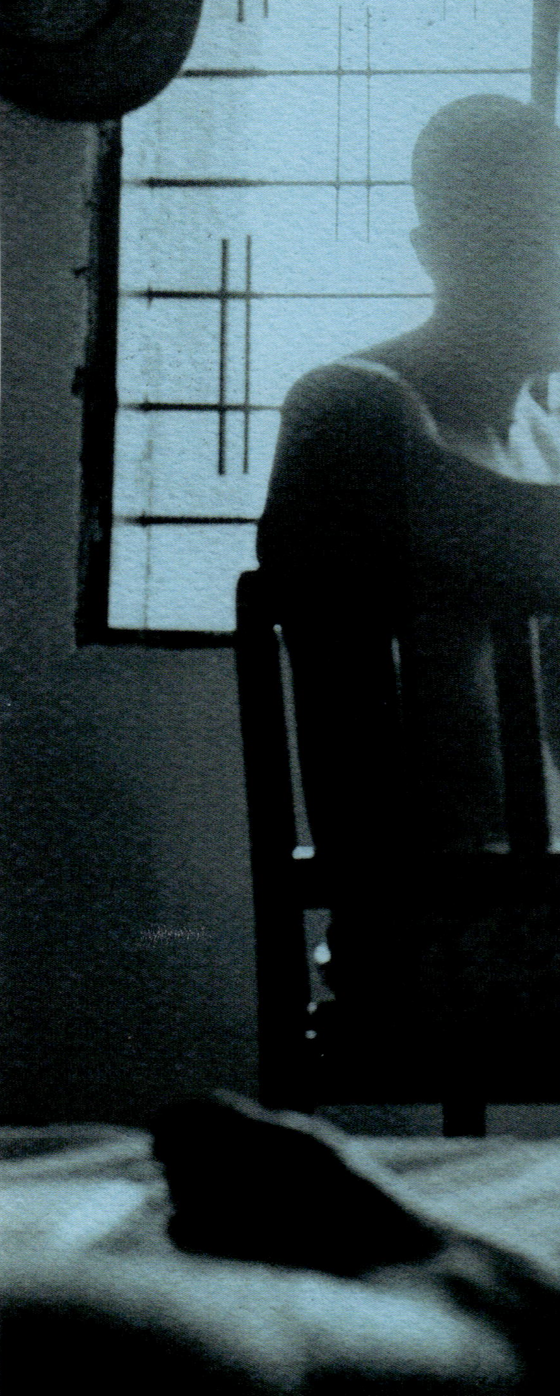

Chiké Frankie Edozien is the author of *Lives of Great Men: Living and Loving as an African Gay Man* (2017). He lives in Accra.

Page 92:
Lyle Ashton Harris,
*Untitled (Readymade, Red Filter, Daily Guide No. 1814, Cover Story, September 2, 2006)*, 2023
Courtesy the artist

This spread:
Eric Gyamfi, *Last page of Giovanni's Room, in Fiifi's room*, 2017–18, from the series *A certain bed*
Courtesy the artist

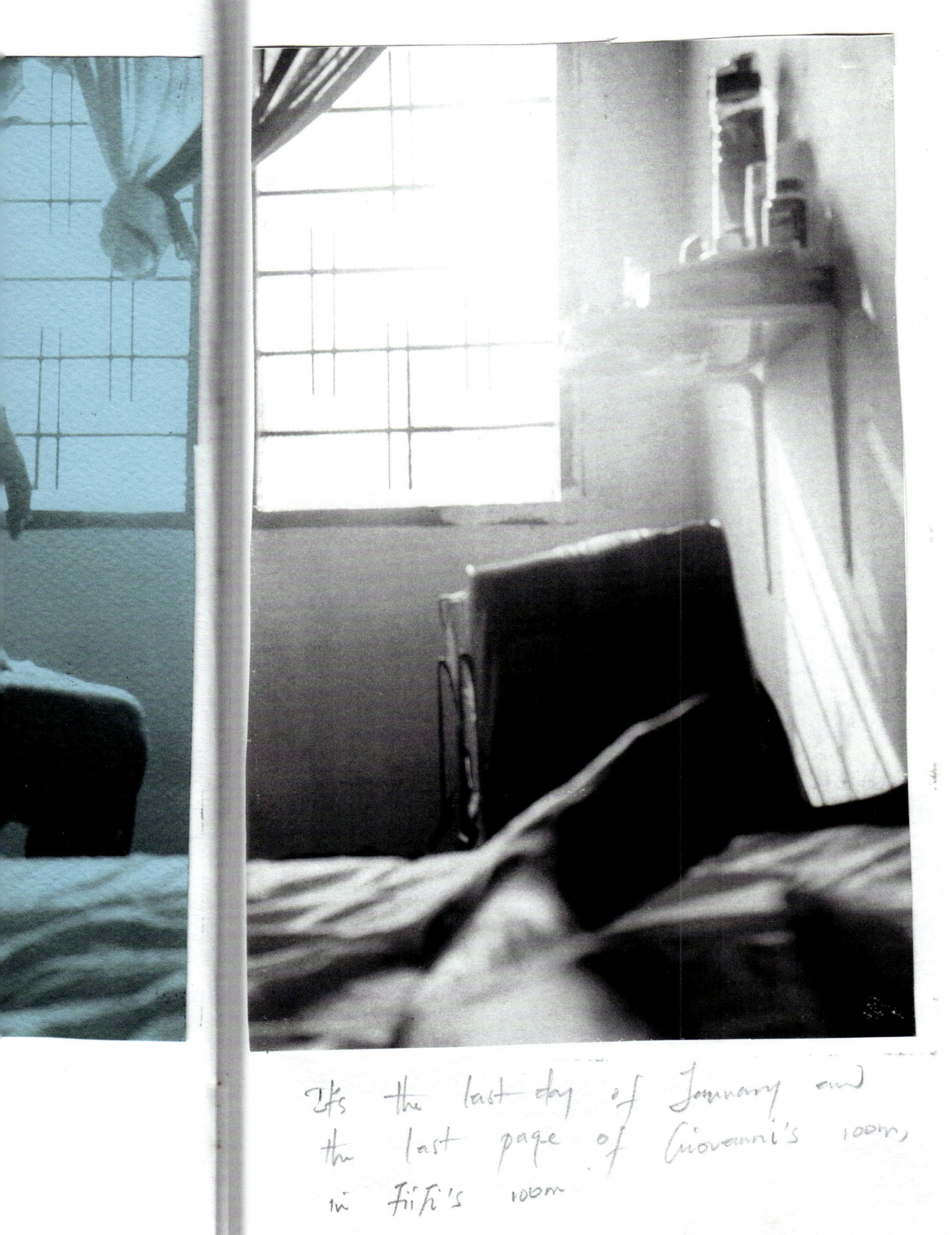

It's the last day of January and the last page of Giovanni's room, in Fifi's room

# Makola's Market Queens

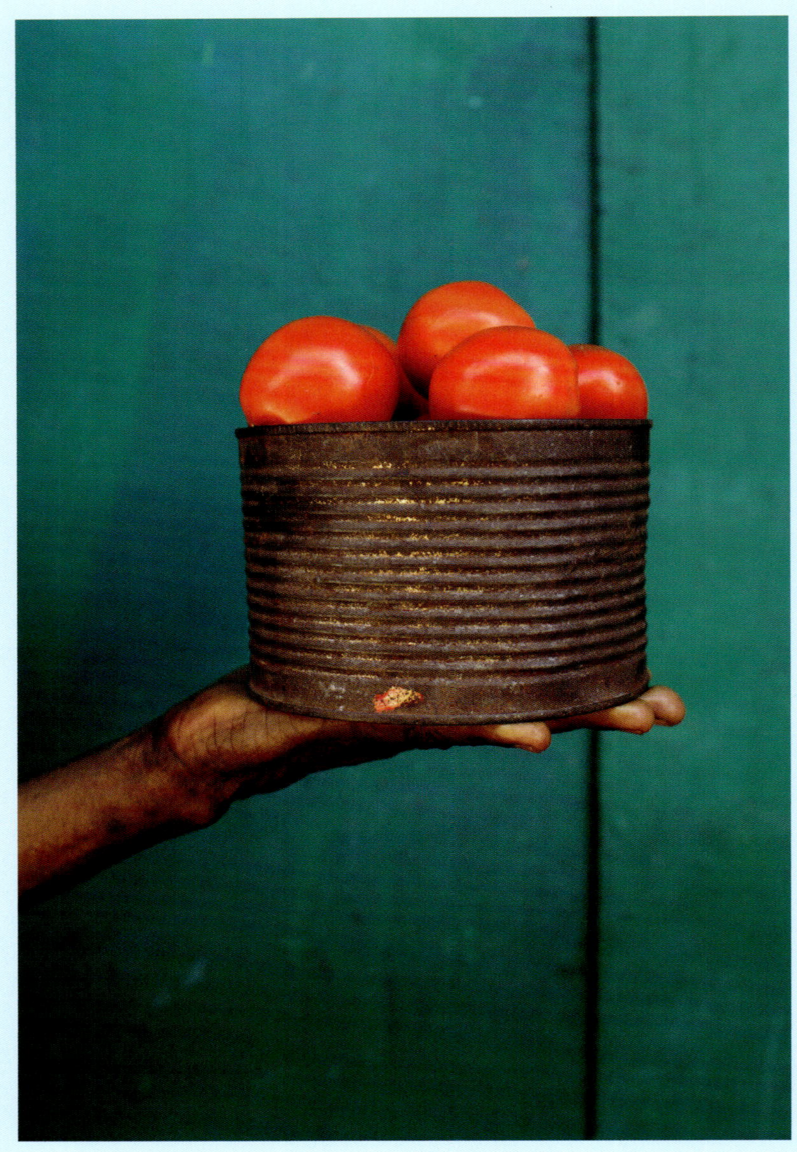

# Misper Apawu

**Nana Ama Agyemang Asante**

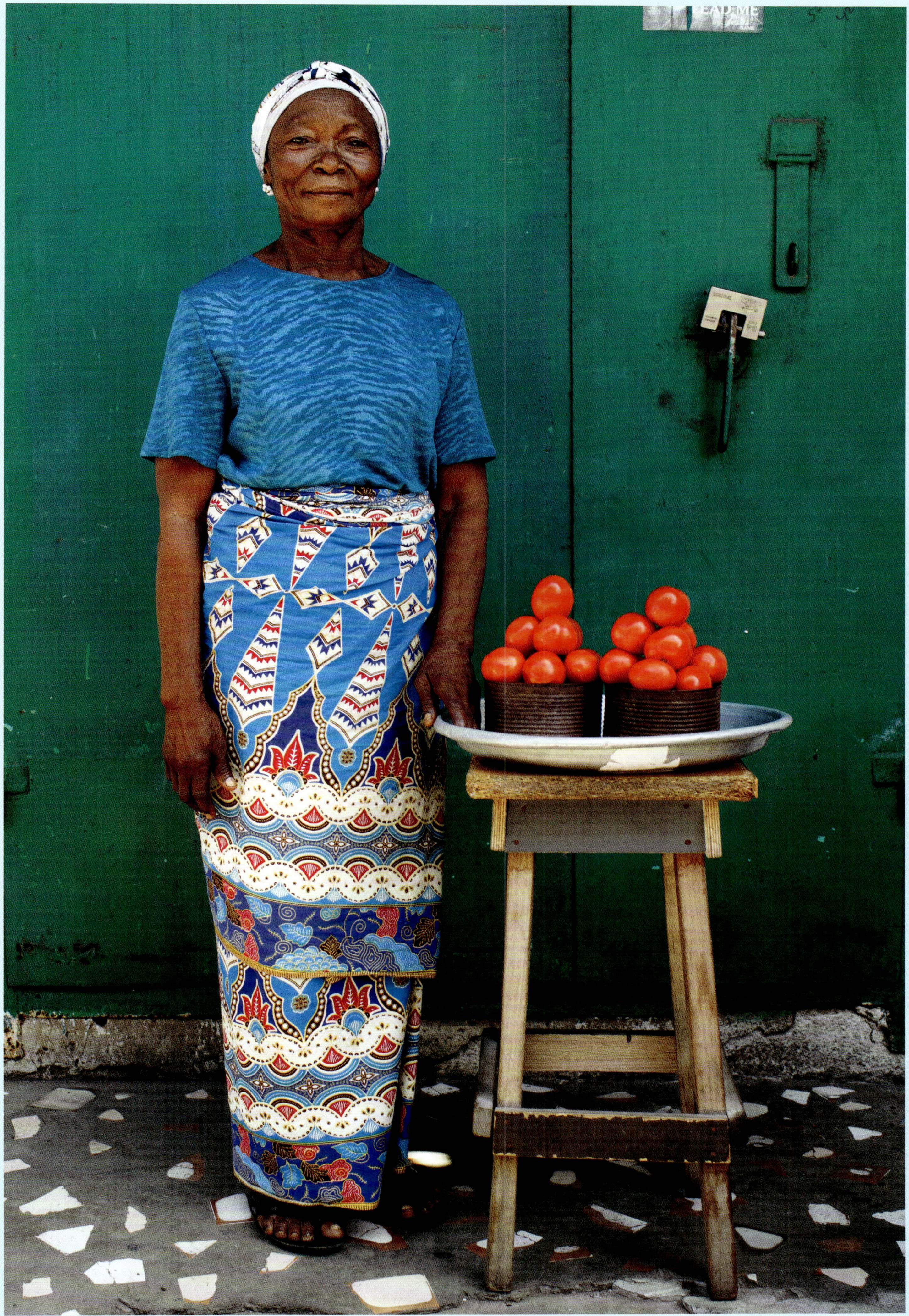

Last spring, the Accra-based photographer Misper Apawu made repeated trips to Makola to produce a series of portraits of women traders. Apawu, whose work has often focused on the lives of women in Ghana, claims that her first encounter with photography occurred in a market in Dambai, a town in the Oti region of Ghana, an experience that changed her life. In her childhood, when she used to sell iced water in the market, she watched the women's faces light up whenever tourists pointed their cameras at them. And when tourists showed the women their pictures, they would beam with delight. The joy Apawu witnessed between the women and the camera inspired her to take up photography as a young adult.

Women in Ghana's markets have built and expanded their businesses on centuries-old systems, including apprenticeships. Alberta Koshie Lamptey, a bead seller, and Lydia Owusu, an avocado seller, learned the trade from their mothers. Makola has changed since they took over their stalls more than a decade ago,

## Makola is located in Accra's central business district, and since being built in 1924 it has been dominated by women.

with an increased number of traders, higher costs of goods, and the lack of a credit system. Like women in markets throughout Ghana, they are grateful for their jobs, financial independence, and the ability to provide for their families. For women such as Elizabeth Darkwa Mensah, Makola has given her not only financial freedom but the opportunity to lead. As president of a wax print sellers' association in Makola, she is part of a team of market queens who manage market facilities, enforce rules, provide financial support, respond to emergencies, and create networking opportunities. Makola, like other markets, is underfunded and underresourced, but its leaders ensure that it runs smoothly.

As influential and visible players in the economy, market women bear the brunt of rising prices, which are often caused by inflation and poor fiscal management. During the 1979 economic crisis, both the government and Ghana's citizens blamed Makola's sellers for rising prices and shortages of essential goods, and for that the market was demolished by soldiers. Elizabeth Darkwa Mensah still remembers the trauma and the challenges that followed when trading resumed in 1987, and she is thankful that Makola has transitioned into a thriving commercial hub in Accra.

It is often said that if you are unable to locate a particular item in Makola Market, or get assistance from a trader who knows where to find it, then the product does not exist—or it's not available in Ghana. But only when you go to Makola does this image of a one-stop shop become apparent. Though chaotic at first glance, the market is clearly structured, so you may wind through hawkers and petty traders to lanes of vendors selling imported fabrics and wax prints, or wigs, hair creams, relaxers, and conditioners—sometimes all at the same table. There are stalls, kiosks, and tabletop shops in the market and open-air areas. You may stumble on wholesalers of beauty products, candy, combs, and spare parts, among other goods that reflect the ingenuity of the traders and a complex system of wholesale, retail, and distribution services.

Makola is located in Accra's central business district, and since being built in 1924 it has been dominated by women. Historically, women from Accra's indigenous Ga ethnic group, who had been trading since the sixteenth century, made Makola a thriving market. Makola is now a much more diverse place, with women from all over Ghana participating in the trading business. Many, including Winnifred Aku Tetteh, a smoked-fish seller, have been working in Makola for more than thirty years. They supply Accra's five million residents with fresh produce, household supplies, clothing, and everything else for their daily needs. The women's success depends on their ability to read cultural shifts and use of a range of marketing techniques while keeping up with global trends. For example, wax print sellers, such as Veronica Agbozo, who source their fabrics and lace from the United States, China, Nigeria, and Togo, among other places, rely on their storytelling skills—beginning with the naming of new patterns to reflect Ghanaian sociocultural realities—to help sell their products.

Nana Ama Agyemang Asante is a journalist covering politics, gender, and business in Ghana.

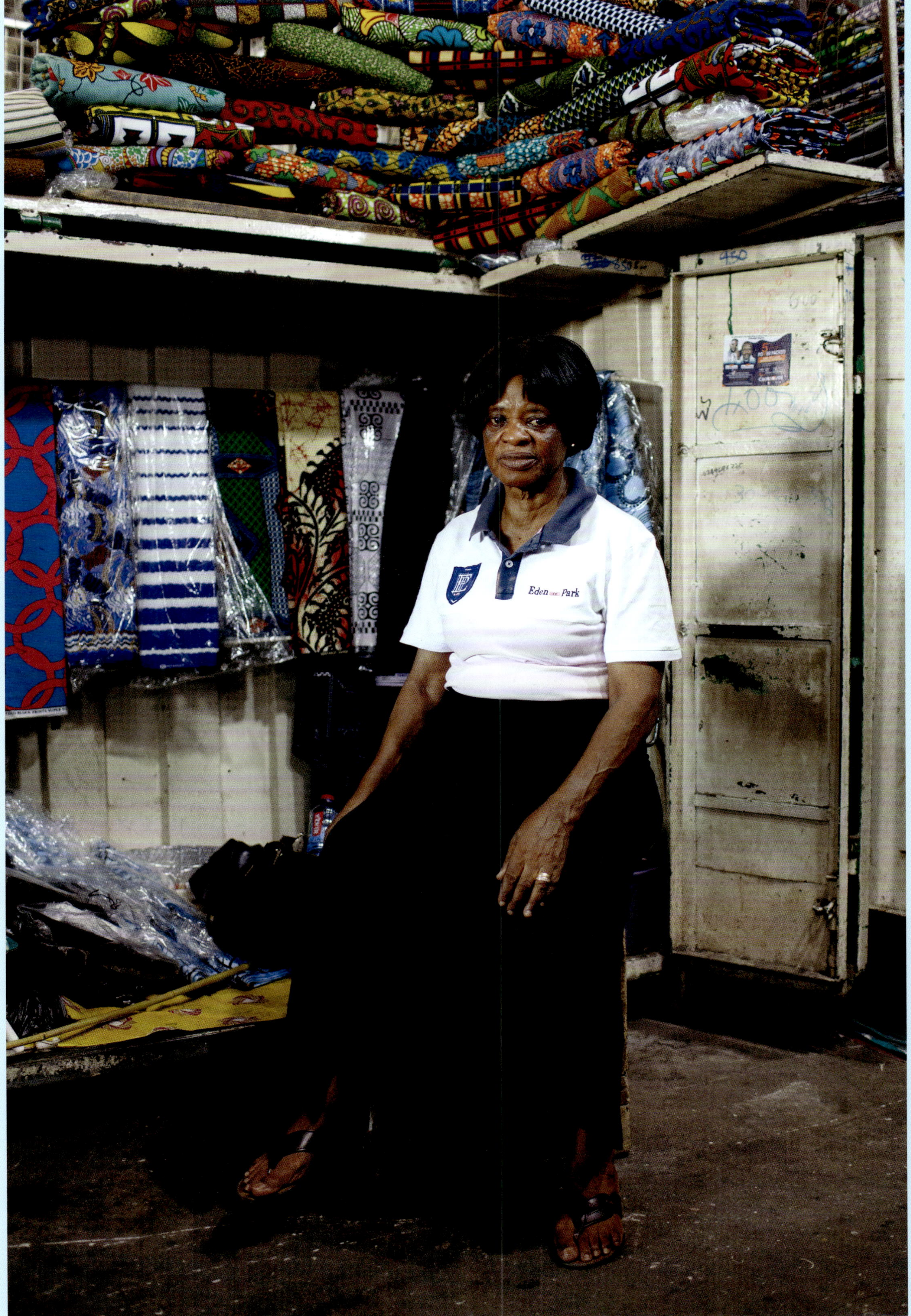

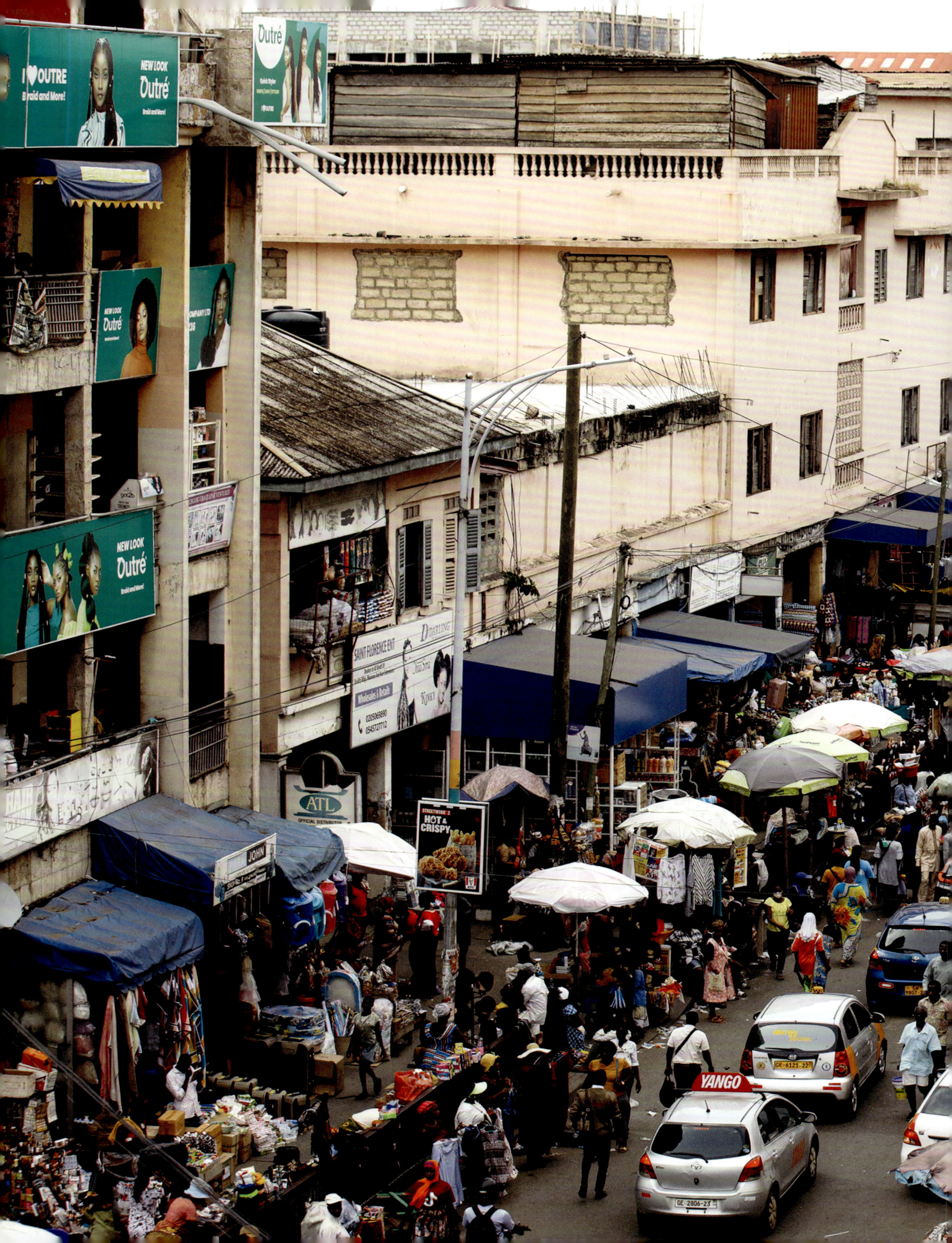

I ♥ OUTRÉ
Braid and More!
NEW LOOK
Outré
Braid and More!
Outré
Quick Styler
NEW LOOK
Outré
NEW LOOK
Outré
Braid and More!
SAINT FLORENCE ENT
DARLING
Wholesale & Retail
ATL
OFFICIAL DISTRIBUTOR
JOHN
STREETWISE 2
HOT & CRISPY
YANGO
GR-6123-22
GE-2806-23

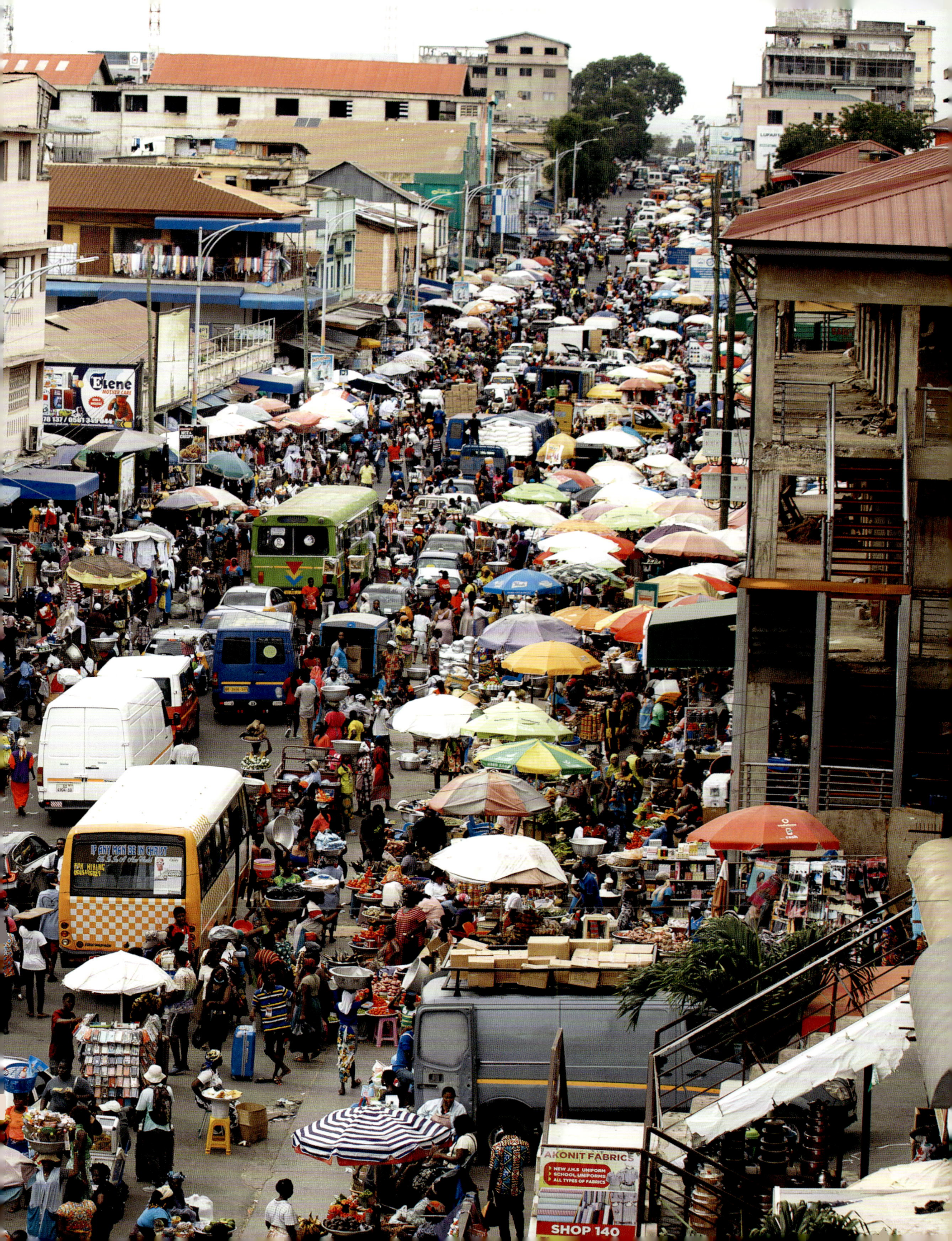

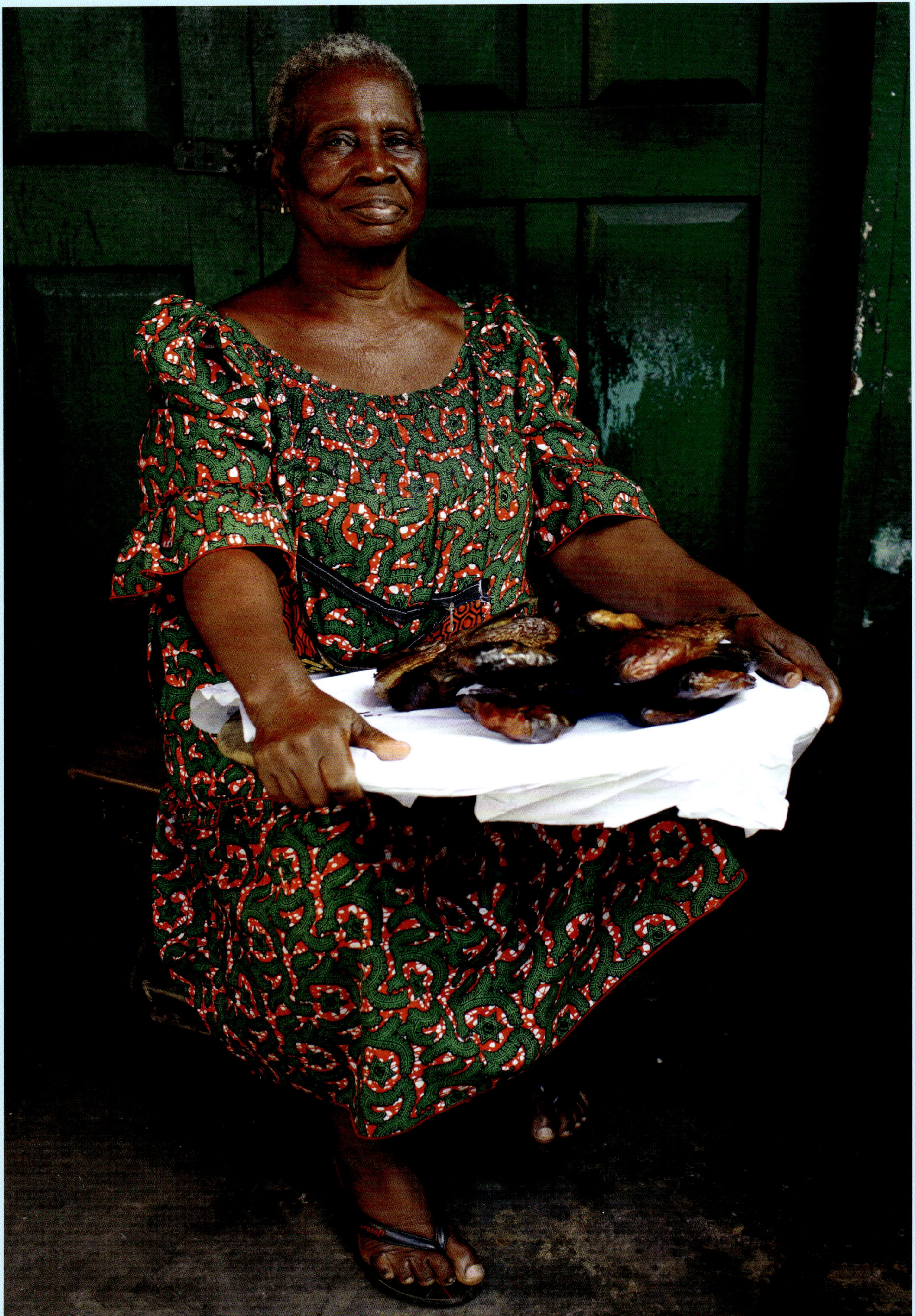

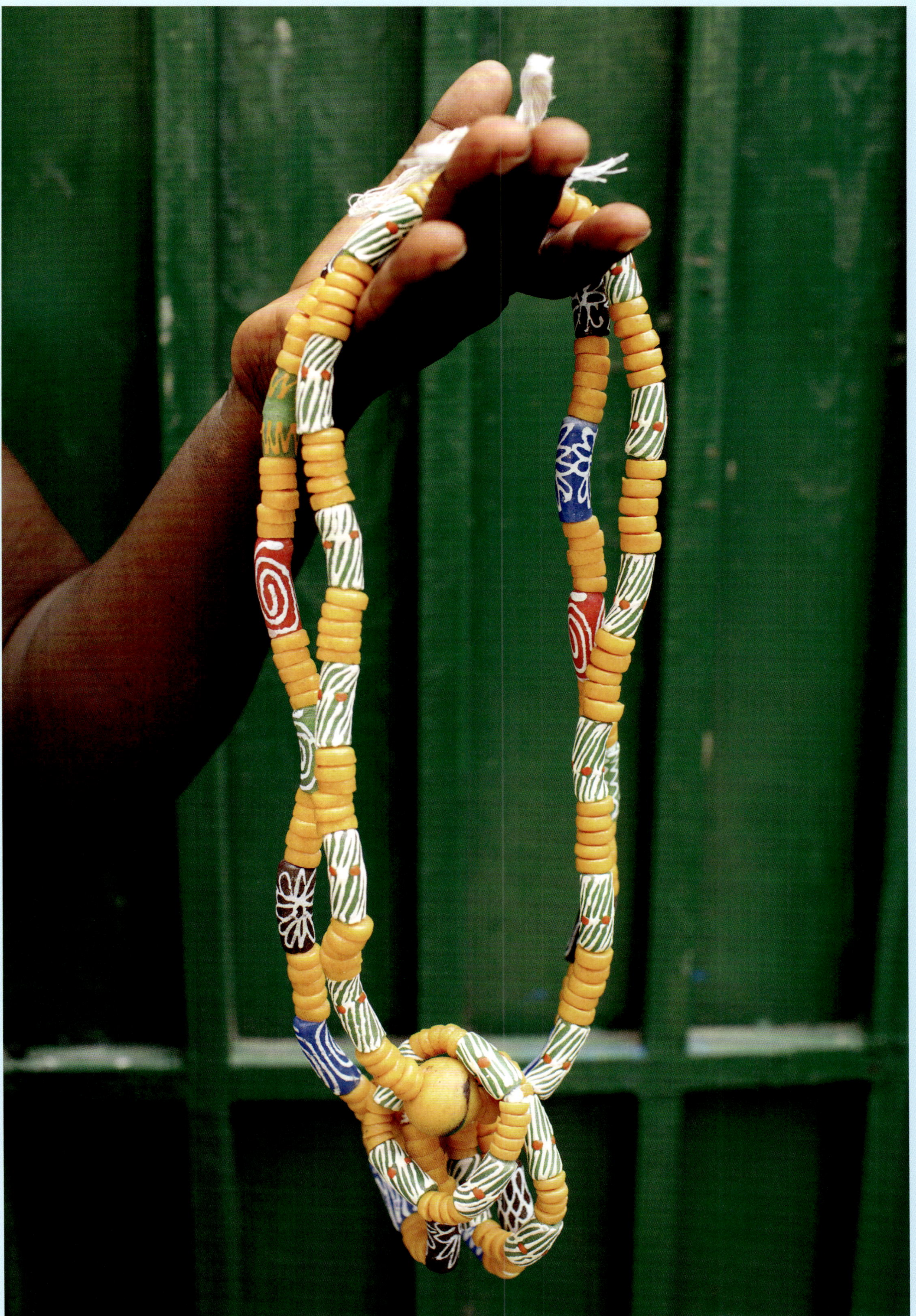

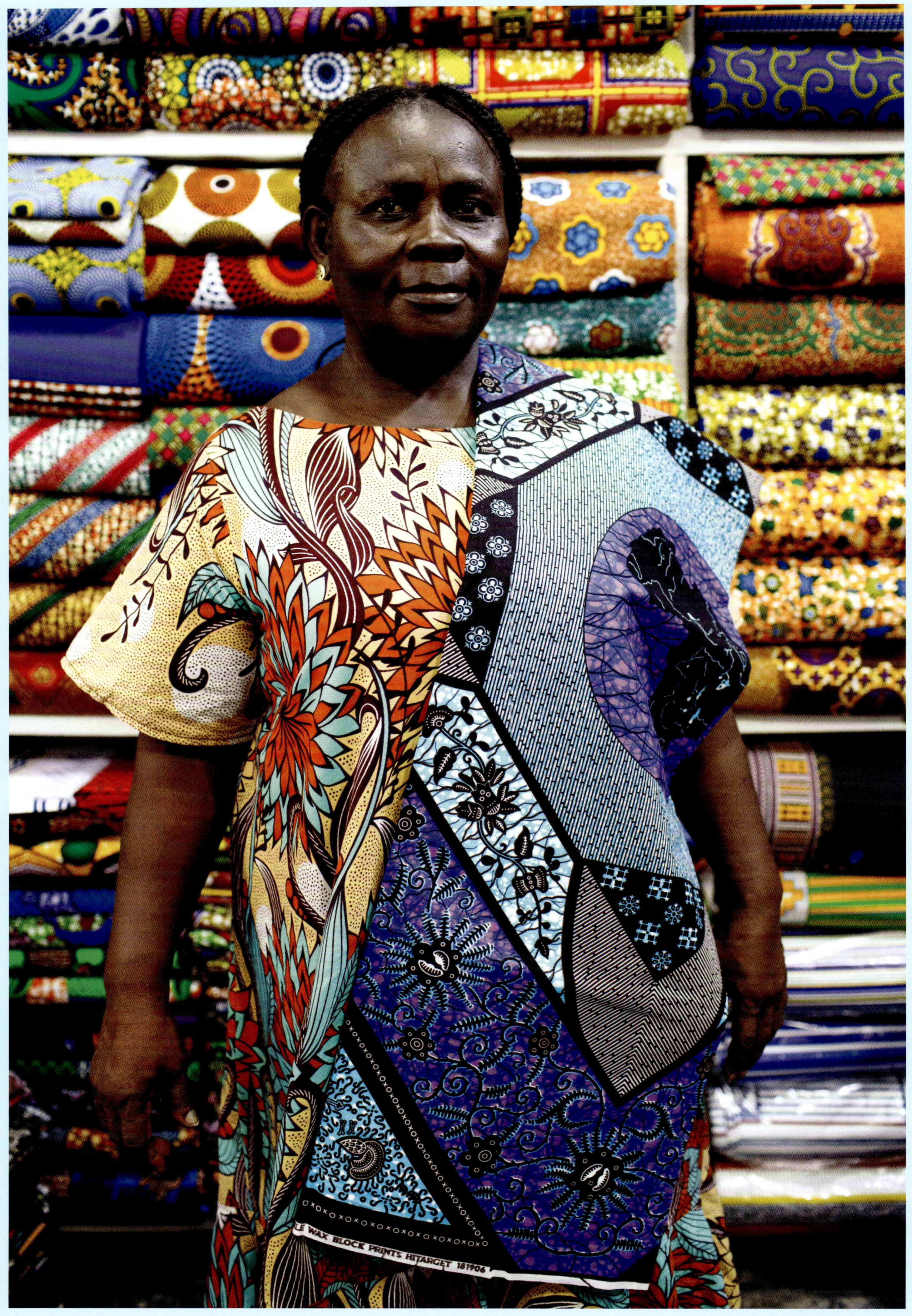

J WAX BLOCK PRINTS HITARGET 181906

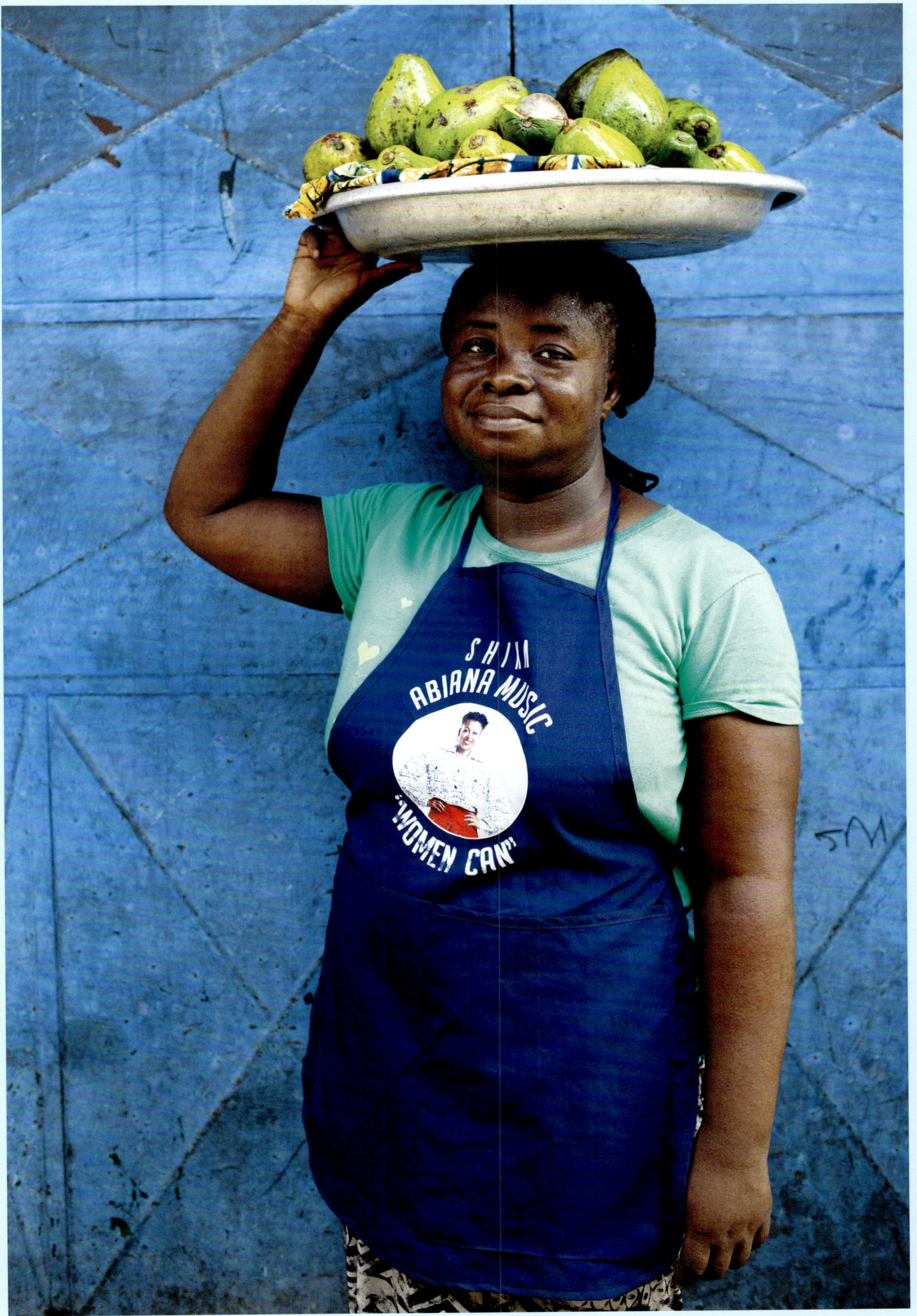
SHIM
ABIANA MUSIC
"WOMEN CAN"

# Lloyd Foster
## *Double Double*

**Nicole Acheampong**

Lloyd Foster's sculptures don't immediately reveal their full faces, which is typical of things that haunt. Last spring, at his solo exhibition at Anton Kern Gallery, in Midtown Manhattan, I had to tiptoe in some corners, crouch in others, to see the undersides of the sculptures that were floating closest to the rafters or the walls. The works are coy, but they're not too precious. They're made of insulation foam embellished with thick streaks of acrylic paint. One is draped in a mosquito net. Each has an inkjet print pasted to one side of the foam, photographs Foster took primarily in Ghana, his family's home country, a place that the artist—who was born in Washington, DC, and raised in Maryland—had never seen until his midtwenties.

Foster takes photographs for a simple reason: to document what he's observed, then return to it later. Before that first trip to Ghana, in 2015, he made street portraits in DC that are much like the ones he now uses for his mixed-media sculptures, black-and-white snapshots that don't differentiate between friends and strangers. Most depict young people posing casually or going about their daily lives. They squint or frown, or they stare beatifically. On their opposite side are crude painted faces, unnervingly gleeful. This series, titled *Double Double* (2023) and adapted for publication in this issue, is a scrapbook of scrambled memories, with images of disparate neighborhoods overlapping one another, and Foster's hand-painted intrusions sprouting from taxicabs, palm leaves, and the brow bones of watchful teenage boys. When installed, the sculptures dangle from the ceiling by thin strands of fishing wire. When you move among them, they move with you.

"I started to think of them as angels," Foster told me recently when we spoke at his studio in Queens, "people you meet in life and may, or may not, see again." That sense of a fragile encounter recalls the project's origin story: Foster's 2015 visit to Ghana was for the funeral of an uncle he didn't know well. Being introduced to Ghana via a traditional homegoing service means being immediately seeped in a unique brew of grief and jubilation. The artist's immersive installations, populated with photographs made on that trip and the many others he's taken since, are of a similar concoction. A gallery of his sculptures, text-filled drawings, and photographs most immediately recalls a busy Accra street, with youths, mothers, and motorcycles clumped in every corner. But it also has the frenzied gloom of a peroxide-bright shrine—not least because several of the artist's two-faced creatures have wings.

On his first Ghana trip, Foster had multiple uncanny encounters. He saw strangers passing by who looked like people he'd known growing up in Maryland. He went to the hometown of his mother, who had passed away when he was a child, and drove along the paths she'd walked when she was young. He took photographs of scenes that gave him déjà vu. "A mom holding her child's hand at the beach might remind me of me and my mom at the lake," he says. Certain silhouettes resonate in his work: the shape of a boy, a baby being cradled or held aloft.

One particular child reappears in multiple iterations, and his image seems like a totem: a small boy, lifted up by an obscure, painted-over figure. Moving through Foster's installation, you find this sculpture again and again. Sometimes, the figure that holds the boy is faceless; sometimes, it smiles mischievously. The boy is always wailing. The juxtaposition is as fragmentary, teasing, and intimate as a memory you can't shake, a place you keep returning to, the kind that moves with you.

All works from the series
*Double Double*, 2023.
**Mixed media**
Installation photographs by
Jason Mandella for *Aperture*.
Courtesy the artist and Anton
Kern Gallery, New York

Nicole Acheampong is a writer and editor whose work has appeared in *Aperture*, *The Atlantic*, and the *New York Review of Books*.

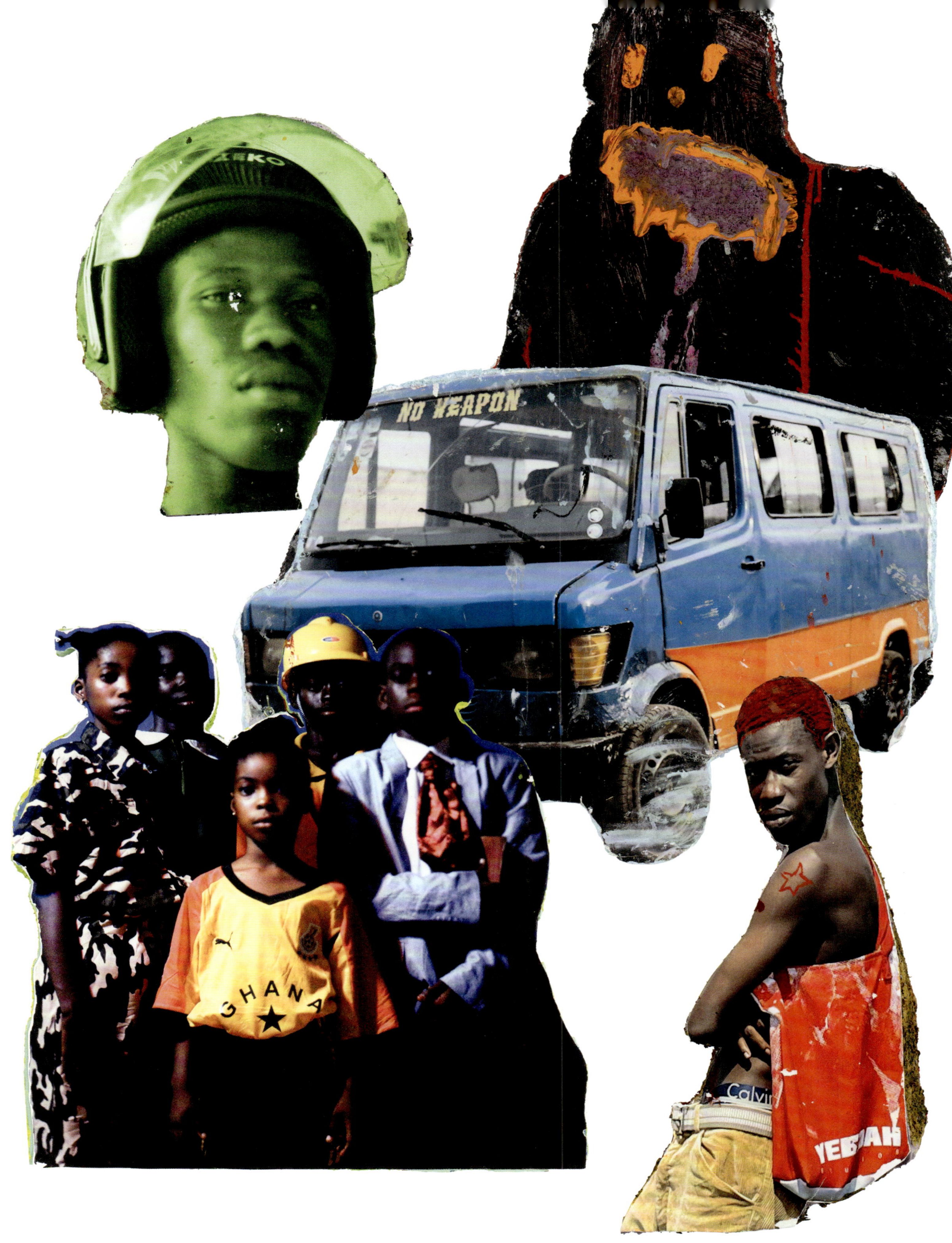

ELKO
NO WEAPON
GHANA
Calvin
YEBOAH

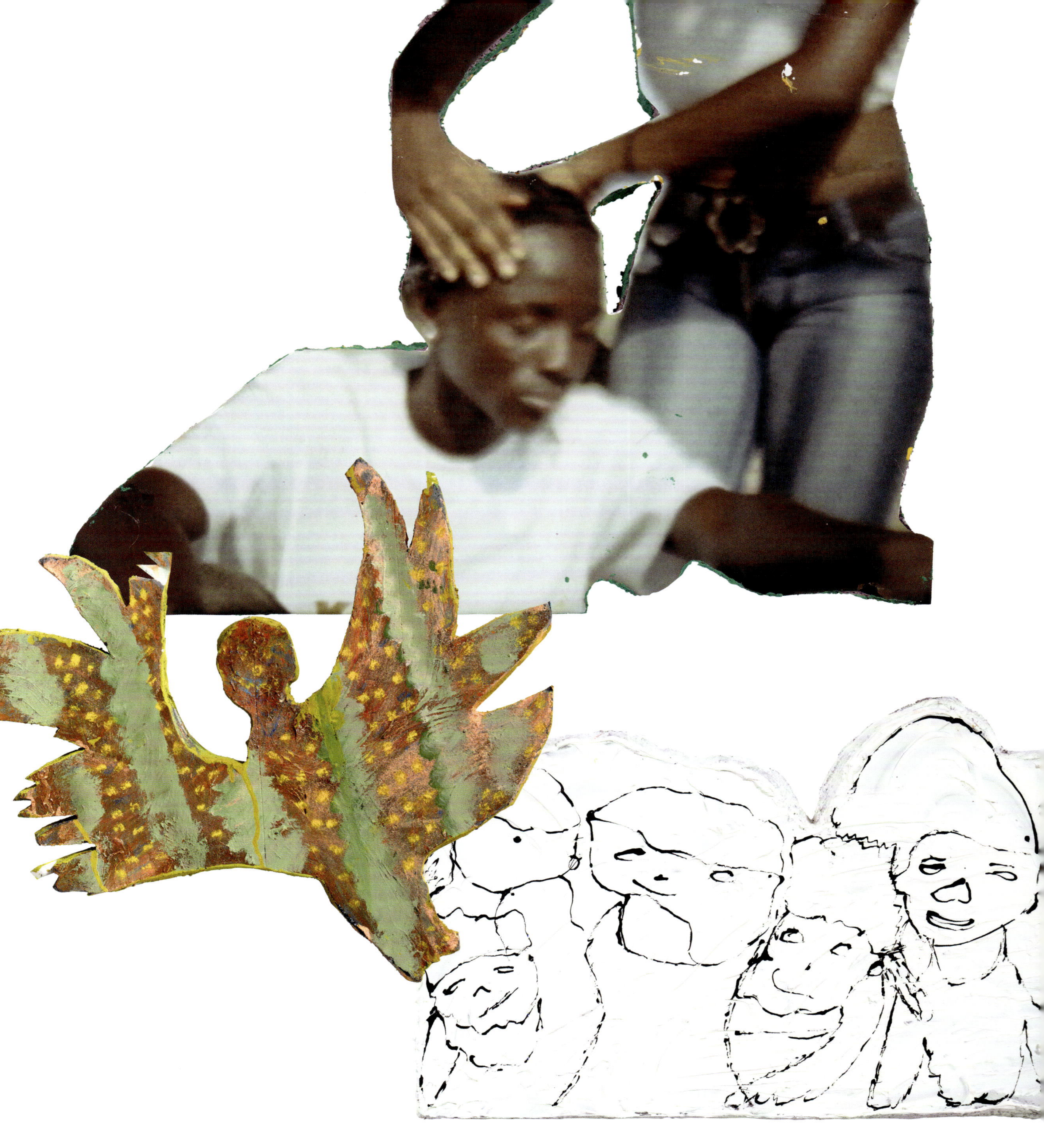

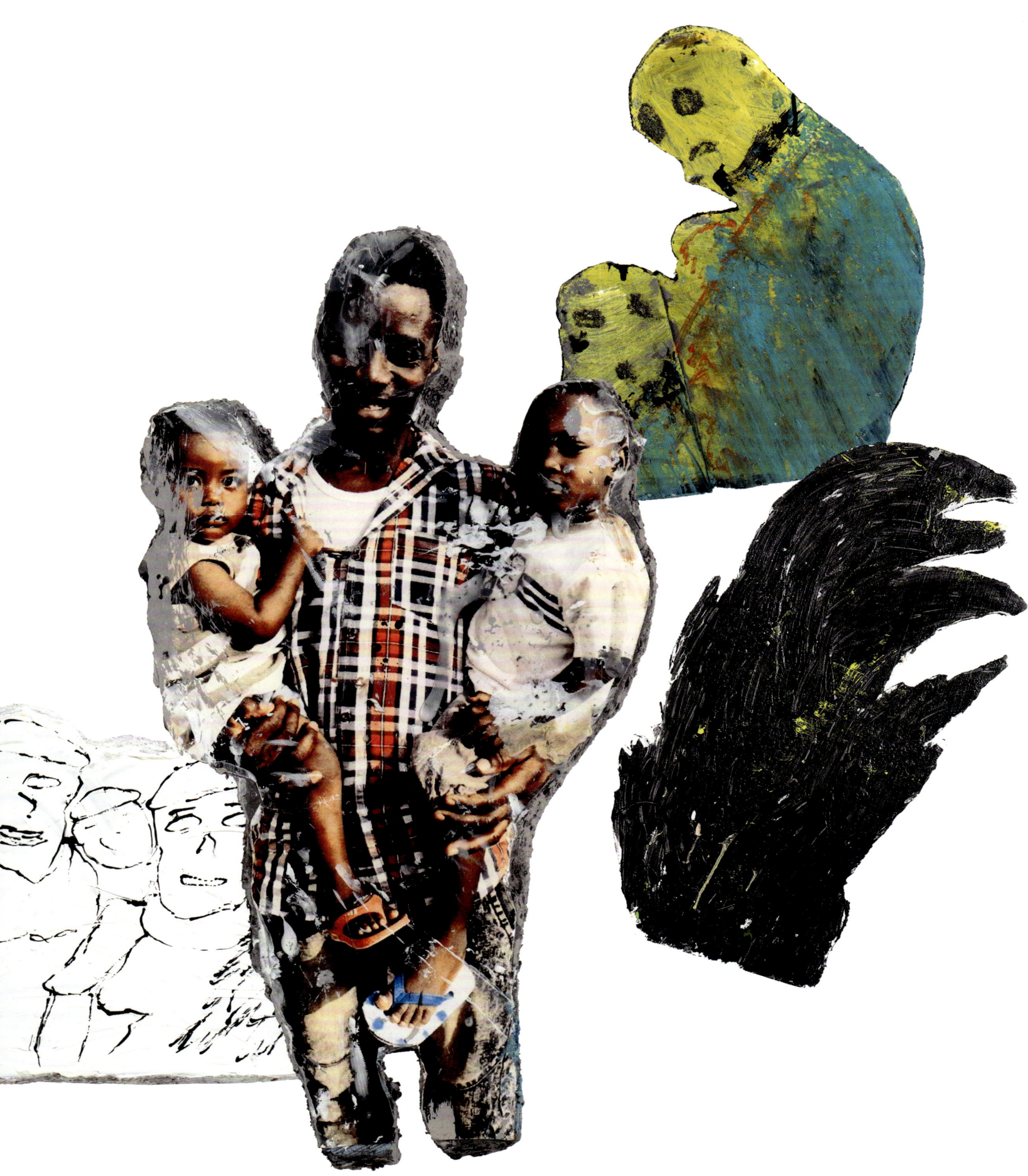

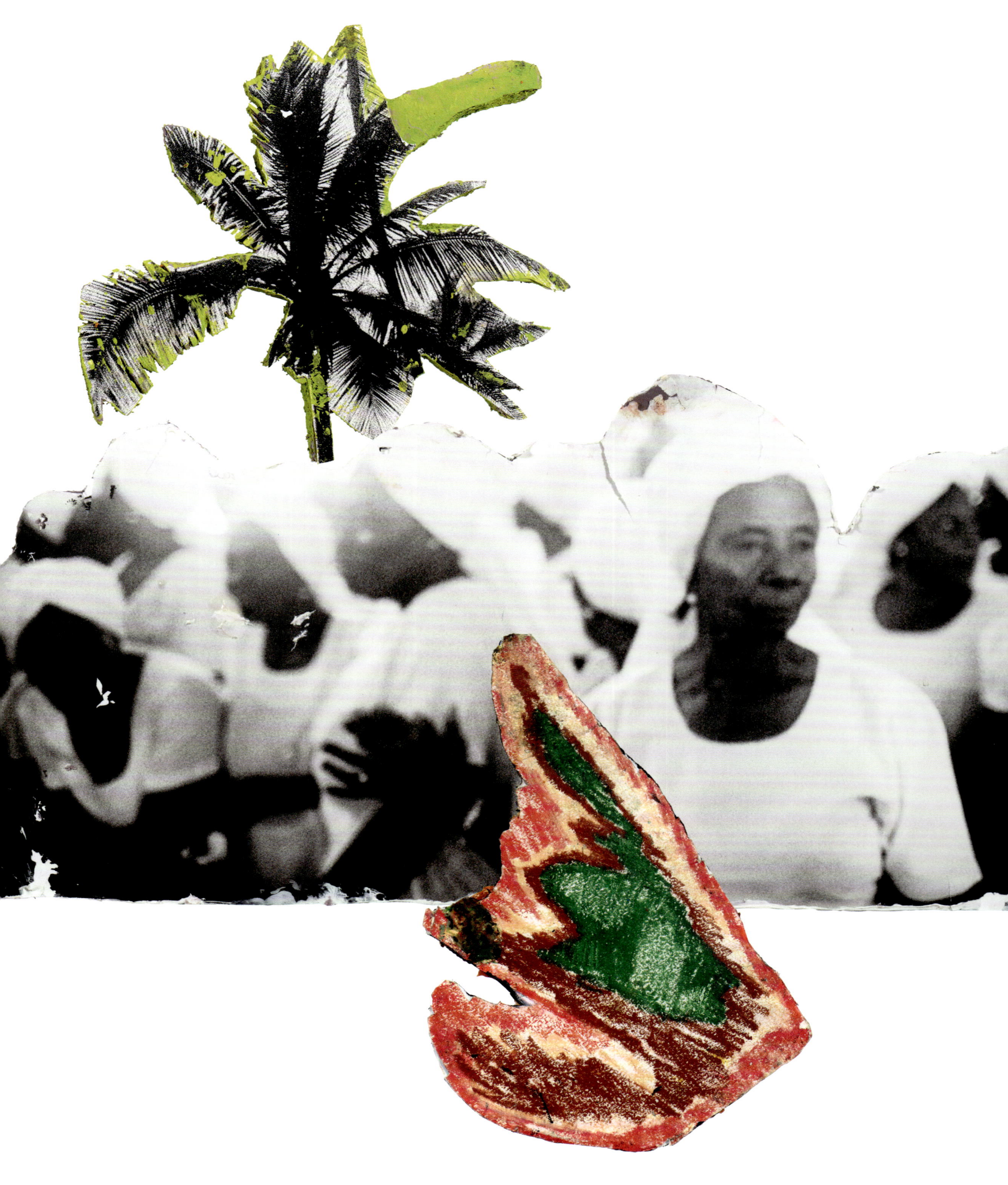

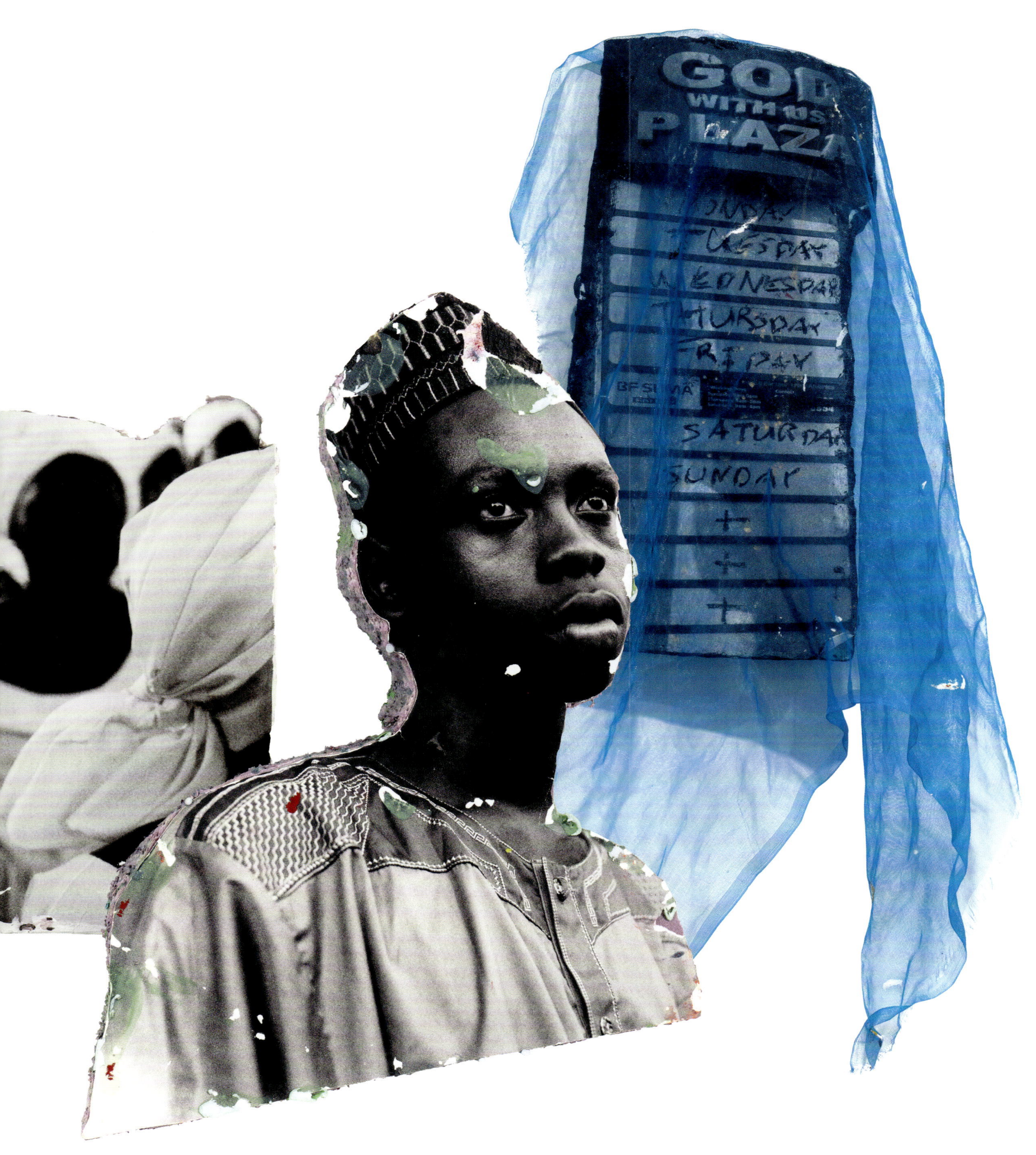
GOD
WITH US
PLAZA
TUESDAY
WEDNESDAY
THURSDAY
FRIDAY
SATURDAY
SUNDAY

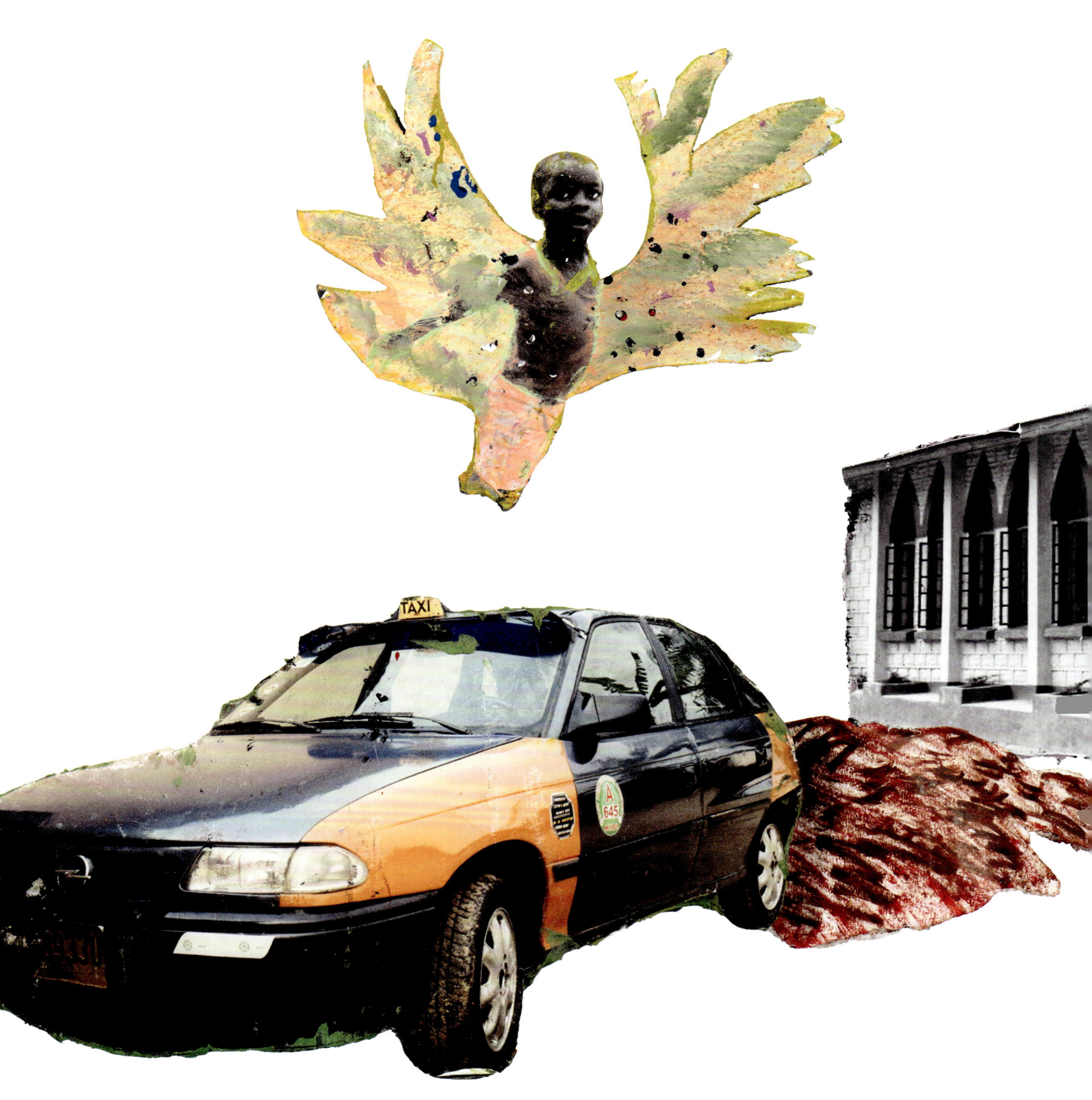

TAXI
A
645

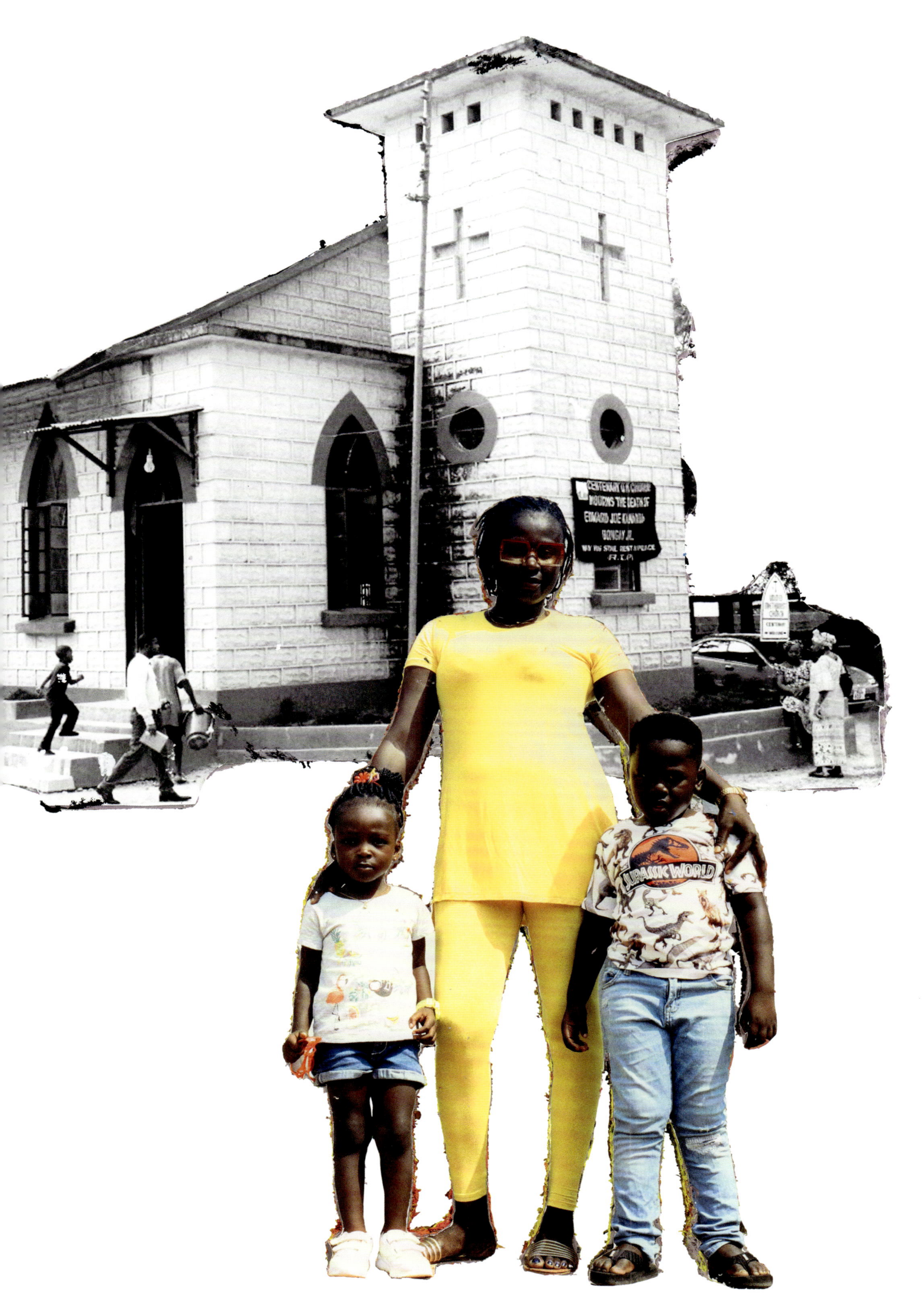

# A Library for the Future

How the Dikan Center has become an oasis for Accra's photography community.
**Ama Benewaa Tawiah**

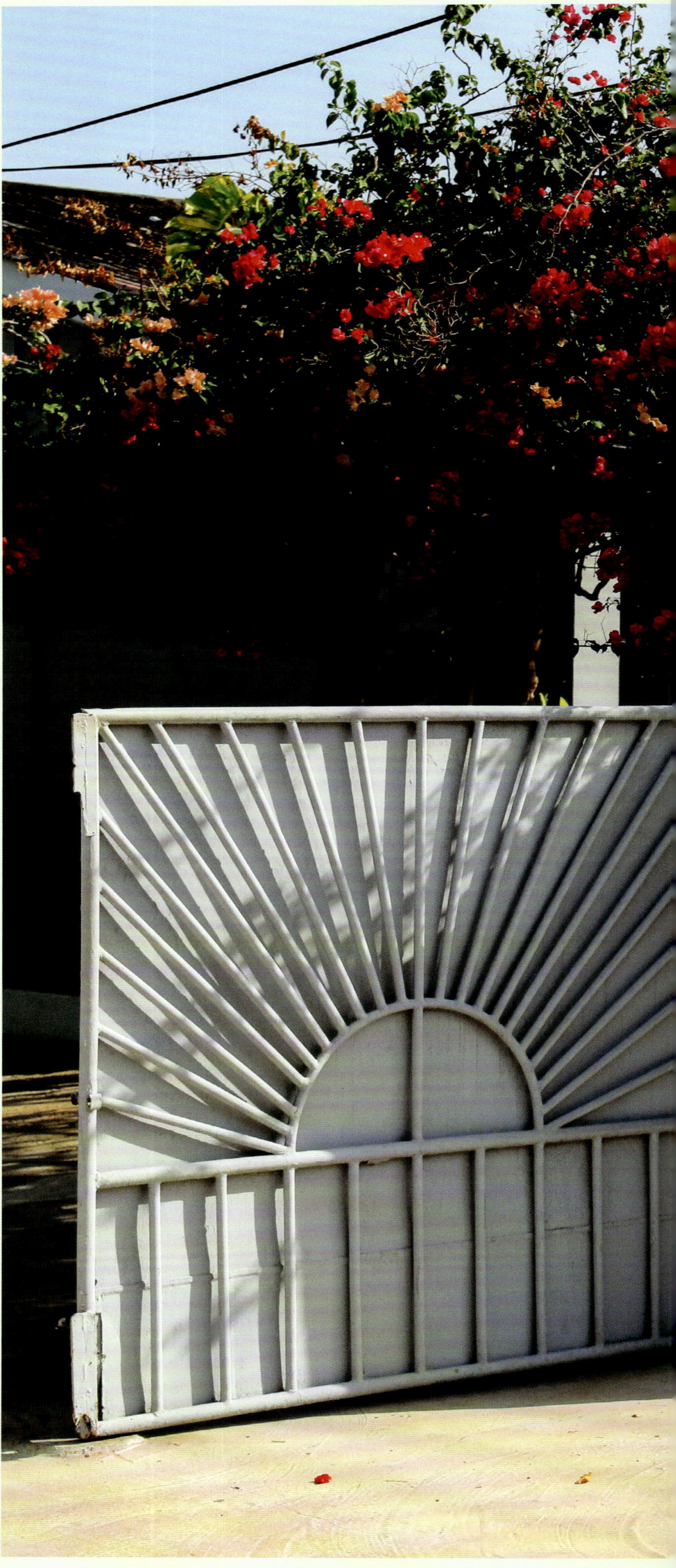

One recent Friday morning, in the library at the Dikan Center, Nana Asomani and his friend and colleague Tiana switched from looking at their computer screens to conversations about some work on which they are collaborating. Both had traveled from different parts of Accra to experience the newly opened photography center. At least once a week, they visit to flip through the thousands of books organized floor to ceiling in the center's impressive library. It is an oasis in a city as fast-paced and noisy as Accra—not long ago, this institution existed only as an idea.

In the last few years, the cultural scene in Ghana has witnessed enormous growth thanks to initiatives by individuals, collectives, and the government. The contemporary art world has expanded with the emergence of spaces such as the Savannah Centre for Contemporary Art; its sister institutions, Red Clay and Nkrumah Voli-ni, in the northern town of Tamale; Artemartis, an Accra-based contemporary art collective and agency; and Accra's artist-run Compound House Gallery, which supports and promotes contemporary art practices in Ghana. Recently, in December 2022, the internationally known painter Amoako Boafo opened dot.ateliers in Accra. This multipurpose three-story structure,

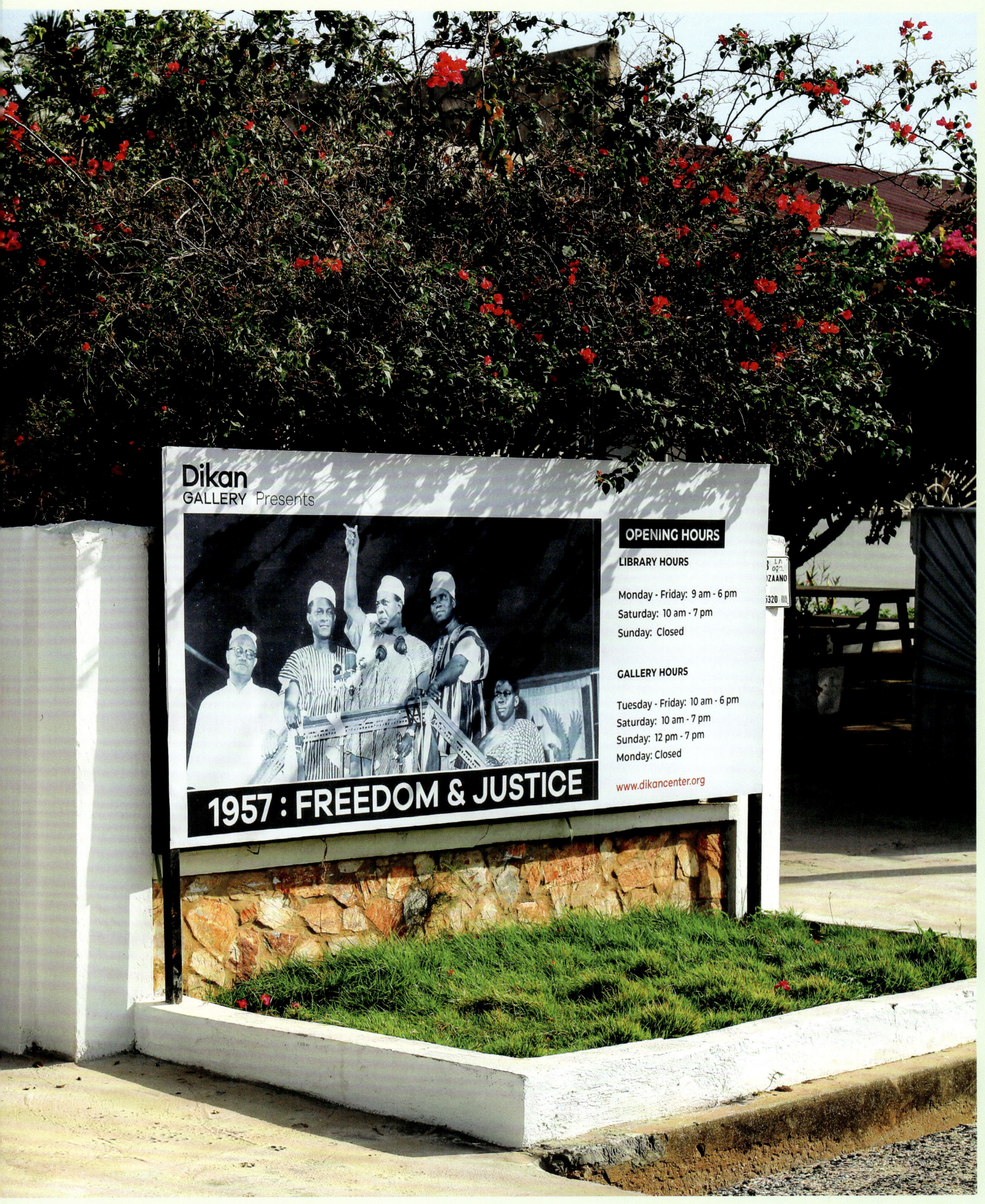

Dikan
GALLERY Presents
OPENING HOURS
LIBRARY HOURS
Monday - Friday: 9 am - 6 pm
Saturday: 10 am - 7 pm
Sunday: Closed
GALLERY HOURS
Tuesday - Friday: 10 am - 6 pm
Saturday: 10 am - 7 pm
Sunday: 12 pm - 7 pm
Monday: Closed
www.dikancenter.org
1957 : FREEDOM & JUSTICE

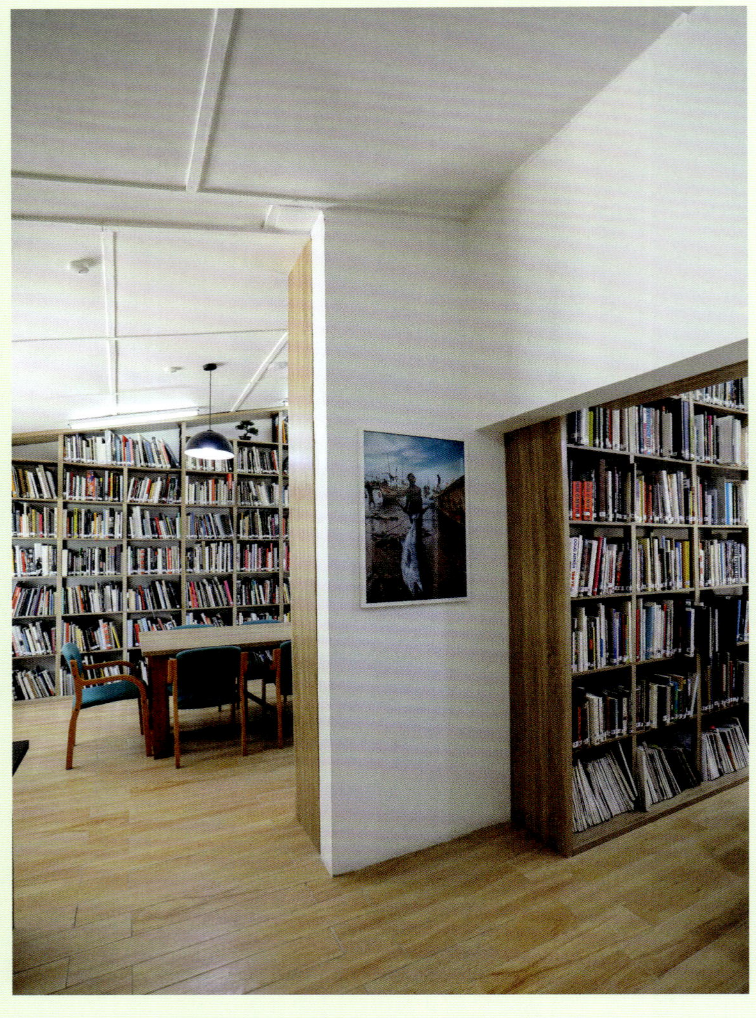

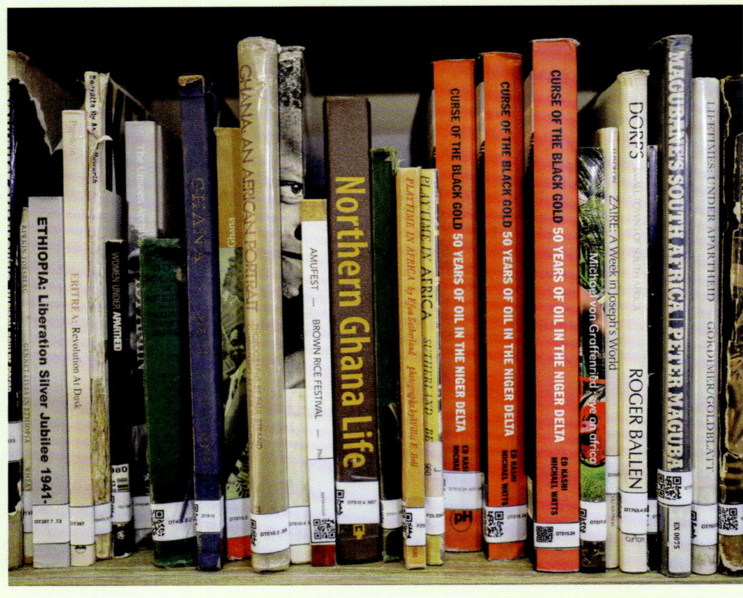

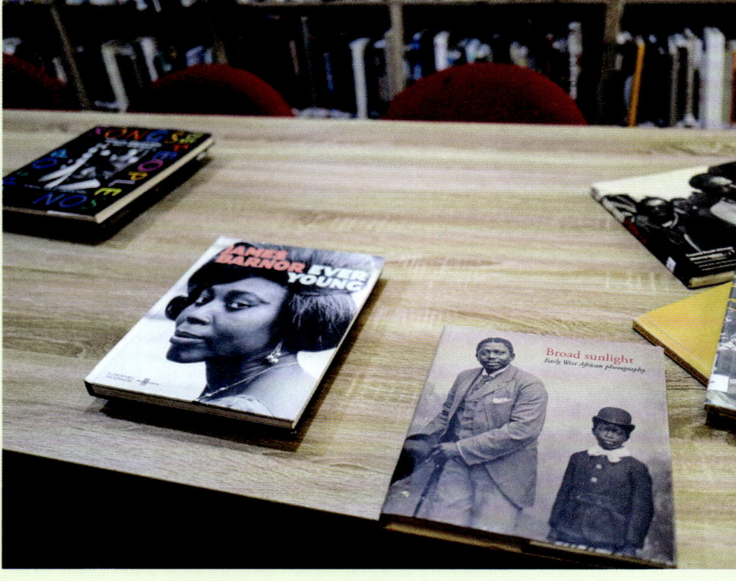

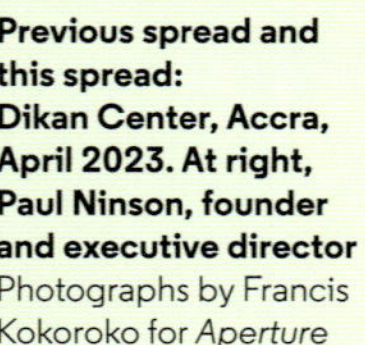

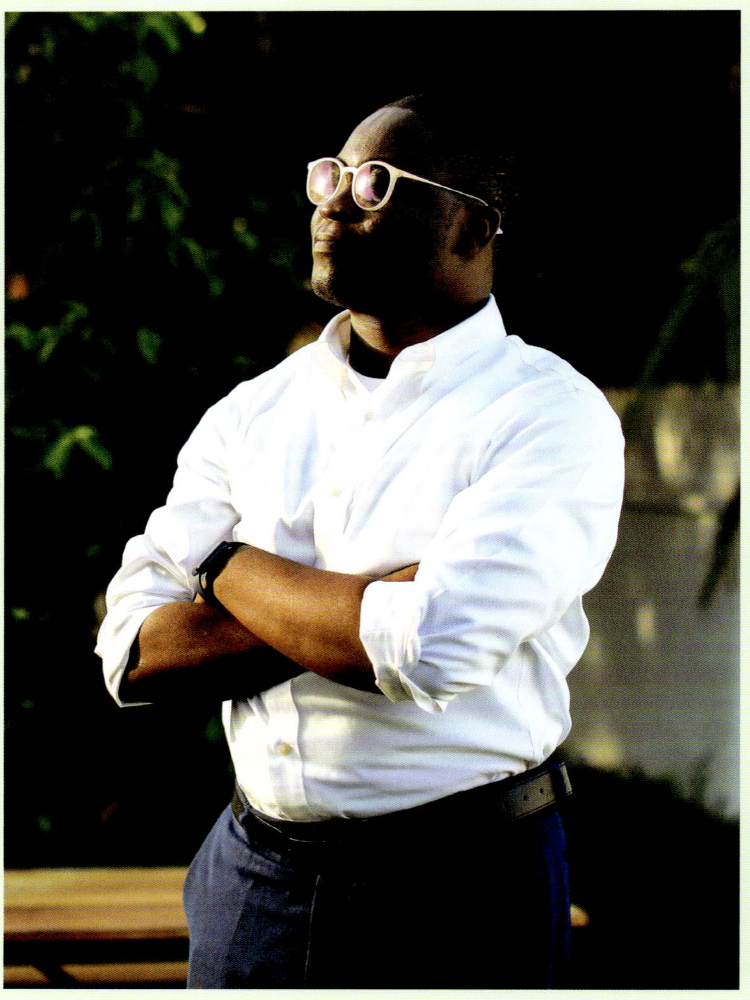

**Previous spread and
this spread:
Dikan Center, Accra,
April 2023. At right,
Paul Ninson, founder
and executive director**
Photographs by Francis
Kokoroko for *Aperture*

down the road from the Dikan Center, houses a studio, gallery, café, and library, as well as a space for art residencies.

The Ga people of Greater Accra say "*loo pii fiteee wonu*," which translates as "too much meat does not spoil the soup." This idea explains why the creation of the Dikan Center is exciting—the institution adds variety to the growing number of artistic spaces the country's creative community needs. It expands on existing projects outside of Accra, such as the Nuku Studio's Center for Photographic Research and Practice, established in 2015 by the photographer Nii Obodai and formally opened in Tamale in 2018. The studio is famous for the Nuku Photo Festival Ghana, which gathers both local and international image makers and visual artists of all levels. A recent photography exhibition there focused on life in northern Ghana and presented a range of photographers.

*Dikan*, an expression from Twi, one of many Ghanaian languages, means "take the lead," which is something the center's founder, Paul Ninson, appears keen to do. In 2019, while studying at the school of the International Center of Photography, New York, Ninson decided to set up Dikan. At that time, he was collecting photography books in the United States, an endeavor that grew into a vision of building a photography library in Ghana to share with young people carving their own paths as image makers. The library project, funded via a crowdfunding campaign organized by Brandon Stanton, founder of the popular Instagram account Humans of New York, required the shipping of thousands of books from the United States to Accra. (There are an estimated thirty thousand books owned by the center.)

The Dikan Center, which in addition to its library also functions as a studio, a classroom for photography workshops, and an exhibition space, officially opened in December 2022 with *Ahennie*, a photography exhibition featuring images by Ninson

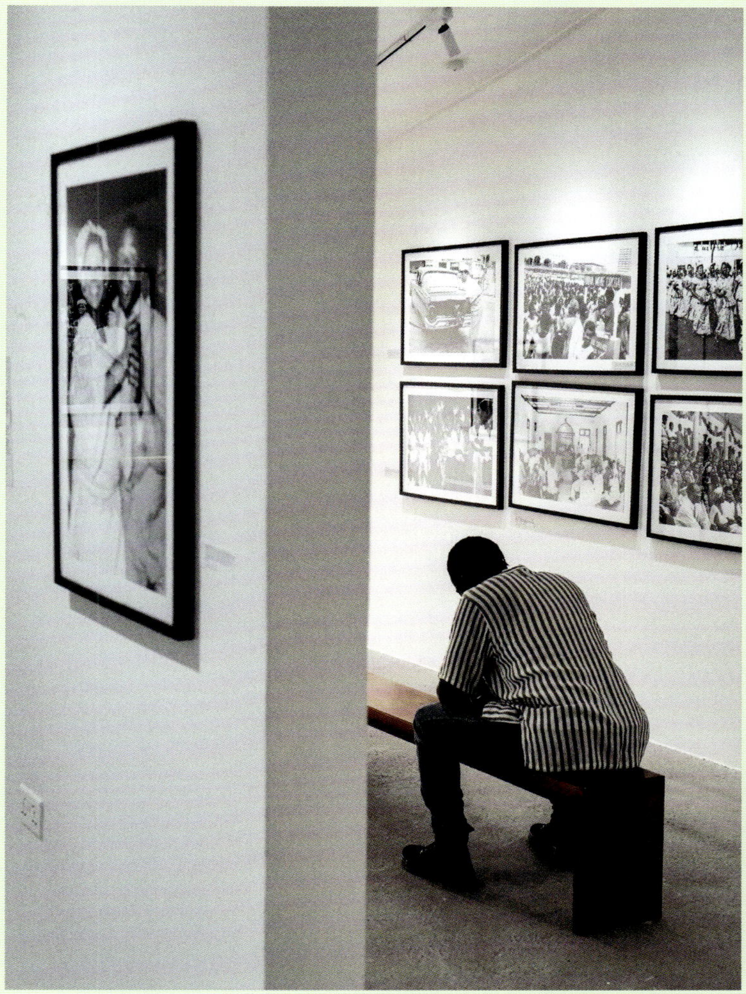

## *Dikan* means "take the lead," which is something the center's founder, Paul Ninson, appears keen to do.

and Emmanuel Bobbie, affectionately known as Bob Pixel. Two months prior, the center soft-launched with Bob Pixel's first solo exhibition, a retrospective titled *Wo Nim Biribi?* (Asante Twi for "Do you know something?"), which celebrated the life and work of the affable photographer, who passed away in 2021. Last March, the center opened *1957: Freedom & Justice*, an exhibition commemorating sixty-six years of Ghana's independence from British rule, where visitors heard E. T. Mensah's "Ghana Freedom" and the famous "At long last, Ghana is free forever" portion of Kwame Nkrumah's independence declaration speech playing on a loop through the speakers connected to a video piece. On the white walls were framed photographs from the 1957 Independence Day celebrations in different parts of the country.

The center's work seems to just be getting started, and photographers are taking advantage of the opportunities offered for education, exhibitions, and research. There are hardly any places like Dikan in Accra. The photographer Ernest Ankomah imagines that the space, beyond exhibiting work by members of Ghana's creative community, might someday serve as a repository for his works, "preserving them for future generations to enjoy." He reckons that as Africa's biggest photography library, Dikan is a "vital resource to gauge the extent to which the African story has been told."

Soon, Dikan will host film screenings and social events aimed at gathering the city's visual-arts community together. The organization will also roll out programs and workshops. The first of them, Women Picturing Africa, a women-only workshop with the photographer Jessica Sarkodie, was held last spring. Ninson hopes that through such collaborations, with artists both in Ghana and beyond, young people can gain a visual education and take charge of telling African stories.

**Ama Benewaa Tawiah is a writer based in Accra.**

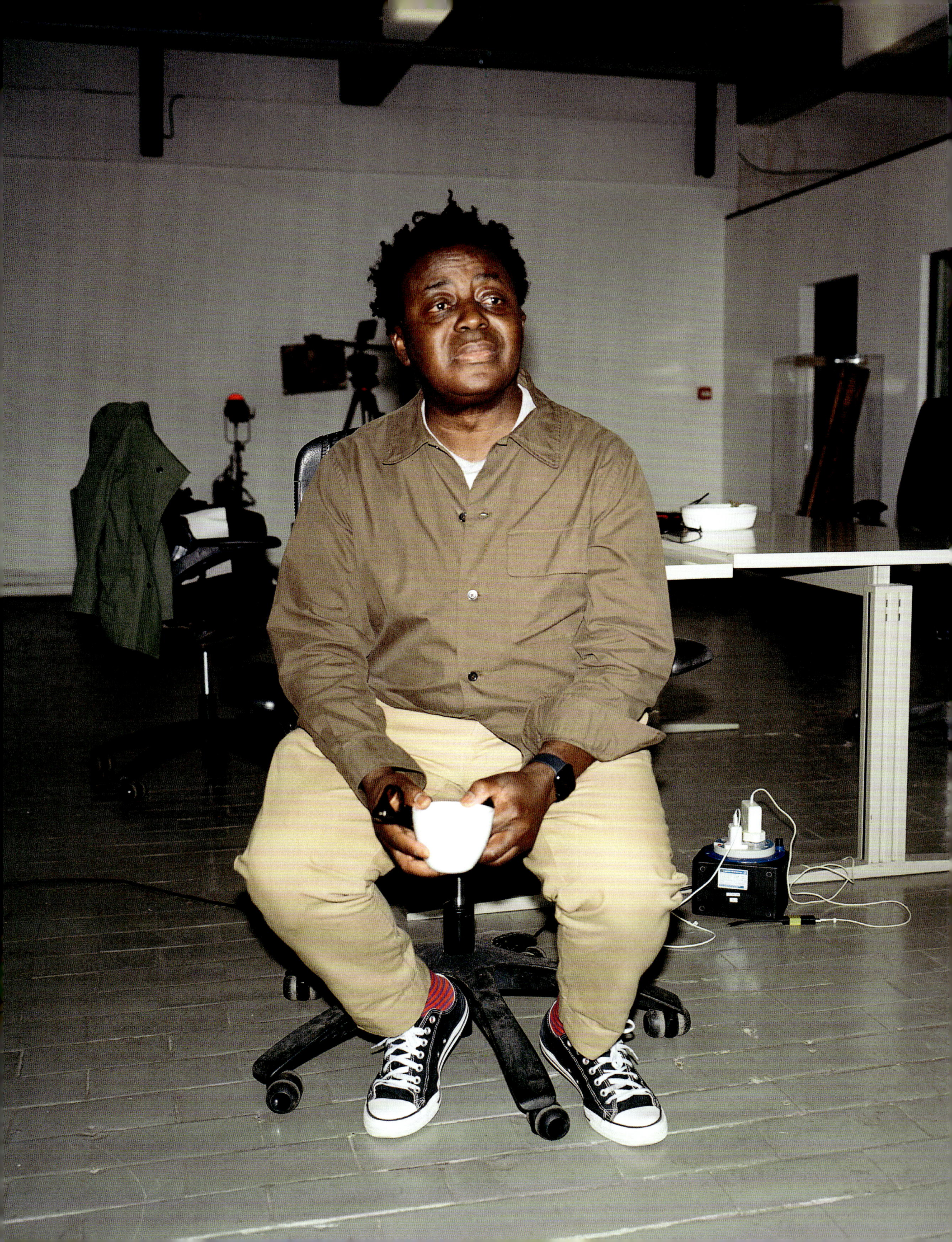

# John Akomfrah
# The Door of Memory

**A Conversation with Vanessa Peterson and Lyle Ashton Harris**

For more than four decades, John Akomfrah has sought to tell myriad tales of migration and belonging. Akomfrah left Ghana for the UK as a young child after the country's first president, Kwame Nkrumah, was overthrown in the 1966 coup, which put his activist mother's life in danger. In a 2012 interview for *The Guardian*, Akomfrah stated that his father's death was due in part to the turmoil and "struggle leading up to the coup." In 1982, he and a group of peers cofounded the organization Black Audio Film Collective. Inspired and energized by the work of theorists such as Paul Gilroy and Stuart Hall, the collective addressed landmark moments in British history with an astute critical gaze, connecting the discrimination that migrants to England faced to the malaise and postindustrial decline of the country.

After the collective dissolved in 1998, Akomfrah continued to write and direct films and video essays, including the three-screen installation *The Unfinished Conversation* (2012) and *The Stuart Hall Project* (2013), both based on the life and work of the pioneering postcolonial scholar. In 2019, Akomfrah was one of six artists invited to show at Ghana's first-ever pavilion at the Venice Biennale, and in 2024 he will represent Great Britain at the international event. Akomfrah's practice and oeuvre is testament to the notion of hybridity: his project is to name the political ghosts and specters that haunt the present day, to confront complex histories—no matter how violent or gruesome—and tackle the bad spirits. Last spring, Akomfrah spoke from London with the writer Vanessa Peterson and the artist Lyle Ashton Harris about the dialogues between Ghana and its diaspora.

Vanessa Peterson: **An interesting place to start would be to talk about your first narrative feature film, *Testament* (1988), which was shot in Ghana and England. The film follows Abena, a political exile who returns to Ghana after the overthrow of Ghana's first president, Kwame Nkrumah, to interview the German director Werner Herzog, who is also in the country, shooting *Cobra Verde*. Abena also seeks to reunite with her former political colleagues. I'd be curious to know what led you to making *Testament*, and the origins of the film.**

**John Akomfrah:** The paradox of the film was that even though I am the most Ghanaian of Ghanaians—born in the year of independence, parents were anticolonial activists completely committed to that project of the transfer of power, both political and cultural—even though all of that was me, and continues to be me, I hadn't really thought about making that film. I, like the character, was in flight from that subject, for all kinds of emotional and psychic reasons. But it was inescapable at a certain point. Even though you might suppose that the reluctance to engage with Ghana was a reluctance to engage with Africa in general, that was the very opposite of the case. I had been tracking and following African cinema and its histories for many years.

I was in Ouagadougou for the Pan African Film Festival when a number of other filmmakers, Haile Gerima being one of them, said to me: "Did you know that Werner Herzog is in Ghana making a film? What are you doing sitting here? Why don't you go and make one, rather than allowing that guy to do your story?" I was like, "Okay. I'm not sure he's going to do my story, but I get the point." It was really via Pan-Africanism that I returned to the nation, and very specifically, it was the urgings of other filmmakers who were all part of that Pan-African movement that took me there.

**Lyle Ashton Harris:** I saw *Testament* when you showed it at CalArts. It seems prescient, if you think about the book *White Malice: The CIA and the Covert Recolonization of Africa* (2021) by Susan Williams, who writes about the Cold War–era involvement of the United States in assassinations and coups

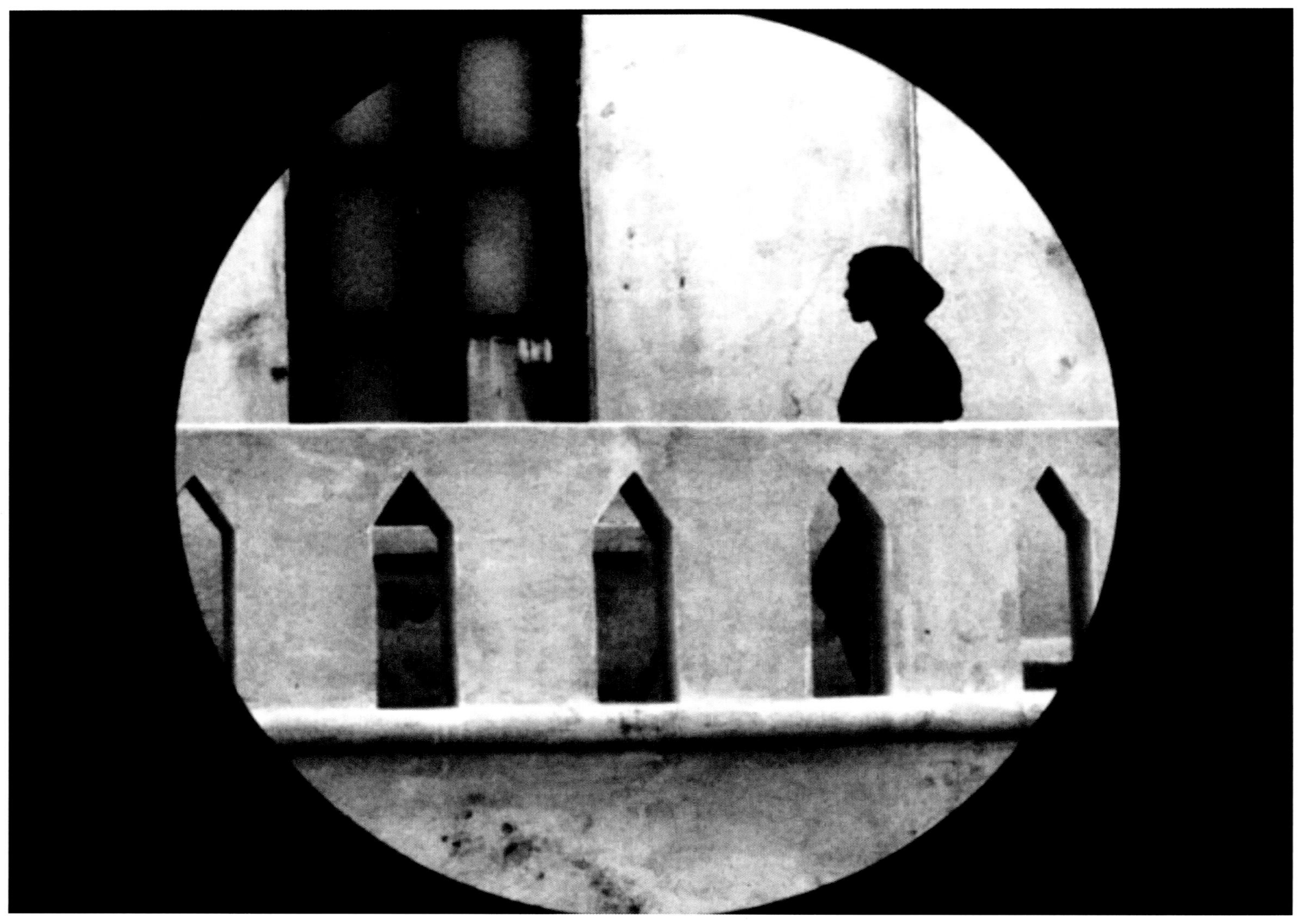

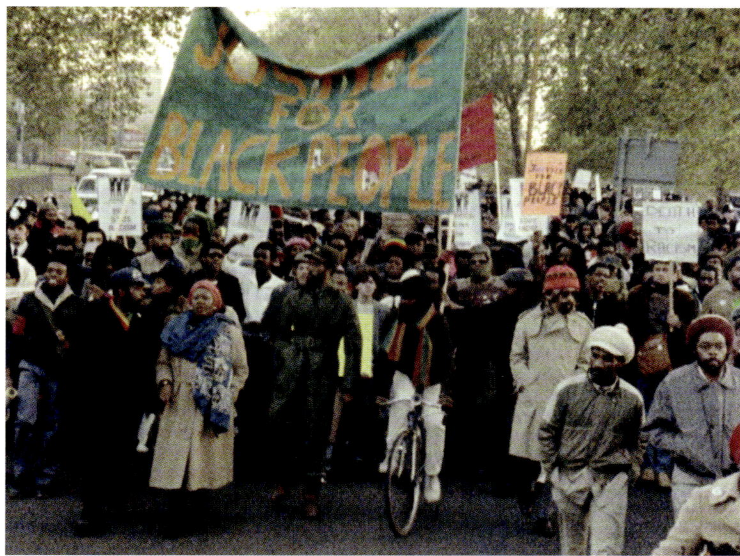

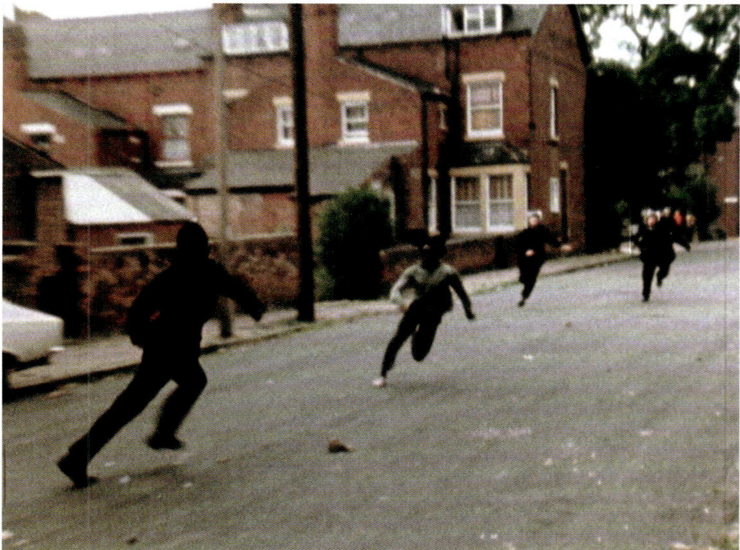

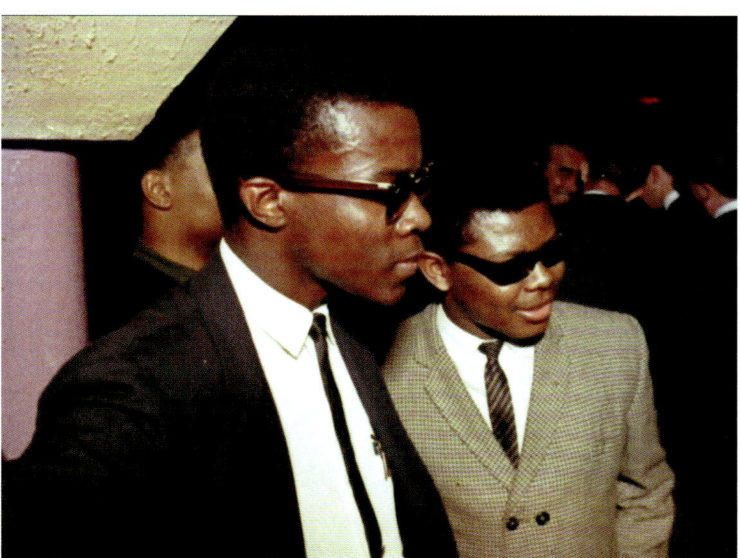

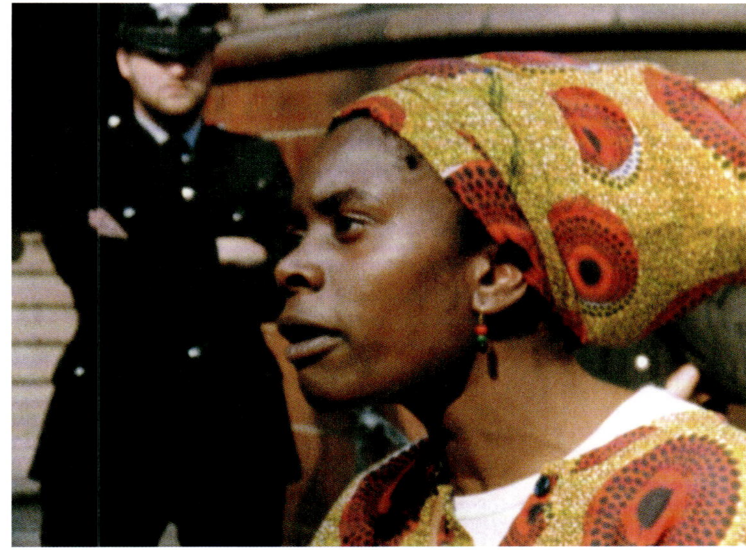



in newly independent African states. You address a lot of similar themes.

**JA:** One of the reasons for avoiding the subject was precisely to do with the terrain that *White Malice* covers. There were a number of living rooms in that African revolution, and I happened to be in probably the epicenter of the living rooms, because both my parents were involved with it, working for the Convention People's Party, founded by Nkrumah in 1944. My mother was at the university, the ideological institute that the film deals with. Many of the subjects later covered by Susan Williams were ones I was intimately familiar with. For instance, I remember having a conversation with my mom in the '70s when I first read Malcolm X's autobiography. She must have seen it on my desk. She said, "Oh, you're reading Malcolm X?" I said, "Yeah." She said, "Oh, I knew him." That blew me away.

Since the '70s, I had known that there were these forces at play on our continent, and specifically in Ghana. I didn't want to go there.

**VP: *Testament* makes me think of autofiction—it's fictional, but it's also playing on deeply biographical elements. Sometimes it's the only way to tell a story, especially one filled with pain and dislocation. To me, that is what writing and directing *Testament* was for you. Did you feel it was a way for you to reckon with your familial circumstances, as well as the legacies of Ghana's turbulent politics? To guard against a sense of amnesia that comes with the passing of time?**

**JA:** Yes, of course. What's been odd for me since we made it in 1987 is that it became a kind of subgenre of African filmmaking. This "returning" film. There were so many films afterward of people returning for one reason or another.

**LAH:** Such as *Sankofa* by Haile Gerima. In actuality, you anticipated his film.

**JA:** Yes. That's very odd. I hadn't even thought about that. But it is true. Including the grandmaster Haile himself. Basically,

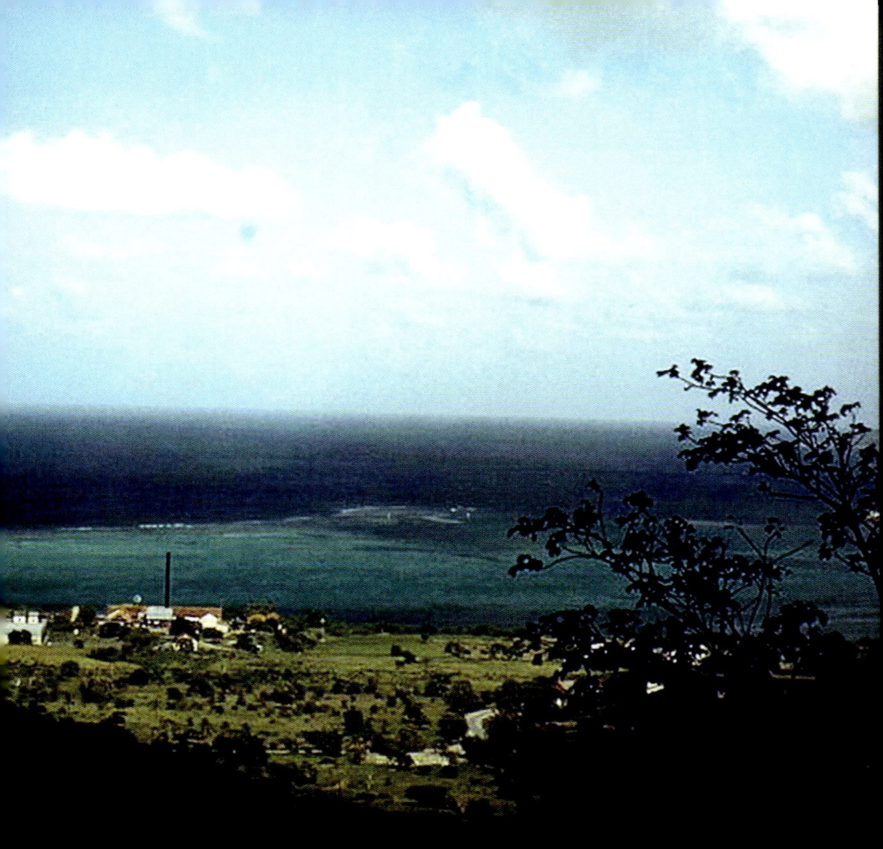

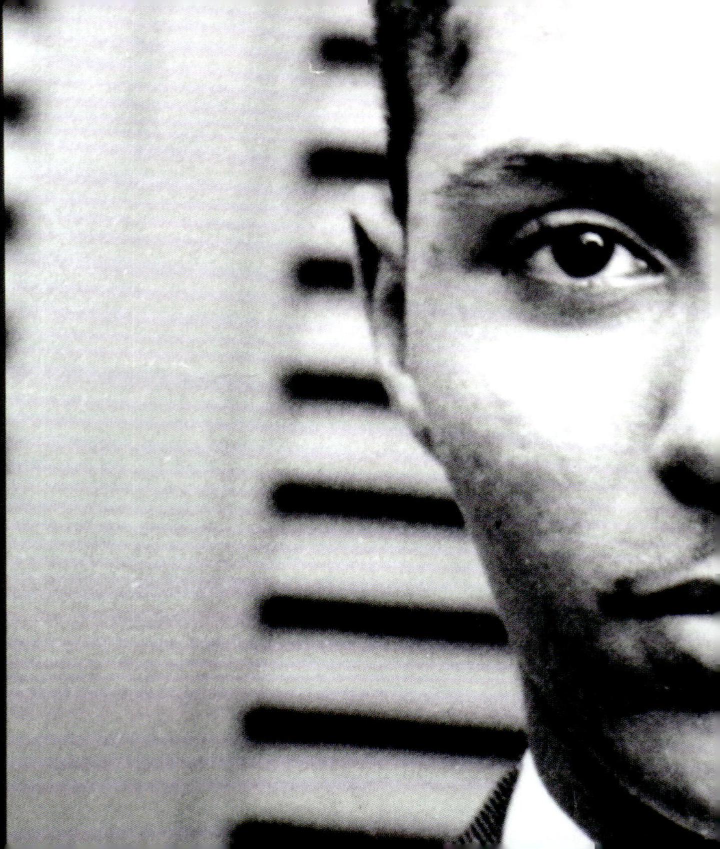

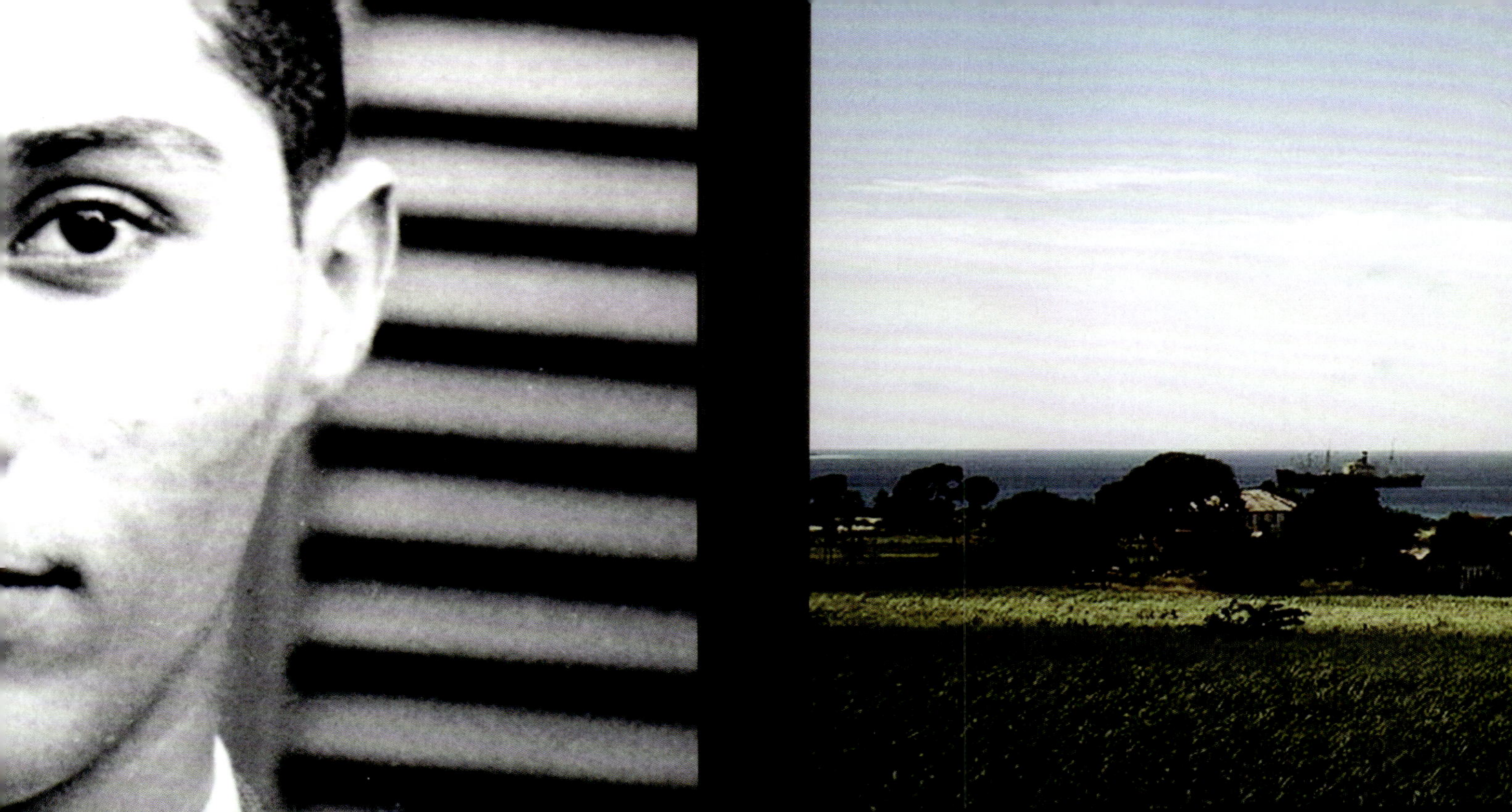

this primal scene of African suffering with its tragedies and its accidents. It was almost Greek in profile, in the sense that there were forces at play that seemed bigger than individuals. One of the ways in which I think many of us exilic kids came to deal with this was via fiction and filmmaking. Many people seemed committed to the idea that there was this hidden country that they felt—a country of ghosts, if you like—where they felt brave enough to go only through cinema or the moving image. That was an extraordinary thing.

**LAH:** With regard to returning-to-Ghana narratives in literature, we can also look at travelogues by Richard Wright, Saidiya Hartman, and Ekow Eshun.

**JA:** Certainly. There was a period when very many people who had either left as children or came of age and were old enough to begin to chart their connections with the continent—for them the moving image was a very good source, as well as literature. I think in the "war zone of memories" here, as *Testament* very clearly says. And in that war zone, the politics of location and identities is crucial. Malcolm was prophetic in all kinds of ways, not just for himself but for my mother and our institute. A year after he died, the military coup happened in Ghana, on March 6, 1966. Everything that that moment stood for was wiped away. You can say that, had Malcolm been alive in '66, and had he wanted to be in Ghana, none of the conditions that made it possible for him to be there would have existed. He wouldn't have been allowed in because the military would have seen him as a troublemaker. Many Pan-African institutions had been shut down for being communist and Marxist. He was prophetic in a way that he hadn't anticipated, because when he spoke about his end, he was actually speaking about the end of a lot more than that.

VP: **And then your life suddenly changed.**

JA: Yes. Following my father's death, we were quite literally in flight, and through a circuitous route via the US, we arrived in this country, begging for shelter, which is so bizarre to me, then and now. The thing that was bizarre to me was the fear of being in Ghana. The fear that something terrible was about to happen to us was palpable. I was very young, but I knew it. I could feel it. Let no one tell you fear does not have a personality, an ontology. It really does. Ghosts do fucking exist, and they do stuff. I was aware, palpably, that we were being stalked by something. I mean, *phantom* is too innocent a word. A kind of ogre. And nothing but flight would save us. I was absolutely relieved when we arrived here, in a way that I think people who now go on boats to leave, to come to this country, would know, would understand. The palpable sense of relief was extraordinary for me.

We arrived here in the late '60s and continued to try to make this place a home.

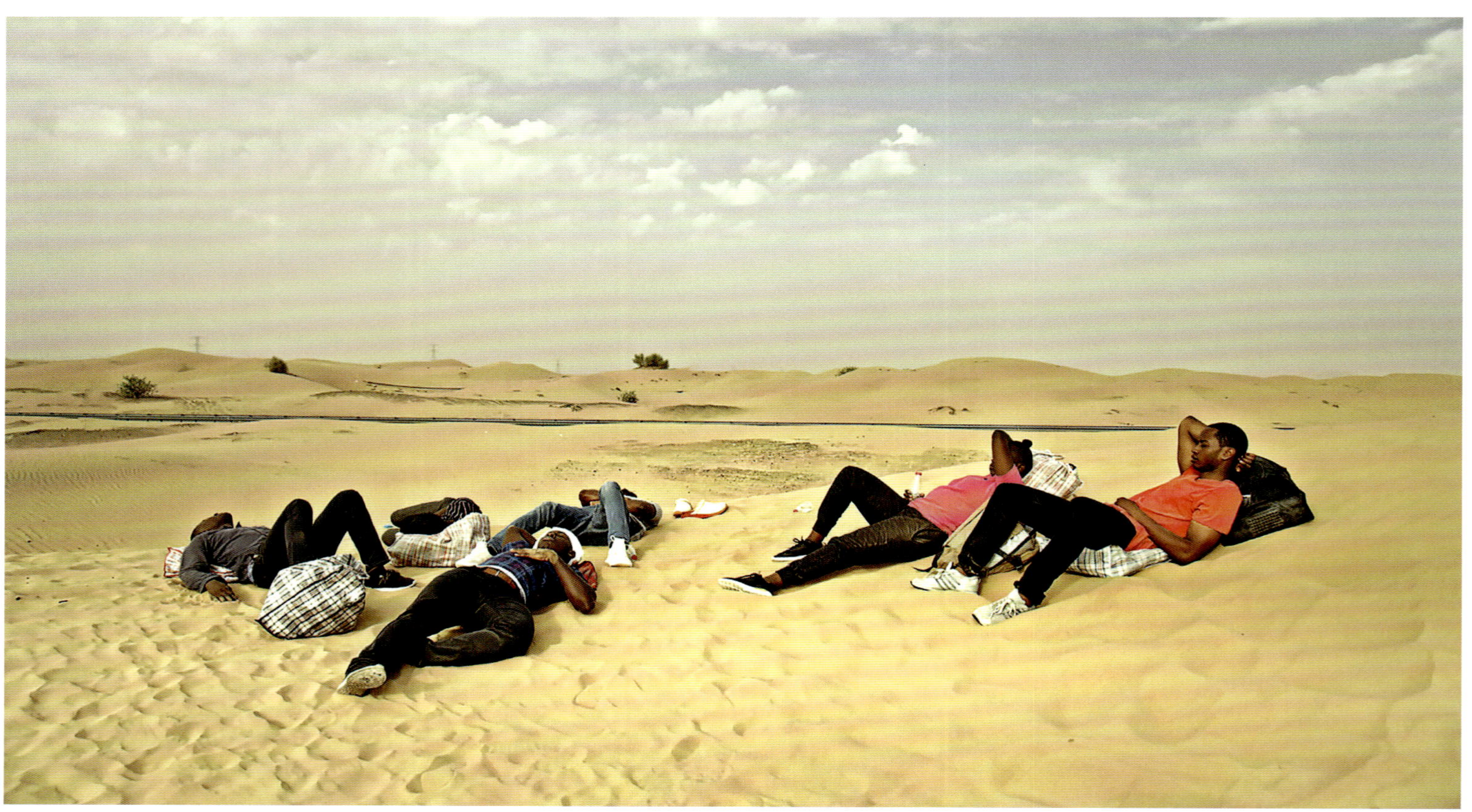

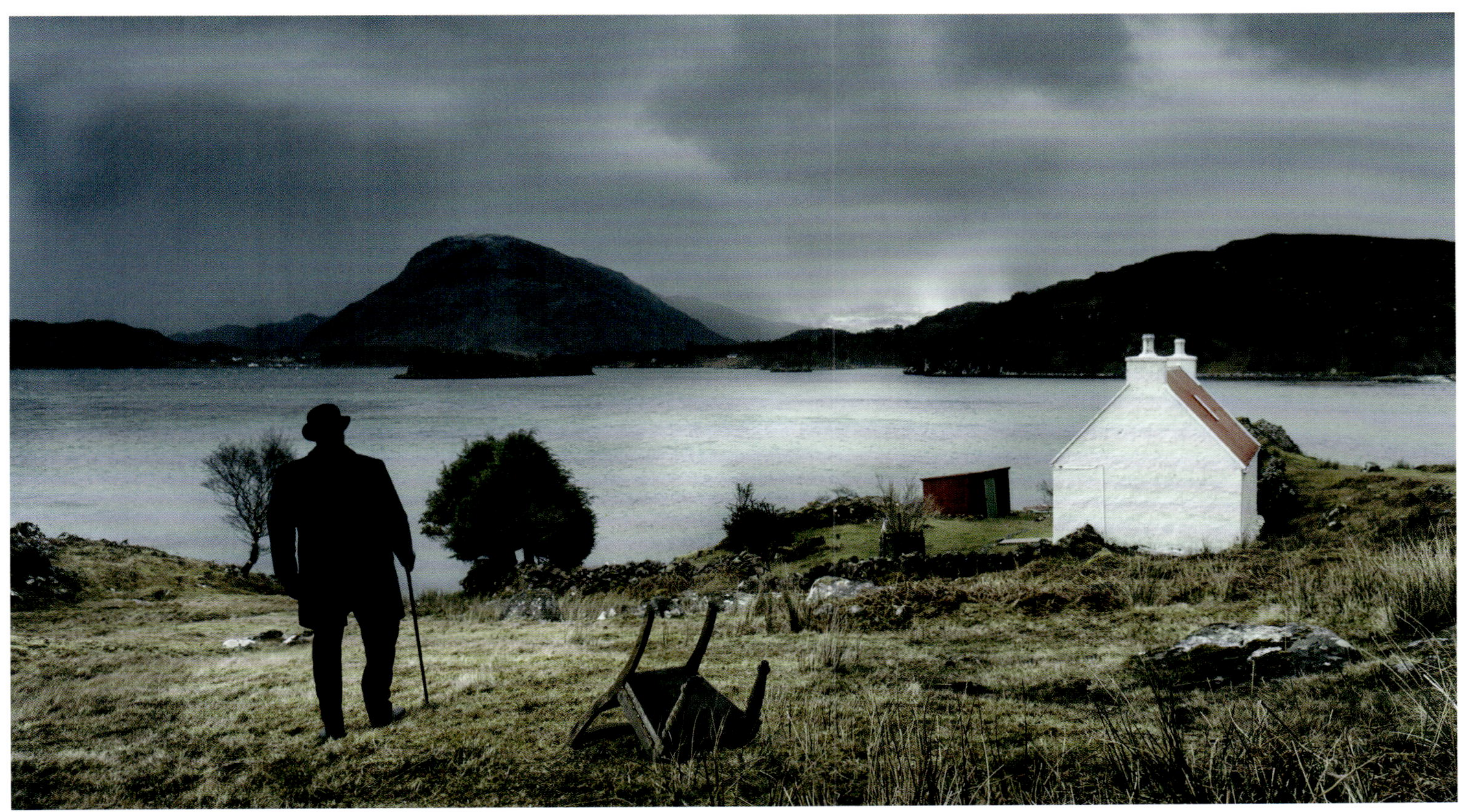

At the time, we consciously tried to create an Accra in London, in our house, which would stand for the Accra that I left. In this weird Faustian bargain that I think most exilic figures make with the historical, you slice a piece of it, a manageable piece, you construct a tableau either in your bedroom or your house or your new town, and that becomes your version of where you've left.

VP: **Did you speak about Ghana?**

**JA:** We spoke about narratives. I remember my mother being obsessed with the narratives of betrayal—who did what, when; how this happened; who was responsible. And it wasn't just a regional thing. It wasn't just a local thing. It was a continental thing. We were in the space of every defeated, every vanquished, every political uprising that didn't happen. I'm including in this all of the ones that were to be, whether it's Angola or South Africa or Zimbabwe—it was just all these places of defeat and the vanquished, which became our country and our continent. In London, you met other people who'd lost their home and were running from violence. There is this incredible, ironic reversal in that period, where you meet all of these folks who had left to go and throw out the British, coming, begging, cap in hand to the British to take them on.

**LAH:** I've used a quote of yours many times, and it has been a guiding force to me:

Still from *Vertigo Sea*, 2015. Video, 48 minutes, 30 seconds, color, sound

**Having been brought up in a Pan-African environment, a lot of things were easier for me to navigate than they might appear at first.**

"The problem with the Black avant-garde is that we're constantly having to reproduce itself, because we don't actually protect it. We don't give a citation. We don't acknowledge it." Starting with *Testament*, there's a thread through all of your work in terms of its radical project of, to Vanessa's point, anti-amnesia. How did you emerge? Why were you chosen by Stuart to be the architect of *The Unfinished Conversation* or *The Stuart Hall Project*?

**JA:** Growing up in a house of the vanquished, of the dismissed, I am aware of what I would call the thing to come, which is the thing that stalks all powerless lives. It's the coming of the disaster, really. All of that made me comfortable with the unpopular. I never had a problem with the avant-garde because many of its conceits had organized my life: asymmetry, bricolage, nonlinearity.

Stuart was one of the few who made generational sense to us. I think it's to do with his purchase on this place, because he got here when he was young and had worked his way into many institutions. He became a product of all of those. When he spoke, we could feel that he inhabited several living rooms at the same time. I wasn't born here, but I always felt more connected with people of my generation here. I didn't see what I was doing as being something from a Ghanaian kid. I knew that I had to make the transition from a Ghanaian kid to a Black British one. But at the same time (and this is the important thing that the people who usually call me Ghanaian are not aware of), most of my generation were doing exactly the same thing. Because their parents had come from somewhere else. It fell on them, as the children, to deliver on the promise of post-migrancy. Sometimes people say to me, "Oh, it's so interesting that you understood Caribbean culture so well that you'd make *Handsworth Songs*." What do you mean? It became clear that Black Britishness was going to be arrived at by a mélange of Caribbean and West African culture.

Having been husbanded, schooled, brought up, and nurtured in a Pan-African environment, a lot of things were easier for me to navigate than they might appear at first. And the navigation wasn't at the expense of being Ghanaian, because no one could remove that. Even as a seven-year-old, I knew that I was forever marked by that place. I knew things that everyone who lives abroad has to contend with. It's typical to meet somebody from the Caribbean who goes back to where they grew up and realizes that they embody everything that that place has lost. The place itself has moved on and doesn't cherish anymore the kinds of fruit that were there that you liked. All that's gone. You have, in a very real sense, become a custodian for that lost life.

VP: **In relation to being a custodian, there are specific references to being Ga— an ethnic group from the Greater Accra region—throughout *Testament*. You reference rivers in relation to memory, for instance. Can you speak more to your relationship with your Ga heritage, and how memory and legacy appear in your work?**

JA: I am aware of huge strands of Ghanaian life that only people like me embody, because it's gone. I remember a time when it was common knowledge that as Ga people, people of the rivers, that our gods were the rivers. I realized that once you lose your memories, everything else will be gone. One of the things I was certain about as a grandson of a Ga elder was what those things mean—what it is to be the high priest of a river, what it means to be an herbalist in a certain kind of tradition. *Testament* was trying to make an oblique reference to a familial past that may not make sense to everybody else. I think there was all kinds of what would now be called ecological consciousness that being Ga entailed. There was an ascetic, frugal relationship with our environment. Quite a lot of it disappears, because the frugality of it was one of the reasons people wanted

**Many generations of people may not necessarily be from Accra but passed through Accra on their journey elsewhere.**

independence—they were sick of living these frugal lives.

VP: **I'm also Ga. My family are from La and Jamestown, where various colonial administrations, such as the British, were based. We've been speaking about anti-amnesia, and now initiatives, such as Year of the Return—when in 2019 Ghana invited African diasporans to return to the country and commemorate four centuries since the beginning of transatlantic slavery—have been put in place to regather and bring those in the United States back to the continent.**

JA: One of my relations with the country at the moment is via a morbid symptom, which is that I go to Ghana frequently, usually to bury someone or to attend memorials. My father had six sisters, five of whom have now passed away in the last fifteen years. I've returned to La every two years or so to bury someone. I flew into Accra a few years ago, and it happened to coincide with the Year of the Return project. The airport was full of hundreds of people—it was the most extraordinary thing. It reminded me of something that I've always felt. We talk about ghosting, phantoms, and unseen guests. There's a real sense in which these figures and apparitions have a right to that landscape. Many generations of people may not necessarily be from Accra but passed through Accra on their journey elsewhere. We're one of these strange spaces where I think our sense of sovereignty needs to be a postmodern one. Our sovereignty cannot simply lie with the living any more than it can lie with just the dead of that place—we have several millions of dead elsewhere who are of that place.

Akufo-Addo, Ghana's president, may have just had economic logic with Year of the Return. Whatever reasons they have, cynical or otherwise, fine. The important thing was that it happened, because someone needed to swing that door of no return the other way. It reduced me to tears because I knew that there would be a day when it wasn't just Maya Angelou and a few friends or Malcolm X who visited—there'd be thousands of people of African origin who feel connected to the place and feel it is indebted to them. And that's right. Because it is. It's indebted to them, in a sense that it has to open the door of memory.

VP: **On a granular note, I'd like to think about hybridity. This is a term that is often used to describe your work and practice. With your relative distance to the country, alongside your project of anti-amnesia, I would love to know what**

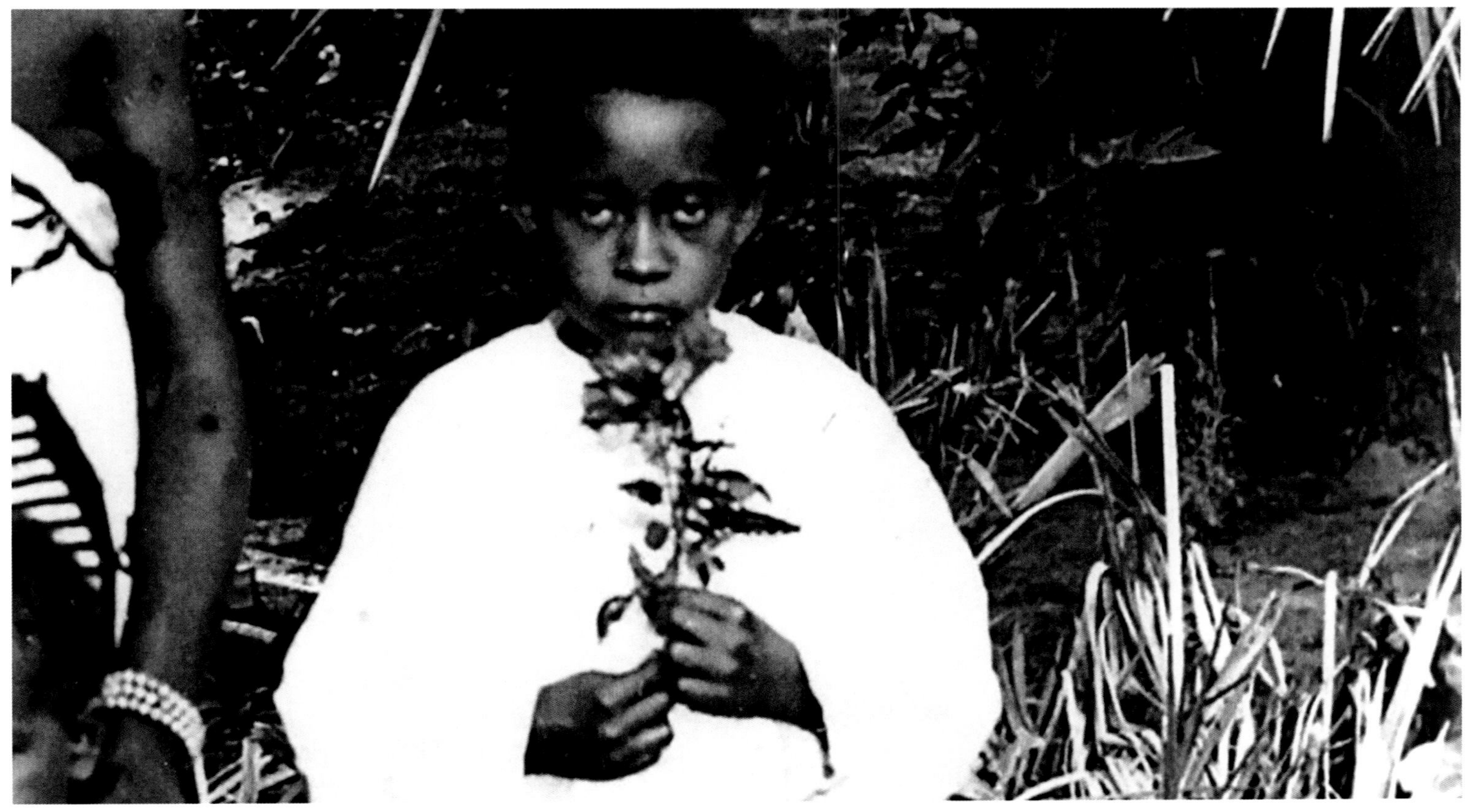

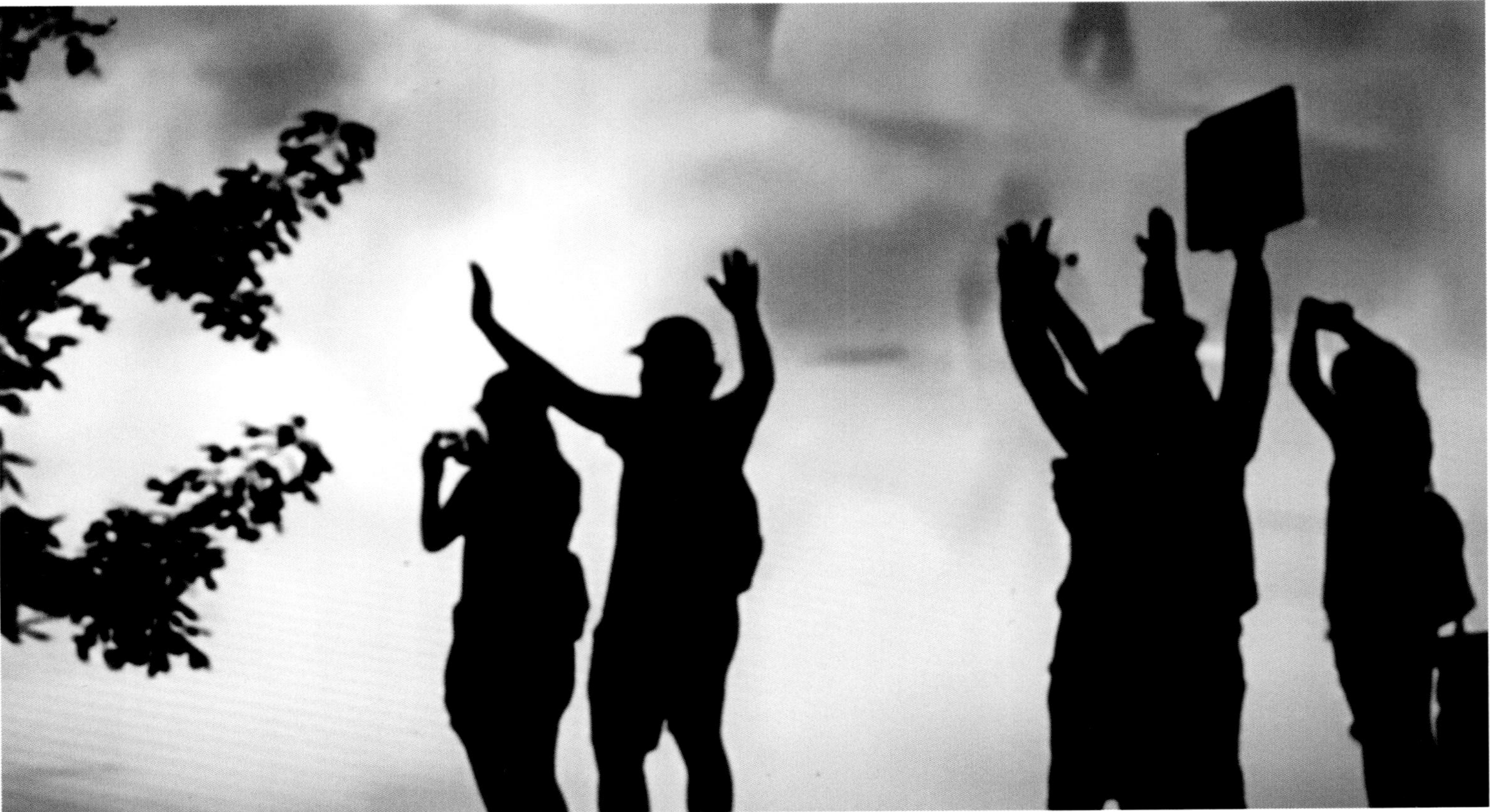

Stills from *Five Murmurations*, 2021. Video, 45 minutes, black and white, sound

**representing Ghana in 2019 at the Venice Biennale brought forth for you.**

JA: The strange thing is that by 2019, a lot had been ironed out for me. Some of the creases of discomfort are gone. One is also aware of this question of temporality. Just about everybody who was involved in my being turfed out is gone. There's no one alive who was an architect of the 1966 coup. So you're aware of being slowly moved to the front of the queue. That seems to me to come with certain obligations. If you've known Nana Oforiatta Ayim, who curated the pavilion; David Adjaye, who designed it; or Okwui Enwezor, an advisor on the project, for as long as I had, and they ask, then you're not just saying yes to a country; you're also saying yes to an ambition of theirs to do something.

Nana made it clear that she was interested in this conversation between Ghana and its diaspora, the old and the young, midcareer and emerging artists. I am, too. I might not live in Ghana, but I am Ghanaian in one very important sense, which is that its future matters to me. I've got relatives who still live there, cousins and aunties. I have very real connections that are ongoing, which make demands on me. For those reasons alone, when someone decides to pull me into a space called the Ghana Pavilion, I thought, Well, I'm not officially, but I'm sort of already there.

If you'd told the younger me that there would be a time when I'd be happy with this, I would have shot you. There was just no way that I wanted to be owned by that place, because it had disowned us in a very violent way, and for me, that was the end of the story. I was quite happy for it to be that. The disavowal of the place or people, it was a disavowal of the connection—the presumed connection between me and it. Providing it didn't try to acknowledge or claim me, I was quite happy for it to be there, doing its own thing. I'd even go there, but when I left, that was it. It's like, Okay, you're there and I'm here. Finished. It's only recently that I've started to understand it. That places don't let you go so easily.

Vanessa Peterson is associate editor of *Frieze*. Lyle Ashton Harris is an artist and a guest editor of *Aperture*'s "Accra" issue.

Installation view of *Five Murmurations*, 2021, Lisson Gallery, New York. Video, 45 minutes, black and white, sound
All works courtesy Smoking Dogs Films and Lisson Gallery

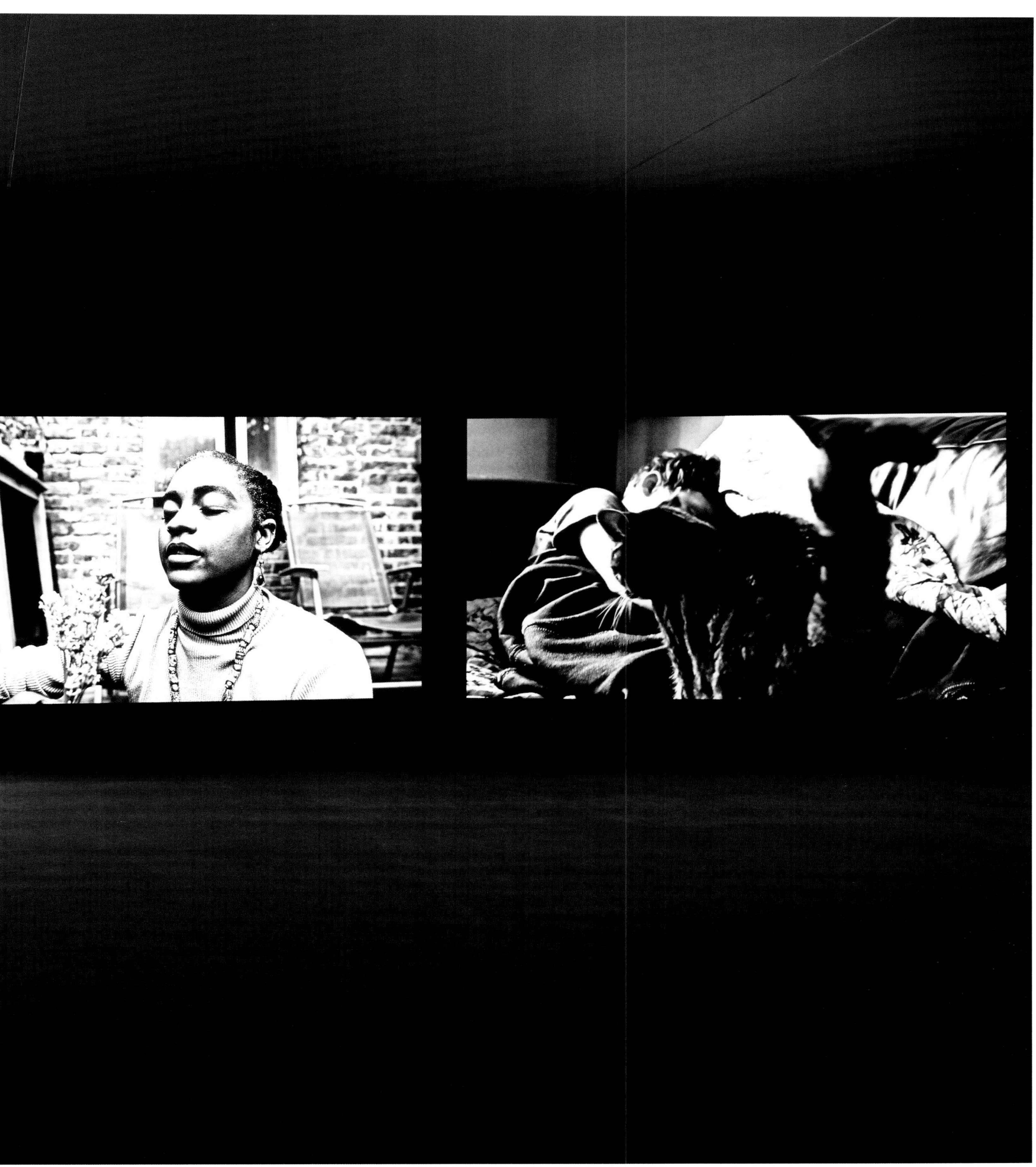

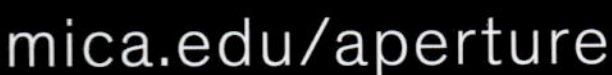

# The Essential Writings
## Stephen Shore

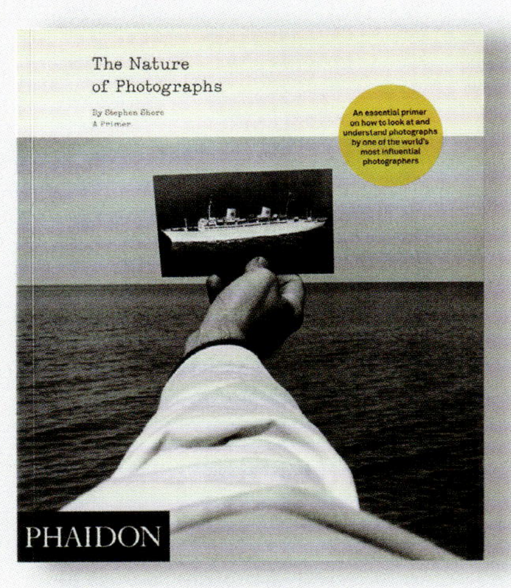

PHAIDON

ISBN: 9780714859040
$29.95 | £19.95 | €24.95

## The Nature of Photographs

A basic primer on how photographs function visually, *The Nature of Photographs* explores how the tools and materials of photography translate the world we see into a photograph.

*It is intelligent and sensitive and knowledgeable—knowledgeable in the sense that it was written by a serious and ambitious photographer, out of the experience of a serious and ambitious photographer.*

—John Szarkowski

## Modern Instances:
## The Craft of Photography
### *Expanded Edition*

An essential handbook for anyone interested in learning more about mastering one's craft and the distinct threads that come together to inform a creative voice.

Modern Instances *is the textbook I've been waiting for. It's about craft and biography, as the subtitle suggests, but it's also a guide for living.*

—Alec Soth

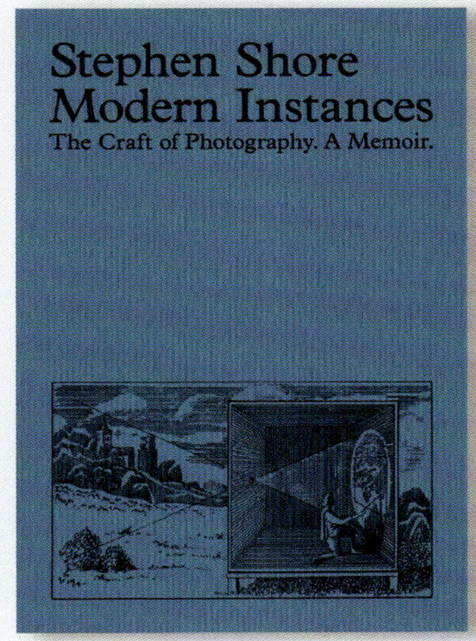

MACK

ISBN: 978-1-915743-20-6
$35 | £25 | €35

# The PhotoBook Review

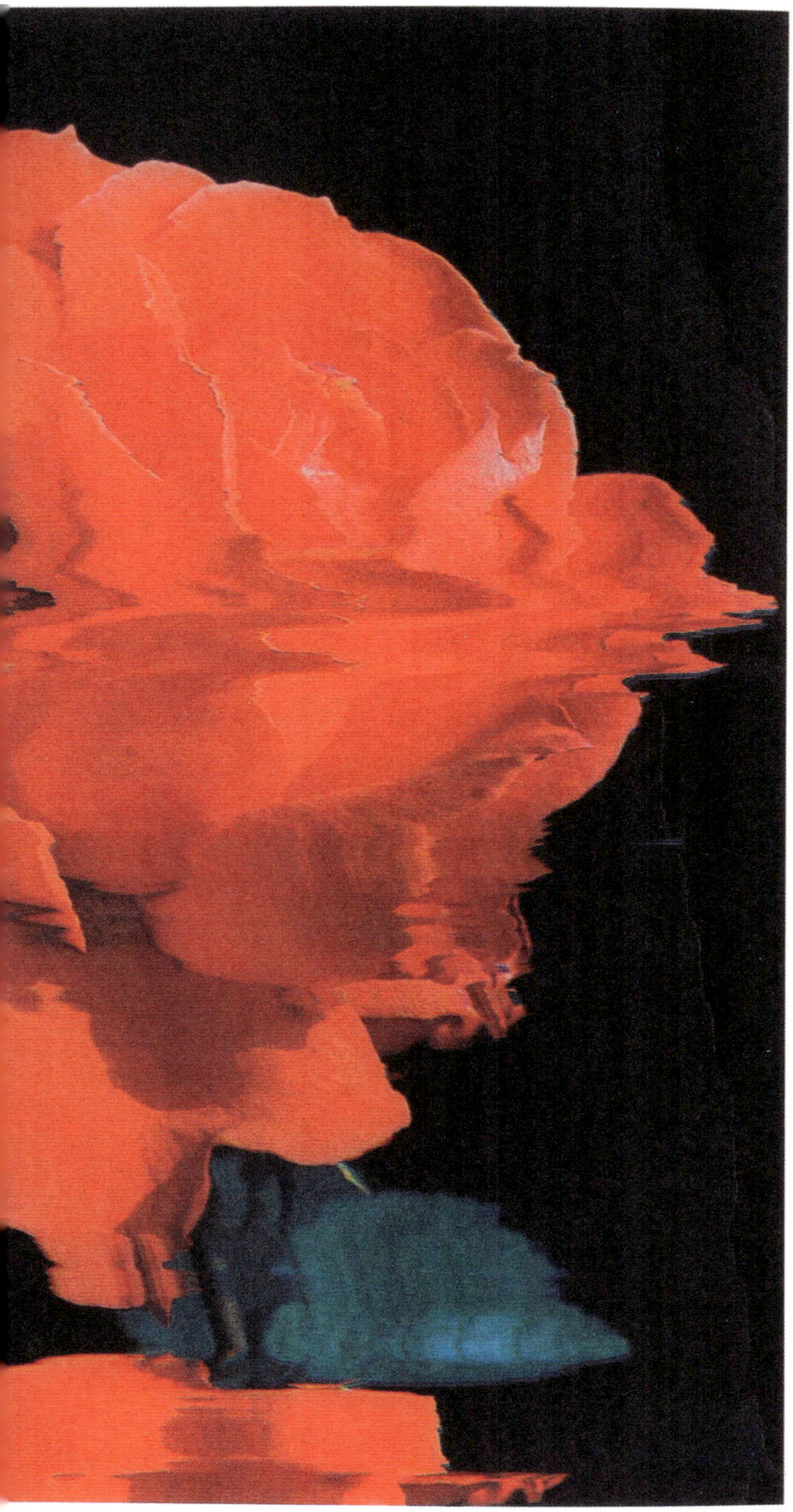

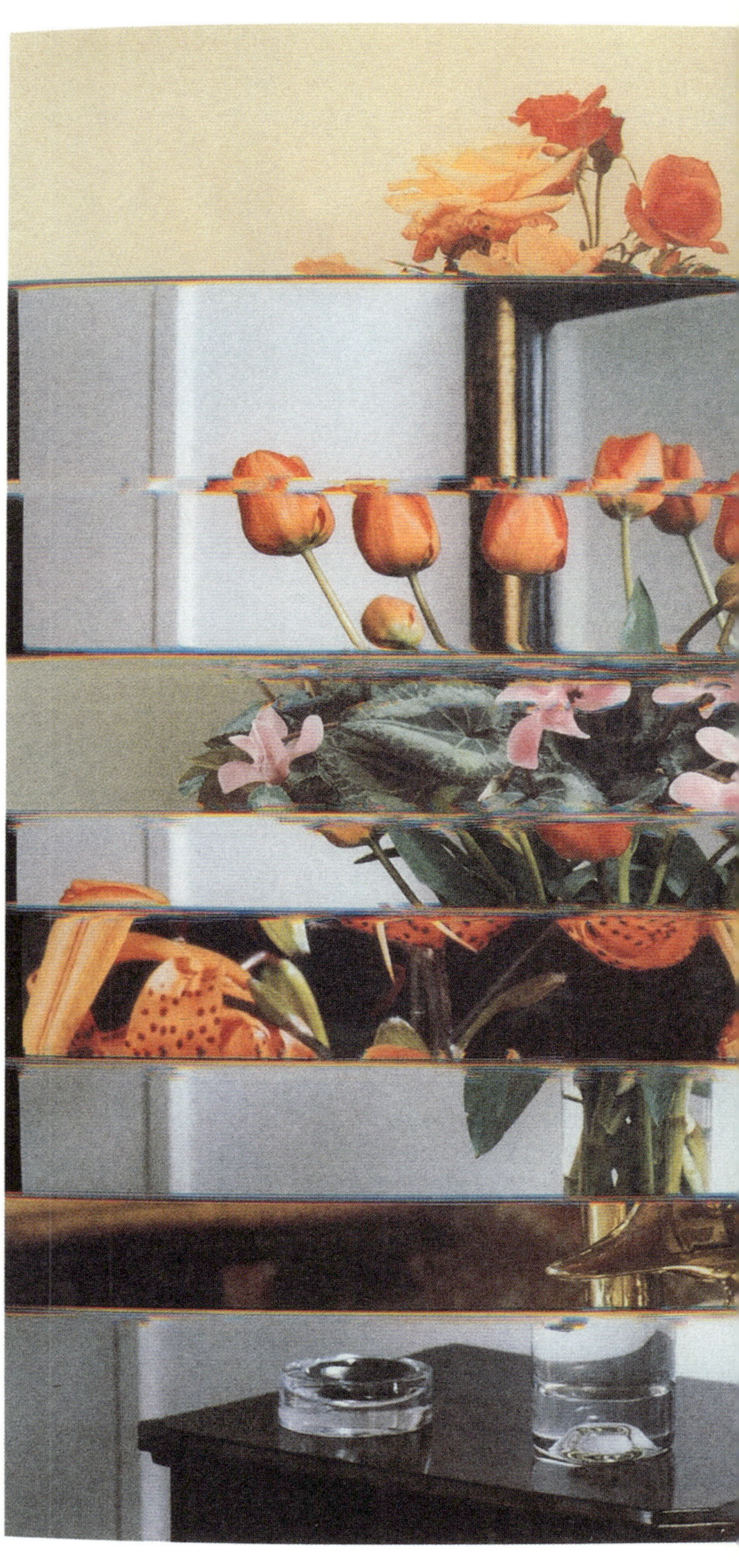

# The Flow of Pictures



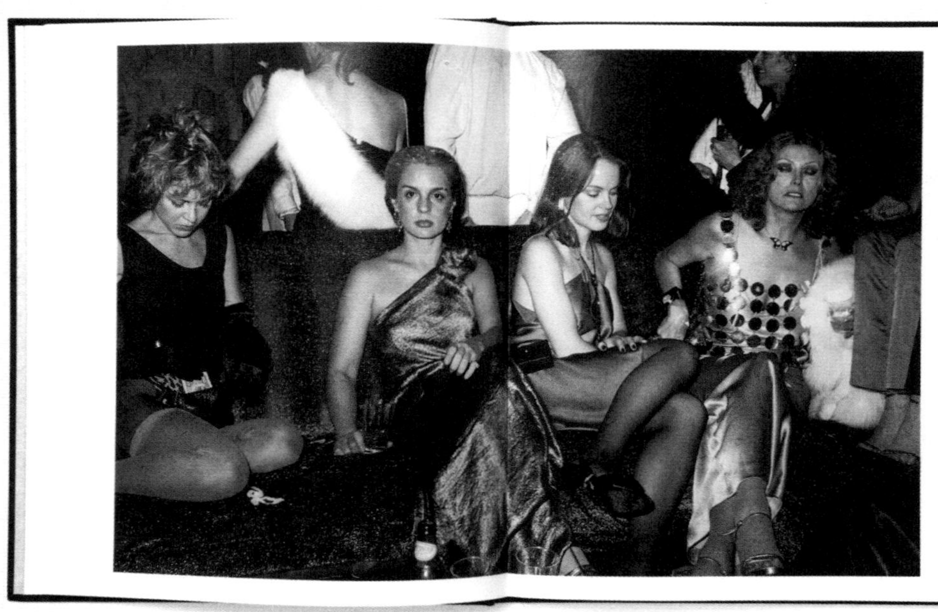

This page:
Spread from Tod Papageorge, *Studio 54*, 2014

Opposite:
Cover of Judith Black, *Pleasant Street*, 2020

Gregory Stanley and Rachel Barker founded their photobook publishing house, Stanley/Barker, based in Shropshire in the West Midlands of England, in 2014. Their first publication, Tod Papageorge's *Studio 54* (2014), sequenced the photographer's unpublished portfolio as a one-night journey into the depths of perhaps the most mythical nightclub ever. Stanley and Barker, who studied photography and art in London, and who are now both in their midthirties, have since published monographs by lesser-known but nonetheless formidable photographers, reviving interest in Mimi Plumb, Judith Black, and Jack Lueders-Booth. Superb black-and-white reproductions and narrative structure have become hallmarks of the Stanley/Barker approach, as well as a sensitivity to the look and feel of a publication held in the hand.

Alistair O'Neill: **First off, could you tell me how you both got into publishing?**

**Rachel Barker:** Greg studied photography, and I studied fine art. Then we met at Blurb, the print-on-demand book company.

**Gregory Stanley:** It was quite fortuitous. We had both graduated and gone to work at probably the worst place to work when you're interested in publishing. But it was 2009, the very start of the golden age of photobooks. We ran a book fair together called Photo Book London, which was the first photobook event in London. But we did it only once. Then, we spent the next three years looking for our first project, because we had a very clear idea of what we thought a photobook could be.

In 2013, we went to Paris Photo and saw Tod Papageorge's Studio 54 images as a wall at Galerie Thomas Zander, and then we spent the next six months convincing Tod

and Thomas to let two twenty-five-year-olds who had no prior experience publish a book about it.

AON: **And now, a decade later, following the pandemic and other changes, how would you describe the photobook market in 2023?**

**GS:** It's returning.

**RB:** It can change rapidly, and we keep our eye on it constantly. With the decisions we make and the books we choose to publish, we have to be sure that in the current market there is an audience for a book and that we are going to be able to sell it. We're just gearing up for the spring 2023 release of Trent Parke's new book, *Monument*, and it's one of our biggest presellers ever. People are really excited about it. So, that's a signifier that there is still a real energy around photography and photobooks and buying them and printing them.

**GS:** We've always seen our role in the publishing community as righting the wrongs of our forebears in terms of finding these projects that should have been books, but they didn't quite get the attention they deserved. We've always thought that we need to make books that people actually want to buy and are important books that need to exist.

**AON: So as much as they are reassessments, they are also contributions to the canon?**

**GS:** Yes, finding where those holes are that shouldn't exist. We do a lot of work with people who were in Massachusetts and the surrounding states in the 1970s, such as Sage Sohier, Mark Steinmetz, Sergio Purtell, Susan Kandel, Paul McDonough, Mike Smith, Joan Albert, Henry Horenstein, Jack Lueders-Booth, and Katherine Turczan. There was such a movement of female artists making incredible images. And for some reason, it didn't quite take off at that time. It's really bizarre. We've been quite fortunate to be able, as you say, to reassess the canon and put that important moment back in place.

**AON: How do you conceive a photobook?**

**GS:** For us, the bookmaking process is always about being as collaborative as possible. It's definitely a three-way collaboration between the artist, us, and the designer. We're always trying to take the artist's work and present it in a way that allows the viewer to have the greatest depth of understanding. We don't want the book to be our taste. We want it to be an extension of the content.

Photographers spent so long making these bodies of photographs—they devoted twenty to thirty years of their lives. So, it's important that the physical object have as much attention to craft and design as possible. But having said that, we keep the insides of our books very simple. Once you get past the title page, what follows are clear, beautifully rendered prints of the photographer's work, because at that point, we're in their headspace. Everything coming before is trying to put the reader in the space where they can appreciate the photographs to the best, fullest extent.

**AON: You mentioned that you're very motivated by the principle of narrative.**

**RB:** Yeah. Probably the book that really inspired what we do was Watabe Yukichi's *A Criminal Investigation* from 2011. When we both looked through it, we were just so

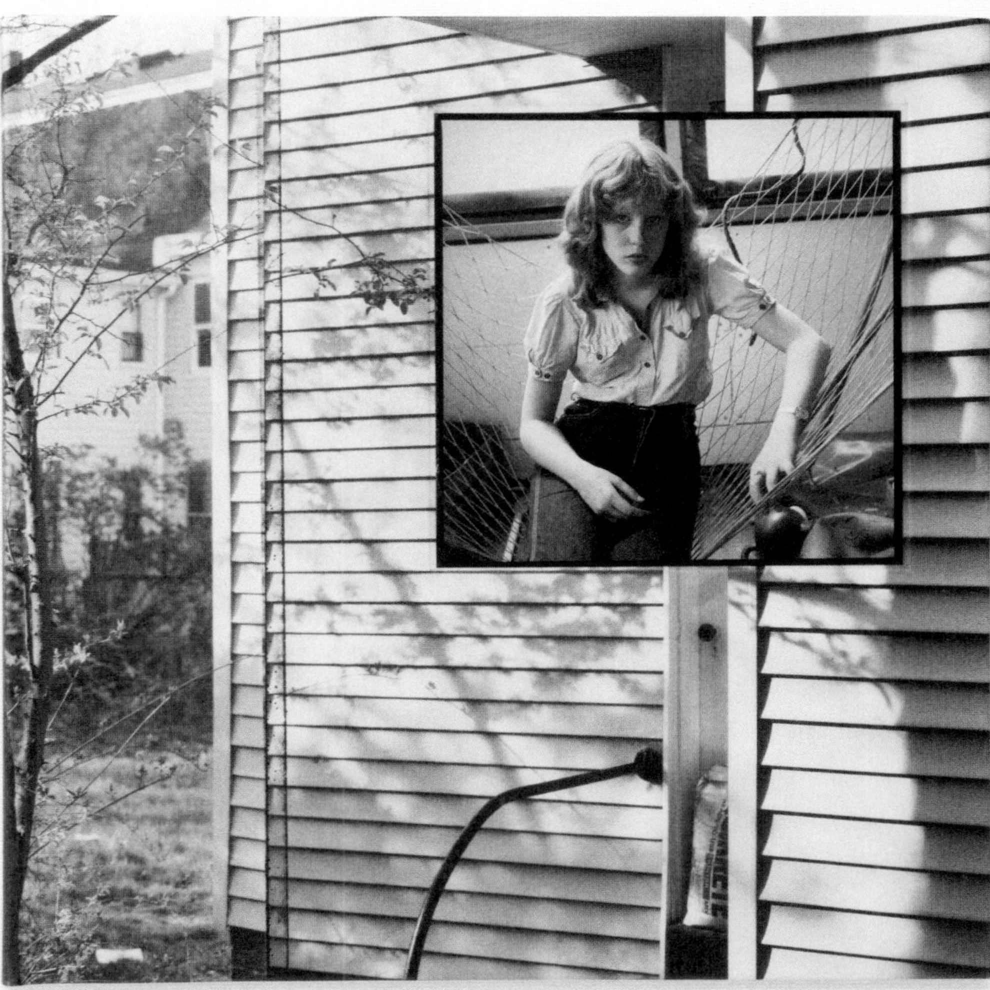

blown away—it is so elegant and simply done. But the detail in it is just amazing, in terms of the points at which it makes you think about the journey you're going on, and the references, such as the typewriter font and the band around it, make the book feel like a criminal dossier.

**GS:** The sequencing.

**RB:** The sequencing, yes. You're following this sort of investigation. It's a story. It's like a novel but visual.

We took a lot from that book and put those ideas into our publications. Looking at the Mark Steinmetz books that we publish; *Carnival* (2019) follows a day at the carnival. When you're looking through its sequence, we take you right from the start, arriving at the carnival, through enjoying the carnival, to the end, when the daylight fades, and the lights of the carnival come on. It's really simple, but it's a pleasurable experience, hopefully, for whoever buys the book and looks through it. They're taken on that journey.

**GS:** There's nothing more boring than "this looks like that." In sequencing, people so often think, Oh, there's a picture of a ball. And then on the next page, There's a picture of a moon. That really takes you out of

experiencing the pictures. Instead, it puts you into a space of trying to find how someone has linked things visually. Whereas we're always trying to get back to—no one talks about it in reviews or anything anymore—the emotional experience of looking through a body of work. We're trying to get people away from *looking* at pictures and toward *experiencing* looking at pictures. If we can give them something very direct, like a journey that they're going to go on, once the brain cops on to this very simple idea, you're no longer looking at the sequence. You're experiencing the pictures and the *flow* of pictures. That's not to say we don't do conceptual editing. We've just edited a Mimi Plumb book, and it's sequenced to the Zen story of the ten ox-herding pictures, like the journey to enlightenment. It was a really interesting way for us to edit a book.

**AON: *Journey* is a really good word to describe it, because it's almost as if the journey you take the reader on is slightly different from, perhaps, the journey that the photographer's portfolio established. Do you think that's a fair distinction?**

**RB:** Yeah, I guess. Sometimes the photographer trusts us with their work,

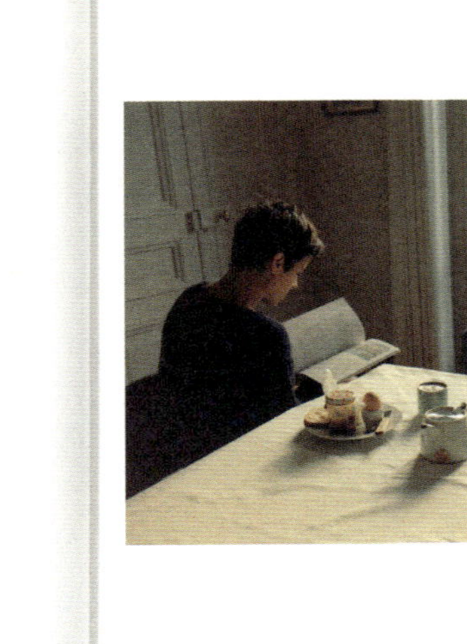



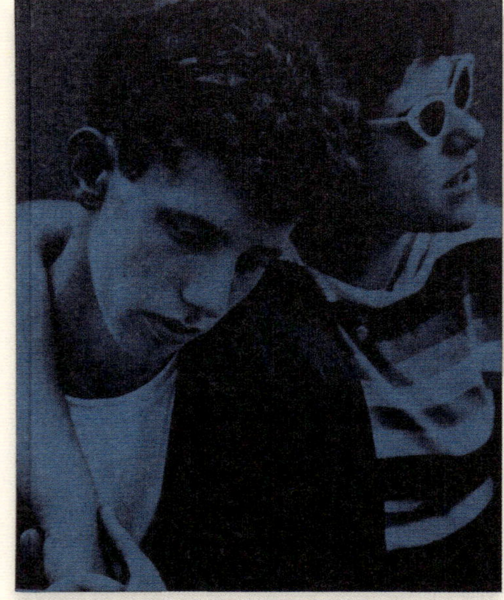

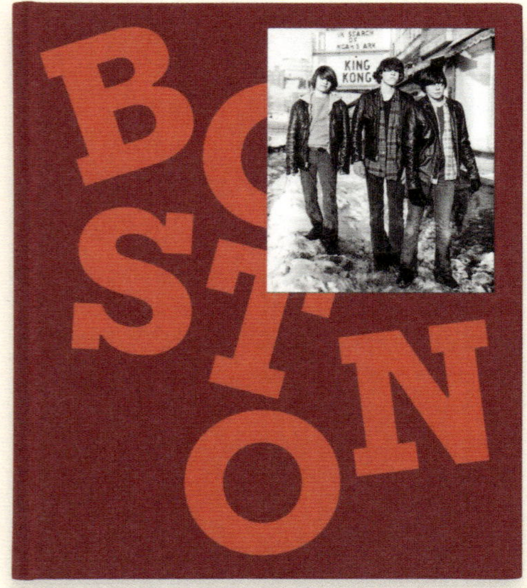


and the sequence we put together perhaps isn't what they brought to us in the first place. I mean, even looking at *Studio 54*, I'm not sure Tod Papageorge ever thought about those images in that sequence—of coming to the nightclub, and then in the middle of the book, you've got the buildup to the real crescendo of the party in full swing, and then you see, as it kind of peters out in the last pages, people lying around on the floor, they've had too much to drink, they're too tired, and then it ends.

**GS**: He didn't have the idea, but he did do forty PDFs of the sequence. We were incredibly fortunate that with the early photographers we published—Tod Papageorge, Bill Henson, Larry Fink, Karen Knorr—it's like having a master class every time you work with one of these people.

**AON: Why do you think sequencing is not up for discussion in the critique of photobooks? What do you think the critique is more attentive to?**

**GS**: I think it's because it's harder to talk about your emotional response to art. It's a really difficult thing to do well in any way that means anything to anyone else. Ten people can look at a book and have ten different emotional responses.

Dave Heath's work—we've published two of his books, *One Brief Moment* (2022) and *Washington Square* (2016)—is people walking along a street, and there's nothing inherently emotionally driven about a street scene. But the way he captures skin and light has such an emotional resonance; it's almost impossible to say how that works. It's like the Minor White quote about looking at photographs to see what else they are, which is difficult and kind of nonsensical at the same time. But that's what's special

about it. We always look for books that are two things. So, to one extent, Dave Heath's books show street scenes; someone who's not interested in photography can totally understand these are pictures on the East Coast in 1967. But someone who's interested in our world can look at them and see unfathomable depths of beauty and sadness.

**AON: It's also about a kind of metropolitan life, a kind of interaction with other human beings that doesn't really exist anymore. It's gone. Washington Square is not like that anymore. As we see in some of these portfolios, there is a sense of loss articulated in the act of looking back and trying to reappraise the canon.**

**One last question. You've got a lot of books piled behind you, and I don't think they're all published by you. So, you enjoy collecting books yourself, I presume? How do you buy books today?**

**GS**: More often than not, the books we buy now are bad books of good photography. Because the type of photography that we love generally wasn't made into beautiful books, since it's from an earlier time period. We tend to buy a lot, just because you see one picture by someone, maybe scrolling through a museum's archive pages, and you think, I bet there's more there, there's got to be more, there's a whole series there. So you buy the book to see, and then you realize there is just that one picture. But then, you've got the book.

**RB**: We come back with a lot of books from events as well. We'll always go in and have a look at other book stands and end up buying more than we need.

**GS**: Yeah, and the bookshelves fill up, and then other rooms get filled with books.

**AON: It's a terrible problem of modern life. It's not the bookcases you have, it's the book towers at the side of them.**

**GS**: If a fire marshal came in, they'd just say, "Oh, what are you doing? There's kindling everywhere."

**Alistair O'Neill** is a professor of fashion history and theory at Central Saint Martins, London.

# Called to the Camera

Spanning more than a century, a new book reveals the inner workings of Black portrait studios.
**Salamishah Tillet**

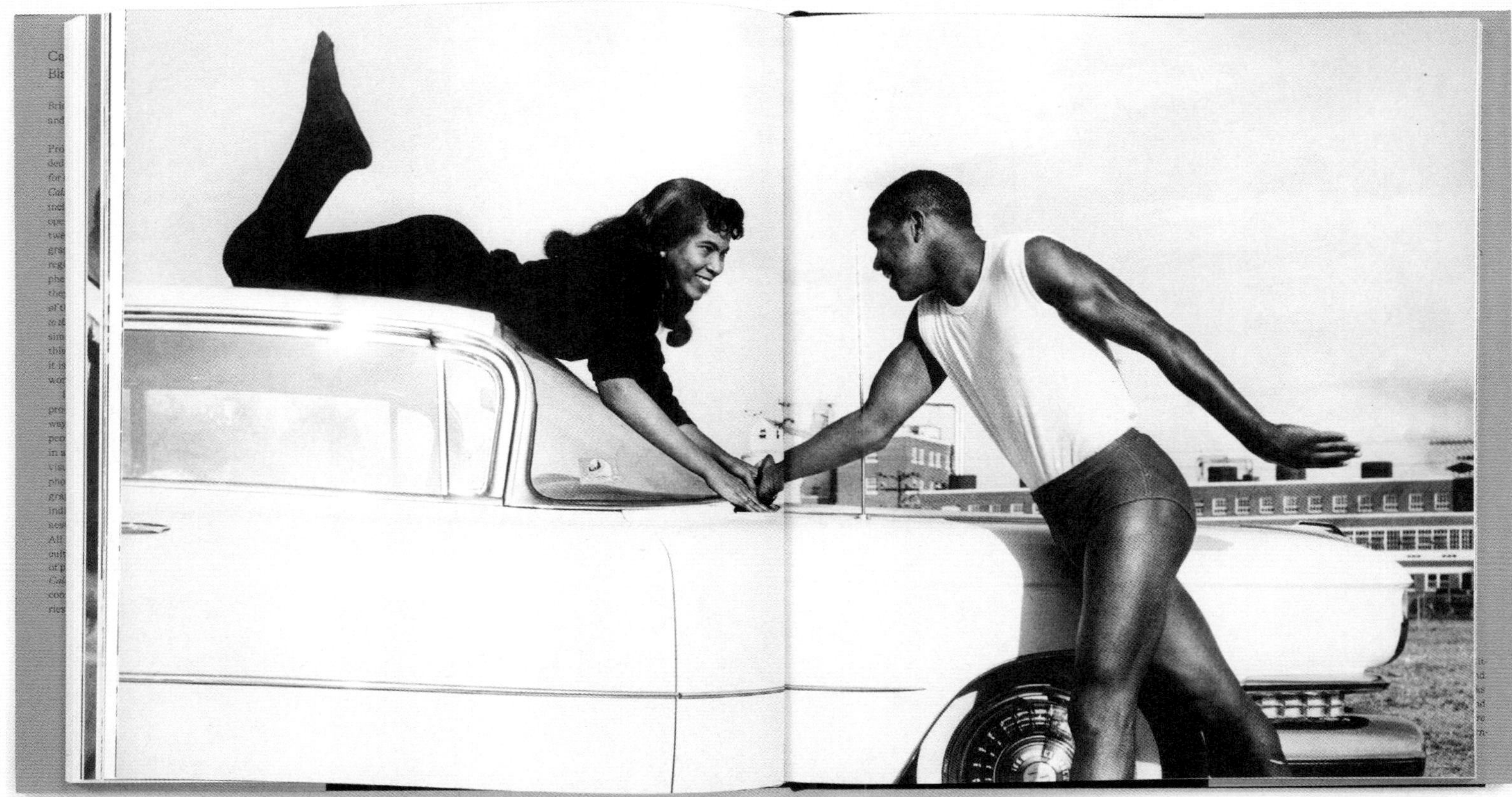

These days, I spend a lot of time in the recently restored Hahne & Company building in downtown Newark, New Jersey. Home to Express Newark, the center for socially engaged art and design that I currently direct, it was abandoned for nearly half a century before being renovated into a hub for everyday Newarkers to meet up, shop, or get their picture taken at our Shine Portrait Studio. Founded in 1858 as the city's first department store, the building is remembered by many African American residents—like my grandmother, who migrated here from North Carolina—as a site of racial discrimination akin to, in many instances, what they long experienced down South. "We didn't shop at Hahne," my grandmother often said. Referring to its competitor around the corner, she'd add: "We only went to Bamberger's."

I've often wondered if the store's racism is why James VanDerZee left so quickly. Moving to Newark from Harlem in 1915, he took his first job in the Hahne's portrait studio as a darkroom assistant and then a portraitist. By 1916, however, he was back in Harlem, setting up his own place—the now iconic Guarantee Photo Studio—at a music conservatory his sister founded in 1911.

Spaces like these, the more than three dozen Black-owned or operated photography portrait studios throughout the United States, are the subject of the remarkable new book *Called to the Camera: Black American Studio Photographers* (**Yale University Press, 2023; 228 pages, $50**). Spanning the first 120 years of photography, the book, edited by the curators, historians, and photographers Brian Piper, Russell Lord,

John Edwin Mason, and Carla Williams, features many photographs published for the first time. This unique collection reveals the inner workings (the toil, the techniques, and the students) of these studios, as well as the intimate portraits of Black life produced inside of them.

The book opens with two images from the Hooks Brothers Studio, the second-oldest continuously operating Black business in Memphis, welcoming visitors from 1907 until the 1970s, and two more from the M. Smith Studio, run by the brothers Morgan and Marvin Smith and located next to the Apollo Theater in Harlem from 1939 to 1968. These black-and-white portraits provide rare insight into some of the aspirations of these early photographers. In the 1950s, the Hooks brothers photographed Black male students working in a darkroom and selecting prints. Lord writes in the book's introduction that such images are about "looking and making, labor and education, the individual and the collective, devotion and joy."

Likewise, the images made in the Smiths' studio from the previous decade—the first featuring a Black woman photographer setting up to shoot her model, or another by Austin Hansen of Morgan Smith himself standing on a lamppost in Harlem with a Speed Graphic camera in hand—underscore how these institutions were also unique places of artistic experimentation and archival documentation. Like the photographs that follow, these earliest examples also remind us of the organizations' critical role in the larger battles over racial representation and the photographic gaze.

When African Americans sought a Black portrait studio, they wanted professional photographs that captured them with dignity and respect and, in doing so, countered the preponderance of racist imagery in American society. This meant that the photographers for whom they sat, dating as far back as the mid-nineteenth century, to portraitists such as Pennsylvania's Glenalvin Goodridge (whose father had been enslaved) or Virginia's James Presley Ball, had to not only master the newly invented form, techniques, and equipment of photography itself but simultaneously innovate the field by opening it up to Black subjects.

Abolitionists understood the power of this new medium. Sojourner Truth sold



## Photographers and their clientele shared a mission: to portray Black people in the best light possible.

cartes-de-visite of herself at lectures to make a living. Frederick Douglass sat for more than 160 photographs, many of them individual portraits, becoming the most photographed man of the nineteenth century. They believed that these images' realism could accurately reflect their humanity back to the world and be an essential weapon in their fight to end slavery. W. E. B. Du Bois recognized that the photographer's identity and political inclinations were as important as the print itself. "The average white photographer does not know how to deal with colored skins and having neither sense of their delicate beauty of tone, nor will to learn, he makes a horrible botch of portraying them," he wrote in 1923 in *The Crisis*, the journal of the NAACP. "From the South especially the pictures that come to us, with few exceptions, make the heart ache."

So within this racial milieu of a segregated nation *and* a racially biased photography tradition, the necessity of the Black portrait studio took on heightened urgency. Unlike the vaudeville stage or the movie or recording studios, which were mostly white-controlled, Black photographers and their Black clientele exercised unique artistic and commercial authorship over their images. They often shared a similar mission: to portray Black people in the best light possible. And as more and more Black portrait studios opened around the country, the style, purpose, and circulation of these images began to vary even more, with photographers picking

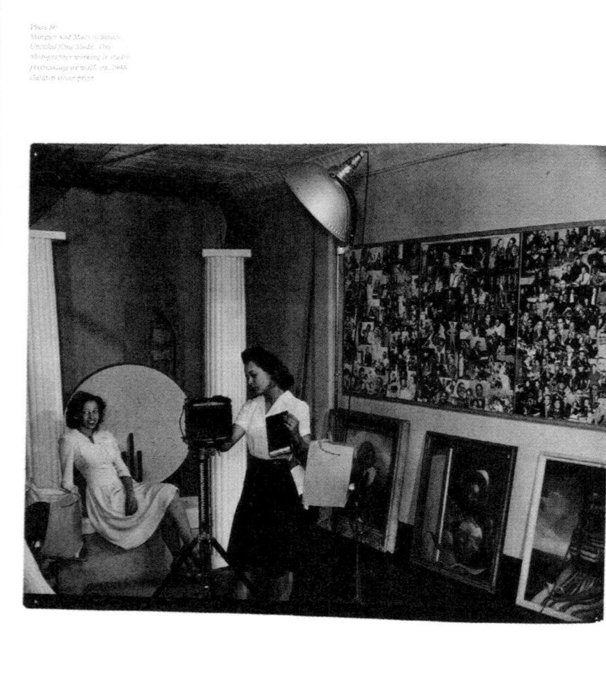

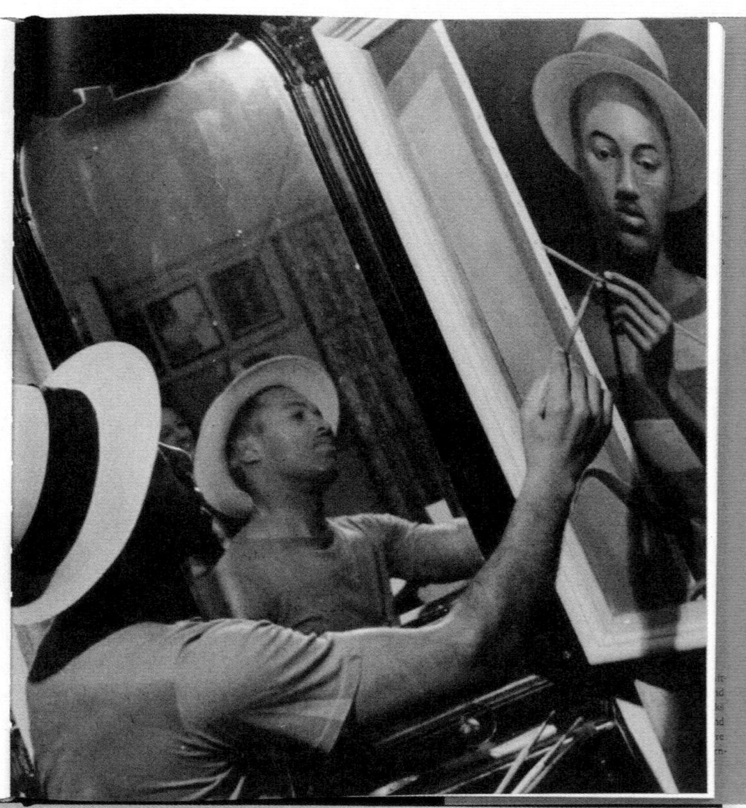

up fashion, advertising, and documentary work.

We see much of this variety in the pages of *Called to the Camera*. Pulling from vast archives, the book includes single portraits such as Ball's daguerreotype from about 1860 of his brother-in-law, VanDerZee's 1924 gelatin-silver print of Marcus Garvey, or an image of the singer Al Green in the Hooks Brothers Studio from about 1968. They are alongside group shots such as a panorama of young Black doctors watching a surgery in an operating theater at the Freedmen's Hospital in Washington, DC, made by Robert Scurlock in his own studio in 1950, or class pictures taken at George W. Carver High School in Memphis. The book's move from the individual to the collective, from the interior to the outside, and staged versus candid, is intentional.

We learn that the Black portrait studios were the primary shapers, teachers, and producers of Black respectability aesthetics. But I also wondered if there was room for artistic experimentation beyond these social and political concerns. In some ways, images of Black photographers working—fixing a smiling model's hair, smoking cigarettes while selecting prints, or quietly meditating in the darkroom— break from this pattern of stateliness by revealing the vitality and joy that went into their process.

Mainly, these portraits were shared among family members. Occasionally, they were made for or put on public display. "We weren't selling messages to white people," the Memphis judge D'Army Bailey is quoted as saying in an essay by Piper. "We were sending messages to each other, sharing evidence of our vision of ourselves to our friends and family and carrying those visions forward to prosperity . . . photography provided an extension of ourselves at our best."

Given this imperative, images that complicate our preconceptions of respectability in general and of Black women's sexuality intrigue me even more. Three very different examples stand out. An unknown photographer's hand-tinted tintype from about 1960 of a Black woman— in a luxurious silk striped dress, her hair half smoothed back while the rest loosely falls on her shoulder—feels both highbrow and casually elegant. Another, a gelatin-silver print by Allen E. Cole titled *Portrait of a Woman, seated*, from about 1925, shows a woman in a strapless silk gown and a finger-wave updo, her bare left arm leaning in, her back partly exposed, her gaze both straight ahead and a bit sultry. Did the photographer elicit such a response? Or did the woman add this flair and sexual appeal all on her own?

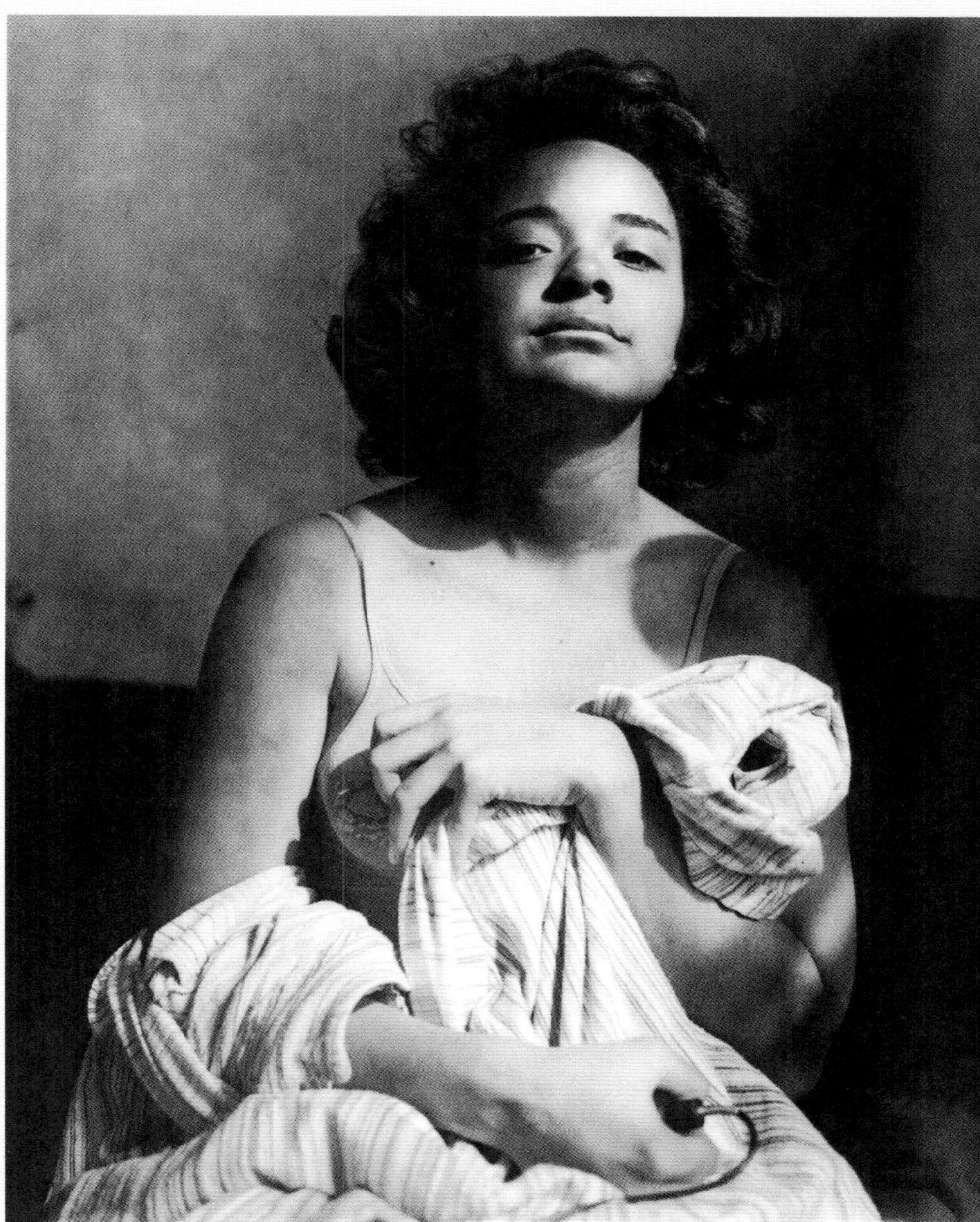

**Carla Williams,** *Untitled (Self Portrait),* **1985**
Courtesy New Orleans Museum of Art

The boldest is, of course, one of the more recent. Carla Williams's 1985 self-portrait features her in a bra, her formerly pin-curled hair now relaxed, her eyes looking downward, and her left hand holding up a robe while her right grasps the cable release. Her essay in the collection hints at the purpose of these images for the sitters as well as for their artists. "We make photographs because photographs make us matter," she writes. "So we primp, we prance, and in the blink of an eye, we strike the pose."

**Salamishah Tillet is a contributing critic at large for the** ***New York Times.*** **She was awarded the Pulitzer Prize for Criticism in 2022.**

# Reviews

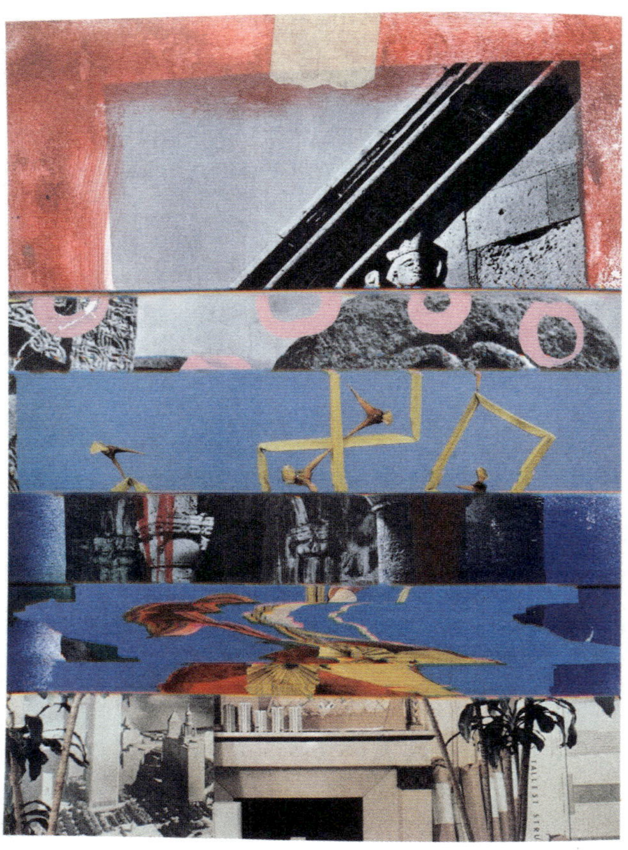

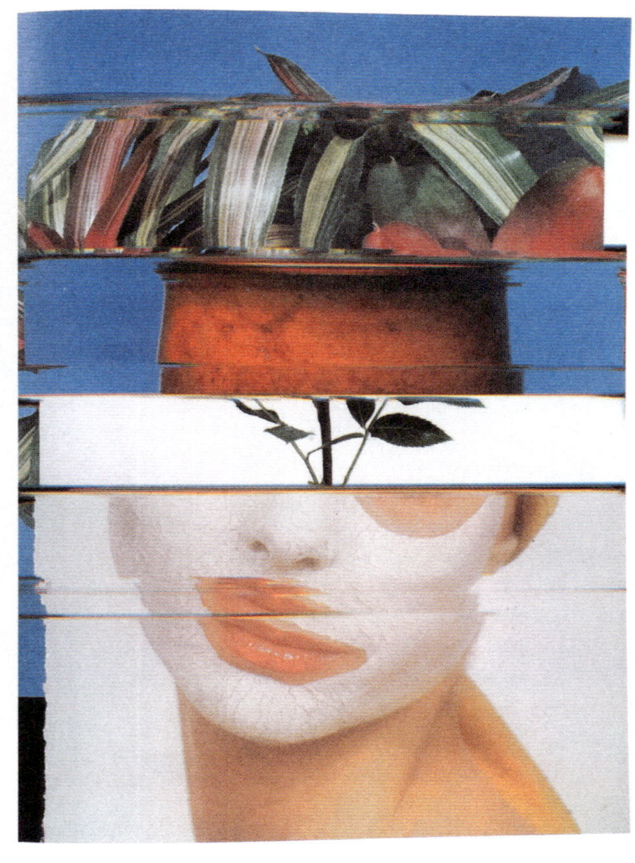



## Nico Krijno

The South African artist Nico Krijno was planning a trip around the world when COVID-19 hit. He found himself stuck at home, in a farmhouse outside Cape Town, isolated from his wife and daughters and accompanied by only his two dogs, a scanner, and his extensive archive. ***Collages 2020–2022* (Art Paper Editions, 2022; 448 pages, €45)**—Krijno's latest and most substantial photobook—was borne out of frustration. Barred from going out to shoot, he began dismantling and recomposing his decade-old archive of photographs, ephemera, and discarded materials. The result is a maximalist doorstopper, edited by the graphic designer and publisher Jurgen Maelfeyt.

In *Collages*, the reader is dropped into a thicket of visual material: prints of foliage and stone busts, mangled by scanning; ad spreads; archival photographs; and occasional interventions with paint. Images that are otherwise distinct in context, style, and source are stitched into grand and glitchy still lifes, reminiscent of the work of Lucas Blalock, John Divola, and Roe Ethridge. Despite each work's rich detail, the overall project's sequencing and size discourage meandering. Instead, the collages have a cumulative effect, with visual ideas and references that speak to one another across pages.

Krijno thinks of his highly physical practice as "a dance." To make the collages, he sets his Epson V850 Pro scanner to a high dpi, slowing the laser to introduce new elements as it wipes the glass surface. In some cases, the final compositions take several minutes and feature up to ten scans. Far from the visual hodgepodge pulled from the internet, Krijno's lockdown collages are the result of careful "foraging" from sources including old South African botany books, fine-art and design catalogs, advertisements, and all kinds of historical and commercial material. He rarely thinks of a collage in isolation, which makes the book form a useful and finite container for his work. Each of Krijno's collages contributes to a greater progression, forming an extended conversation, or, as he puts it, "an accumulation of improvised failures, even the dirt on the scanner." —**Varun Nayar**

## Matthias Brunner

One day in April 1991, the Swiss film curator Matthias Brunner and his boyfriend, the art dealer Thomas Ammann, were checking out of the Mamounia Hotel in Marrakech, Morocco, when they ran into a celebrity. "What a shock," Brunner recalled of meeting Jean-Paul Belmondo, the French New Wave star of Jean-Luc Godard's *Breathless* and *Pierrot le Fou*, who was "dressed in tiny red shorts so tight they would have gotten him arrested in Egypt." Brunner and Ammann were "*à bout de souffle*" upon spotting an idol from their youth—and that's just one of numerous such insouciant encounters in ***Magnificent Obsessions Saved My Life* (Edition Patrick Frey, 2022; 426 pages, €82)**, Brunner's delirious memoir about art, film, and the tragic drama of late twentieth-century gay culture.

For decades, Brunner programmed art-house cinemas in Zurich and later curated film screenings for Art Basel. In 2011, he began to create a multimedia installation called *Magnificent Obsession*, an homage to the Douglas Sirk film from 1954 starring Rock Hudson, which traces what Brunner saw as the "love affair" between movies and literature. That experiment in quotation and editing was an overture to the book. "Instead of writing an autobiography," Stefan Zweifel insists in the foreword, Brunner has invented a new genre, the "autopictography," by connecting "a series of hard cuts, with life on the screen and in front of the screen constantly superimposed and layered." Chapters open with full-bleed stills from midcentury classics covered with florid cursive titles ("Those Were the Days"), while snapshots from Brunner's life intermingle with film posters and artworks by Nan Goldin, Richard Hamilton, Jack Pierson, and Andy Warhol.

Other than cinema, Ammann was Brunner's *amour fou*. They met in Zurich in 1973, in a scene, Brunner writes, like one from Jacques Demy's 1964 musical romance *The Umbrellas of Cherbourg*. Together, they lived an immensely privileged life in the art world and on the film-festival circuit, lunching with Jackie Onassis and spending holidays on a yacht in Naples. That would all come to an end when Ammann died of AIDS in 1993, which Brunner describes in devastating detail. Doctors couldn't save Ammann's life, but film saved Brunner's—though he had a taste for auteurs who overwhelmingly are white, and his gaze lingers unerringly on masculine, athletic men. Still, *Magnificent Obsessions* is evidence that "anyone who wanted to could always find great solace in art."
—Brendan Embser

## Masahisa Fukase

Some books compel a reader to pick them up for reasons both irresistible and undefinable. For all its unassuming appearance, the diary-size ***Masahisa Fukase: 1961–1991, Retrospective* (AKAAKA, 2023; 216 pages, $24)** is one of those books. The unadorned cover is simply foil-stamped in black on a vibrant yellow, faux-linen case. On the back is a matte, tipped-on, black-and-white image of Yoko Wanibe, Fukase's second wife, from a series he took of her every day from their apartment window as she left for work. Wanibe looks directly at the photographer through the lens pointing at her from above; she is bent over in laughter and gesturing as if to say, Enough already! The series documents her daily departures, her poses, side-eye glances, and chic 1970s-era looks in a typological progression.

*Retrospective* also includes selections from other key series in the Fukase oeuvre— *Slaughter* (1963), *Yūgi* (*Homo Ludence*, 1971), *Kazoku* (*Family*, 1971–89), and, of course, his best-known work, *Karasu* (*Ravens*, 1976–82). It is the inclusion of the series about Yoko, however, that anchors this latest retrospective book. (The series had been removed from widespread circulation since its original publication in magazines and books in the late 1970s.) It's a photographic pas de deux that stands among the pantheon of works focusing on the relationship between a photographer and their subject-turned-

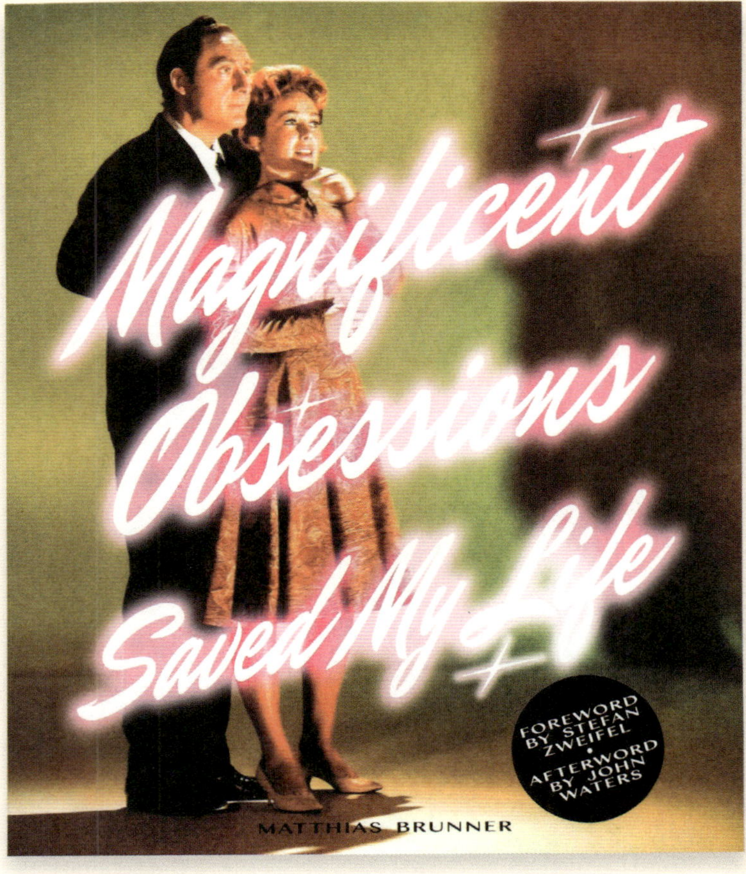



Cover of Matthias Brunner, *Magnificent Obsessions Saved My Life* (Edition Patrick Frey, 2022)

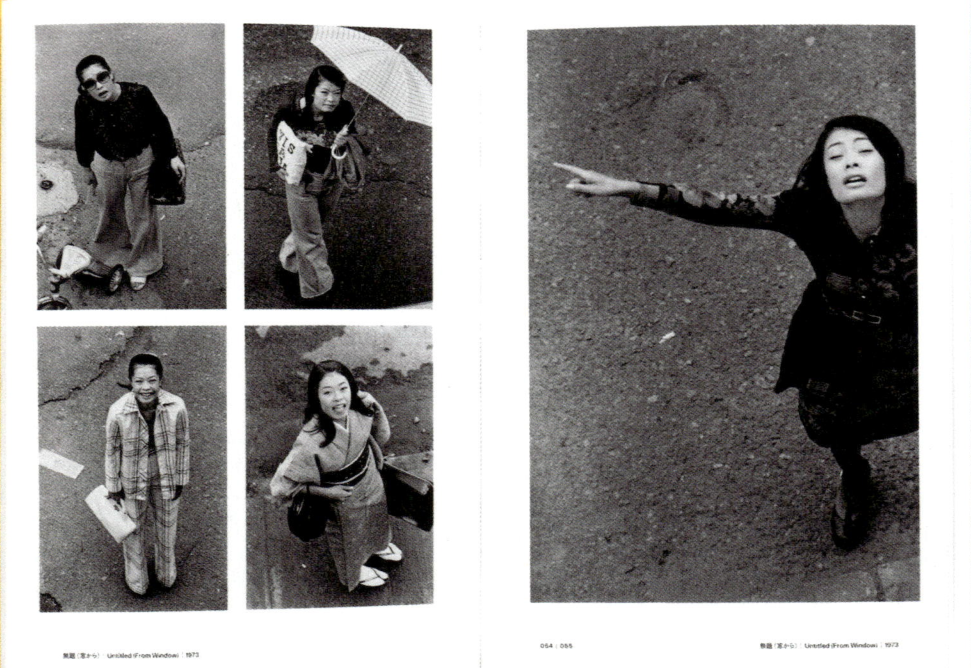



obsession—Seiichi Furuya and his wife, Christine Gössler; Roni Horn and Margrét Haraldsdóttir Blöndal; Edward Weston and Charis Wilson. But the Yoko series turns less on erotic vulnerability than on the comic forbearance of a reluctant and somewhat exasperated muse.

In the years following Fukase's sudden and unfortunate incapacitation in 1992, and his death in 2012, Tomo Kosuga, the founder and director of Masahisa Fukase Archives, based in Tokyo and Amsterdam, has spearheaded a drive to catalog and champion Fukase's legacy. His efforts have resulted in a bonanza of international books and shows. This particular survey was published on the occasion of a retrospective exhibition at the Tokyo Photographic Art Museum based on its Fukase holdings. For the reader familiar with the in-depth survey published in 2018, simply titled *Masahisa Fukase*, this latest volume serves as a useful supplement. For those new to the photographer's work, it's a valuable, bite-size introduction to his wit, his weirdness, and his most iconic images. **—Lesley A. Martin**

---

## B. Ingrid Olson

For an architect whose ideas loom large over the field, Le Corbusier hardly built in the United States. One exception is the Carpenter Center for the Visual Arts at Harvard University, an austere, gray-concrete, ramped building that interrupts the archetypal Ivy League campus. B. Ingrid Olson, an artist working at the intersection of photography and sculpture, recently staged two simultaneous installations—*History Mother* and *Little Sister* (both 2022)—

Top:
**Spread from Masahisa Fukase, *Masahisa Fukase: 1961–1991, Retrospective* (AKAAKA, 2022)**

Bottom:
**Cover of B. Ingrid Olson, *History Mother, Little Sister* (Carpenter Center for the Visual Arts, 2023)**

at the museum, a space she considers to be a sculpture in its own right.

Olson's first photographs looked at architecture—close-up images of light fixtures in the stacks of the library at the Art Institute of Chicago. Later works feature disorienting depictions of her own body, reflected, refracted, distorted, and fragmented. Images appear within images; the body is pictured at times as an unfamiliar, estranged form. The Carpenter exhibition also featured the artist's fiberboard reproductions of reliefs, as well as a series of new sculptures that respond to the building, playing on moments in architectural design connected to entering and exiting. Some pieces have humorously anthropomorphizing titles: *Why does my vestibule hurt?* (2020–22).

These seem to point to the negotiations between space and the artist's body—not to mention the viewer's when confronted with her work. In the handsome exhibition catalog ***History Mother, Little Sister* (Carpenter Center for the Visual Arts, 2023; 184 pages, \$40)**, which toggles between vertical and horizontal layouts, Olson reflects on her art, which is at once cerebral and physical: "I think there is a latent invitation in a lot of the work, in the recessed forms that might accommodate a body or the photographic images that offer the possibility of sharing the first-person perspective. These qualities might prompt the question, How close can I get? Can I touch it?" In this tactile publication, you certainly can. **—Michael Famighetti**

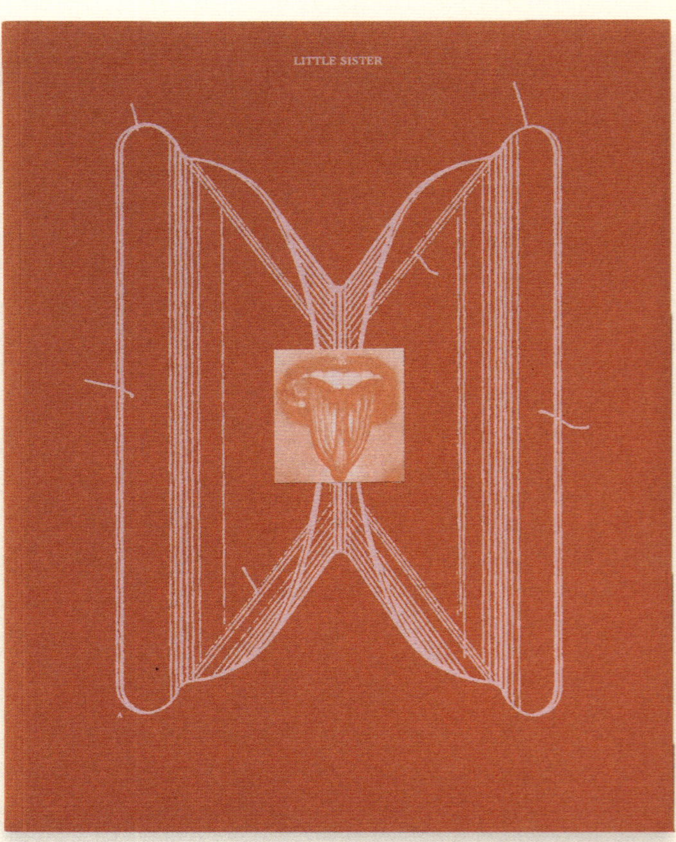

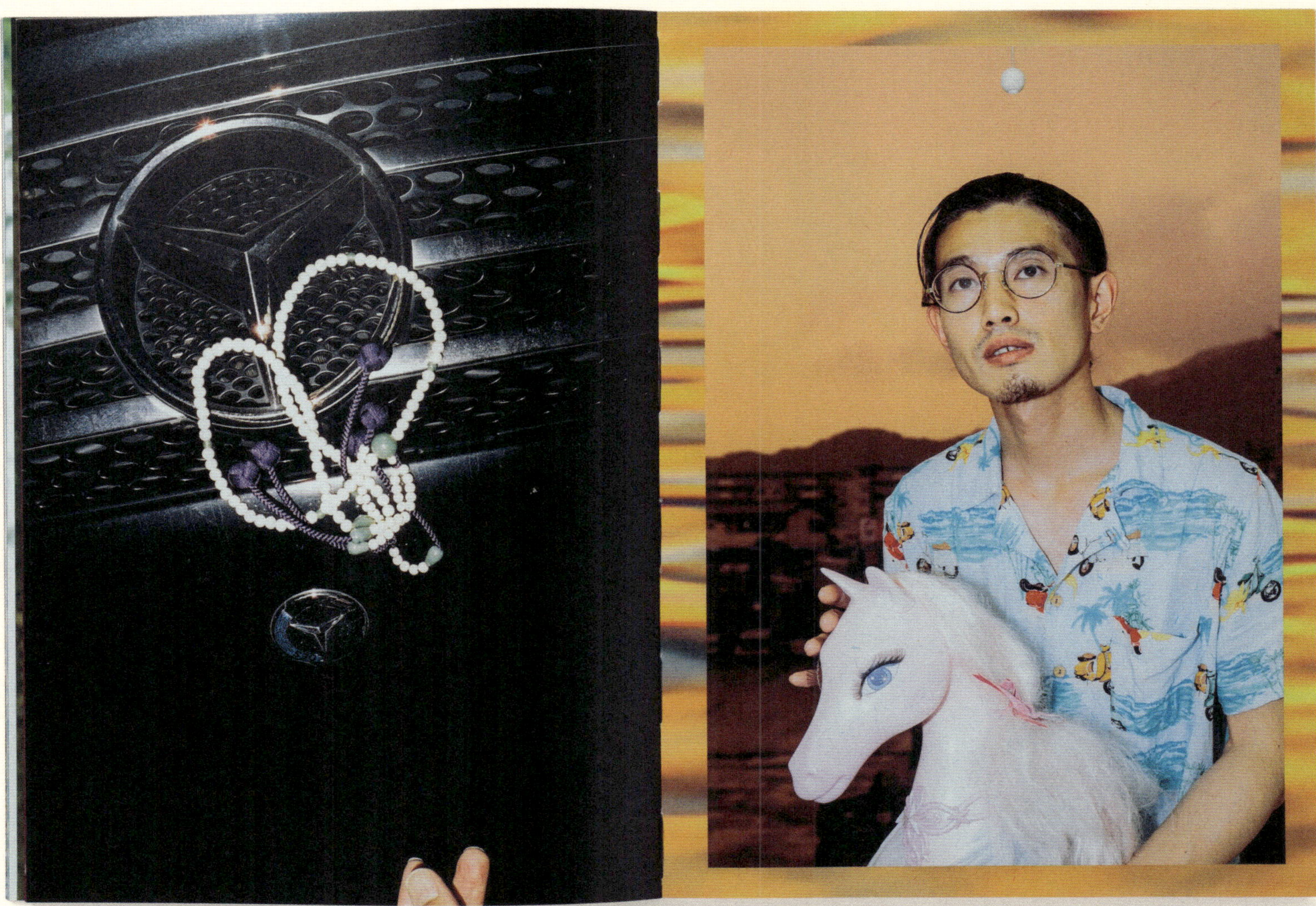

Spread from Kenta Nakamura, 銀河に埋める (*Ginganiumeru – Release into the Galaxy*) (GAP4 Publishing, 2022)

## Kenta Nakamura

When Kenta Nakamura, a photographer based in Tokyo and Fukuoka, Japan, who started his career as a systems engineer, declared to his family that he wanted to become a photographer, it was his grandmother who was the most surprised. She told Nakamura about his grandfather, who had abandoned the family before Nakamura could know him, and his own passion for photography. Nakamura was shocked by the similarities he would discover between his grandfather's aesthetic sensibilities and his own, even though the two never met. Later, as he made images of his grandmother donning a Snow White costume for his project *Snow Silver* (2013–17), he was struck by a peculiar feeling that his grandfather was there, evoked somehow by his act of photographing.

This sense of simultaneity and meta-physical transference informs the structure of Nakamura's eccentric and idiosyncratic first book, 銀河に埋める (***Ginganiumeru – Release into the Galaxy***) (**GAP4 Publishing, 2022; 136 pages, $36**). Nakamura shoots for the Japanese photo studio LOBJET and also maintains a dedicated personal practice; he combines both sensibilities to great effect in his book, which entangles photographs that are often bizarre and offbeat. In one spread, a flash illuminates a baby lying on the floor between two pizzas, and a portrait of two people is obstructed by a large overlaid angel emoji. The variety of Nakamura's photographs and sequencing, combined with full-bleed images (some are bordered by boisterous, abstract patterns) and a near-illegible title typeface, gives the impression that Nakamura wants to launch the viewer into a fugue state, a kind of harmonic dissonance—or controlled chaos.

An epilogue by Kyohei Yanashita relays a surreal story about a man who experiences the so-called Mandela Effect—when people believe in an event that hasn't actually occurred—at a dan dan noodle restaurant. The story's narrator echoes the sentiments of the reader of *Ginganiumeru* as they navigate Nakamura's images: "I noticed something odd about my surroundings: billboards, bus stops, and neon signs downtown were all written in characters I could not read," Yanashita writes. "I wondered if I had wandered into another world." —**Noa Lin**

# Endnote
## Kwame Anthony Appiah

The philosopher, writer, and *New York Times Magazine* columnist Kwame Anthony Appiah grew up in Ghana at a time of dynamic change for the newly independent country. His books have shaped a generation of thought about the complexity of African history and culture—and about the role of Ghanaians on the world stage.

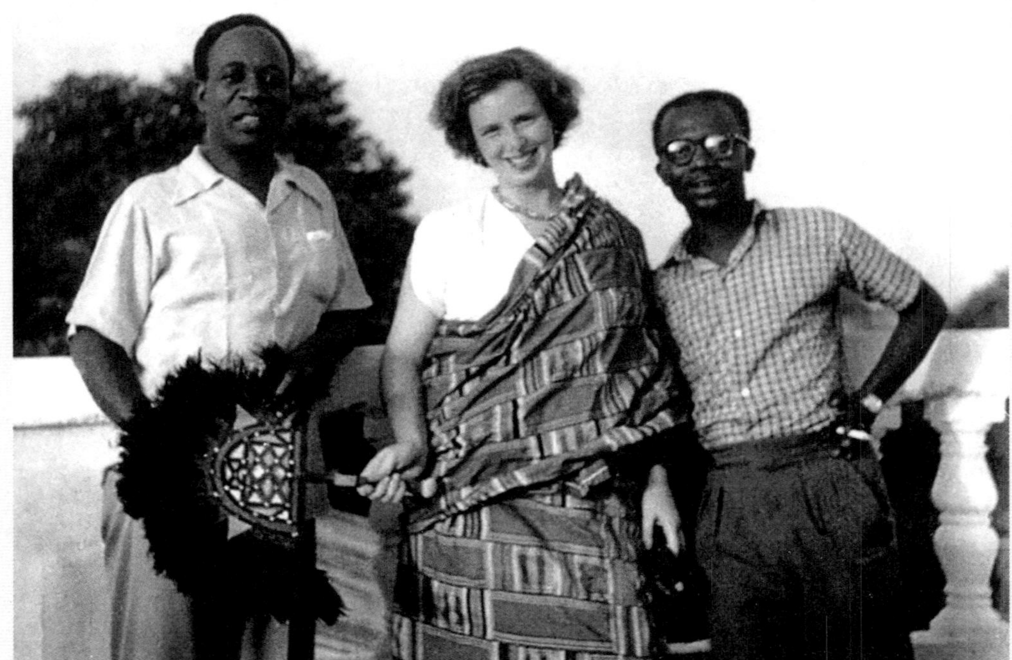

Kwame Nkrumah, Peggy Appiah, and Joseph Appiah, Accra, early 1950s
Courtesy Kwame Anthony Appiah

**What do you look forward to doing when you return to Ghana?**

I do nostalgic things. I go to the campus of Tech, the Kwame Nkrumah University of Science and Technology, in Kumasi, where I went to primary school. One of my main pleasures in Kumasi was visiting the old Queen Mother of the Asante, Nana Afia Kobi Serwaa Ampem II, who died in 2016, at age 109. She was very fond of my mother, referring to her as "husband." My mother was the only person who regularly kissed her when she saw her, so the Queen Mother would laugh and say, "Ah, here's my husband."

**When you're in Accra or Kumasi today, what aspects of the cities strike you as transformed?**

There's a part of downtown Accra now that has taller buildings, and restaurants and malls, and so on, which didn't really exist until recently. One thing I noticed in Kumasi is that there are a lot more veiled women than when I was growing up. Islam is changing in Ghana, as it is everywhere. And the traffic is terrible [*laughs*].

**Why do you feel Ghana has become a destination for diaspora tourism?**

In the early 1960s, Maya Angelou was there, Maryse Condé was there, and, of course, W. E. B. Du Bois was there. Ghana is an incredibly friendly place, and people are welcoming to strangers. And there are all those castles along the coast—places from which the ancestors of Black people in the New World were taken.

**Earlier this year, Uganda passed antigay legislation that drew worldwide condemnation. A similar law was recently proposed in Ghana. What do you think about these political developments?**

Having grown up in Ghana as a gay person, I felt that the situation was sort of like the 1960s in the United States, that is, you could get into trouble if there were cops who wanted to bully you. But, on the whole, you could live a fairly satisfactory gay life, at least in the city. The fact is that gay sex is illegal under colonial laws, which have never been repealed. My sense of all this in Ghana is that politicians are just mobilizing homophobia in the way that populist politicians around the world often do. It's a cheap shot, it gets people excited. So, it's extremely brave of LGBTQ Ghanaians to speak out.

**You are currently advising on the redevelopment of the W. E. B. Du Bois Memorial Centre for Pan-African Culture in Accra. What does that site mean to you?**

My father was involved in the 1945 Pan-African Congress, in Manchester, which Kwame Nkrumah came to, and that's where he met Du Bois. My father and Nkrumah were intimate friends. So that sense of Du Bois as a wider connection to the diaspora was something that I grew up with. In the 1990s, when the scholar Henry Louis Gates Jr. and I were in Ghana, we laid a wreath on Du Bois's grave at the site. Since then, we've been trying to find ways to see if the center can be refurbished. Now, there's a design by the architect David Adjaye.

**Do you see a relationship between the castles where enslaved people were taken and the future Du Bois Memorial Centre?**

It's a great site of diaspora memory— a literal site of return, because some of Du Bois's ancestors went from Africa to the New World, and then he moved to Accra and became a Ghanaian citizen. He had a state funeral in Ghana. That's one of the representative moments in the history between the diaspora and the continent.